THE

WATERLOO ROLL CALL.

WITH BIOGRAPHICAL NOTES AND ANECDOTES.

BY

CHARLES DALTON, F.R.G.S.,

AUTHOR OF "HISTORY OF THE WRAYS OF GLENTWORTH," "LIFE OF GENERAL SIR
EDWARD CECIL," "MEMOIR OF CAPTAIN JOHN DALTON, COMMANDANT OF
TRICHINOPOLY, 1752–1753"; AND EDITOR OF "ENGLISH ARMY
LISTS AND COMMISSION REGISTERS, 1661–1714,"
"THE BLENHEIM ROLL," ETC.

Second Edition,

REVISED AND ENLARGED.

LONDON:

EYRE AND SPOTTISWOODE,

Government and General Publishers,

EAST HARDING STREET, E.C.

1904

THE
WATERLOO ROLL CALL.

Dedicated

TO

GEORGE TANCRED, ESQUIRE

(LATE CAPTAIN SCOTS GREYS),

OF

WEENS, ROXBURGHSHIRE.

PREFACE TO SECOND EDITION.

TIME does not diminish the interest of Waterloo, for that combat of giants is indissolubly connected with Napoleon—the greatest master of the art of war the world has ever known.

Since the publication of my ROLL CALL in 1890, I have received much additional information from the relatives of Waterloo officers. This has enabled me to bring out the present revised and enlarged edition. And I wish particularly to mention that many of the obituary notices of Waterloo officers given in the following pages were collected by the late Mr. J. W. O'Brien, of the British Museum Library (formerly in the ranks of the 4th Dragoon Guards), whose annotated copy of the ROLL CALL came into my possession by purchase. Mr. O'Brien's researches were not made at my instigation or wish, but having been made, and brought to my notice, I thought it advisable to secure and utilise this copy of my book containing the aforesaid MS. entries.

A special feature of the Second Edition is the list of non-commissioned officers and men (given in Part III.) who served at Waterloo, and subsequently received commissions in the British army.

CHARLES DALTON.

September 1*st*, 1904.

CONTENTS.

PART I.

INTRODUCTION TO FIRST EDITION.

Ah ! Je les tiens donc, ces Anglais !—NAPOLEON.

NEVER since the days of Oliver Cromwell had any name caused so much fear in England as did that of Napoleon Bonaparte. From 1802 until his first downfall, in 1814, a spirit of alarm and uneasiness pervaded all classes in Great Britain, from the King and his Ministers down to the most illiterate peasant. Those who were witnesses of, and participators in, this panic have now passed away, but the national pride which our victory over Napoleon at Waterloo excited in every Briton's breast is as strong as ever, and will last till the crack of doom.

In July, 1803, a little pamphlet, entitled *Important Considerations for the People of this Kingdom,* was published in London, and " sent to the officiating minister of every parish in England." This pamphlet, which bears the Royal Arms of England, was an appeal from the Government to the Nation, and a diatribe against Napoleon. Mark the closing lines of this appeal : " Shall we, who are abundantly supplied with iron and steel, powder and lead—shall we, who have a fleet superior to the maritime force of all the world, and who are able to bring two millions of fighting men into the field—shall we yield up this dear and happy land, together with all the liberties and honours, to preserve which our fathers so often dyed the land and the sea with their blood ? . . . No, we are not so miserably fallen ; we cannot, in so short a space of time, have become so detestably degenerate ; we have the strength and the will to repel the hostility, to chastise the insolence of the foe. Mighty, indeed,

must be our efforts, but mighty also is the need." The idea of
a French invasion was slow in forcing its way into the minds
of the uneducated classes in England. When they first heard of
such a possibility they thought it of no more consequence than
the invasion of Scotland by Charles Edward Stuart with a mere
handful of Frenchmen at his back. They also thought less of the
projected descent from having heard so much in 1797, and during
the Rebellion in Ireland in 1798, of a French army coming to the
relief of the National party in that kingdom :—

> "For the French are on the sea,
> Says the Shan Van Vaugh,
> And Ireland will soon be free,
> Says the Shan Van Vaugh."

And yet nothing had come of all this talk! But when the nation
at large had fully grasped the possibility of a Napoleonic invasion,
Pitt had no difficulty in raising the sinews of war. No fewer than
300,000 men enrolled themselves in volunteer corps and defence
associations. The army and navy were increased, and everything
was done that was possible to counteract the power of that
wonderful man, who, in the short space of a few years, had,
speaking metaphorically, built a Great Wall of China round the
British Isles, shutting the English out of the commerce of Europe.
Our preparations were none too soon. In 1805 the battle of
Austerlitz established the supremacy of Napoleon over Austria
and Russia. Fortunately for England, Nelson's crowning victory
at Trafalgar indefinitely postponed Napoleon's invasion scheme ;
but we were still engaged in a gigantic war, single-handed,
with half of Europe our declared, and the other half our
enforced, enemies. Nelson was dead ; Pitt was dying from the
weight of anxieties which pressed upon him in this tremendous
crisis ; Hanover had been taken from us. The outlook was
very gloomy, and affairs became more complicated in 1807, when
the military expeditions, arranged by Lord Grenville's ministry,
against Constantinople and Egypt, had turned out failures,
and resulted in the Turks declaring war against us and con-
fiscating all British property. And yet in 1807 Napoleon
had not yet reached the zenith of his power. For the next

five years he held the destinies of nearly the whole of Europe
in his own hands. Monarchies of long standing were dis-
established and new kingdoms—Napoleonic kingdoms—were
raised up in their place. Immense French armies traversed
Europe from Portugal to the heart of Russia, and every capital
within that limit was, in its turn, subjugated to the French
yoke. But in 1808 two British Generals stemmed the tide of
French conquest in the Peninsula, viz., Sir John Moore and Sir
Arthur Wellesley. The first met a soldier's death at Corunna,
and the latter was superseded by an incapable commander. But
the British Government soon found that they had made a
grievous mistake, and Wellesley was again entrusted with the
supreme command in Portugal. Then commenced that series of
brilliant campaigns which liberated Portugal and Spain from the
Napoleonic grasp, and only ceased after the battle of Toulouse
by Napoleon's abdication at Fontainebleau. In the spring of
1814 England had a large army, composed for the most part of
seasoned veterans, who were fit for anything and worth millions.
When war broke out again, in the spring of 1815, at least half of
the Peninsular army had been disbanded—dispersed—and not
to be had at any price. Some of the best of the old Peninsular
regiments had been sent to America in 1814, and several of
them—the gallant 43rd Light Infantry being one—did not reach
Waterloo in time to take part in the battle. Raw levies took
their place, and foreign auxiliaries helped to bring up
Wellington's army in Flanders to the required strength. Of
Wellington's 106,000 barely one-third were British. The remainder consisted of "King's German Legion," "Hanoverian
Levies," "Brunswick Contingent," "Nassau Contingent," "Dutch
and Belgian Troops," and "Nassauers in Dutch service." Of
this polyglot force the German Legion, both cavalry and infantry,
were deserving of the highest praise for their conduct on
Waterloo Day. They formed part of the British army for nearly
a dozen years, and many British officers held commissions in
the "Legion." I have been obliged to leave out the German
Legion officers in the following ROLL CALL (excepting those
who served on the Staff), and it would be invidious, when all
did so well, to pick out the British officers who served in the

"Legion" at Waterloo and record their services when those of their German brother-officers are omitted. I cannot even make an exception of Colonel (afterwards Baron) Hugh Halkett, who, like a knight in the olden days of chivalry, singled out a French general (Cambronne) in single combat, and took him prisoner.

The Hanoverian levies did well also, excepting one regiment, which refused to charge the French when commanded so to do. And this was doubtless owing to the *lâcheté* of their colonel, who, when ordered to lead his regiment to the charge, declined to do so, saying he had no confidence in his men. It is related that Captain Horace Seymour, who had brought this officer Lord Uxbridge's orders, addressed "a few words of plain Saxon" to him, "which no gentleman ought to have listened to unmoved," but the only effect they had on the Hanoverian was to hasten his departure to the rear. The Brunswick Contingent fought at a disadvantage at Waterloo, having lost their brave leader (the Duke of Brunswick) at Quatre Bras. Of the Nassau, Dutch, and Belgian troops it is only fair to say that they were, mostly, utterly useless at Waterloo. The glamour of Napoleon was upon them. They had lately been in his service, and had a settled conviction that Wellington would be defeated and his army cut to pieces. "Come over to us, brave Belgians!" shouted a French regiment at Waterloo to their Belgian opponents in the battle. But the "brave Belgians" preferred making "a retrograde movement for strategical reasons," and retired from the field, carrying news of Wellington's defeat to Brussels.

Now for Napoleon's army : This consisted on the 15th of June of about 128,000 men*—mostly veterans who had served in many campaigns, and to whom defeat was rare. Add to this, that they all belonged to one nation, and were all equally devoted to their beloved emperor. "No army," says Colonel Chesney, in his *Waterloo Lecture*, "was probably ever so well furnished with leaders as his, as none had ever the like experience wherewith to train them." It is no slight to Wellington to say that Napoleon was, for rapid and offensive warfare, by far the first general of his

---

* Lord Wolseley, in his *Decline and Fall of Napoleon*, says the French army consisted of about 123,000 men of all arms and 344 guns.—ED.

day. In defensive warfare Wellington was much in advance of
his great rival. Taking the words out of Philip the Second's
mouth, Wellington might have with truth said, "Time and I
against any other two." Once more : Wellington himself told
Earl Stanhope that he considered the presence of Napoleon with
the French army at Waterloo fully equivalent to an additional
force of 30,000 men ! Now this was the total of the force sent
under Marshal Grouchy, on the 17th June, to follow the Prussian
army, which had been defeated at Ligny by Napoleon on the
previous day, and which was supposed to be in full retreat on
Namur and Liége, so that, in round numbers, Napoleon was himself considered equal to a whole army corps ! If the British had
a Picton, the French had a Ney, who was considered almost
Napoleon's equal in handling troops in the field, and who had
pressed us so sorely at Quatre Bras, on the 16th of June, when
only half our army had arrived at that position. Then as a leader
of cavalry Lord Uxbridge was well matched by Kellermann, whose
fame as a cavalry general dated from Marengo. And General
Mouton (Count Lobau) was an infantry leader of whom any army
might have been proud. It was he who, at the head of the
Imperial Foot Guards, had wrested the victory from the Prussians
on the bloody field of Lützen, in 1813, and saved the French
army from a reverse. Enough has now been said to show what a
splendid army the British had opposed to them on the 18th of
June, 1815. "I have them at last, these English !" exclaimed
Napoleon, in a transport of joy, early in the morning of that day,
when he saw our army drawn up in position, with their backs to
the forest of Soignies. But he underrated Wellington's general-
ship, nor could he foresee how the British generals, officers, and
men of all ranks would fight that memorable day, when the eyes
of all Europe were upon them, because upon the issue of that
contest depended the fate of empires and kingdoms, as well as the
future peace of the world. And knowing, as we all do, what glory
the victory at Waterloo brought to our countrymen and our
country, we must be generous enough to give the brave Prussians
the full share due to them for their co-operation on that day. Had
it not been for them, Waterloo would have been as barren a victory
as Borodino, and Napoleon would have retreated in as good

order, probably, as Blucher was able to do after his defeat at
Ligny.   As it was, our troops bore the whole brunt of the battle
without losing an inch of ground, and the arrival of the Prussians,
at the close of the day, sealed the fate of Napoleon.*

   In offering this, the first annotated Waterloo Army List, to the
British public, I must ask their indulgence for any omissions and
errors it may contain.   Although I have spared no trouble in the
matter, there must be, I well know, a few names of British
Waterloo officers who have escaped my notice.   But when the
following list is compared with the very defective lists given by
Siborne and George Jones (the foundation of all other lists), I
think the following ROLL CALL will be found infinitely more
trustworthy.   I have also added the regimental and army commissions of the Waterloo officers up to the date of the battle, and
the honours and promotions bestowed after Waterloo.   The war
services of *many* of these same officers now appear in print for the
first time, and are not to be found in the *Military Calendar* of
field officers which was published in 1820, nor in Hart's *Army
Lists*, which date from 1840, and are such valuable works of
reference.   Of course, a large proportion of the names I have
annotated, genealogically, are names of well-known families of the
present time, but there are also many names in the following
ROLL CALL which belong to families that are now extinct or
lost sight of.   I have endeavoured to rescue as many names
from oblivion as time would allow, but there are a certain
number of whom I can give no information beyond their obituary
notices :

> "Here lies Pat Steele.   That's very true.
> Who was he?   What was he?   What's that to you?"

As regards the orthography of the names in the regimental lists,
I am not responsible, as they are copied from the "official"

---

* "I should not do justice to my feelings, or to Marshal Blücher and the
Prussian Army, if I did not attribute the success of this arduous day to the
cordial and timely assistance I received from them."— *Wellington's despatch
to Earl Bathurst.*

Army List. The same rule applies to the precedence of the different regiments.

I am indebted to Colonel F. A. Whinyates, late R.H.A., for some interesting information regarding artillery officers, and to George Tancred, Esq., late captain Scots Greys, for the Waterloo muster-roll and some memoranda relating to the Scots Greys.

CHARLES DALTON.

32 WEST CROMWELL ROAD, LONDON, S.W.
June 1, 1890.

ABBREVIATIONS.

Par.   = Peninsular.

Pa.   = Peninsula.

G.C.H.   = Knight Grand Cross of Hanover.

K.C.H.   = Knight Commander of Hanover.

K.H.   = Knight of Hanover.

K.M.T.   = Knight of Maria Theresa of Austria.

K. St. A. = Knight of St. Anne of Russia.

K. St. V. = Knight of St. Vladimir of Russia.

K. St. G. = Knight of St. George of Russia.

K.T.S.   = Knight of the Tower and Sword of Portugal.

K.M.B.   = Knight of Maximilian of Bavaria.

K.W.   = Knight of Wilhelm of Holland.

W. after an officer's name = Wounded.

K.   „   „   = Killed.

M.I. = Monumental inscription.

THE WATERLOO ROLL CALL.

STAFF.

COMMANDER-IN-CHIEF.
F.-M. Arthur, DUKE OF WELLINGTON, K.G., G.C.B., &c.

MILITARY SECRETARY.
Lt.-Col. Lord Fitzroy Somerset, 1st Ft. Gds., w.

AIDES-DE-CAMP.
Lt.-Col. J. Fremantle, 2nd Ft. Gds.
Lt.-Col. C. F. Canning, 3rd Ft. Gds., к.
Hon. Sir Alexander Gordon, K.C.B., 3rd Ft. Gds., к.
Lt. Lord George Lennox, 9th Lt. Dns.
Hered. Prince of Nassau-Usingen.

EXTRA AIDES-DE-CAMP.
Maj. Hon. Henry Percy, 14th Lt. Dns.
Capt. Lord Arthur Hill, h. p.
Lt. Hon. George Cathcart, 6th Dn. Gds.

GENERAL.
H.R.H. The Prince of Orange, w.

AIDES-DE-CAMP.
Lt.-Col. Baron Tripp, 60th Foot.
Capt. Lord John Somerset, h. p.
Capt. Hon. Francis Russell, h. p.

EXTRA AIDES-DE-CAMP.
Capt. The Earl of March, 52nd Foot.
Capt. Viscount Bury, 1st Ft. Gds.
Lt. H. Webster, 9th Lt. Dns.

LIEUTENANT-GENERAL.
The Earl of Uxbridge, G.C.B., w.

AIDES-DE-CAMP.
Major W. Thornhill, 7th Hussars, w.
Capt. H. B. Seymour, 18th Hussars, w.

EXTRA AIDES-DE-CAMP.
Capt. T. Wildman, 7th Hussars, w.
Capt. J. Fraser, 7th Hussars, w.

LIEUTENANT-GENERAL.
Lord Hill, G.C.B.

AIDES-DE-CAMP.
Lt.-Col. C. Hill, R. H. Gds., w.
Major R. Egerton, 34th Foot.
Major C. H. Churchill, 1st Ft. Gds.
Capt. D. Mackworth, 7th Foot.

EXTRA AIDE-DE-CAMP.
Capt. Hon. O. Bridgeman, 1st Ft. Gds., w.

LIEUTENANT-GENERAL.
Sir Thomas Picton, G.C.B., k.

AIDES-DE-CAMP.
Capt. Algernon Langton, 61st Foot, w.
Capt. J. Tyler, 93rd Foot, w.
Capt. N. Chambers, 1st Ft. Gds., k.

EXTRA AIDE-DE-CAMP.
Capt. B. Price, h. p.

LIEUTENANT-GENERAL.
Sir Henry Clinton, G.C.B.

AIDES-DE-CAMP.
Capt. F. Dawkins, 1st Ft. Gds.
Capt. J. Gurwood, 10th Hussars, w.

LIEUTENANT-GENERAL.

Charles, Count Alten, K.C.B.

AIDES-DE-CAMP.

Lt. W. Havelock, 43rd Foot, w.
Bt. Maj. A. Heise, 2nd Lt. Batt. K.G.L.

LIEUTENANT-GENERAL.

Sir Charles Colville, G.C.B.

AIDES-DE-CAMP.

Capt. J. Jackson, 37th Foot.
Lt. F. W. Frankland, 2nd Ft. Gds.

EXTRA AIDE-DE-CAMP.

Capt. Lord James Hay, 1st Ft. Gds.

MAJOR-GENERAL.

V. Count Alten.

AIDE-DE-CAMP.

Lt. Baron Estorff, 2nd Dns. K.G.L.

MAJOR OF BRIGADE.

Capt. Einem, K.G.L.

MAJOR-GENERAL.

Sir John Vandeleur, K.C.B.

AIDE-DE-CAMP.

Capt. W. Armstrong, 19th Lt. Dns.

MAJOR OF BRIGADE.

Maj. M. Childers, 11th Lt. Dns.

MAJOR-GENERAL.

Maj.-Gen. Cooke, w.

AIDE-DE-CAMP.

Capt. G. Disbrowe, 1st Ft. Gds.

EXTRA AIDE DE-CAMP.

Ensign Augustus Cuyler, 2nd Ft. Gds.

MAJOR-GENERAL.

Sir James Kempt, K.C.B., w.

AIDE-DE-CAMP.

Capt. Hon. Charles Gore, 85th Foot.

MAJOR OF BRIGADE.

Capt. Charles Eeles, 95th Foot, к.

MAJOR-GENERAL.

Hon. Sir Wm. Ponsonby, K.C.B., к.

AIDE-DE-CAMP.

Lt. B. Christie, 5th Dn. Gds.

EXTRA AIDE-DE-CAMP.

Maj. D. Evans, 5th W. I. Regt.

MAJOR OF BRIGADE.

Maj. T. Reignolds, 2nd Dns., к.

MAJOR-GENERAL.

Sir John Byng, K.C.B.

AIDE-DE-CAMP.

Capt. H. Dumaresq, 9th Foot, w.

MAJOR OF BRIGADE.

Capt. Wm. Stothert, 3rd Ft. Gds., к.

MAJOR-GENERAL.

Sir Denis Pack, K.C.B., w.

AIDE-DE-CAMP.

Maj. E. L'Estrange, 71st Foot, к.

MAJOR OF BRIGADE.

Bt.-Maj. Charles Smyth, 95th Foot, к.

MAJOR-GENERAL.

Lord Edward Somerset, K.C.B.

AIDE-DE CAMP.

Lt. H. Somerset, 18th Hussars.

MAJOR-GENERAL.

Sir John Lambert, K.C.B.

AIDE-DE-CAMP.

Lt. T. Baynes, 39th Foot.

MAJOR OF BRIGADE.

Maj. H. G. Smith, 95th Foot, w.

MAJOR-GENERAL.

Sir Colquhoun Grant, K.C.B., w.

AIDE-DE-CAMP.

Lt. R. Mansfield, 15th Hussars, w.

EXTRA AIDE-DE-CAMP.

Capt. W. Moray, 17th Lt. Dns., w.

MAJOR OF BRIGADE.

Capt. Jones, h. p.

MAJOR-GENERAL.

Sir James Lyon, K.C.B.

AIDE-DE-CAMP.

Lt. Jas. McGlashan, 2nd Lt. Batt. K.G.L.

MAJOR OF BRIGADE.

Capt. Richter, 1st Ceylon Regt.

MAJOR-GENERAL.

Maj.-Gen. P. Maitland.

AIDE-DE-CAMP.

Ensign Lord Hay, 1st Ft. Gds., k.

MAJOR OF BRIGADE.

Capt. J. Gunthorpe, 1st Ft. Gds.

MAJOR-GENERAL.

Maj.-Gen. G. Johnstone.

AIDE-DE-CAMP.

Capt. C. G. Gray, 95th Foot.

MAJOR OF BRIGADE.
Capt. S. Holmes, 78th Foot.

MAJOR-GENERAL.
Maj.-Gen. F. Adam, w.

AIDE-DE-CAMP.
Lt. R. P. Campbell, 7th Foot.

EXTRA AIDE-DE-CAMP.
Capt. C. Yorke, 52nd Foot.

MAJOR OF BRIGADE.
Maj. Thos. Hunter-Blair, 91st Foot, w.

MAJOR-GENERAL.
Sir Colin Halkett, K.C.B., w.

AIDES-DE-CAMP.
Capt. H. Marschalk, 1st Lt. Batt., K.G.L., к.
Capt. A. Home, 2nd Lt. Batt., K.G.L.

MAJOR OF BRIGADE.
Capt. W. Crofton, 54th Foot, к.

MAJOR-GENERAL.
Sir Hussey Vivian, K.C.B.

AIDE-DE-CAMP.
Capt. Edward Keane, 7th Hussars.

EXTRA AIDE-DE-CAMP.
Lt. C. A. Fitzroy, R. H. Gds.

MAJOR OF BRIGADE.
Capt. Thos. Noel Harris, h. p., w.

ADJUTANT-GENERAL.
Maj.-Gen. Sir Edward Barnes, K.C.B., w.

AIDE-DE-CAMP.
Maj. Andrew Hamilton, 4th W. I. Regt.

DEPUTY ADJUTANT-GENERAL.

Col. Sir John Elley, K.C.B., R. H. Gds., w.

ASSISTANT ADJUTANTS-GENERAL.

Lt.-Col. J. Waters, Unattached, w.
Lt.-Col. Sir George H. Berkeley, K.C.B., 35th Foot, w.
Lt.-Col. Sir Guy Campbell, Bt., 6th Foot.
Lt.-Col. Sir Noel Hill, K.C.B., 1st Ft. Gds.
Lt.-Col. D. Barclay, 1st Ft. Gds.
Lt.-Col. H. Rooke, 3rd Ft. Gds.
Lt.-Col. E. Currie, 90th Foot, κ.
Maj. A. Wylly, 7th Foot.
Maj. G. Evatt, 55th Foot.
Maj. W. Darling, h. p.
Maj. F. Breymann, 2nd Lt. Batt. K.G.L.

DEPUTY ASSISTANT ADJUTANTS-GENERAL.

Capt. Hon. E. S. Erskine, 60th Foot, w.
Capt. Lord Charles Fitzroy, 1st Ft. Gds.
Capt. C. A. F. Bentinck, 2nd Ft. Gds.
Capt. George Black, 54th Foot.
Capt. H. Blanckley, 23rd Foot.
Capt. Hon. Wm. Curzon, 69th Foot, κ.
Lt. Jas. Henry Hamilton, 46th Foot, w.
Lt. John Harford, 7th Rl. Veteran Batt.
Lt. E. Gerstlacher, 3rd Hussars, K.G.L.
Lt. Jas. Rooke, h. p.

DEPUTY JUDGE ADVOCATE.

Lt.-Col. Stephen Arthur Goodman, h. p.

DEPUTY QUARTERMASTER-GENERAL

Col. Sir Wm. Howe de Lancey, K.C.B., κ.

ASSISTANT QUARTERMASTERS-GENERAL.

Col. the Hon. Alex. Abercromby, 2nd Ft. Gds., w.
Col. F. E. Hervey, 14th Lt. Dns.
Lt.-Col. Robt. Torrens, 1st W. I. Regt.
Lt.-Col. Sir Charles Broke, K.C.B. (Permanent).
Lt.-Col. Sir Jeremiah Dickson, K.C.B. (Permanent).

Lt.-Col. Lord Greenock (Permanent).
Lt.-Col. John George Woodford, 1st Ft. Gds.
Lt.-Col. C. Grant, 11th Foot.
Lt.-Col. Sir Wm. Gomm, K.C.B., 2nd Ft. Gds.
Lt.-Col. Sir Henry Hollis Bradford, K.C.B., 1st Ft. Gds., w.
Lt.-Col. Sir George Scovell, K.C.B., h. p.
Lt.-Col. D. Kelly, 73rd Foot.
Maj. Wm. Campbell, 23rd Foot.
Maj. Hon. George Lionel Dawson, 1st Dn. Gds., w.
Maj. Chas. Beckwith, 95th Foot, w.
Capt. Jas. Shaw, 43rd Foot.
Capt. J. Jessop, 44th Foot, w.

DEPUTY-ASSISTANT QUARTERMASTERS-GENERAL.

Capt. E. T. Fitzgerald, 25th Foot, w.
Capt. Richard Brunton, 60th Foot.
Capt. Thos. Wright, Rl. Staff Corps, w.
Capt. H. MacLeod, 35th Foot, w.
Capt. J. J. Mitchell, 25th Foot, w.
Capt. W. Moore, 1st Ft. Gds.
Capt. Geo. Hillier, 74th Foot.
Capt. W. G. Cameron, 1st Ft. Gds.
Capt. F. Read, Rl. Staff Corps.
Lt. P. Barrailler, 33rd Foot.
Lt. Basil Jackson, Rl. Staff Corps.
Lt. A. Brauns, Rl. Staff Corps.

COMMANDANT AT HEAD-QUARTERS.

Col. Sir Colin Campbell, K.C.B., 2nd Ft. Gds.

STAFF.

COMMANDER-IN-CHIEF.

F.-M. Arthur, Duke of WELLINGTON, K.G., G.C.B., &c.

Born in Dublin, 1st May, 1769. 3rd son of Garrett, 1st Earl of Mornington, by Anne, eldest dau. of Arthur (Hill), 1st Viscount Dungannon.
Educated at Eton and Angers Military Academy. Like Clive, he
was " a heaven-born general." His fame far exceeded the many
titles he won by his genius. " I am going to dine with Wellington
to-night," said a young Irish staff officer to a group of brother
officers at the close of a hard-fought battle in Spain. "Give me at
least the prefix of Mr. before my name," said Lord Wellington, who
happened to ride by at the moment and had overheard the jubilant
remark. " My Lord," replied the officer, "we do not speak of Mr.
Cæsar, or Mr. Alexander, so why should I speak of Mr. Wellington?"
The Duke d. at Walmer Castle, 14th Sept., 1852, and was buried in
St. Paul's Cathedral. He had m., in 1806, the Hon. Catherine Pakenham, 3rd dau. of Edward, 2nd Lord Longford, and by her, who d. in
1831, left issue.

MILITARY SECRETARY.

Lt.-Col. Lord Fitzroy Somerset, 1st Ft. Gds., w.

Youngest son of Henry, 5th Duke of Beaufort. Was Wellington's
A.D.C. and "right hand" throughout the campaign in Spain and
Portugal. Lost his right arm at Waterloo, from a shot fired from the
top of La Haye Sainte farmhouse after its capture by the French.
Created Baron Raglan a month after Wellington's death. F.-M. and
C.-in-C. of the British army in the Crimea in Nov., 1854. D. in the
Crimea during the siege of Sebastopol, at a farmhouse overlooking
the plains of Balaklava. In the principal room is still to be seen a
marble slab with the inscription, "In this room died F.-M. Lord
Raglan, G.C.B., Commander-in-Chief of the British Army in the
Crimea, 28th June, 1855." Lord Raglan's body was brought to England
and interred at Badminton with his ancestors. He had m., in 1814,
Lady Emily Harriet Wellesley-Pole, 2nd dau of Wm., 3rd Earl of
Mornington, and by her, who d. 1881, left issue.

AIDES-DE-CAMP.

Lt.-Col. J. Fremantle, 2nd Ft. Gds. (1st Batt.)

Served as A.D.C. to Wellington at Vittoria, and brought home the
despatch. Eldest son of Col. Stephen Fremantle, by Albinia, dau. of
Sir John Jeffrys, Bart.; C.B. M., 17th Feb., 1829, Agnes, 3rd dau. of
David Lyon. Died a maj.-gen. on ret. list.

Lt.-Col. C. F. Canning, 3rd Ft. Gds., k.

3rd son of Stratford Canning, by Mehetabel Patrick, of Summerhill,
Dublin, and brother of the subsequently celebrated diplomatist,
Viscount Stratford de Redcliffe. Had acted as A.D.C. to Wellington

in the Pa., and it was by the former's special request that the Duke took him again on his personal staff just before Waterloo.

> " Dying lamented CANNING lay,
> On MARCH he wistful gaz'd.
> 'How fares the Duke?' 'How goes the day?'
> 'All well'—his head he raised."

Lt.-Col. Hon. Sir Alexander Gordon, K.C.B., 3rd Ft. Gds., K.

It is said that when Wellington was roused from sleep by Dr. Hume early on the morning after Waterloo and told that Gordon had died from the effect of his wounds, he burst into tears.   Alex. Wm. Gordon was 3rd son of George, Lord Haddo, by Charlotte, youngest daughter of Wm. Baird, of Newbyth.   He had served as A.D.C. to his uncle, Sir David Baird, at the capture of the Cape of Good Hope and in several subsequent campaigns.

Lt. Lord George Lennox, 9th Lt. Dns.

2nd son of Charles, 4th Duke of Richmond, by Lady Charlotte Gordon, eldest daughter of Alexander, 4th Duke of Gordon.   He and his eldest brother took an active part in the drama of the 18th June, whilst the duke, his father, and Lord Wm. Pitt Lennox, his younger brother, were spectators of a battle in which they were unable to play a more active part. (See notes to 35th Regt. of Foot.) Lord George m., 29th June, 1818, Louisa, dau. of the Hon. F. Rodney, and had issue.   Was M.P. for West Sussex, 1832-41, and Gent. of the Bed-chamber to Prince Albert. D. 1873.

Hered. Prince of Nassau-Usingen.

Son of Duke Bernard of Nassau, who sent a contingent of Nassau troops to fight at Waterloo.   In the Wellington Despatches is a letter from Wellington to Duke Bernard, in July, 1815, in which he speaks highly of the bravery of the young Prince.

EXTRA AIDES-DE-CAMP.

Maj. Hon. Henry Percy, 14th Lt. Dns.

Sent home with the Waterloo Despatch, and recd. the bonus usual on such occasions and a brevet of Lt.-Col. A Jew—an agent of Rothschild, who was at Ghent when news was brought to Louis XVIII. of the defeat of the French army, drew his own conclusions from the king's happy face which he saw through a window—set off at once for London and did his little business on the Stock Exchange a few hours before Percy reached the metropolis. 5th son of Algernon, 1st Earl of Beverley, by Isabella, 2nd dau. of Peter Burrell, of Beckenham.   Was A.D.C. to Sir J. Moore at Corunna.   C.B.   D. unm. 15 April, 1825.

Capt. Lord Arthur Hill, h. p.

2nd son of Arthur, Marquis of Downshire, by Mary, Baroness Sandys in her own right. Succeeded his mother as Baron Sandys in 1836. Lt.-Gen and Col.-in-Chf. 2nd Dns.   D. unm. 1860.

Lt. Hon. George Cathcart, 6th Dn. Gds.

3rd son of William, 10th Baron, and 1st Earl, Cathcart, by Elizabeth, dau. of Andrew Elliott, Gov. of New York.   Bn. 12th May, 1794.   M., 1824, Lady Georgiana Greville (dau. of Louisa, Countess of Mansfield, by

her 2nd husband, the Hon. Robert Greville), and had issue. G.C.B.
Lt.-Gen., Com. of the forces at the Cape of Good Hope. Commanded the
4th Division of the British Army in the Crimea, and fell at Inkerman.
He was a worthy descendant of the founder of his family—Sir Alan de
Cathcart—whose bravery at the battle of Loudoun Hill is thus recorded
in an old rhyme :—

> " A knight that then was in his rout,
> Worthy and witht, stalwart and stout,
> Courteous and fair, and of good fame,
> Sir Alan Cathcart was his name."

GENERAL.

H.R.H. the Prince of Orange, w.

Bn. 6th Dec., 1792. Appointed a maj.-gen. in the Brit. Army in Dec.,
1813. Succeeded his father, William I. King of Holland (who d. in 1843),
as William II. Became a F.-M. of England in 1845. D. in 1849, and
was succeeded by his son, the reigning King of Holland.

AIDES-DE-CAMP.

Lt.-Col. Baron Tripp, 60th Foot.

Ernest Otto, Baron Tripp, C.B., was maj. in the 60th Rifles and brevet
lt.-col. He d. 1816.

Capt. Lord John Somerset, h.p.

Brother to Lord Fitzroy Somerset. Bn. 30th Aug., 1787. M., 4th Dec.,
1814, Lady Catherine Annesley, and had issue. Col., 10th Jan., 1837.
D. 3rd Oct., 1846, whilst holding the appointment of Inspecting Field
Officer, Recruiting District.

Capt. Hon. Francis Russell, h. p.

Placed on h. p., 2nd Garrison Batt., 28th April, 1814. Restored to f. p.
as capt., 57th Regt., in 1816. Afterwards capt. and lt.-col., Coldstream
Guards. Eldest son of Lord Wm. Russell, who was murdered by his
valet in 1840. In the *Army List* for 1815 is styled " Honourable." May
have been a royal page.

EXTRA AIDES-DE-CAMP.

Capt. the Earl of March, 52nd Foot.

At the siege of Ciudad Rodrigo, the Earl of March, then a lt. in the
13th Lt Dns., and serving as A.D.C. to Visct. Wellington, entered the
breach as a volunteer with the storming party of the 52nd. The Prince
of Orange and Lord Fitzroy Somerset were Lord March's companions in
this adventure. On the following morning, when breakfasting with
Wellington, they received a gentle reproof, being staff officers, for thus
risking their lives. Succeeded his father as 5th Duke of Richmond in
1819. Placed on h. p., 25th July, 1816. Served in the Pa. with the
52nd Regt. and was severely wounded at the battle of Orthes. M.,
10th April, 1817, Lady Charlotte Paget, eldest dau. of the 1st Marquis of
Anglesey, and had issue. A.D.C. to the Queen. K.G. Lt.-col. in the
army, and col. Sussex Militia. D. 21st Oct., 1860.

Capt. Viscount Bury, 1st Ft. Gds.

Eldest son of William Charles, 4th Earl of Albemarle, by the Hon. Eliz. Southwell, dau. of Edward, Lord de Clifford. Bn. 2nd June 1794. Served in the Pa. M., 4th May, 1816, Frances, dau. of Charles Steer, of Chichester. Succeeded as 5th earl in 1849. D. s. p. 15th March, 1851.

Lt. H. Webster, 9th Lt. Dns.

Afterwards Col. Henry Vassall Webster, K.T.S., 2nd son of Sir Godfrey Webster, Bart., by Eliz. Lady Holland, dau. and heir of Robt. Vassall, of Jamaica. Made a Knt. of Wilhelm of the Netherlands for his services at Waterloo. M. Grace, dau. of Samuel Boddington. Killed himself in a fit of insanity, 19th April, 1847.

LIEUTENANT-GENERAL.

The Earl of Uxbridge, G.C.B., w.

"The Prince Murat of the British Army." This brilliant cavalry leader served with distinction in the early part of the war in the Pa. The way he handled the cavalry at Waterloo is a matter of history known to every Briton. Wounded in the right knee during the last charge; his right leg was amputated after the battle and buried under a tree. A board was afterwards affixed to this tree with this verse :—

> " Here lies the Marquis of Anglesey's leg ;
> Pray for the rest of his body, I beg."

Was created Marquis of Anglesey 23rd June, 1815. Bn. 17th May, 1768. Succeeded his father as 2nd Earl of Uxbridge in 1812. Attained the rank of F.-M. in Nov., 1846. Was twice m., and left issue by both wives. D. 29th April, 1854. Bd. in Lichfield Cathedral.

AIDES-DE-CAMP.

Maj. W. Thornhill, 7th Hussars, w.

2nd son of Bache Thornhill, of Stanton-in-Peak, near Bakewell, by Jane, dau. of Edward Gould, of Mansfield Woodhouse. Promoted lt.-col. of 7th Hussars 12th Aug., 1819. K.H. He had received his brevet lt.-colcy. in June, 1815, at Lord Anglesey's request. D. at Wimborne, 9th Dec., 1850.

Capt. H B. Seymour, 18th Hussars, w.

"The strongest man in the British Army," who is said to "have slain more men at Waterloo than any other single individual." Was taken prisoner on the 18th June, but rescued by some of our cavalry sent by Wellington himself for the purpose. He is the identical " Capt. Trevanion" in Charles Lever's *Harry Lorrequer*, who was grossly insulted by a French officer—a noted bully—at a restaurant in Paris a few weeks after Waterloo. After repeated insults the French bully ordered a glass of brandy, and, whilst sitting just opposite Trevanion, drank it off, saying, in a loud vo'ce that could be heard all over the café, "A votre courage, Anglais." "Trevanion slowly rose from his chair, displaying to the astonished Frenchman the immense proportions and gigantic frame of a man well known as the largest officer in the British Army. With one stride he was beside the chair of the Frenchman, and with the speed of lightning, he seized his nose by one hand while with the other he grasped his lower jaw, and, wrenching open his mouth with the strength of an ogre, he spat down his throat." The bully's jaw was broken by his adversary's iron grasp, and he disappeared to be seen no more.

Horace Beauchamp Seymour was transferred, in 1815, to a troop in the 1st Life Gu rds. Was put on h. p. 1819, K.C.H. ; M.P. for Lisburn. 3rd son of Adml. Lord Hugh Seymour, by Lady Anne Waldegrave, dau. of 2nd Earl Waldegrave. M. twice, and by his first wife (Eliz., dau. of Sir L. Palk, Bt.) was father of Adml. Lord Alcester. D. at Brighton 23rd Nov., 1851.

EXTRA AIDES-DE-CAMP.

Capt. T. Wildman, 7th Hussars, w.

Purchased the Newstead Abbey estate for £95,000 from Mr. Clawton, who had bought it of Lord Byron for £14,000. Eldest son of Thos. Wildman of Bacton Hall, Suffolk, by Sarah, dau. of Henry Hardinge, of Durham. Served at Corunna and in many of the subsequent engagements. M., 1816, Louisa Preisig, a Swiss lady. D. s. p., 20 Sept. 1859.

Capt. J. Fraser, 7th Hussars, w.

Aftds. Sir James John Fraser. Bart. Succeeded his brother, Sir Wm. Fraser. in 1827. Son of Wm. Fraser (a direct descendant of 1st Lord Lovat), who was created a bart. in 1806, by Elizabeth Farquharson. M. Charlotte, only child of D. Craufurd. D. 5th June, 1834, and was succeeded by his son, Wm. Augustus.

LIEUTENANT-GENERAL.

Lord Hill, G.C.B.

The 2nd son and 4th chi'd of a family of sixteen. His father was Sir John Hill, a Shropshire bart. His mother, the dau. and co-heir of John Chambré, of Petton, in the same county. Bn. 11th Aug., 1772, at The Hall, in the village of Prees, in Shropshire. Entered the 53rd Regt. as lieut., in 1793. Was A.D.C. to Gen. O'Hara, at Toulon. Commanded the 90th Regt. at the age of 23. Appointed to a brigade command in the Pa., in 1808, and to a division in 1809. Greatly distinguished himself at Arroyo and Almaraz—victories that were entirely his. K.C.B. In 1814 was created a baron of England. At Waterloo had a horse shot under him—was rolled over and severely bruised. In a letter to his sister, dated 24th July, 1815, he said : " I verily believe there never was so tremendous a battle fought as that at Waterloo." C.-in-C. 1828-42. Created a viscount. 1842, with remainder to his nephew, Sir Rowland Hill. D., unm., 10th Dec., 1842, at Hardwick Grange.

AIDES-DE-CAMP.

Lt.-Col. C. Hill, R. H. Gds., w.

Brother to the above. Bn. 6th Dec., 1781. As a Maj.-Gen. commanded the forces at Madras. Equerry to H.R.H. the Duchess of Kent. D. unm., 20th Jan, 1845.

Maj. R. Egerton, 34th Foot.

9th and youngest son of Philip Egerton, of Oulton, Cheshire, by Frances, dau. and co-heir of Sir Griffith Jefferies, Knt. As a subaltern served in North America with the 29th Foot, and in South America with the 89th

Foot. Served with the 2nd Batt. 34th Foot in the Pa., in 1809. In 1810 was appointed to the Staff of Wellington's army. In 1812 was A.D.C. to Lord (then Sir Rowland) Hill, and served in that capacity at Waterloo, and with the army of occupation in France. In 1828 Lord Hill chose Col. Egerton for his first A.D.C. and private sec. C.B. Par. medal with 8 clasps. Col.-in-Chf. 46th Foot. M., 1st Dec., 1814, Arabella, youngest dau. of H. Tomkinson, of Dorfold. D. at Eaton Banks, Cheshire, aged 72, 21st Nov., 1854.

Maj. C. H. Churchill, 1st Ft. Gds.

Col. Chatham Horace Churchill, C.B., appears to have sprung from the Dorsetshire family of this name. This officer, who took a prominent part in the Waterloo drama, evinced the enthusiasm which characterized his great namesake a century before. "By G—, they deserve to have Bonaparte !" he was heard to exclaim, as he watched the French "Invincibles" ride into the jaws of death. Writing home to his family the day after the battle he said : "I had rather have fallen yesterday as a British Infantryman, or a French Cuirassier, than die ten years hence in my bed!" He d. in action at Gwalior, India, 27th Dec., 1843, whilst holding the appointment of Q.-M.-G. in India. He left a dau., Louisa, who m. Lt.-Col. John Michel, who became F.-M., 1886. See Appendix.

Capt. D. Mackworth, 7th Foot.

Aftds. Sir Digby Mackworth, Bart. As a subaltern in 7th Fusiliers, was at the battle of Albuera, and was one of the 150 men who remained unwounded in the 7th and 23rd Regts. at the close of the action. Succeeded his father. Sir Digby, in 1838. K. H. Lt.-Col. 1837. Was twice married and left issue. Died at Glen Usk, co. Monmouth, 1852, aged 63.

EXTRA AIDE-DE-CAMP.

Capt. Hon. O. Bridgeman, 1st Ft. Gds., w.

3rd son of Orlando, 2nd Baron Bradford, by Lucy Elizabeth, dau. of 4th Visct. Torrington. M., 1817, Selina, dau. of Francis, Earl of Kilmorey, and had issue. Placed on h. p. 1819. D. 1827.

LIEUTENANT-GENERAL.

Sir Thomas Picton, G.C.B., K.

Son of Thos. Picton, of Poyston, co. Pembroke. The leader of the "fighting" third division in the Par. War. Victory and glory went hand in hand with this heroic leader, whose memory is so dear to every Briton. Received a probably mortal wound at Quatre Bras. but concealed the fact from everyone, excepting an old servant, in order that he might be present at what he foresaw was to be a tremendous struggle. Fell whilst gloriously leading a charge of infantry to repel "one of the most serious attacks made by the enemy on our position." It is said that on the morning of the 18th June, one of the first questions asked by Napoleon of his Staff was : "*Où est la division de Picton?*" A few hours later, the broken ranks and decimated companies of many French regts. answered the question. Picton's body was conveyed to England and interred in the burial ground of St. George's, Hanover

Square. In 1859 his remains were finally deposited in St. Paul's Cathedral. Pensions were granted to the sisters of Sir Thos. Picton, G.C.B., in consideration of his great services.

AIDES-DE-CAMP.

Capt. Algernon Langton, 61st Foot, w.

3rd son of Bennet Langton, of Langton, co. Lincoln, by Mary, dowager Countess of Rothes. Wounded at Quatre Bras. Made a bt.-maj. On h. p. 1817. Took holy orders. M. Mary Anne, sister of Edward Drewe, of Grange, co. Devon, and had issue a son, Bennet. D. 1829.

Capt. J. Tyler, 93rd Foot, w.

Picton's first A.D.C. in the Pa. Was by his General's side when he was killed at Waterloo. Sent home with the body. Made bt.-maj. for Waterloo. Placed on h. p. 1820. Appointed junior maj. of the 97th Regt. in 1829. Belonged to a Glamorganshire family. D. 4th June, 1842.

Capt. N. Chambers, 1st. Ft. Gds., K.

Son of George Chambers by the Hon. Jane Rodney, eldest dau. of the "Great" Lord Rodney by his 2nd wife, Henrietta Clies. Killed a few minutes after Picton fell.

EXTRA AIDE-DE-CAMP.

Capt. B. Price, h. p.

Barrington Price commenced his career in the 43rd Regt., and was present at Vimiero and Corunna. Capt. 102nd Regt. 1811; h. p. 50th, 1815. D. in London, 21st Jan., 1816. Grandson of Robert Price, of Foxley, who married, in June, 1746, Sarah, dau. of John, 1st Visct. Barrington. It is worthy of note that it was a Welsh gentleman of the name of Price who was the first to smoke tobacco in the streets of London.

LIEUTENANT-GENERAL.

Sir Henry Clinton, G.C.B.

2nd son of Sir H. Clinton, K.C.B., the C.-in-C. of the Brit. forces in America during the war, by Harriet, dau. and co-heir of Thos. Carter. Received the thanks of Parliament for his services at Waterloo. M., in 1799, 2nd dau. of Francis, Lord Elcho. D. s. p. 11th Dec., 1829.

AIDES-DE-CAMP.

Capt. F. Dawkins, 1st Ft. Gds.

4th son of Henry Dawkins, M.P. for Aldborough, by Augusta, dau. of Gen. Sir H. Clinton, Commander of the forces in North America. Bn. 1796. M., 1836, Ann, eldest dau. of Gen. Sir Howard Douglas, Bart., and had issue. Dep. Q.-M.-G. in the Ionian Islands, 1837. Col. in the army, 1841. D. 1847.

Capt. J. Gurwood, 10th Hussars, w.

As a subaltern in 52nd Regt., commanded the forlorn hope, at the lesser breach, at the assault on Ciudad Rodrigo, and received a severe wound in his head. On this occasion he took the Governor, Gen. Barrié, prisoner, whose sword was presented to Gurwood by Wellington. Came of poor but honest parents in the East Riding of Yorkshire. Was a frequent visitor at Langton Hall, near Malton, the seat of his friend, Col. (aftds. Maj.-Gen.) Norcliffe, K.H., who persuaded Gurwood to sit to Morton, the painter, for his portrait, which is still at Langton. Editor of *The Wellington Dispatches.* C.B. and Col. Dep. Lt. of the Tower. D. at Brighton, 25 Dec., 1843. Bd. in the Tower Chapel.

LIEUTENANT-GENERAL.

Chas., Count Alten, K.C.B.

Served throughout the Par. War with the German Legion. Specially mentioned in the Waterloo dispatch. Aftds. Minister of War and Inspector-Gen. Hanoverian army.

AIDES-DE-CAMP.

Lt. W. Havelock, 43rd Foot, w.

"*El chico blanco*" of the Par. War. Bn. 1795. Eldest son of Wm. Havelock, of Ingress Park, Kent. Ensign, 43rd Regt., 12th July, 1810. K.H. Killed in action at Ramnuggur, India, 22nd Nov., 1848, whilst commanding 14th Lt. Dragoons. The following account of the sanguinary action with the Sikh army is given in the *Annual Register* for 1848 :—" A more fearful sight was perhaps never witnessed on a field of battle, for the British army stood drawn up silent spectators of the bloody conflict of 450 sabres against an army amounting to more than 15,000 men with heavy cannon. . . . the gallant Havelock, in the front of his regt., charged amidst the undeviated fire from the batteries of the enemy, and was almost cut to pieces."

Bt.-Maj. A. Heise, 2nd Lt. Batt. K.G.L.

Aftds. Lt.-Col. Sir Augustus Heise, K.C.H. D. at Tübingen, in State of Wurtemburg, 1st Aug., 1819.

LIEUTENANT-GENERAL.

Sir Charles Colville, G.C.B.

Commanded the Reserves at Hal, on 18th June, and was not present at Waterloo. Commanded the British troops at the siege of Cambray, and accompanied the allied army to Paris. 2nd son of John, 9th Baron Colville (and father of 11th Baron), by Amelia Webber. Served in the Pa., and was wounded when commanding the principal attack on "Badajoz's breeches," 6th April, 1812. Bn. 7th Aug., 1770. M. 16th Feb., 1818, Jane eldest dau. of Wm. Mure, of Caldwell, co. Ayr. G.C.B. ; G.C.H. ; K.T.S. ; Col. 5th Foot ; Gen. and Gov. of Mauritius 1828. D. 27th May, 1843, at Hampstead.

AIDES-DE-CAMP.

Capt. J. Jackson, 37th Foot.

Capt. 6th Dn. Gds. 4th Dec., 1817. Aftds. Gen. Sir James Jackson, G.C.B., and Col.-in-Chf., K.D.G. Served in the Pa. and in Arabia, and was for some time Lt.-Gov. at the Cape of Good Hope. 3rd son of Col. George Jackson, of Enniscoe, by Maria, only dau. and heir of Wm. Rutledge, of Foxford, co. Mayo. D. 31st Dec., 1871.

Lt. F. W. Frankland, 2nd Foot.

Aftds. Sir Fredk. Wm. Frankland, Bart., of Thirkelby, co. York. Descended from Oliver Cromwell, through his daughter Frances Cromwell's marriage with Sir John Russell, Bart. Served at Pampeluna, the battles of the Pyrenees, Nivelle, Nive, Bidassoa, and Toulouse. Sir Frederick m. Katharine, only dau. of Isaac Scarth, and left at his decease, in 1878, a son, the late Sir Wm. Frankland, Bart., R.E., of Thirkelby.

EXTRA AIDE-DE-CAMP.

Capt. Lord James Hay, 1st Ft. Gds.

2nd son of George, 7th Marquis of Tweeddale, by Lady Hannah Maitland, dau. of 7th Lord Lauderdale. M., 1813, Eliz., only child of James Forbes, of Seaton, co. Aberdeen. Lt.-gen. and col. 86th Regt. D. 17th Aug., 1862, leaving issue.

MAJOR-GENERAL.

V. Count Alten.

Count Victor Alten distinguished himself in the Pa. D. at Osnabruck, a lt.-gen. in the Hanoverian Service.

AIDE-DE-CAMP.

Lt. Baron Estorff, 2nd Dns., K.G.L.

D. at Osnabruck, 28th April, 1827.

MAJOR OF BRIGADE.

Capt. Einem, K.G.L.

Afterwards Lt.-Col. Gottfried von Einem. D. 23rd Aug., 1820.

MAJOR-GENERAL.

Sir John Vandeleur, K.C.B.

Only son of Richard Vandeleur of Rutland, Queen's Co., a captain 9th Lt. Dns., by Elinor, dau. of John Firman of Firmount. Bn. 1763. Served under Lord Lake in India; commanded a cavalry brigade in the Pa., and received the gold cross. G.C.B. for Waterloo. Gen. and Col.-in-Chf. 16th Lt. Dns. in 1830. M., 1829, Catherine, dau. of Rev. John Glasse, and had issue. D. 1st Nov., 1849.

AIDE-DE-CAMP.

Capt. W. Armstrong, 19th Lt. Dns.

The 19th Dragoons was Sir John Vandeleur's old regt. Wm. Armstrong was placed on h. p. as capt. in the Royal African Corps in 1819. In the h. p. list 1830.

S 5473.   C

MAJOR OF BRIGADE.

Maj. M. Childers, 11th Lt. Dns.

Eldest son, by a 2nd marriage, of Chas. Walbanke-Childers, who assumed the latter name on inheriting the estates of his grandfather, Leonard Childers, of Carr House, co. York. Michael Childers became jun. lt.-col of 11th Dns. in 1820. C.B. Col. 1837. D. at Sand Hutton, co. York, 9th Jan., 1854, unm.

MAJOR-GENERAL.

Maj.-Gen. George Cooke, w.

Son of Col. G. Cooke, of Harefield Park, Mdx., and brother of Sir H. F. Cooke (private sec. to Duke of York) and Adl. Sir Edward Cooke. His mother was Penelope, sister of Adl. Boyer. Appointed ens. 1st Guards, 1784. In 1794 served in Flanders, and was A.D.C. to Maj.-Gen. (aftds. F.-M.) Hulse. As lt.-col. in the Guards was sev. wnded. when serving in Holland in 1799. Held a command in the Pa. under Sir T. Graham. Appointed maj.-gen. 4th June, 1811. Lost his right arm at Waterloo. K.C.B. 22nd June, 1815 ; K. St. George of Russia, &c. ; Col.-in-Chf. 40th Foot. D. 3rd Feb., 1837, at Harefield, Mdx.

AIDE-DE-CAMP.

Capt. G. Disbrowe, 1st Ft. Gds.

The Desboroughs, or Disbrowes, were brought into notice during the Civil Wars when John Desborough, a noted Republican, exchanged his plough for a sword, and attained high renown as a soldier. The Gen.'s family came still more into notice when he married Cromwell's youngest sister. George Disbrowe was placed on h. p. as lt.-col. 1821, K.H. He was 2nd son of Edward Disbrowe, of Walton-upon-Trent, co. Derby, by Lady Charlotte Hobart, youngest dau. of George, 3rd Earl of Buckinghamshire. Col. G. Disbrowe d. about 1875.

EXTRA AIDE-DE-CAMP.

Ens. Augustus Cuyler, 2nd Ft. Gds.

Bn. 14th Aug., 1796. 2nd son of Gen. Cornelius Cuyler, who was created a Bart. in 1814 ; lt. and capt. same regt. 1817 ; lt.-col. h. p. 1826.

MAJOR-GENERAL.

Sir James Kempt, K.C.B., w.

Bn. in Edinburgh about 1764. Son of Gavin Kempt, of Batley Hall, Hants. Entd. army 1783. A.D.C. to Abercromby in Holland. Accompanied Sir Ralph to the Mediterranean and served as his A.D.C. and military sec. until that Gen.'s death. Served under Lord Hutchinson in Egypt in similar position. Commanded a brigade in the 3rd division in the Pa. Received the gold cross with three clasps ; G.C.B. for Waterloo ; Gov. Nova Scotia ; Gov.-Gen. Canada ; Master-Gen. of the Ordnance ; Col.-in-Chf. 1st Foot, 7th Aug., 1846. D. in London 20th Dec., 1854, leaving £120,000 in personalty.

Capt. the Hon. Charles Gore, 85th Foot.

Bn. 1793. Began his career in 6th Regt. Foot. Exchanged to 43rd Regt. Joined this regt. in the Pa. 1811, and was one of the storming party of Fort San Francisco, at the investment of Ciudad Rodrigo. A.D.C. to Sir Andrew Barnard at Salamanca, and in a similar capacity to Sir J. Kempt at Vittoria and subsequent battles. Accompanied Kempt to Canada in 1814, and returned just in time to fight at Waterloo, where he had three horses shot under him. Son of Arthur Gore, 2nd Earl of Arran, by his 3rd wife, Eliz. Underwood. G.C.B.; K.H.; Gen. and col. 6th Foot; Lt.-Gov. Chelsea Hospital. M. 1824 Sarah, dau. of Hon. James Fraser of Nova Scotia, and had issue. D. 4th Sept., 1869.

MAJOR OF BRIGADE.

Capt. Charles Eeles, 95th Foot, K.

Brother of Lt.-Col. Wm. Eeles, K.H., who. d. in command of 1st Batt. Rifle Brigade in 1837.

MAJOR-GENERAL.

The Hon. Sir William Ponsonby, K.C.B., K.

Lost his life at Waterloo from being badly mounted. Whilst leading a cavalry charge against the "Polish Lancers" his horse stuck in a heavy ploughed field and was unable to extricate itself. "He took a picture and watch out of his pocket and was just delivering them to his A.D.C. to give his wife when the lancers were on him." Both Ponsonby and his companion were immediately killed by the Polish cavalry, who, later in the day, were almost annihilated by the Heavy Brigade which Ponsonby had commanded. He was 2nd son of Wm., 1st Baron Ponsonby, of Imokilly, co. Cork, by Hon. Louisa Molesworth, 4th dau. of F.-M. Viscount Molesworth. M. 20th Jan., 1807, Hon. Georgiana Fitzroy, dau. of Charles, 1st Baron Southampton, and had a son, born posthumous, 6th Feb., 1816, who succeeded as 3rd Baron Ponsonby.

AIDE-DE-CAMP.

Lt. B. Christie, 5th Dn. Gds.

Braithwaite Christie was promoted capt. in 5th D.G. 3rd July, 1817, and in 1824 was senior capt. in the regt. He d. at Belmont 23rd Sept., 1825. He was 3rd son of Adl. Alexander Christie of Baberton (2nd son of Archibald Christie of Stenton), by Eliz., dau. of Adl. Richard Braithwaite.

EXTRA AIDE-DE-CAMP.

Maj. D. Evans, 5th W.I. Regt.

Afterwards the celebrated Sir De Lacy Evans of British Legion and Crimean fame. Bn. at Moig, Ireland, 1787. Educated at the Military Academy, Woolwich. Gained distinction in the Par. War by volunteering for storming parties. Served in the American War of 1812. Fought at Bladensburg, where Gen. Ross gained fame for himself and his descendants. At Washington, with a very small force of infantry, De Lacy Evans captured the Congress House. Was engaged at Balti-- more and New Orleans, and returned in time for Waterloo, where he had two horses shot under him. Commanded British Legion in Spain 1835-7 and 2nd division in Crimea. G.C.B., and was decorated with various Spanish orders ; was also a Grand Officer of the Legion of Honour ; Col.-in-Chf. 21st Fusiliers 1853. D. 9th Jan., 1870. Bd. in Kensal Green Cemetery, M.I. See Appendix.

MAJOR OF BRIGADE.

Maj. T. Reignolds, 2nd Dns., K.

Doubtless was the officer mentioned above as being with Sir W. Ponsonby when he was killed, as there were none of that Gen.'s A.D.C.s killed at Waterloo. He left orphan children to whom a pens. was granted.

MAJOR-GENERAL.

Sir John Byng, K.C.B.

Youngest son of George Byng, of Wrotham Park, Middx. (grandson of George, 1st Viscount Torrington), by Anne, dau. of Wm. Connolly, of Castletown, Ireland. Twice received the thanks of Parliament for his eminent services in the Pa. and at Waterloo, and an augmentation to his arms for himself and his descendants by royal grant. G.C.B.; G.C.H. ; K.M.T. ; K.S.G. ; P.C.; F.-M., Oct., 1855 ; Col.-in-Chf. 29th Foot ; Governor of Londonderry and Culmore. M. 1st Miss Mackenzie, and had issue ; m. 2ndly, 1809, Marianne. 2nd dau. of Sir Walter James Bart., and had issue. Created Baron Strafford in 1835, and Earl of Strafford in 1847. D. 3rd June, 1860.

AIDE-DE-CAMP.

Capt. H. Dumaresq, 9th Foot, w.

Fought in 13 battles during the Par. War. Also at the sieges of Burgos and Badajoz, and assaults on forts of Salamanca. On the two former occasions served as a volunteer with the Engineers, and on the latter was again a volunteer ; being foremost in the assault of that redoubt, he received from the officer commanding at Vittoria convent the terms of his capitulation, which document he delivered to Lord Wellington. Was a lt.-col. after nine years' service (so gazetted in June, 1817). Was shot through the lungs at Hougoumont, but, being at the time in charge of a message to Wellington, he went on to the Duke and delivered it. Ball never extracted. D. in New South Wales 5th March, 1838, age 46, whilst holding the post of manager of the Australian Agricultural Co. He was a native of Jersey. M. 19th Aug., 1828, Eliz. Sophia Danvers, and left issue.

MAJOR OF BRIGADE.

Capt. Wm. Stothert, 3rd Ft. Gds., K.

In 1814 this officer was sev. wnded. in the attack on Bergen-op-Zoom. The only family bearing this name, that the Editor has been able to trace, came from Kirkcudbrightshire.

Sir Denis Pack, K.C.B., w.

Only son of the Very Rev. Thos. Pack, Dean of Ossory, by Catherine dau. and heiress of Denis Sullivan, of Berehaven, co. Cork. Five times received the thanks of Parliament for his military services. Was one of the most dashing leaders of a brigade in the Par. War. "He was scarred with wounds and covered with glory." Commanded the 71st Regt. at Buenos Ayres when that city was retaken by the Spaniards, and was sev. wnded. and taken prisoner. When he escaped from prison, Pack was appointed to the command of a provisional battalion stationed at Colonia. His fidgety and irascible temper somewhat tried those who had to serve under him. One morning there appeared written in chalk on the door of a barn the following distich :—

> "The devil break the gaoler's back
> That let thee loose, sweet Denis Pack."

For his services at Waterloo he was made Col.-in-Chf. of the York Chasseurs. M. 10th July, 1816, Lady Eliz. Beresford, youngest dau. of George, 1st Marquis of Waterford, and had issue. His 2nd son was Lord Beresford's heir, and assumed the surname of Beresford. Sir Denis d. 24th July, 1823.

AIDE-DE-CAMP.

Maj. E. L'Estrange, 71st Foot, к.

Edmund L'Estrange was a hero in every sense of the word. He was eldest son of Capt. Anthony L'Estrange of the 88th Regt.—one of the Irish representatives of the ancient family of Le Strange, of Hunstanton, co. Norfolk. Was A.D.C. to Sir Denis Pack in the Par. War, and his especial gallantry, on several occasions, attracted the notice of Wellington. Made a brevet maj. at the early age of 26. His right leg was shattered by a round shot at Waterloo, and he died soon after suffering amputation. Had he lived, a great future was in store for him. A pension was granted to his mother whom he had supported.

MAJOR OF BRIGADE.

Bt.-Maj. Chas. Smyth, 95th Foot, к.

Bn. 8th Jan., 1786. Distinguished himself in the Par. War, and was promoted brevet maj. in 1815. D. from wounds received at Quatre Bras. 4th son of the Rt. Hon. John Smyth, of Heath Hall, near Wakefield, by Lady Georgiana Fitzroy. eldest dau. of 3rd Duke of Grafton.

MAJOR-GENERAL.

Lord Edward Somerset, K.C.B.

Commanded the 4th Lt. Dns. in the Par. War. In the first Cavalry charge at Waterloo, Lord Edward Somerset lost his cocked hat, and went to the charge bare-headed. On his return, whilst looking for his hat, a cannon-ball took off the flap of his coat and killed his horse. He donned a Life Guard's helmet and wore it during the battle. Bn. in 1776. 4th son of Henry, 5th Duke of Beaufort. M., 1805, Louisa, youngest dau. of 2nd Visct. Courtenay. G.C.B., K.T.S. Col.-in-Chf. 4th Lt. Dns. 1836. D. 1st Sept., 1842, leaving issue.

Lt. H. Somerset, 18th Hussars.

Afterwards Lt.-Gen. Sir Henry Somerset, K.C.B. and K.H.   Col.-in-Chf. 25th Foot.   Bn. 30th Dec., 1794.   Eldest son of Lord Charles Somerset, by 4th dau. of Visct. Courtenay.   M., 1st April, 1817, Frances, dau. of Adml. Sir H. Heathcote, and had issue.   Served in the first Kaffir War, and was afterwards C.-in-C. at Bombay.   D. 15th Feb., 1862, leaving issue.

MAJOR-GENERAL.

Sir John Lambert, K.C.B.

2nd son of Capt. Robert Lambert, R.N. (2nd son of Sir John Lambert, 2nd Bart.), by Catherine, dau. of Edward Byndloss, of Jamaica.   Succeeded to the command of the British troops before New Orleans, in Jan. 1815, on the deaths of Generals Pakenham and Gibbs, who nobly fell whilst heading an attack on the "Crescent City."   The disorganised state of the British troops, and the utter impracticability of forcing the American entrenchments, induced General Lambert to retreat, which he was able to do without meeting with any opposition, having captured Fort Bowyer.   With their natural love of exaggeration, the Americans magnified both their victory and our defeat :—

> "The English had ten thousand,
>   Jackson only one ;
> But what was that to Jackson
>   When him they turned their backs on ? "

By a forced march from Ostend, Lambert's brigade arrived at Waterloo just as the battle was commencing.   G.C.B.   Col.-in-Chf. 10th Foot, 1824.   M., 19th Oct., 1816, a dau. of John Mount, of Brocklehurst, in the New Forest.   D. at Thames Ditton, 14th Sept., 1847, leaving issue.

AIDE-DE-CAMP.

Lt. T. Baynes, 39th Foot.

Promoted capt. in 1824, and placed on h. p. 20th Nov., 1828.   D. at Brussels, 27th May, 1847.

MAJOR OF BRIGADE.

Maj. H. G. W. Smith, 95th Foot, w.

Afterwards the renowned Sir Harry George Wakelyn Smith, Bart., G.C.B. and Col.-in-Chf. Rifle Brigade.   Bn. at Whittlesea, Isle of Ely ; son of a local surgeon.   Entered the 95th Rifles in 1805.   Was present at the capture of Monte Video.   Served at twelve general actions in the Pa. and was afterwards A.A.G. in America.   Served at Bladensburg and the destruction of Washington.   Sent home with despatches.   Went out again under Sir E. Pakenham, and was present at the attack upon the enemy's lines near New Orleans.   Promoted brevet lt.-col. for his services at Waterloo.   Commanded a division in the Kaffir War of 1834-5.   In 1840 was A.-G. in India.   K.C.B. for battle of Maharajpore. G.C.B. for the Sutlej Campaign.   Created a baronet for his victory at Aliwal.   C.-in-C. at Cape of Good Hope in Kaffir War of 1848.   He m., in 1816, a young Spanish lady, Juana Maria de los Dolores de Leon, who

THE WATERLOO ROLL CALL. 23

had appealed to him for protection on the day after the assault on
Badajoz in Apr. 1812. D. in London, without issue, 12th Oct., 1860,
and was buried at Whittlesea. M. I., in St. Mary's Church.

Sir Colquhoun Grant, K.C.B., w

"Descended from the Grants of Gartenbeg." In order to show the
antiquity of the great "Clan Grant," one of the name asserted that the
verse in the Old Testament, saying, "There were giants in the earth in
those days" had been wrongly translated, and that it ought to read :
"There were *Grants* in those days." This genealogical flight reminds
one of the story of a negro servant, Deemers by name, who, hearing his
Yankee master everlastingly talking of his ancestors, cut into the
conversation one fine morning when waiting at table with the following :
"Massa, an ancestor of mine is mentioned in de Bible ; I heard de
minister read out last Sunday a chapter about a coloured man—one
nigger Deemers !"

Colquhoun Grant commanded the 72nd Regt. in the expedition to the
Cape of Good Hope, under Sir David Baird, in 1806, and on 8th Jan.
was wounded in the action with the Batavian army. In Sir D. Baird's
despatch, announcing the victory of the British troops, occurs this
passage : "Your lordship will perceive the name of Lt.-Col. Grant among
the wounded ; but the heroic spirit of this officer was not subdued by his
misfortune, and he continued to lead his men to glory as long as an
enemy was opposed to the 72nd Regt." The following is an authentic
anecdote :—

Sir Colquhoun Grant, being in command of a regt. at Clonmel, he
gave offence in some way to an honest shopkeeper, named Mulcahy, who
struck him on the parade, in presence of his whole corps. The officers
rushed forward to seize the delinquent, but Sir Colquhoun interposed,
declaring that he had been the aggressor, and as the gentleman thought
proper to resent his conduct in so gross a manner, it remained for him to
seek the usual reparation. "Oh !" exclaimed Mulcahy, "if it's for fighting you are, I'll fight you ; but it shall neither be with swords nor
pistols, nor anything else but my two fists" (and fine big mutton fists
they were, sure enough). "Well, then," replied the gallant officer,
"with all my heart. By insulting you, I have put myself on a level with
you, and of course cannot refuse to meet you on your own terms. Come
along, sir." The men were dismissed ; and Col. Grant, accompanied by
his adversary and some mutual friends, repaired to the mess-room, where
he very speedily closed up Mr. Mulcahy's peepers, and sent him home
perfectly satisfied. That was the proudest day of Mulcahy's life, and
many a time has he boasted of the black eye he got from a K.C.B., as if
it were an honourable ordinary emblazoned upon his escutcheon. "Ever
since that morning," would he say, "let me meet Sir Colquhoun Grant,
where I might, in town or country, among lords or ladies, dressed in plain
clothes or dizened out in gold and scarlet, he would give me his hand and
say, 'How are you, Billy?'"

In Aug., 1808, Grant was appointed lt.-col. of the 15th Lt. Dns., and
served in the Pa. Had five horses shot under him at Waterloo. G.C.B.,
G.C.H. Col.-in-Chf. 15th Hussars, 1827. Lt.-Gen. Succeeded to a
large property at Frampton, co. Dorset, 1833. M. Marcia, dau. of

Rev. J. Richards, of Long Bredy, co Dorset, and had an only surviving child, Marcia, who eloped with Richard Brinsley Sheridan in May 1835. Sir C. Grant d., 20th Dec., 1835.

AIDE-DE-CAMP.

Lt. R. Mansfield, 15th Hussars, w.

Eldest son of Francis Mansfield, of Castle Wray, by Margaret West, grand-dau. of John Leonard, of co. Fermanagh. Left the army soon after obtaining his troop in 15th Hussars. D. 12th Nov., 1854.

EXTRA AIDE-DE-CAMP.

Capt. W. Moray, 17th Lt. Dns., w.

Representative and possessor of the estates of the ancient House of Abercairnie. 2nd son of Col. Charles Moray, by the elder dau. and heir of Sir Wm. Stirling, Bart., of Ardoch. Promoted brevet maj. 19th June, 1817. Placed on h. p., 10th Nov., 1821. Succeeded his elder brother in 1840. Assumed the additional surname of Stirling. M. the Hon. Fanny Douglas, dau. of Archibald, Lord Douglas. D. s. p., 9th Feb., 1850.

MAJOR OF BRIGADE.

Capt. Jones, h. p.

Capt. Charles Jones, of 15th Hussars, was placed on h. p. in 1814. He appears to have been brought back to f. p. after 1817 as capt. in the York Chasseurs, and to have been again placed on h. p., 29th March, 1821. In 1830 his name was still on h. p. list.

MAJOR-GENERAL.

Sir James Lyon, K.C.B.

It is to be recorded of this officer that he had served on board the fleet under Lord Howe, and was present at the glorious action of 1st June, 1794—his regt. being at that time employed as marines. Was with the reserve at Hal, and did not share in the great battle of 18th June. G.C.H. Governor of Barbadoes, 1828. Col.-in-Chf., 24th Foot, 1829. D. at Brighton, 14th Oct., 1844.

AIDE-DE-CAMP.

Lt. Jas. McGlashan, 2nd Lt. Batt. K.G.L.

Promoted capt. in same regt., 22nd Aug., 1815. Exchanged with Capt. Richter, of 1st Ceylon Regt., 25th Dec., 1815. Left the army soon after 1817.

MAJOR OF BRIGADE.

Capt. Richter, 1st Ceylon Regt.

George Richter was placed on h. p. from 2nd Lt. Batt. K.G.L., 24th Feb 1816. Was on the h. p. list in 1830. D. as bt. maj. 23rd May, 1833.

MAJOR-GENERAL.

Major-Gen. Peregrine Maitland.

Son of Thos. Maitland, of Shrubs Hall, in the New Forest. Joined the 1st Regt. of Foot Guards in 1792. Commanded the 1st Brigade of Guards at the battle of Nive. The example he set, both at Quatre Bras and Waterloo, had much to do with the victory then obtained over the French. When Napoleon's " Old Guard " made that gigantic and final effort, on the evening of June 18th, to retrieve the fortunes of the day, it was Maitland's brigade which checked their advance and drove them headlong down the bloody slope. " Now, Maitland, now's your time ! " said Wellington, as the leading column of the French Guards approached the crest of the slope where the British Guards were stationed—the front rank kneeling. How Maitland responded is told in the words of Col. J. H. Stanhope in his letter to the Duke of York :—" Were it possible for me to add anything to the reputation of Maitland by stating the gallantry he has shown, cheering on with his hat off, I could dwell long on the subject." Made K.C.B., 22nd June, 1815. Received the Russian Order of St. Vladimir and the Dutch Order of Wilhelm. C.-in-C. at Madras, 1836. Gov. and C.-in-C. at Cape of Good Hope, 1843. Col.-in-Chf., 17th Foot same year. M. firstly, 1803, Hon. Louisa, 2nd dau. of Sir Edward and the Baroness Crofton. She d. 1805. He m. secondly, in 1815, Lady Sarah Lennox, 2nd dau. of 4th Duke of Richmond. D., 30th May, 1854.

AIDE-DE-CAMP.

Ens. Lord Hay, 1st Ft. Gds., K.

Killed at Quatre Bras. Had ridden and won a race at the Grammont Races on 13th June, and was dead on the 16th. Was acting as adjutant to Lord Saltoun. His horse, a fine thoroughbred, refused a fence, and tried to wheel round. As Lord Saltoun was passing down a path close by, a body fell across his horse's neck and rolled off. It was poor Hay, who had been picked off by a French cavalry skirmisher, who was, in his turn, shot dead by a Grenadier. James, Lord Hay, eldest son of William, 16th Earl of Errol, by his 2nd wife—Alicia, youngest dau. of Samuel Eliot, of the Island of Antigua—was born 7th July, 1797. In *The History of the Grenadier Guards* he is erroneously called "Lord James Hay." The latter officer, also in the 1st Guards, lived for many years afterwards.

MAJOR OF BRIGADE.

Capt. J. Gunthorpe, 1st Ft. Gds.

Promoted capt. and lt.-col., 26th Dec., 1821. Retired from the army, 1833. His elder brother, Lewis, of same regt., was killed in the campaign in Holland, 1799.

MAJOR-GENERAL.

Major-Gen. G. Johnstone.

George Johnstone was appointed a lt. in the Royal Marines, 5th March, 1776. Served at New York and Halifax, and was in several sea engagements in the Indian Ocean. In 1792 he received a company in the

New South Wales Corps, and embarked for that colony, where he served several years. Being at Hal, with the Reserves, he was not present at Waterloo. In his obituary notice in the *Scots' Magazine*, he is described of "Riggheads." He d. in Edinburgh, 19th Dec., 1825.

AIDE-DE-CAMP.

Capt. C. G. Gray, 95th Foot.

Charles George Gray served in the Pa., and was wounded at Badajoz. Promoted bt.-major 21st Jan., 1819. In 1830 was major on the un-attached list, and on 27th May, 1836, became lt.-col. Retd. in 1837.

MAJOR OF BRIGADE.

Capt. S. Holmes, 78th Foot.

Served in the Pa. and led a forlorn hope at Burgos. Stephen Holmes was placed on h. p. 25th April, 1816. Brought back to f. p. as capt. 90th Regt., 3rd Feb., 1820. R. h. p. with rank of major, 24th Dec., 1825. In 1838, as lt.-col., recd. the appointment of Dep. Inspector Gen. of the Irish Constabulary. K. H. D. in 1839.

MAJOR-GENERAL.

Major-Gen. Frederick Adam, w.

Bn. 1781. 4th son of the Rt. Hon. Wm. Adam, of Blair Adam, Lord Lieut. for co. Kinross, by 2nd dau. of 10th Lord Elphinstone. Received an ensign's commission in 1795, but continued his education and studied "the art of war" at the Milit. Academy, Woolwich. Made lieut. in the 26th Foot, 1796, and capt., 1799. Served with the 27th Foot in Holland from July to October, 1799, and was present in several actions. Served four months in 9th Foot, as capt., and then exchanged to the Coldstream Guards. Served in Egypt, and was promoted major in 1803, and in 1805, at age of 24, purchased the command of 21st Foot. Served in Sicily, and at battle of Maida. Appointed A.D.C. to the Prince Regent in 1811. In 1813 obtained command of a brigade in the army, and was sent to Spain. His command lay on the eastern side of the Pa., where there was a great lack of good commanders. Adam maintained his reputation, despite several reverses. When the French stormed and took Ordal, 12th Sept., 1813, he had his left arm broken and his left hand shattered. Made maj.-gen. 1814. The rout of the Old Guard at Waterloo by General Adam's Brigade was the turn-ing-point of the battle, and ensured victory. G.C.B., G.C.M.G., P.C., Gen. and Col.-in-Chf. 21st Foot. Gov. Ionian Islands. D. 17th Aug., 1853, very suddenly at Greenwich railway station. His widow d. 26th May, 1904.

AIDE-DE-CAMP.

Lt. R. P. Campbell, 7th Foot.

Robert Preston Campbell fired the last gun at Waterloo, and the gun was a French one ! It was one of the guns captured by the 71st Regt. in the *sauve qui peut* of the French, and was turned against their re-treating masses by some men of the 71st under Lieut. Torriano and discharged by Campbell (Siborne, vol. II., p. 234). Was placed on h. p. 25th Feb., 1816, but given a company in the Ceylon Rifles, 27th March, 1823. D., as capt, in that regt., 1825.

EXTRA AIDE-DE-CAMP.

Capt. C. Yorke, 52nd Foot.

Aftds. F. M. Sir Charles Yorke, G.C.B., Col.-in-Chf. Rifle Bde. Son of Col. Yorke (who had once held the appointment of Lieut. of the Tower), by Juliana, dau. of John Dodd. Placed on h. p. 25th Feb., 1816. Brought back to f. p. as capt. 52nd Regt. L.I., 2nd July, 1818. Succeeded Sir W. Gomm as Constable of the Tower. D. in London, 20th Nov., 1879, aged 90.

MAJOR OF BRIGADE.

Maj. Thos. Hunter-Blair, 91st Foot, w.

A most gallant and able officer. Served in the Pa.; was wounded and made prisoner at Talavera, and detained in France until the peace of 1814. Made a bt.-lt.-col. for his services at Waterloo. He was brother to Sir David Hunter-Blair, 3rd Bart. of Dunskey, co. Wigtown, and m., 1820, Miss Eliza Norris. D. a maj.-gen. and C.B., 31st Aug., 1849, at Leamington.

MAJOR-GENERAL.

Sir Colin Halkett, K.C.B., w.

Bn. 7th Sept., 1774. Eldest son of Frederick Halkett, a maj.-gen. in the British Service, who had also served in the Dutch army, by Georgina, dau. and heir of George Seton. Raised the German Legion, and served with distinction in the Pa. Had four horses shot under him at Waterloo. G.C.B. and G.C.H. Col.-in-Chf. 31st Regt., 1838. Gov. of Jersey and aftds. C.-in-C. at Bombay. M. Letitia (Crickett), widow of Capt. Tyler, R.A., and had issue. He d., 24th Sept., 1856, being then Gov. of Chelsea Hospital.

AIDES-DE-CAMP.

Capt. H. Marschalk, 1st Lt. Batt., K.G.L., K.

Henry von Marschalk was killed whilst gallantly assisting Baron Baring to defend La Haye Sainte, which was captured by the French after a noble resistance.

Capt. A. Home, 2nd Lt. Batt., K.G.L.

Alexander Home was one of the many Scotchmen who had joined the German Legion. D., at Hanover, 12th Oct., 1821, as capt. in the Hanoverian Rifle Guards

MAJOR OF BRIGADE.

Capt. W. Crofton, 54th Foot, K.

Walter Crofton left a widow and four children. Pens. of £100 per ann. granted to Mrs. Harriet Crofton, the widow, whose maiden name was Wauchope. The late Rt. Hon. Sir Walter Frederick Crofton, born in 1815, was a son of the above gallant Irish officer.

THE WATERLOO ROLL CALL

MAJOR-GENERAL.

Sir Hussey Vivian, K.C.B.

Richard Hussey Vivian, eldest son of John Vivian, of Truro, Cornwall, Warden of the Stannaries, by Betsey, only surviving child of the Rev. Richard Cranch; was born 28th July, 1775, and entered the army as ensign in the 20th Foot, in July, 1793. Served in Holland in the campaigns of 1795 and 1799. On 1st Dec., 1804, was appointed a lt.-col. in 7th Lt. Dns. Served with his regt. in the retreat from Corunna. In 1813 commanded the 7th Dns. in the Pa., and in Nov. of same year was appointed to the command of a cavalry brigade, and was present at the battle of the Nive. Was sev. wnded. in the advance upon Toulouse. In the dispatch on this occasion, Lord Wellington observes: "Col. Vivian had an opportunity of making a most gallant attack upon a superior body of the enemy's cavalry, which they drove through the village of Croix D'Orade." When the 18th Hussars were approaching two squares of the Old Guard at Waterloo, Gen. Vivian rode up to the regt. with the brief address: " Eighteenth, you will follow me." The 18th responded, in expressive language, that they were ready to follow the general *anywhere*. The charge was made on the cavalry and guns, and was eminently successful. G.C.B. and G.C.H. Was created a baronet 1828, and a baron in the peerage of England, 1841. Col.-in-Chf. 12th Dns. Master-Gen. of the Ordnance, 1835-41. Was twice married, and left issue by both wives. D., 20th Aug., 1842.

AIDE-DE-CAMP.

Capt. Edward Keane, 7th Hussars.

Made a bt.-maj. for his services at Waterloo. 3rd son of Sir John Keane, 1st Bart., by Sarah, dau. of John Kelly. His elder brother, General Sir John Keane, was created a peer of England, as Baron Keane of Ghuznee, in Afghanistan, 1839. Was lt.-col. of 6th Dns., 1825-33. R. h. p. 29th March, 1833. Reappointed to the Gren. Guards, and retd., in 1838, as col. D., 2nd Nov., 1866. M., 17th Jan., 1818, Anna, 3rd dau. of Sir Wm. Fraser, Bart., of Ledechune, co. Inverness.

EXTRA AIDE-DE-CAMP.

Lt. C. A. Fitzroy, R. H. Gds.

Aftds. Lt.-Col. Sir Charles Augustus Fitz-roy, K.C.B. and K.C.H., Capt. Gen. and Gov. of New South Wales. Eldest son of Lord Charles Fitz-roy, by Frances, dau. of Edward Miller Mundy, of Shipley, co. Derby. Bn. 10th June, 1796. Placed on h. p. as lt.-col. in 1825. M., 1st, 11th March, 1820, Lady Mary Lennox, eldest dau. of 4th Duke of Richmond, and had issue. He d., 16th Feb., 1858.

MAJOR OF BRIGADE.

Capt. Thos. Noel Harris, h. p., w.

Son of Rev. Hamlyn Harris, rector of Whitehall, co. Rutland. Served in the Pa. Went to Germany in 1813, and served with the Prussian army until the surrender of Paris in 1814. Was at Leipsic and all the battles with Blucher in 1814. Sent to London by lt.-gen. Sir Charles Stewart 30th March, 1814, with despatches announcing the taking of

Paris by the Allied Sovereigns. Recd. the Prussian Order of Merit, and the Russian Orders of St. Anne and St. Vladimir, for his services with the Allied Army. Lost his right arm at Waterloo, and was otherwise severely wounded. R. h. p. 1830, as col. K.C.H. Was chief magistrate at Gibraltar for some years, and a groom of His Majesty's Privy Chamber. Was married three times. His first wife was Mary Thomson (*née* White), widow of Robert Thomson, of Camphill, co. Renfrew. D., at Updown, Eastry, 23rd March, 1860. An interesting memoir of Sir T. N. Harris was compiled by C. B. Harris, Esq., grandson of the above veteran.

ADJUTANT-GENERAL.

Maj.-Gen. Sir Edward Barnes, K.C.B., w.

Known at Waterloo as " our fire eating adjutant-general." His family appears to have been of Irish extraction. His father was a brother of the Robert Barnes whose two daughters and co-heirs married into the good old family of Johnston, of Kilmore, co. Armagh. In 1794 we find Edwd. Barnes maj. in 99th Foot. As lt.-col. of 46th Foot, he comded. a bde. at the capture of Martinique and Guadaloupe. Served on the staff in Spain and Portugal, and comded. a bde. at the battles of Vittoria, Pyrenees, Nivelle, Nive and Orthes. His forward gallantry, on 2nd August, 1813, on the Heights of Eschalar, when, with a small force, he attacked a large part of the French army, in a strong position, occasioned a distinguished officer to say : " Barnes set at the French as if every man had been a bull-dog and himself the best bred of all." In 1819 was on the staff in Ceylon, and in 1824 was appointed Gov. of that island. Held this appointment until 1831, and so endeared himself to the natives that his departure was universally lamented, and a monument was erected in his honour. Was C.-in-C. in India from 1831 to May, 1833, with the local rank of general. M.P. for Sudbury. G.C.B. and Col.-in-Chf. 78th Regt. It is worthy of note that the present Army and Navy Club owed its existence to the joint exertions of Sir Edward Barnes and Adml. Bowles, who may be termed the founders ef this club. Sir Edward m., in 1824, Maria, eldest dau of Walter Fawkes, of Farnley Hall, Otley, and had issue. D. in London, 19th March, 1838.

AIDE-DE-CAMP.

Maj. Andrew Hamilton, 4th W. I. Regt.

Made a bt. lt.-col. for Waterloo. M. 1816, Anne, eldest dau. of Wm. Ord, of Fanham, Newminster Abbey, and Whitfield, co. Northumberland, and had issue. Served as A.D.C. to Sir Edward Barnes in Ceylon, and d. 1821.

DEPUTY ADJUTANT-GENERAL.

Col. Sir John Elley, K.C.B., R. H. Gds., w.

This distinguished general entered the army as a private soldier and rose by his own merits. He commanded the rear guard of the cavalry at Talavera. Was employed on the staff from 1807 to 1819, when he resumed the command of his old regt.—the Horse Guards. K.C.B. ; K.C.H. ; K.M.T., &c. Lt.-Gen. and Col.-in-Chf. 7th Hussars. He represented Windsor in Sir Robert Peel's Govt. D. 23rd Jan., 1839, unm., at

Chalderton Lodge, near Amesbury. Left large bequests to charities; also money to provide plate for the 7th Hussars and 17th Lancers.

ASSISTANT ADJUTANTS-GENERAL.

Lt.-Col. J. Waters, Unattached, w.

Afterwards Lt.-Gen. Sir John Waters, K.C.B. In the Par. War he was attached to the Portuguese army and was taken prisoner. When Wellington heard of this officer's capture, he quietly remarked, " Col. Waters will not remain long in the hands of the enemy." Being a reckless and dare-devil rider Waters made so sure of his speedy escape that he mockingly told his captors they would not have him on their hands for long. Such proved the case, for having managed to get his spurs sharpened, he literally " rode away " from his pursuers one fine morning, and they saw him no more. D. 21st Nov., 1842. His heir was his brother Edmond Thomas Waters, of Tyvree and Stormy, co. Glamorgan, who d. 1848, leaving issue.

Lt.-Col. Sir George H. Berkeley, K.C.B., 35th Foot, w.

Eldest son of Adml. Sir George Berkeley. Served in the Pa. Was for a short time Surveyor-Gen. of the Ordnance, and M.P. for Devonport. D. a maj.-gen. and col. of the 35th Foot, 25th Sept., 1857.

Lt.-Col. Sir Guy Campbell, Bt., 6th Foot.

Eldest son of Lt.-Gen. Colin Campbell, lt.-gov. of Gibraltar, by Mary, eldest dau. and co-heir of Col. Guy Johnson. Entered the 6th Foot, of which Gen. Colin Campbell was col., at an early age; and for his distinguished conduct in the Pa., when serving as maj. of the 6th Foot, was created a baronet in May, 1815 : C.B. and gold medal for the Pyrenees. M., 1st, the eldest dau. and co-heir of Montagu Burgoyne, of Marks Hall, and had issue. M., 2ndly, in 1820, Pamela, eldest dau. of the late Lord Edward Fitz-gerald, and had issue. Maj.-gen. in the army. D. at Kingstown, Ireland, 25th Jan., 1849.

Lt.-Col. Sir Noel Hill, K.C.B., 1st Ft. Gds.

Afterwards lt.-col. of the 13th Lt. Dns., and commandant of the Cavalry Depôt. Bn. 24th Feb., 1784. 7th son of Sir John Hill, Bart., and brother of Lord Hill. Served with distinction in the Pa., and commanded the 1st Portuguese Regiment, which he soon brought into a state of efficiency. In 1814 was transferred to a company in the 1st Foot Guards. Made K.C.B. and K.T.S., and after Waterloo was nominated a Knight of the Bavarian Order of Maximilian Joseph. Appointed D.A.G. in Canada, 1827. Succeeded Sir John Brown in the command of the cavalry depôt at Maidstone, and d. there, 8th Jan., 1832. Bd. with military honours at Maidstone. By his wife (4th dau. 'of 1st Baron Teignmouth), Sir Noel left several children.

Lt.-Col. D. Barclay, 1st Ft. Gds.

Col. Delancey Barclay, C.B , was for some years A.D.C. to the King and to the Duke of York. He d. at his house at Tillingbourne, near Dorking, 29th March, 1826.

Lt.-Col. H. Rooke, 3rd Ft. Gds.

Afterwards Maj.-Gen. Sir Henry Willoughby Rooke, C.B., and K.C.H., of Martinsherne, Berks, and afterwards of Pilston House, co. Monmouth. Bn. 2nd August, 1782. Younger son of Col. Charles Rooke (who raised a regiment called the "Windsor Volunteers," and was allowed by George III. to reside in the "Stone Tower" of Windsor Castle, where he d., 1827) by Elizabeth, dau. of Ambrose Dawson, of Langcliffe and Bolton Hall, co. York, by Mary, sister of Sir Willoughby Aston, Bart. The Rookes have been in the army for six successive generations : and that distinguished sailor, Adm. Sir George Rooke, who took Gibraltar in 1704, also belonged to this family. Sir H. W. Rooke m., in 1804, his first cousin, Selina Rooke (dau. and heir of Henry Rooke), and had issue. He d. 2nd May, 1869.

Lt.-Col. E. Currie, 90th Foot, к.

Edward Currie, junior maj. of the 90th Foot, and bt. lt.-col., was a scion of the Annandale family of that name who resided at Dalebank. He was the tenth of a family who had sacrificed their home in their country's service. Received his first commission when only thirteen, from the Duke of York, in consequence of the meritorious services of his father in the army. Fought under Abercromby in Egypt, and was A.D.C. to Lord Hill in the Pa. Received the thanks of the C.-in-C. for his bravery at Talavera, Almarez, and Aroyo de Molinos.

Maj. A. Wylly, 7th Foot.

Afterwards Lt.-Col. Alexander Campbell Wylly, C.B., of the 95th Regt. Served in Spain and Portugal as A.D.C. to Sir Edward Pakenham ; also in the American campaign in similar capacity. Sent home after Pakenham's death with despatches from Sir John Lambert, in which he (Wylly) was very honourably named. D. in Malta, 10th Nov., 1827.

Maj. G. Evatt, 55th Foot.

Col. George Evatt began his military career as a private in a foot regt. His gallantry and ability, shown in many engagements, procured him a commission, and he became capt. and bt.-major in the 55th Regt. On 25th June, 1816, he was appointed commandant of the Royal Military Asylum, Southampton, and d. there, 29th Oct., 1840.

Maj. W. Darling, h. p.

Wm. Lindsay Darling served at the reduction of Guadaloupe in 1810, and during the latter part of the Par. War was on the staff. Was A.A.G. to Sir C. Colville's division in June, 1815, and served at the storming of Cambray. Attained the rank of gen. and was appointed Col.-in-Chf. 98th Regt. in 1854. D. 7th Jan., 1864.

Maj. F. Breymann, 2nd Lt. Batt., K.G.L.

Frederick Leopold Breymann served in the Pa., and was wounded both at Talavera and Burgos. Placed on h. p. as maj. in Feb., 1816. Made C.B. for Waterloo. D. at Tesperhude, near Lauenburg, Denmark, 24th Jan., 1821.

DEPUTY-ASSISTANT ADJUTANTS-GENERAL.

Capt. the Hon. E. S. Erskine, 60th Foot, w.

Esme Stuart Erskine was sev. wnded. and taken prisoner on 17th June, 1815. He was brought before Napoleon, who asked him many questions, and showed a perfect knowledge of the strength of the British army. The conversation being ended, Erskine was put in charge of a guard, and a surgeon sent to attend to his wounded arm, which had to

be amputated. Bn. 1789. 4th son of Baron Erskine, Lord Chancellor,
by Frances, dau. of Daniel Moore, M.P. Was promoted bt.-maj. for
Waterloo, and transferred, in 1816, to 2nd Ceylon Regt. and made bt.
lt.-col. same year. M., 1809, Eliza, dau. of Lt.-Col. Smith, and had
issue. D. 26th August, 1817.

Capt. Lord Charles Fitzroy, 1st Ft. Gds.

2nd son of 4th Duke of Grafton by Lady Charlotte Waldegrave. Bn.
28th Feb., 1791. Served in the Pa. R. h. p. as maj. and bt. lt.-col.
27th Foot, 1821. M.P. Bury St. Edmunds. Vice-Chamberlain of the
Household. M. 25th Oct., 1825, Lady Anne Cavendish, 2nd dau. of 1st
Earl of Burlington, and had issue. D. at Hampton, 17th June, 1865.

Capt. C. A. F. Bentinck, 2nd Ft. Gds.

Made bt.-maj. for Waterloo. 2nd son of John Charles Bentinck, a count
of the Roman Empire, by Lady Jemima de Ginkel, dau. of the Earl of
Athlone. Bn. 4th March, 1792. Served in Pa., and under Lord Lynedoch in Flanders, as adjt. of his regt. Attained rank of lt.-gen. and
Col.-in-Chf. 12th Foot in 1857. M. 30th Jan., 1846, Countess Caroline,
eldest dau. of Count of Waldeck-Pyrmont, and had issue. D. 28th Oct.,
1864.

Capt. George Black, 54th Foot.

D. as capt. in same regt. in 1825.

Capt. H. S. Blanckley, 23rd Foot.

Henry Stanyford Blanckley was promoted brevet-maj. 21st June, 1817.
Exchanged to the 13th Lt. Dns., and d. 1820.

Capt. Hon. Wm. Curzon, 69th Foot, к.

Third son of Nathaniel, 2nd Baron Scarsdale, by his 2nd wife (Felicité
de Wattines). He met his fate at Waterloo with almost "military glee."
In falling from his horse, he called out gaily to Lord March, who had
been galloping by his side, "Good bye, dear March."

Lt. Jas. Henry Hamilton, 46th Foot, w.

Promoted captain 26th March, 1823, and transferred to 45th Regiment.
D. 3rd Jan. 1827.

Lt. John Harford, 7th Rl. Veteran Batt.

Probably rose from the ranks. His name is not in the 1812 *Army List.*
His regt. was reduced in 1816, and he was placed on ret. f. p., which
denoted distinguished service. In the *Army List* for 1824, and succeeding years, his name is spelt "Hurford." D. 1839.

Lt. E. Gerstlacher, 3rd Hussars, K.G.L.

Eberhard Gerstlacher joined the K. G. L. in March, 1813. Served in
North Germany, 1813-14. Made brevet-capt. for Waterloo. Living at
Carlsruhe in 1837.

Lt. Jas. Rooke, h. p.

Only son of Gen. James Rooke, Col.-in-Chf. 38th Regt., who was M.P.
for co. Monmouth in five Parliaments, by Eliz. Brown. Lieut. Rooke
was attached to the Prince of Orange's staff at Waterloo, as an extra
A.D.C. For his services on this occasion was appointed, 11th Aug.,
1815, a lieut. in the Staff Corps of Cavalry. In 1817 he joined the

Venezuelan Independent Army, and was given the rank of col. by Gen. Bolivar, who commanded the " Patriots." D. of a wound received in action in 1819. Was twice married, and left issue by his 1st wife.

DEPUTY JUDGE ADVOCATE.

Lt.-Col. Stephen Arthur Goodman, h. p.

Junior maj. 48th Regt., 26th Dec., 1813. Placed on h. p. with brevet rank of lt.-col. in 1814. D. in British Guiana 2nd Jan., 1844, whilst holding the post of Vendue-Master of Demerara and Esequibo.

DEPUTY QUARTERMASTER-GENERAL.

Col. Sir Wm. Howe De Lancey, K.C.B., K.

The De Lanceys were descended from a wealthy Huguenot family, who went from Caen, in Normandy, to America, after the revocation of the Edict of Nantes. In the short space of sixty years this family produced three celebrated soldiers, viz., Gen. Oliver De Lancey, a leading American loyalist, who fought on the British side during the War of Independence, and, settling in England, d. at Beverley, 1785. In another generation, an Oliver De Lancey distinguished himself as a Christine leader in the Spanish war, and was killed at the siege of San Sebastian in 1837. The third distinguished soldier of this family was the above Wm. Howe De Lancey, who was only son of S. De Lancey, Gov. of Tobago, by Cornelia his wife, who d. in 1817. His early career was one of renown, and in 1799 we find him maj. of the 45th Regt., at the age of 21. On 4th April, 1815, he was married, in Scotland, to the beautiful Magdalen Hall, dau. of Sir James Hall, Bart., of Dunglass, by Lady Helen Douglas, dau. of 4th Earl of Selkirk. The return of Napoleon from Elba once more called De Lancey to the seat of war. Leaving his fair young wife, he proceeded, in May, to Brussels, whither he was followed, the first week in June, by his bride. At Waterloo, when riding by Wellington's side, the wind of a cannon ball knocked him off his horse. This, it was afterwards found, had separated the ribs from the back-bone, and caused a fatal injury. Wellington caused De Lancey to be removed to a hut in a blanket. For some days hopes were entertained of his recovery, and he was devotedly nursed by his sorrow-stricken wife, whose perilous drive to the battle-field, and her experiences, were lately given in the *Illustrated Naval and Military Magazine*, from an old MS. narrative written by herself. After lingering ten days, the hero died.

> " Fair lady's love, and splendid fame,
> De Lancey did enthral,
> His loyal heart alike they claim,
> They sigh to see him fall."

ASSISTANT QUARTERMASTERS-GENERAL.

Col. Hon. Alex. Abercromby, 2nd Ft. Gds., w.

Bn. 4th March, 1784. 4th son of Sir Ralph Abercromby, of Tullibody, who fell at Aboukir, by Mary Anne, dau. of John Menzies, of Ferntoun, Perthshire, who was created a baroness in 1801. As Lieut.-Col. of the 28th Foot, commanded a bde. in the Pa., and received the gold cross. K.T.S. Made C.B. for Waterloo. M.P. for Clackmannanshire, 1817–18. D. 27th Aug., 1853.

S 5473.   D

Col. F. E. Hervey, 14th Lt. Dns.

Afterwards Col. Sir Felton Elwell Hervey-Bathurst, Bart. He was eldest son of Felton Lionel Hervey, by Selina, only dau. and heir of Sir John Elwell, Bart. After Waterloo was appointed A.D.C. to Wellington, which post he held during the British occupation in France. The following anecdote is from *Reminiscences of Wellington and Anecdotes of his Staff*, by Lord Wm. Lennox :—" Felton Hervey, of the 14th, who had lost an arm when in pursuit of the enemy flying from Oporto, always mounted himself and his orderly upon English hunters, so as to make his escape should he at any time be unexpectedly surrounded. Upon one occasion, when reconnoitring, Hervey rode up, by mistake, to a small detachment of French cavalry. Fortunately for him, the men were dismounted, and busily employed in cooking their rations ; but no sooner was the colonel discovered, and his rank recognized, than the order to mount was given. Hervey and his orderly, finding the odds greatly against them, immediately started off at a tremendous pace to reach our lines. The French dragoons were quickly in their saddles, for the prize was worth gaining, and amidst wild shouts and loud halloes, gave chase to their flying foes. The noise attracted the attention of some of the enemy's lancers, who, being posted nearer the English forces, were enabled to cut off the retreat of the fugitives. The clattering of the horses' hoofs, who had thus joined in the pursuit, sounded like a death-knell to the two gallant soldiers. ' Your only chance, colonel,' said the faithful orderly, ' is to make for that ravine.' Hervey followed the suggestion ; the ravine was narrow, with only room for one horse to enter. No sooner had he gained it than, on looking round, a terrible sight presented itself. The devoted soldier, knowing that the life of his commanding officer could alone be saved by the sacrifice of his own, had placed himself across the narrow opening, and was literally pierced and cut to pieces. The delay thus occasioned enabled Hervey to pursue his flight. Gaining the open, he charged a stiff fence, and was soon out of sight of his pursuers." He m.. 1817, Louisa Catherine, 3rd dau. of Richard Caton, of Maryland, U.S.A.; was created a baronet, with remainder to his brother Frederick, 3rd Oct., 1818, and d. s. p. 24th Sept., 1819.

Lt.-Col. Robt. Torrens, 1st W. I. Regt.

Afterwards Lt.-Col. of 38th Regt. and Adjt.-Gen. in India. C.B. Belonged to the Londonderry family of this name, and was a near relative of Sir Henry Torrens, K.C.B., the Adjt.-Gen. In 1836 Col. Torrens was appointed a Commissioner by Parliament, for carrying out their scheme for the colonisation of South Australia.

Lt.-Col. Sir Charles Broke, K.C.B. (Permanent).

2nd son of Philip Broke, of Nacton, Suffolk. Served in the expeditions to Hanover and South America ; also in the Pa. K.C.B. in Jan., 1815. Decorated with the Russian Order of St. Vladimir and the Dutch Order of Wilhelm, for his gallantry at Waterloo. In 1822 took the surname of Vere, in addition to that of Broke. A.D.C. to King Wm. IV., and K.C.H.; M.P. for East Suffolk. His elder brother was created a bart. in 1813, in consideration of the gallant victory he had achieved 1st June, 1813, as capt. of the " Shannon" ship of war, over the American frigate " Chesapeake." Sir C. Broke-Vere d. a maj.-gen. 1st April, 1843.

Lt.-Col. Sir Jeremiah Dickson, K.C.B. (Permanent).

Joined the 2nd Dn. Gds., as cornet, in 1798. Served in the Pa., and was A.Q.M.G. to the army in Spain, and received the gold cross and one clasp. Promoted col. 27th May, 1825 ; appointed Q.M.G. in India, 12th July 1827, maj.-gen. 1837, and Col.-in-Chf. 61st Regt., 1844. M. 15th March, 1818, Jemima, youngest dau. of Thos. Langford Brooke, of Mere Hall, co. Chester. Sir Jeremiah's parentage is unknown, but from his Scripture name we may conclude that "Job Dickson," ens. 67th Regt., in 1811, was a near relative. Sir Jeremiah d. in March, 1848.

Lt.-Col. Lord Greenock (Permanent).

Charles Murray, Lord Greenock succeeded his father, in 1843, as 2nd Earl Cathcart, G.C.B., Gen. and Col.-in-Chf. 1st D. G. Received the gold medal for Barrosa. Gov. Edinburgh Castle, Comr. of the Forces and Gov.-Gen. in North America. Bn. 1783 ; d. at St. Leonard's 16th July, 1859, having m., 30th Sept., 1818, in France, Henrietta, 2nd dau. of Thos. Mather, and left issue.

Lt.-Col. John George Woodford, 1st Ft. Gds.

Bn. at Chatham, 28th Feb., 1785. Younger son of Col. John Woodford, by his 2nd wife (Susan, dau. of Cosmo, Duke of Gordon) and widow of 9th Earl of Westmoreland. D.A.Q.M.G. at Corunna, and with Sir J. Moore when the latter was wounded. Wounded same day, and horse shot. Was attached to Gen. Sir C. Colville's division, but was sent, on the evening of 17th June, by his gen. to Wellington, to ask him if the British troops at Hal should join the main army. Only reached Waterloo a few hours before the battle commenced. Acted as extra A.D.C. to Wellington at Waterloo. C.B. and Col. Maj.-Gen. in 1837. K.C.B. and K.C.H. D. 22nd March, 1879.

Lt.-Col. C. Grant, 11th Foot.

Colquhoun Grant joined the 11th Foot in 1795, and attained the rank of Lt. Col. of 54th Regt. in 1821. C.B. for Waterloo. Son of Duncan Grant, of Lingeston, N.B. D. at Aix-la-Chapelle in the spring of 1829.

Lt.-Col. Sir Wm. M. Gomm, K.C.B., 2nd Ft. Gds.

Afterwards F.-M. Sir Wm. Maynard Gomm, G.C.B., Constable of the Tower and Col.-in-Chf. 13th Regt. L. I.; also D.C.L. and LL.D. This veteran soldier and philanthropist was son of Lieut.-Col. Wm. Gomm, who had served in America in the 46th Regt. The family is undoubtedly of French origin. As far back as 1685 we find Sir Bernard de Gomme appointed Master Surveyor of the Ordnance. Wm. M. Gomm entered the army, as ensign, in 1794, and at the age of 14 carried the colours of the 9th Foot—the Holy Boys—into action in Holland. Served in the Pa., and received the gold cross and one clasp. The charger he rode at Waterloo, by name "George," survived until 1841, aged 33, and was buried under a stone seat in the garden at Stoke Park, near Windsor. The veteran charger's veteran master held the high post of C.-in-C. in India, and received a F.-M.'s baton in Jan., 1868. He d. at Brighton, 15th March, 1875, full of years and good works. By his wife Eliz. (eldest dau. of Lord Robert Kerr), whom he m. in 1830, he had no issue.

Lt.-Col. Sir Henry Hollis Bradford, K.C.B., 1st Ft. Gds., w.

Bn. 25th June, 1781. 3rd and youngest son of Thos. Bradford, of Wood-lands, near Doncaster and Ashdown Pk., co. Sussex, by Eliz., dau. of

D 2

Wm. Otter, of Welham, co. Notts ; served in the Pa., Knt. of the Dutch Order of Wilhelm, and of the Russian Order of St. Vladimir. D. at La Vacherie, near Lillière, France, 7th Dec., 1816, of wounds recd. at Waterloo. Bur. at Storrington, Sussex.

Lt.-Col. Sir George Scovell, K.C.B., h. p.

Aftds. G.C.B., Col.-in-Chf. 4th Lt. Dns., and Gov. Rl. Milit. College, Sandhurst. Served in the Pa., and was present at Corunna as D.A.Q.M.G. Recd. the gold cross and one clasp ; also the silver war medal with eight clasps, and 4th class of St. Vladimir of Russia. D. at Henley Park, Guildford, 17th Jan., 1861.

Lt.-Col. D. Kelly, 73rd Foot.

Dawson Kelly joined the 47th Regt. as ens. in 1800. Became major of the 73rd in 1811. Towards the close of the battle of Waterloo a sergeant of his regt. came and told him that all the officers of the 73rd were killed or wounded. Although serving on the staff, Kelly immediately returned to take over the command. C.B. and bt.-lt.-col. On h. p. 15th Jan., 1818. Bt.-col. 1837. D. same year at Dungannon, Ireland. He was 5th son of Thos. Kelly, of Dawson's Grove, co. Armagh, by his wife, Jane Waring. M.I. in Armagh Cathedral. Communicated by Lt.-Col. G. H. Johnston, late 15th Foot.

Maj. W. Campbell, 23rd Foot.

Was A.D.C. to Gen. Craufurd in the Pa. D. a C.B. and maj.-gen. 3rd June, 1852.

Maj. Hon. George Lionel Dawson, 1st Dn. Gds., w.

3rd son of John, 2nd Visct., and 1st Earl of Portarlington, by Lady Caroline Stuart, dau. of 3rd Earl of Bute. Bn. 28th Oct. 1788. Promoted bt.-lt.-col. 4th Dec., 1815. Placed on h. p. 17th Aug., 1820. C.B. Assumed the additional surname of Damer 14th March, 1829. M., 20th Aug., 1825, Mary, dau. of Lord Hugh Seymour, and had issue. D., 14th April, 1856.

Maj. Chas. Beckwith, 95th Foot, w.

Son of Capt. John Beckwith, 23rd Lt. Dns., and nephew of Sir George and Sir T. S. Beckwith. Bn. at Halifax, N.S., 2nd Oct., 1789. His mother was a sister of Judge Haliburton (Sam Slick). Brigade-maj. to the celebrated Light Division in the Pa. Lost his left leg at Waterloo. Was a frequent visitor at Apsley House. Being one day left alone in the Duke's library his attention was called to Gilly's *Waldensee*, which book graphically described the neglected state of the Waldensee inhabitants. His interest was touched, and soon after he took up his abode among those "primitive Christians of the Alps." Beckwith did much for the good of the people, by whom he was greatly beloved. He d. as maj.-gen. at Torre, 19th July, 1862. See *Memoir of General Beckwith, C.B.,* by M. Meille, translated, London, 1873. Also Foster's *Yorkshire Pedigrees.*

Capt. Jas. Shaw, 43rd Foot.

Aftds. Sir James Shaw-Kennedy, K.C.B. Bn. 1788. Educated at the Military College at Marlow. Joined the 43rd L.I. as ens., 1805. Served with this regt. at Copenhagen, and proceeded to the Pa. in 1808. Served at Corunna, and in 1809 was adjt. Was A.D.C. to Gen. Robert Craufurd during 1809 and 1810. Present at siege of Ciudad Rodrigo. "Stood with Gen. Craufurd when, in the assault of that fort and place, he placed himself on the crest of the glacis, where he fell mortally wounded." Served at the siege and storming of Badajoz, at Salamanca, and other actions. "On 18th June, 1815, he was allowed, in presence of Wellington, to form the 3rd Division (to which he was attached), in a new and unusual order of battle, to meet the formidable masses of cavalry seen forming in its front, and in this formation the division resisted, successfully, repeated attacks of Napoleon's cavalry." Commanded at Calais during the three years of the Army of Occupation. Organised the constabulary force of Ireland. Bt. maj. for Waterloo. M., 1820, Mary, dau. of David Kennedy, and assumed his wife's name. D. a lt.-gen. and Col.-in-Chf. 47th Regt., 30th May, 1865.

Capt. J. Jessop, 44th Foot, w.

Served as A.D.C. to Gen. Dunlop in the Pa. The late Gen. Sir George L'Estrange thus speaks of John Jessop in his *Recollections* (published in 1873) :—"A splendid officer, a perfect gentleman, particularly handsome, and a capital good fellow." Made C.B. for Waterloo. Placed on h. p. as bt.-maj., 44th Regt., 1821. D. at Butterley Hall, Derbyshire, in Sept., 1869, aged 90.

DEPUTY-ASSISTANT QUARTERMASTERS-GENERAL.

Capt. E. T. Fitzgerald, 25th Foot, w.

Edward Thos. Fitzgerald, K.H., 2nd son of Charles Fitzgerald, of Turlough Park, Castlebar, was bn. 22nd Dec., 1784. Placed on h. p. as bt. maj., 1818. M., 20th Nov., 1811, Emma, dau. of Edmond Green, of Medham, in the Isle of Wight, and had issue. D., at Castlebar, 1845, as lt.-col. h. p.

Capt. Richard Brunton, 60th Foot.

The name of Brunton is to be found in the Lowlands of Scotland. The above officer, who bore this name, served in the Pa., and obtained his company in the 60th in 1813. Exchanged to the 13th Lt. Dns. 1819. Maj. in 1826, and lt.-col. of same regt. 1830. M. 30th June, 1829, Eliz., eldest dau. of Rev. Josiah Thomas, Archdeacon of Bath (by Susanna Harington), and widow of Major Wallace, of the Madras Cavalry, who was shot on parade in India by a sepoy of his regt. Col. Brunton d. at Bath, 1846, leaving issue by his wife, who re-married Edward Downe, of Abbeyside, Dungarvan.

Capt. Thos. Wright, Rl. Staff Corps, w.

Promoted maj., 25th June, 1830. Placed on h. p. 5th Nov. same year. Alive in 1846.

Capt. H. G. MacLeod, 35th Foot, w.

Aftds. Sir Henry George MacLeod, K.H. Col. h. p. 1838. Was knighted by William IV., on being appointed Lt.-Gov. of St. Christopher's. Had previously served in Canada as A.D.C. to the Duke of Richmond. D. at his residence, near Windsor, 20th Aug., 1847. He was 4th son of Gen. Sir John MacLeod, G.C.H., R.A., and had served six years in the R.A.

Capt. J. J. Mitchell, 25th Foot, w.

This officer was for some years capt. in the 1st Royals. None of the Army Lists give his Christian names—only the enigmatical initials "J. J."

He was placed on the Irish Half Pay List, in 1816, as capt. in the 25th Foot, and his name disappeared altogether from the Army List soon after that date.

Capt. W. G. Moore, 1st Ft. Gds.

Aftds. Lt.-Gen. Sir Wm. George Moore, K.C.B. Col.-in-Chf. 60th Rifles. Eldest son of Francis Moore, Under-Sec. of War, by Frances, Countess of Eglinton (dau. of Sir Wm. Twysden, Bart.). This Francis Moore was youngest brother of the famous Sir John Moore "of Corunna celebrity." Bn. 1795. Educated at Harrow. Served as A.D.C. to Sir John Hope at siege of Bayonne, and was severely wounded and taken prisoner while attempting to assist his general when dismounted and wounded in the sortie of 14th April, 1814. D. at Petersham, 23rd Oct., 1862.

Capt. Geo. Hillier, 74th Foot.

Aftds. lt.-col. of the 62nd Regt. Served in Canada as A.D.C. to Sir P. Maitland, and, subsequently, as D.Q.M.G. in Jamaica. Of Devizes, Wilts. M. before 1820, and left, with other issue, the present Lt.-Col. G. E. Hillier. D. in Bengal, 15th June, 1840.

Capt. W. G. Cameron, 1st Ft. Gds.

Son of Lt.-Gen. Wm. Neville Cameron, H.E.I.C.S., by Charlotte, dau. of Sir Wm. Gordon, 7th Bart. of Embo, co. Sutherland. Capt. Wm. Gordon Cameron lost his right arm at Waterloo and had other severe wounds. K.H., made bt. lt.-col., 7th July, 1825, and placed on h. p. the following day. D. at Christchurch, Hants, 26th May, 1856.

Capt. F. Read, Rl. Staff Corps.

Francis Read d. a capt. in the same regt., 4th June, 1829. He appears to have been a relative of Lt.-Col. Wm. Read, who d. at Madras, 21st Aug., 1827, whilst holding the appointment of D.Q.M.G. Another of the same family (Constantine) was a Lieut. in Rl. Staff Corps, 1830.

Lt. P. T. de Barrailler, 33rd Foot.

Peter Toussaint de Barrailler was, as his name implies, of Gallic origin. The irony of fate decreed that he should use his sword against the Gallic army in 1815. His name disappeared from the Army List a few years after Waterloo.

Lt. Basil Jackson, Rl. Staff Corps.

The following memoir of this distinguished veteran appeared in the *Illustrated London News* of 9th Nov., 1889 :—" A gallant military veteran, who has died at the great age of ninety-four, was reckoned one of the four surviving officers of the British Army present at the battle of Waterloo. Colonel Basil Jackson, born at Glasgow on June 27, 1795, was son of Major Basil Jackson ; he entered the Military College in 1808, and, having received his commission as ensign, did not join a Line regiment, but was transferred to the Royal Staff Corps, where he learned the duties of the Quartermaster-General's Department and engineering. In that branch of the Army he was employed in Holland and Belgium, in 1814 and 1815, and in the Waterloo campaign did good service in clearing the roads, and on the Duke of Wellington's Staff. He accompanied the army to Paris, and was afterwards selected to go to St. Helena with Napoleon. In that island he remained till about a year and a half before Napoleon's death. At a later period he was employed in Nova Scotia and in Canada, taking part in the construction of the Rideau Canal. He held the Professorship of Military Surveying in the East India Company's Military College at Addiscombe during twenty years. After retiring from the army he lived at Hillsborough, near Ross, in Herefordshire.' M. 28th March, 1828, the dau. of Col. Muttlebury, C.B.

Lt. A. Brauns, Rl. Staff Corps.

Probably a son of the Col. John Brauns, of the German Legion, who was killed at the battle of Talavera. The above officer bore the names of "Augustus Christ. Gotleib." Was placed on h. p. as lieut., in 1819. Living 1846.

COMMANDANT AT HEAD-QUARTERS.

Col. Sir Colin Campbell, K.C.B., 2nd Ft. Gds.

5th son of John Campbell, of Melfort, by Colina, dau. of John Campbell, of Auchalader. In 1792 he ran away from Perth Academy, and entered himself on the books of a ship bound for the West Indies. He was met in the fruit market at Kingston, Jamaica, by his brother Patrick (aftds. an admiral), a lieut. on board a man-of-war, who brought him home. In 1793 became a midshipman on board an East Indiaman. Two years later we find him serving as a lieut. in the 3rd Batt. Breadalbane Fencibles, and in 1799 he was appointed ens. in a West India Regt. Exchanged to the Ross-shire Buffs, and as capt.; served under Sir A. Wellesley at the storming of Ahmednuggur, where his distinguished gallantry won him a brevet majority. At Assaye he had two horses shot under him, and was severely wounded. He accompanied Sir A. Wellesley to the Peninsula, and was for a considerable time on the staff of the army. For his services in Spain he obtained the gold cross with six clasps, and in Jan., 1815, was made K.C.B. He was a splendid soldier, but a bad French scholar. "When he wished his dinner to be arranged on the table, he used, as it were, to address the dishes, '*Bif-teck venez ici! Petits pâtés allez là!*'" (anecdote by Wellington). Was Governor of Ceylon from 1840-7. During his residence there he frequently heard from his great chief, Wellington, his attached friend. "We are both growing old," wrote the Duke to Campbell; "God knows if we shall ever meet again. Happen what may, I shall never forget our first meeting under the walls of Ahmednuggur." Sir Colin returned to England in June, 1847, and d. on the 13th of same month, in London, aged seventy-one, and was buried in St. James's Church, Piccadilly.

BRITISH AND HANOVERIAN ARMY

AT

WATERLOO,

As formed in Divisions and Brigades on the 18th June, 1815.

CAVALRY.

Commanded by Lieut.-Gen. the Earl of UXBRIDGE, G.C.B.

1st Brigade.—Commanded by Major-Gen. Lord EDWARD SOMERSET, K.C.B.

1st Life Guards	Lieut.-Col. Ferrior.
2nd „	Lieut.-Col. the Hon. E. P. Lygon
Royal Horse Guards (Blue) . .	Lieut.-Col. Sir Robert Hill.
1st Dragoon Guards	Lieut.-Col. Fuller (Col).

2nd Brigade.—Major Gen. Sir WILLIAM PONSONBY, K.C.B.

1st, or Royal Dragoons . . .	Lieut.-Col. A. B. Clifton.
2nd (or Royal N. B.) Dragoons .	Lieut.-Col. J. I. Hamilton.
6th, or Inniskilling Dragoons .	Lieut.-Col. J. Muter (Col.)

3rd Brigade.—Major-Gen. W. B. DORNBERG.

23rd Light Dragoons	Lieut.-Col. the Earl of Portarlington (Col.).
1st „ K.G.L. .	Lieut.-Col. J. Bulow.
2nd „ „ .	Lieut.-Col. C. de Jonquiera.

4th Brigade.—Major-Gen. Sir JOHN O. VANDELEUR, K.C.B.

11th Light Dragoons	Lieut.-Col. J. W. Sleigh.
12th „	Lieut.-Col. the Hon. F. C. Ponsonby (Col.).
16th „	Lieut.-Col. J. Hay.

5th Brigade.—Major-Gen. Sir COLQUHOUN GRANT, K.C.B.

7th Hussars	Col. Sir Edward Kerrison.
15th „	Lieut.-Col. L. C. Dalrymple.
2nd „ K.G.L.	Lieut.-Col. Linsingen.

6th Brigade.—Major-Gen. Sir HUSSEY VIVIAN, K.C.B.

10th Royal Hussars. . . . . Lieut.-Col. Quentin (Col.).
18th Hussars . . . . Lieut.-Col. the Hon. H. Murray.
1st „ K.G.L. . . . . Lieut.-Col. A. Wissell.

7th Brigade.—Col. Sir F. ARENSCHILDT, K.C.B.

13th Light Dragoons . . . . Lieut.-Col. P. Doherty.
3rd Hussars, K.G.L. . . . . Lieut.-Col. Meyer.

Col. BARON ESTORFF.

Prince Regent's Hussars . . . Lieut.-Col. Count Kielmansegge.
Bremen and Verden Hussars . Col. Busche.

BRITISH HORSE ARTILLERY.

Batteries . . . .
{ Major Bull's (Howitzers).
Lieut.-Col. Webber Smith's.
Lieut.-Col. Sir Robert Gardiner's.
Capt. Whinyates's (with rockets).
Capt. Mercer's.
Major Ramsay's.

INFANTRY.

First Division.

Major-Gen. GEORGE COOKE.

1st Brigade.—Maj.-Gen. P. MAITLAND.

1st Foot Guards, 2nd Batt. . . Major H. Askew (Col.).
„ „ 3rd „ . . Major Hon. Wm. Stewart.

2nd Brigade.—Major-Gen. Sir J. BYNG.

Coldstream Guards, 2nd Batt. . Major A. G. Woodford (Col.).
3rd Regt. Foot Guards, 2nd Batt. Major F. Hepburn (Col.).

ARTILLERY.

Lieut.-Col. ADYE.

Batteries . . . .
{ Capt. Sandham's Foot Battery.
Major Kuhlman's Horse „ (K.G.L.)

Second Division.

Lieut.-Gen. Sir H. CLINTON, G.C.B.

3rd Brigade.—Major-Gen. F. ADAM.

52nd Foot, 1st Batt. . . . . Lieut.-Col. Sir J. Colborne, K.C.B.
71st „ „ . . . . Lieut.-Col. T. Reynell.
95th „ 2nd Rifles . . . . Major J. Ross (Lieut.-Col.).
95th „ 3rd „ . . . . Major A. G. Norcott (Lieut.-Col.).

1st Brigade, K.G.L.—Col. Du Plat.

1st Line Batt., K.G.L.	. . .	Major W. Robertson.
2nd „ „	. . .	Major G. Muller.
3rd „ „	. . .	Lieut.-Col. F. de Wissell.
4th „ „	. . .	Major F. Reb.

3rd Hanoverian Brigade.—Col. Halkett.

Milᵃ Batt. Bremervorde	. . .	Lieut.-Col. Schulenberg.
Duke of York's, 2nd Batt.	. .	Major Count Munster.
„ 3rd „	. .	Major Baron Hunefeld.
Milᵃ Batt., Salzgitter .	. . .	Major Hammerstein.

ARTILLERY.

Lieut.-Col. Gold.

Batteries	. ·	{ Capt. Bolton's Foot Battery (British). { Major A. Sympher's Horse ditto (K.G.L.).

Third Division.

Lieut.-Gen. Baron Alten.

5th Brigade.—Major-Gen. Sir Colin Halkett, K.C.B.

30th Foot, 2nd Batt.	. . . .	Major W. Bailey (Lieut.-Col).
33rd „		Lieut.-Col. W. K. Elphinstone.
69th „ 2nd Batt.	. . . .	Lieut.-Col. C. Morice (Col.).
73rd „ „	. . . .	Lieut.-Col. W. G. Harris (Col.).

2nd Brigade K.G.L.—Col. Baron Ompteda.

1st Light Batt., K.G.L.	. . .	Lieut.-Col. L. Bussche.
2nd „ „ „	. . .	Major G. Baring.
5th Line „ „ „	. . .	Lieut.-Col. W. B. Linsingen.
8th „ „ „	. . .	Major Schroeder (Lieut.-Col.).

1st Hanoverian Brigade.—Major-Gen. Count Kielmansegge.

Duke of York's 1st Batt.	. .	Major Bulow.
Field Batt. Grubenhagen	. .	Lieut.-Col. Wurmb.
„ Bremen.	. . . .	Lieut.-Col. Langrehr.
„ Luneburg .	. . ·	Lieut.-Col. Kleucke.
„ Verden .	. . . .	Major De Senkopp.

ARTILLERY.

Lieut.-Col. Williamson.

Foot Batteries ·	. ·	{ Major Lloyd's (British). { Capt. A. Cleves's (K.G.L.).

Fourth Division.

Lieut.-Gen. Hon. Sir CHARLES COLVILLE, K.C.B.

4th Brigade.—Col. MITCHELL.

14th Foot, 3rd Batt. . . . . Major F. S. Tidy (Lieut.-Col.).
23rd ,, 1st ,, ... Lieut.-Col. Sir Henry W. Ellis, K.C.B.
51st ,, ... Lieut.-Col. H. Mitchell (Col.).

6th Brigade.—Major-Gen. JOHNSTONE.

35th Foot, 2nd Batt. . . . . Major C. M'Alister.
54th ,, ... Lieut.-Col. J., Earl Waldegrave.
59th ,, 2nd Batt. . . . . Lieut.-Col. H. Austin.
91st ,, 1st ,, ... Lieut.-Col. Sir W. Douglas, K.C.B. (Col.).

6th Hanoverian Brigade.—Major-Gen. LYON.

Field Batt. Calenberg . . . .
,, Lanenberg . . . Lieut.-Col. Benort.
Mila Batt. Hoya . . . . . . Lieut.-Col. Grote.
,, Nieuberg . . . .
,, Bentheim . . . . Major Croupp.

ARTILLERY.

Lieut.-Col. HAWKER.

Foot Batteries . . . . . . { Major Brome's (British).
{ Capt. von Rettberg's (Hanoverian).

Fifth Division.

Lieut.-Gen. Sir THOMAS PICTON, G.C.B.

8th Brigade.—Major-Gen. Sir JAMES KEMPT, K.C.B.

28th Foot, 1st Batt. . . . . Sir C. Belson (Col.).
32nd ,, ,, ... Major J. Hicks (Lieut.-Col.).
79th ,, ,, ... Lieut.-Col. N. Douglas.
95th ,, ,, ... Lieut.-Col. Sir A. F. Barnard, K.C.B. (Col.).

9th Brigade.—Major-Gen. Sir DENIS PACK, K.C.B.

1st Foot, 3rd Batt. . . . . . Major C. Campbell.
42nd ,, 1st ,, ... Lieut.-Col. Sir Robert Macara, K.C.B.
44th ,, 2nd ,, ... Lieut.-Col. J. M. Hamerton.
92nd ,, 1st ,, ... Lieut.-Col. J. Cameron (Col.).

5th Hanoverian Brigade.—Col. VINCKE.

Mila Batt. Hameln. . . . . Lieut.-Col. Kleucke.
,, Hildesheim . . . Major Rheden.
,, Peina . . . . . Major Westphalen.
,, Giffhorn . . . . Major Hammerstein.

ARTILLERY.

Major HEISE.

Foot Batteries . . . . . . $\left\{\begin{array}{l}\text{Major Rogers's (British).} \\ \text{Capt. Braun's (Hanoverian).}\end{array}\right.$

Sixth Division.

10*th Brigade.*—Major-Gen. J. LAMBERT.

4th Foot, 1st Batt.	Lieut.-Col. F. Brooke.
27th ,, 1st ,, ...	Capt. John Hare (Major).
40th ,, 1st ,, ...	Major A. Heyland.

4*th Hanoverian Brigade.*—Col. BEST.

Milᵃ Batt. Luneburg	Lieut.-Col. de Ramdohr.
,, Verden	Major Decken.
,, Osterode	Major Baron Reden.
,, Minden	Major De Schmidt.

ARTILLERY.

Lieut.-Col. BRUCKMANN.

Foot Batteries . . . . . . $\left\{\begin{array}{l}\text{Major Unett's (British).} \\ \text{Capt. Sinclair's (British).}\end{array}\right.$

REGIMENTAL LISTS.

1st LIFE GUARDS.

(2 *Squadrons*.)

	Rank in the Regiment.	Army.
MAJOR AND LIEUT.-COLONEL.		
[1] Samuel Ferrior, K.	22 June, 1809	
CAPTAINS.		
[2] John Whale, w.	13 Nov. 1809	
[3] Montague Lind, K.	22 June, 1810	
[4] Edward Kelly, w.	2 Aug. 1810	13 Sept. 1805
[5] John Berger	20 May, 1813	Maj., 4 June, 1814
LIEUTENANTS.		
[6] George Randall	15 Apr. 1811	
[7] William Mayne	26 Sept. 1811	
CORNETS AND SUB-LIEUTENANTS.		
[8] William Stewart Richardson, w.	23 Feb. 1813	
[9] Samuel Cox, w.	1 June, 1814	
[10] George Story	3 Apr. 1815	4 Aug. 1814
QUARTERMASTERS.		
[11] [Wm.] Dobson, w.		
— Towers, K.		
— Slingsby, K.		
ASSISTANT SURGEONS.		
[12] Richard Gough	22 Sept. 1812	
[13] John Haddy James	27 Oct. 1812	
VETERINARY SURGEON.		
[14] Francis Dalton	20 May, 1813	

*Scarlet. Facings blue. Lace **gold**.*

[1] Is said to have led his regt. to the charge no less than eleven times, "And most of the charges were not made till after his head had been laid open by the cut of a sabre and his body was pierced with a lance."

[2] Exchanged to 16th Dgns. as maj. (commission dated 18th June, 1815). Quitted the service before 1st March, 1817.

[3] Only son of Edward George Lind, of Stratford Place.

[4] Bn. at Portarlington, Queen's County, 1771. At Waterloo he encountered and killed the col. of the 1st Regt. of French Cuirassiers, stripped him of his epaulettes, and carried them off as a trophy. Made brevet-maj. for Waterloo and Knight of St. Anne of Russia. Exchanged into 23rd Light Dgns. and served as A.D.C. to Gen. Lord Combermere at the siege of Bhurtpore. D. at Mullye, 6th Aug., 1828, as col. on staff. His widow d. 22nd Nov., 1860.

[5] Quitted the service 14th Dec., 1815.

[6] Promoted capt. 18th June, 1815. H. p. 13th Oct., 1825. Living in 1847.

[7] Promoted capt. 14th Dec., 1815. Out of the regt. before 1824.

[8] Promoted lieut. 5th June, 1815. Lieut. in the 55th Foot, 24th Oct., 1822. Capt. 24th Dec., 1825. H. p. same date.

[9] Afterwards Capt. Samuel Fortnam Cox, of Sandford Park, Oxfordshire. M., 1820, Mary Emily, dau. of Sir Robert Sheffield, Bart. R. h. p. 1829. D. 22nd Nov., 1849.

[10] This officer had been taken prisoner during the preceding war, and been kept a prisoner for seven years at Verdun, in France. In the first charge made by the Life Guards at Waterloo, Lt. Story was in the act of raising his sword to cut down a French soldier, when the latter suddenly threw down his firelock and thus accosted him : " Monsieur, ne me tuez pas ; je vous connois à Verdun ; sauvez-moi la vie en grâce ! " Story immediately recognised the speaker, and not only spared the French soldier's life, but likewise that of his comrade—also from Verdun—and sent them as prisoners to the rear. In May, 1815, Story obtained permission from the Prince Regent to accept and wear the Russian Order of St. Vladimir of the 4th class. Retired about 1825, and d. at Maidenhead 20th Feb., 1828.

[11] Retd. on f. p. in 1828. D. in Dec., 1849.

[12] Retd. on h. p. 25th Dec., 1818. Living in 1830.

[13] Serving in 1816. Out of the regt. in 1817.

[14] Serving in 1817. Out of the regt. in 1818.

2ND LIFE GUARDS.

(2 *Squadrons.*)

	Rank in the Regiment.	Army
MAJOR AND LIEUT.-COLONEL.		
[1] Hon. Edward P. Lygon	27 Apr. 1815	
CAPTAINS.		
[2] William Boyce	30 Apr. 1812	Maj., 4 June, 1814
[3] Richard Fitzgerald, K.	18 May, 1812	{ Lt.-Col., 4 June, 1814
[4] Hon. Henry Edw. Irby	22 Sept. 1812	7 Aug. 1806
[5] James P. M. Kenyon	23 Sept. 1812	
LIEUTENANTS.		
[6] Richard Meares	23 Sept. 1802	10 Mar. 1808
[7] William Elliott	27 Nov. 1802	
[8] Samuel Waymouth, w.	28 Mar. 1813	
[9] Chum. (*sic*) Barton	30 Jan. 1814	
CORNETS AND SUB-LIEUTENANTS.		
[10] Abraham Kenyon	24 June, 1813	
[11] Thomas Marten	22 Nov. 1813	
[12] Alexander McInnes	16 June, 1814	
[13] Josiah Clues, Adjt.	12 Apr. 1815	
QUARTERMASTERS.		
— Bradley, K.		
— Beamond, K.		
SURGEON.		
[14] Samuel Broughton	22 Sept. 1812	
ASSISTANT-SURGEON.		
[15] Thomas Drinkwater	22 Sept. 1812	
VETERINARY SURGEON.		
[16] Jeremiah Field	24 Apr. 1813	

Scarlet.   Facings blue.   Lace gold.

[1] 4th son of Edward Lygon, of Worcester (who was created Baron and Earl Beauchamp), by Catherine, only dau. of James Dennis. For his forward gallantry at Waterloo was made C.B. and a K. St. V. of Russia. Was aftds. Inspector-gen. of cavalry. Gen. and Col.-in-Chf. 13th Lt. Dgns. D. 11th Nov., 1860.

[2] Placed on h. p. 24th April, 1817.

[3] 4th and only surviving son of — Fitzgerald, of the County Clare. Was for ten years detained in France with others of his family. Returned to England 1812, and purchased a troop in the 2nd Life Guards. Served in the Pa. Shot whilst gallantly leading his squadron against the enemy. Buried at Waterloo. M. I. in church there. His widow brought out a coffin to remove his remains to England ; but it proved too short, and the body was re-interred. His will, dated at Paris, 30th Nov., 1810, was proved by his sister, Catherine, 3rd Aug., 1815. His widow (Georgina Isabella Sinclair) resigned her pension in favour of her husband's three sisters.

[4] Son of 2nd Baron Boston. Bt.-maj. for Waterloo. Was taken prisoner as his horse fell in returning from the charge, but escaped soon afterwards. Retd. as lt.-col., and died at Calais, 1821.

[5] Placed on h. p. 10th Oct., 1816. M., Sept., 1817, Julia, only dau. of Gen. Rainsford, and had issue. His name does not appear in the Kenyon pedigree given in Foster's *Lancashire Families*. D. at Brandon, 20th Jan., 1830, aged 45.

[6] Placed on h. p. as capt 24th Dec., 1818.

[7] Promoted capt. 14th April, 1818. Appointed capt. in the 17th Foot 20th Jan., 1821. Serving in 1824. Out of said regt. before 1830.

[8] Severely wounded and taken prisoner in a charge against the French cuirassiers. Lieut. in 88th Foot, 13th Oct., 1825 ; h. p. in Dec., 1825. Capt. in 30th Foot, 8th Feb., 1839. Retd. in 1741 as lt.-col. unattached. D. as col. 26th Dec., 1863.

[9] Chambré Brabazon Barton. 2nd son of Thos. Barton of Grove, M.P. for Fethard before the Union. Capt. 1818. Lt.-col. h. p. 1825. D. 1834.

[10] Younger brother to J. P. Kenyon. On h. p. 2nd D.G., 1817. Lieut. 2nd W. I. Regt., 13th Dec., 1833.

[11] Bn. at Winchilsea, 29th Dec., 1797. Had exceptionally high interest in early life. Cornet in the regt. 1813. Lt.-col. Rl. Dns. in 1835. Aftds. Maj.-Gen. and Col.-in-Ch. 6th Dns. K.H. Resided at Beverley. M. Miss Ellison, and d. s. p. 22nd Nov., 1868

[12] Son of Thos. McInnes of Edinburgh, architect, by Jane Nicholson, sister to Lt.-Gen. Robt. Nicholson, E.I.C.S., who distinguished himself at the siege of Baroach in the E. Indies. Cornet McInnes, who had served at Vittoria, assumed the name and arms of Nicholson by Rl. Licence in 1821. He m. Cecilia Innes, eldest dau. and co-heir of Peter Innes of Fraserfield, in Shetland. She d. in 1842. In the *Gentleman's Magazine* for 1862 occurs the following notice :—

"Feb. 9th.—In the Charterhouse, aged 82, Alexander Nicholson, Esq., formerly Captain 2nd Life Guards, late of East Court, Charlton King's, near Cheltenham, and of Ufford, Suffolk. Descended from an old family long settled at Loan End, near Norham, co. Durham."

[13] Placed on h. p. as lt., 83rd Foot, 25th Jan., 1817. Living in 1830.

[14] Grandson of the Rev. Thos. Broughton, rector of St. Mary Redcliffe, Bristol. Succeeded Mr. Moore (elder bro. to Sir John Moore) as surgeon, F.R.S. D. after having his leg amputated 20th Aug., 1837.

[15] Out of the regt. in 1818.

[16] Placed on h. p. 25th Dec., 1818. Living in 1846.

ROYAL REGIMENT OF HORSE GUARDS.

	Rank in the	
COLONEL.	Regiment.	Army.
Arthur,Duke of WELLINGTON,*K.G.*1 Jan. 1813		F.-M., 21 June, [1813
LIEUT.-COLONELS.		
Sir John Elley, K.C.B., w.	6 Mar. 1806	Col., 7 Mar. 1813
[1] SirRobt.Chambre Hill,Knt.w.	13 May, 1813	1 Jan. 1812
MAJOR.		
[2] Robert Christopher Packe K.	13 May, 1813	
CAPTAINS.		
[3] John Thoyts	22 Aug. 1805	
[4] William Robert Clayton	27 Apr. 1809	
Clement Hill, w.	4 Apr. 1811	Lt.-Col., 30 Dec.
[5] William Tyrwhitt Drake	29 Aug. 1811	[1813
LIEUTENANTS.		
[6] John B. Riddlesden	4 Apr. 1811	
[7] William Cunliffe Shawe, w.	26 Dec. 1811	
[8] Everard William Bouverie, w.	15 Oct. 1812	
Charles Augustus Fitzroy	16 Oct. 1812	
[9] Henry Ellis Boates	28 Jan. 1813	
[10] Tathwell Baker Tathwell	9 Sept. 1813	
[11] George Smith	18 Nov. 1813	
[12] Hon. George John Watson	24 Mar. 1814	
CORNETS.		
[13] John Kirkby Picard	2 Sept. 1813	
[14] James Arnold	1 Sept. 1814	
QUARTERMASTERS.		
[15] Thomas Varley, w.	20 Mar. 1806	
[16] Peter Watmough	22 Feb. 1809	
[17] Thomas Hardy	13 Feb. 1812	
[18] Jonas Varley, w.	18 May, 1813	
[19] Thomas Troy	5 Aug. 1813	
SURGEON.		
[20] David Slow	18 July, 1805	23 Aug. 1799
VETERINARY SURGEON.		
[21] John Seddall (*sic*)	10 Oct. 1812	

Blue. Facings scarlet. Lace gold.

[1] 4th son of Sir John Hill, Bart., and brother to Lord Hill. C.B. for Waterloo. Col., 1st Jan., 1819. Of Prees Hall, Salop. M., 5th Feb., 1801, Eliza, dau. of Henry Lumley, and had issue. D. 5th March, 1860.

[2] 2nd son of Charles Packe, of Prestwold, co. Leicester. M.I. in St. George's Chapel, Windsor.

[3] 3rd son of John Thoyts, of Sulhamstead, Berks, by Mary, dau. of Thos. Burfoot, Treasurer of Christ's Hospital. Bn. 2nd Nov., 1771. Matriculated at B.N.C., Oxford, 23rd March, 1789. Cornet R. H. Gds., 14th Feb., 1800. Served in the Pa. His horse was shot under him at Waterloo, and he was taken prisoner. Detained at Charleroi for some days by the French rear-guard. Promoted maj., 18th June, 1815, and bt. lt.-col. same date. Retd. 1820. D. May, 1849. Bd. at Kensal Green.

[4] Eldest son of Sir W. Clayton, Bart., by Mary, dau. of Sir Wm. East, Bart. Succeeded as 5th Bart. in 1834. M., in 1817, Alice, dau. and co-heir of Col. O'Donel, son of Sir Neil O'Donel, Bart., and had issue. Served in the Pa. Attained rank of maj.-gen. 1858. D. 1866.

[5] 2nd son of Robert Tyrwhitt Drake, of Shardeloes, Bucks. Lt.-col. 22nd June, 1820. M., 22nd Aug., 1832, Emma, dau. of Joseph Halsey, and had issue. D. 21st Dec., 1848.

[6] Served in the Pa., and was present at Vittoria and Toulouse. Attained rank of col. h. p., 23rd Nov., 1841. Living 1874.

[7] Eldest son of Joseph Cunliffe Shawe. Capt. same regt., 1816. M. — Pattenson, of Selwood, Bath, and had issue.

[8] Aftds. Gen. and Col.-in-Chf. 15th Hussars. Of Delapré Abbey, North-ampton. Son of Edward Bouverie. Bn. 13th Oct., 1789. M., 3rd April, 1816, Charlotte, dau. of Col. Hugh O'Donel. D. s. p. 18th Nov., 1871.

[9] Of Rose Hill, Denbigh. Killed out hunting, 8th Dec., 1838. Lt.-col. h. p. 1828.

[10] Was taken prisoner at Waterloo, but effected his escape two days after. It is on record that he captured a French eagle, which was retaken by his captors. See *Stamford Mercury*, 4th Aug., 1815.

[11] Aftds. maj. and bt.-lt.-col. same regt. Living 1846.

[12] Aftds. 4th Baron Sondes, of Lees Court, Kent. Bn. 20th Jan., 1794. Quitted the service 1816. M., 24th July, 1823, Eleanor, 5th dau. of Sir Edward Knatchbull, Bart., and had issue. Assumed the surname of Milles, D. 17th Dec., 1874.

[13] Quitted the service as lieut. R.H.G. in 1821.

[14] Reduced with his tp. in 1818.

[15] Placed on h. p. 12th Dec., 1822. Appointed a Military Knight of Windsor. D. at Windsor 25th March, 1841, aged 69.

[16] Retd. on f. p. before 1830 and d. 1841.

[17] Placed on h. p. 25th Aug., 1822. D. in 1855.

[18] Serving in 1824. Out of the regt. before 1830.

[19] Retd. f. p. 1829. Living in 1846.

[20] Serving in 1824. Out of the regt. in Jan., 1826.

[21] *Siddall.* D. at Windsor 2nd Oct., 1856, aged 69. " He served 52 years in the Royal Horse Guards, and was the last surviving Waterloo officer of the regiment."—*Naval and Military Gazette.*

E 2

1ST (OR THE KING'S) REGIMENT OF DRAGOON GUARDS.

	Rank in the Regiment.	Army.
LIEUT.-COLONEL.		
1 William Fuller, K.	22 Aug. 1805	Col., 4 June, 1813
CAPTAINS.		
2 Henry Graham, K.	12 June, 1799	Maj., 4 June, 1811
3 Michael Turner, w.	4 July, 1805	
4 James Frank Naylor, w.	15 May, 1806	
5 William Elton	11 May, 1809	
6 John Dorset Bringhurst, K.	24 Oct. 1811	Maj., 12 Apr. 1814
7 John Paget Sweeny, w.	9 Jan. 1812	
8 Robert Wallace	20 Oct. 1814	
9 Thomas N. Quicke	8 Dec. 1814	
Hon. George L. Dawson	6 Apr. 1815	Maj., 10 Mar. 1814
10 George Battersby, K.		2 Sept. 1813
LIEUTENANTS.		
11 James Leatham	12 June, 1806	
12 William Stirling	19 Mar. 1812	
13 Ralph Babington	18 June, 1812	
14 Francis Brooke, K.	31 Dec. 1812	
15 Robert Toovey Hawley	30 Sept. 1813	
16 Thos. Coventry Brander	30 Mar. 1814	
17 Thos. Shelver, Adjt., K.	31 Mar. 1814	
18 Edward Hamill	17 Nov. 1814	
19 Wm. d'Arcy Irvine, w.	15 Feb. 1815	
20 Jos. Edward Greaves	16 Feb. 1815	
21 John N. Hibbert	30 Mar. 1815	
22 George Quicke	3 May, 1815	
23 Thos. Falkiner Middleton	4 May, 1815	
CORNETS.		
24 Hon. H. B. Bernard, K.	15 June, 1814	
25 Wm. Warburton Huntley	16 June, 1814	
QUARTERMASTER.		
26 John Brown	15 June, 1815	
SURGEON.		
27 John Going	17 Dec. 1801	
ASSISTANT-SURGEONS.		
28 William M'Auley	16 Aug. 1810	8 Feb. 1810
29 Robert Pearson	13 May, 1813	

Scarlet. Facings blue. Lace gold.

[1] In his will, dated 14th March, 1813, and proved in London, 21st Aug., 1815, he mentions his brothers Joseph, Richard, and George. The first-named was left sole executor and residuary legatee.

[2] Pens. of £100 per ann. granted to his widow, Maria Graham.

[3] Promoted maj. 7th Sept., 1815. Out of the regt. in 1818.

[4] Retd. as bt.-maj. in 1820. D. in 1854.

[5] Lt.-col. h. p. 5th Nov., 1825. 2nd son of the Rev. Sir Abraham Elton, Bart. Bn. 6th Jan., 1785. D. 15th Nov., 1848.

[6] Of Woodstone, co. Huntingdon. Administration of his personalty and effects was granted, on 22nd Nov., 1815, to his widow, Frances Maria Bringhurst. M.I. at Waterloo.

[7] Promoted maj. 28th Aug., 1823. On h. p. 1825.

[8] Resided in York, and was a well-known figure in York society. Bn. 1st Nov., 1789. 6th son of John Wallace, of Sedcop House, Kent, who was uncle of the Rt. Hon. Thos. Wallace (created Baron Wallace, 1828). When charging with his regt. at Waterloo, a French trumpeter was passed lying on the ground. Few of the regt. forbore to have a slash at their fallen enemy, as they galloped past ; but Robert Wallace was merciful. "I did not slash at him," said the kind-hearted old colonel, in narrating the incident, "but the trumpeter slashed at me !" Promoted maj. in same regt. 1828. K.H. M. Henrietta Ellis (sister to Thos. Ellis, M.P. for Dublin), and had issue. D., as col., 25th March, 1863.

[9] 4th son of John Quicke, of Newton St. Cyres, by Emily, dau. of Alex. Cumming. M., 1823, Sophia, dau. of John Evered. On h. p. 1827. D. 1830.

[10] Bn. 20th April, 1788. Youngest son of John Battersby, of the Westmeath family. Fell in the last cavalry charge.

[11] Promoted capt. 19th July, 1815. Placed on h. p. 28th April, 1825. Living in 1860 as a lt.-col., retd.

[12] Promoted capt. same regt. 20th July, 1815. Placed on h. p. 12th Feb., 1818. Bn. 1789. Son of Wm. Stirling, of Keir and Cawder, by his 2nd wife (Jean, dau. of Sir John Stuart, Bart.). Was twice married. The only issue of the first marriage was the late Wm. Stuart Stirling Crawford, who married the D.-Duchess of Montrose.

[13] A cadet of the ancient Leicestershire family of this name. Promoted capt. 6th Sept., 1815.

[14] Bn. 1794. Eldest son of Sir H. Brooke, of Colebrooke, Bart.

[15] Promoted capt. 30th Dec., 1826. On h. p. 1828. See pedigree of this family in the *Genealogist*, Vol. I.

[16] Capt., 15th Lt. Dns., 1st June, 1839. Retd. on h. p. in 1840. D. at Somerford Grange, near Christchurch, 12th Nov., 1861.

[17] Had been appointed adjt., Feb., 1812.

[18] Capt. 19th Dec., 1822. Exchanged to 66th Foot 19th June, 1823. Capt. h. p. 28th June, 1827.

[19] Of Castle Irvine, Irvinestown, Fermanagh. He adopted the surname of D'Arcy. Retired from the army 2nd Jan., 1817. M., 1817, Maria, dau. of Sir Henry Brooke, of Colebrooke, Bart., and had issue. D. 23rd June, 1857.

[20] Of Thornhill and Woodlands, co. York. 2nd son of George Bustard Greaves, by Ellen, dau. and heir of Joseph Clay, of Bridge House, co. York. Assumed the name of Elmsall in 1817. Capt. 1820. On h. p. 1821. M., 19th Feb., 1824, Hannah, youngest dau. of Adam Lawson, of Cramlington, and had issue. D. 5th July, 1851, as a maj., retd. list.

[21] Of Chalfont Park, co. Bucks. 3rd son of Robert Hibbert, of Birtles Hall, co. Chester, by Letitia, dau. of John Nembhard, of Jamaica. M., 6th Aug., 1833, Jane, eldest dau. of Sir Robert Alexander, Bart. D., 3rd Jan., 1886.

[22] Younger brother to the above Capt. Quicke. D. at Southsea 18th Sept., 1838.

[23] Placed on h. p. in 1816.

[24] Bn. 5th Dec., 1797. 5th son of 1st Viscount Bandon, by the only dau. of Richard, 2nd Earl of Shannon.

[25] Capt. 3rd D. G., 16th March, 1832.

[26] H. p. 30th March, 1838. D. 21st Feb., 1851.

[27] Left the regt. in March, 1817.

[28] Left the regt. in 1816.

[29] Appointed surgeon to 87th Foot, 13th Aug., 1830. Placed on h. p. in 1847.

1st (or ROYAL) REGIMENT OF DRAGOONS.

	Rank in the	
	Regiment.	Army.
LIEUT-COLONEL.		
1 Arthur Benjamin Clifton	22 Nov. 1810	25 July, 1810
MAJOR.		
2 Philip Dorville	17 Oct. 1811	Lt.-Col., 4 June, 1814
CAPTAINS.		
3 Charles Edward Radclyffe, w.	1 Dec. 1804	Maj., 4 June, 1814
4 Alex. Kennedy Clark, w.	13 Dec. 1810	
5 Paul Phipps	25 July, 1811	
6 Edward Chas. Windsor, k.	18 June, 1812	
LIEUTENANTS.		
Charles Foster, k.	18 Nov. 1807	
7 Henry Robert Carden	13 Apr. 1809	
8 George Gunning, w.	7 Dec. 1809	2 Sept. 1807
9 Townshend Richard Kelly, w.	25 Oct. 1810	
10 Sigismund Trafford	25 July, 1811	
11 Samuel Windowe, w.	21 Nov. 1811	
12 Cornthwaite Ommaney, w.	17 Apr. 1815	13 Aug. 1812
13 Charles Blois, w.	18 Apr. 1815	2 Sept. 1813
14 Stephen Goodenough, w.	19 Apr. 1815	6 Jan. 1814
CORNETS.		
15 Richard Magniac, k.	2 Sept. 1813	
16 William Sturges	30 Dec. 1813	
17 Charles Butler Stevenson	24 Mar. 1814	
18 Hon. John Massey	31 Mar. 1814	
19 John C. Sykes, k.	19 Jan. 1815	
T. — Shipley, Adjt., k.	19 Jan. 1815	
QUARTERMASTER.		
20 William Waddell	8 July, 1813	
SURGEON.		
21 George Steed	17 Jan. 1811	
ASSISTANT-SURGEON.		
22 Thomas Prosser	9 Dec. 1813	29 Aug. 1811
VETERINARY SURGEON.		
23 Wm. Ryding	2 June, 1804	2 May, 1800

Scarlet. Facings blue. Lace gold.

[1] 3rd son of Sir Gervase Clifton, Bart., of Clifton, Notts, representative of a very ancient family. Served throughout the Par. War, and received the gold medal and one clasp for Fuentes d'Onor and Vittoria. On the death of Sir Wm. Ponsonby at Waterloo, the command of the 2nd Cavalry Brigade devolved upon Col. Clifton. G.C.B., K.C.H., K.S.A., gen. in the army and Col.-in-Chf. 1st Dgns. D. 7th March, 1869, unm.

[2] The name of Dorville has only been known in England for a little over a century ; but it is that of a well-known Norman family which flourished for six hundred years in France prior to its exodus from France to North Germany, for religious causes, early in the 17th century. From Germany the " d'Orvilles " migrated to Holland, where the family left its mark in the person of the learned James Philip Dorville, professor of history and languages to a Dutch university, and likewise a Sicilian explorer, whose valuable book on Sicily (with rare illustrations), written in the purest Latin, is treasured, with other Dorville books, in the Bodleian Library. The professor's son, John Dorville, quitted Holland and settled in England. He bought the Ravenscourt Estate at Fulham. M. Anne Gibson (grand-daughter of Edmund Gibson, Bishop of London), and had three sons, the two younger of whom were Philip and Thomas, both of whom entered the army and did good service in the Par. War—the former being for some time on Lord Anglesey's staff, and the latter in the 1st Foot Guards. At Waterloo Col. Dorville commanded the two squadrons of the 1st Dgns. " which rushed into the second column of the enemy, consisting of about 4,000 men, and after a desperate fight returned with a French eagle." In this gallant charge Col. Dorville had the scabbard of his sword shot away, and a bullet passed through the breast of his coat. Had three horses shot under him. On the death of Sir Wm. Ponsonby the command of the " Union Brigade " devolved on Col. Muter, of the 6th Dgns., who, being soon after wounded, was replaced by Col. Clifton, and Col. Dorville succeeded to the command of the 1st Dgns. Made C.B. for Waterloo. Retd. on h. p. 8th March, 1827. M. Miss Dewar, of Clapham, and left at his death, 10th Nov., 1847, three daughters, who bequeathed the High Croft Estate at Malvern to their cousin, Admiral Dorville, the late possessor, the last male representative of an ancient family, on every page of whose eventful career in the navy the word " Hero " is plainly visible.

[3] "A most scientific and dexterous swordsman." Did good work in the famous charge of his regt. at Waterloo. A musket ball lodged in his knee, which could never be extracted, and helped to shorten his life. Made bt.-lt.-col. for Waterloo. H. p. list 1820. Appointed maj. of brigade to the Inspector-Gen. of Cavalry in Great Britain. D. 24th Feb., 1827.

[4] Aftds. Lt.-Gen. Sir Alexander Clark-Kennedy, of Knockgray, co. Kirkcudbright, A.D.C. to the Queen, K.C.B., and K.H. Served in the Pa. It was this officer, and not Corporal Stiles, who *personally* captured the French eagle of the 105th Regt. at Waterloo, after a desperate fight, in which he was severely wounded, and handed it over to Corporal Stiles (of whom see memoir in Part III.), to convey it to the rear. Bn. 1782. Son of John Clark, of Nunland, by Anne, dau. and co-heir of Alex. Kennedy, of Knockgray. M., 21st Dec., 1816, Harriet, dau. and co-heir of John Randall, and had issue. D. in Jan., 1864.

[5] 3rd son of Thos. Phipps, of Leighton House, Wilts, by Penelope, dau. of Lewis Clutterbuck, of Widcombe House, Bath. Bn. 18th Jan., 1789. Served in the Pa. Aftds. lt.-col., h. p. 1829, and K.H. M. Mrs. Kingston (*née*

Saunders), widow of Benjamin Kingston, and had. issue. D. 22nd Nov., 1858.

[6] Son of Edward Windsor, of Shrewsbury. A pen. of £50 per ann. was granted to his mother, Dorothy Windsor, she having expended all her fortune in buying her son's commission.

[7] Bn. 8th Feb., 1789. 2nd son of Col. Sir John Carden, 1st Bart. of Templemore, co Tipperary, who raised and commanded the 30th Regt. of Lt. Dgns., which regt. was reduced at the Peace of Amiens. Succeeded his brother as 3rd Bart. in 1822. M., 10th March, 1818, Louisa, only child of Frederick Thomson, of Dublin, and had issue. Was placed on h. p. as Capt. 1st Dgns. in 1816. D. in March, 1847.

[8] Eldest son of George Gunning, of Frindsbury, J.P. and D.L. for Kent. Ensign 17th Foot, 1804. Served in the Pa., and commanded the Grenadier Company of the 9th Foot at battle of Vimiera. Exchanged to 1st Dgns. 1809. Commanded his troop at Waterloo in the famous charge, where he was sev. wnded. He always claimed that he gave the order to Corporal Stiles to seize the eagle of the 105th French regt. from the officer who held it. (See Part III.) H. p. 1822. D. at Brighton, 5th Jan., 1849.

[9] Capt. h. p. 19th Jan., 1826. D. 5th April, 1854.

[10] Eldest son of Sigismund Trafford, of Wroxham Hall, Norfolk, Half-pay in 1816. Capt., h. p. in 1842. D. 14th Feb., 1852, at his residence, Rue de Lille, Paris.

[11] *Wyndowe.* Capt. 11th July, 1822. Serving in 1825. Out of the regt. before 1830.

[12] Capt. 24th Lt. Dgns., 24th Dec., 1818. Half-pay same date. D. at Chichester 14th Sept., 1833.

[13] Capt. 25th Sept., 1823. Major 27th Oct., 1829. Retd. 1st Sept., 1830. Was subsequently Lt.-Col. East Suffolk Militia. Eldest son of Sir Chas. Blois, 6th Bart. of Grundisburgh Hall, Suffolk. Succeeded as 7th Bart. in 1850. D. unm. in 1855.

[14] Capt. 20th July, 1826. Serving in 1830.

[15] Returned as "missing" in the *London Gazette* but was never again heard of. His gallantry at Waterloo is referred to in the *Gentleman's Magazine*, 1815.

[16] Lieut. 20th July, 1815 Exchanged to the Scots Greys 14th Sept., 1815. Capt. 4th April, 1822. Serving in 1830.

[17] Left the regt. in 1816.

[18] In 1822 was appointed to a troop in the Cape Corps. Placed on h. p. 1826. Lt.-col., retd. 1841. 3rd son of Hugh, 3rd Baron Massey. M., 12th April, 1828, Eliz., youngest dau. of Edward Homewood, and had issue. D. in Dublin 7th March, 1848.

[19] Grandson of Joseph Sykes of West Ella, Hull, brother of the Rev. Sir Mark Sykes, 1st Bart.

[20] Retd. f. p. 1828. Living in 1846.

[21] Retd. h. p. Sept. 1825. Living in 1846.

[22] Retd. on h. p. 18th Jan., 1816. Living in 1825.

[23] Serving in 1830.

2ND (OR ROYAL NORTH BRITISH) REGIMENT OF DRAGOONS.

	Rank in the	
LIEUT.-COLONEL.	Regiment.	Army.
1 James Inglis Hamilton, K.	16 June, 1807	Col., 4 June, 1814
MAJOR.		
2 Isaac Blake Clarke, w.	16 June, 1807	Lt.-Col., 4 June, 1814
3 Thomas Pate Hankin, w.	4 Apr. 1808	Lt.-Col., 4 June, 1814
CAPTAINS.		
4 Edward Cheney	3 May, 1800	Maj., 1 Jan. 1812
5 James Poole, w.	25 May, 1803	Maj., 4 June, 1813
6 Robert Vernor, w.	23 Nov. 1804	Maj., 4 June, 1814
Thomas Reignolds, K.	25 Dec. 1804	Maj., 4 June, 1814
7 Charles Levyns Barnard, K	2 Feb. 1815	
8 Thomas Charles Fenton	6 Feb. 1815	
9 Edward Payne	5 Apr. 1815	
LIEUTENANTS.		
10 Henry McMillan, Adjt.	10 Apr. 1805	
11 John Mills, w.	5 May, 1808	
12 Francis Stupart, w.	14 Dec. 1809	
13 Geo. Home Falconar	21 Nov. 1811	
14 James Wemyss	15 Sept. 1814	19 Nov. 1812
15 James Carruthers, K.	9 Feb. 1815	
16 Archibald J. Hamilton, w.	16 Mar. 1815	11 June, 1812
17 Thos. Trotter, K.	16 Mar. 1815	
18 James Gape	3 May, 1815	
19 Charles Wyndham, w.	4 May, 1815	
20 Jas. Reg. Torin Graham	8 June, 1815	
CORNETS.		
21 Edward Westby, K.	12 May, 1814	17 Feb. 1814
22 F. C. Kinchant, K.	18 Jan. 1815	
23 Lemuel Shuldham, K.	19 Jan. 1815	

2ND (OR ROYAL NORTH BRITISH) REGIMENT OF DRAGOONS—*continued*.

	Rank in the	
	Regiment.	Army
PAYMASTER.		
24 William Dawson	13 Oct. 1814	
QUARTERMASTER.		
25 John Lennox	3 June, 1813	
SURGEON.		
26 Robert Dann, M.D.	4 Aug. 1814	
ASSISTANT-SURGEON.		
27 James Alexander	9 Jan. 1812	
VETERINARY SURGEON.		
28 John Trigg	17 Dec. 1807	23 Dec. 1797

Scarlet. Facings blue. Lace gold.

[1] Second son of Sergt.-Major Wm. Anderson of the 21st Fusiliers. Born in camp at Tayantroga, America, 4th July, 1777, and bapt. 28th Aug. same year. On the return of the 21st to Scotland the sergt.-major was discharged with a pension and settled at his native city, Glasgow. Gen. James Inglis Hamilton, the colonel of the 21st, who was a Lanarkshire man, being on a visit to Glasgow some years later, happened to meet his former sergt.-major and gave him money for educational purposes. Later on he took little James Anderson to his family seat at Murdestoun and introduced him to his maiden sister Miss Christina Hamilton. The general and his sister educated James Anderson and his brothers at Glasgow Grammar School. Through his patron's army interest James Anderson was appointed Cornet in the Scots Greys at the age of fifteen under the name of James Inglis Hamilton. (*Old Reminiscences of Glasgow*, Vol. I.) Lieut. 4th Oct. 1793. Capt. 15th April, 1794. Major 17th Feb., 1803. Lt.-Col. 16th June, 1807. Bt.-Col. 4th June, 1814. Col. Hamilton had both arms cut off in the charge at Waterloo, and he snatched the reins with his mouth (Col. Clerke's letter to the Misses Anderson). Hamilton's body was found on the field—shot through the heart in addition to other wounds, and rifled. His trusty sword was gone, but the scabbard and silken sash remained. These relics were transmitted to Lieut. Jno. Anderson, the colonel's brother, who d. at Glasgow 3rd Dec., 1816, from wounds recd. at Salamanca. The Treasury remitted £200 to the Misses Anderson in Dec., 1829; and the Waterloo Fund gave a pension to Col. Hamilton's widow (*née* Clerke), who was an English lady.

[2] Promoted lt.-col. of the regt. 20th July, 1815. C.B. Retd. 11th Oct., 1821. D. at St. Peter's, Isle of Thanet, 7th Jan., 1850, aged 76.

[3] Knighted by the Prince Regent in 1816. Lt.-Col. of the regt. 11th Oct., 1821. D. at the cavalry barracks, Norwich, 20th Oct., 1825, aged 59. By his wife Sarah, dau. of John Reade, he had no issue, she having d. with her child in her first confinement.

⁴ Commanded the regt. for the last three hours of the battle, and in twenty minutes' time had five horses killed under him. C.B. Col. Eldest son of Robert Cheney, of Meynell Langley, co. Derby, by his second marriage with Bridget Leacroft. D. at Gaddesby, co. Leicester, 3rd March, 1847, leaving issue by his marriage with Elizabeth Ayre.

⁵ Taken prisoner at Waterloo. Quitted the service in consequence of mental derangement, 17th Feb., 1817, with the bt. rank of lt.-col.

⁶ This officer's name is erroneously spelt "Vernon" in the Army Lists. Left the service in 1817, and afterwards resided at Musselburgh.

⁷ 2nd son of Henry Barnard, of Cave Castle, co. York, whose family had long been settled in Yorkshire, by Sarah Eliz., eldest dau. and co-heir of Roger Gee, of Bishop Burton, in the same county. Formerly served in the 38th Foot, and was placed on h. p. 1st Dgn. Gds. 1814.

⁸ Brought into the regt. from h. p. 4th Lt. Dgns. Quitted the service 1819. M., 1817, Harriet, dau. of George Rooke. Resided at Chepstow. D. 5th Feb., 1841.

⁹ Quitted the service a few months after Waterloo.

¹⁰ Promoted capt. 18th July, 1815. Placed on h. p. 19th Sept., 1816. Living in 1842.

¹¹ Promoted capt. 19th July, 1815.

¹² Promoted capt. 20th July, and placed on h. p. 25th March, 1816.

¹³ There is some doubt as to whether this officer was actually present at Waterloo, as in a contemporary list of officers of the Scots Greys who served at this battle, in the handwriting of Lieut. J. R. T. Graham of this regt., Lieut. Falconar is noted as being "on baggage guard at Brussels." It is noticeable, however, that Falconar's name appears in the original "Waterloo Muster-roll" of the regt. given in Part II.; and it may be that he re-joined the Greys before the close of the battle. Placed on h. p. 25th March, 1816. D. at Woodcot, co. Haddington, 15th Sept., 1820.

¹⁴ Promoted capt. 10th Oct., 1816, and Maj. 10th June, 1826. H. p. 1827. It fell to his lot to command his troop in the final charge at Waterloo, and, though severely wounded in the arm, led his men into the midst of the conflict. Afterwards held the appointment of High Constable of Durham, and d. at Durham 1st Oct., 1847.

¹⁵ A scion of the ancient family of Carruthers, in Annandale. The late head of this family, who d. 1878, was formerly an officer in the Scots Greys.

¹⁶ Son and heir of Gen. John Hamilton, of Dalzell, by Anne, dau. of R. Mathews. Bn. 28th Oct., 1793. Served in the Pa. Was twice md., and by 2nd wife was father of John Glencairn Hamilton, created a baron 15th Aug. 1886. D. 11th Jan., 1834.

¹⁷ Bn. 1795. Son of Lt.-Gen. Alex. Trotter, of Morton Hall, Midlothian. Killed by a French officer with whom he was fighting.

¹⁸ Son of Rev. James Gape, of St. Albans, who was grandson maternally of 1st Viscount Grimston. Promoted capt. 19th June, 1817.

¹⁹ Afterwards lt.-col. of the regt. Appointed keeper of the Crown jewels in the Tower of London. D. there 15th Feb., 1872, aged 77.

²⁰ Son of James Graham, Esq., of Barrock Lodge and Rickerby, Cumberland. Appointed cornet in the Scots Greys, 20th Jan., 1814, when 15 years of

age. He took part in the battle during the whole day, and late at night commanded the party sent back to the field to succour the wounded and bury the dead. M. Eliz. Jane, dau. of James Saurin, D.D., Lord Bishop of Dromore, and had issue. Promoted capt. 16th March, 1820 ; h. p. 1821 ; major in 1837. D. in Kensington, 20th Jan., 1865. Bd. in Brompton Cemetery. The reredos in Stanwix Church, Cumberland, was erected in memory of Major Graham. It is an interesting historical fact that the Graham family received and sheltered Prince Charles Edward at Barrock, after his defeat at Penrith, in Dec., 1745, for a night. The old chair in which the Prince slept, and the remains of his plaid (which plaid he gave Mrs. Graham when he thanked her on leaving in the morning), are now in the possession of Miss Graham, to whom the Editor is indebted for the above details of her father and ancestors. It is said that the Prince fought at Culloden in someone else's plaid—having given away his own.

[21] 3rd son of Wm. Westby, of Thornhill, co. Dublin.

[22] Son of Rev. Francis Kinchant, of Easton, co. Hereford.

[23] Got separated from his troop when charging. He was a cadet of the Shuldhams, of Moigh House, co. Longford, and a cousin of Capt. J.A. Schreiber, of 11th Lt. Dgns., who met and spoke to him just before the battle commenced. Was bd. on the field by men of his own regt. under Lieut. Graham.

[24] Out of the regt. in 1829.

[25] Left the regt. 7th Dec., 1826.

[26] Left the regt. 27th Feb., 1817.

[27] Placed on h. p. from 28th Foot 1st March, 1821.

[28] Left the regt. in May, 1826.

6TH (OR INNISKILLING) REGIMENT OF DRAGOONS.

		Rank in the	
LIEUT.-COLONEL.		Regiment.	Army.
[1] Joseph Muter, w.		4 June, 1813	Col., 4 June, 1814
MAJOR.			
[2] Fiennes S. Miller, w.		25 May, 1809	Lt.-Col., 4 June, [1814
CAPTAINS.			
[3] Henry Madox		19 Dec. 1805	
[4] Wm. Frederick Browne, w.		7 May, 1807	2 Apr. 1807
[5] Thomas Mackay		3 Dec. 1807	
[6] Wm. Frederick Hadden		28 Jan. 1808	14 Jan. 1808
[7] Edward Holbech		25 May, 1809	
[8] Hon. Sholto Douglas		23 Aug. 1810	24 May, 1810
LIEUTENANTS.			
[9] Theophilus Biddulph		22 May, 1806	
[10] Augustus Saltern Willett		27 Aug. 1807	
[11] John Linton		25 Jan. 1809	
[12] Henry Wm. Petre		26 Jan. 1809	
[13] Alexander Hassard, w.		23 Apr. 1812	
[14] Samuel Black		8 July, 1813	
[15] Richard Down		31 Mar. 1814	
[16] Paul Ruffo, w.		3 May, 1815	
CORNETS.			
Michael Clusky, Adjt., K.		9 Jan. 1812	
[17] John Delancy Allingham		7 Oct. 1813	
PAYMASTER.			
[18] Wm. Armstrong		18 Oct. 1813	
QUARTERMASTER.			
[19] James Kerr		9 Dec. 1813	
SURGEON.			
[20] John Bolton		14 Sept. 1791	
ASSISTANT-SURGEON.			
[21] Wm. Henry Ricketts		16 Mar. 1809	
VETERINARY SURGEON.			
[22] Richard Vincent		25 Nov. 1797	

Scarlet. Facings yellow. Lace silver.

[1] Son of Col. Muter. Took the surname of Straton in lieu of that of Muter, about 1816, on succeeding to the property of his aunt, Miss Straton, at Kirkside, near Montrose, N.B. On the death of Sir Wm. Ponsonby, at Waterloo, the command of the "Union Brigade" devolved on this officer. C.B. and K.C.H. Col.-in-Chf. 6th Dgns.; F.R.S., Edinburgh; lt.-gen. D. 23rd Oct., 1840. Left about £70,000 to Edinburgh University.

[2] Eldest son of Fiennes S. Miller, of Radway Grange, Kineton, by Henrietta, 2nd dau. of Capt. Joseph Meade, R.N. Sev. wnded. at Waterloo while commanding the regt. C.B. Retd. before 1824. M., 23rd May, 1819, Georgina Sibella, 5th dau. of Rev. Philip Story, and had issue. D. Sept., 1862.

[3] Commanded his regt. the last few hours of the battle. Made bt.-maj. for Waterloo. Promoted lt.-col. 1825. K.H. Attained rank of col. on retd. list 1838. M. Miss Williams. D. at Bath 18th March, 1863, aged 81.

[4] Quitted the service in 1819.

[5] Bt.-maj. 19th July, 1821. Serving in 1825. Out of the regt. before 1830.

[6] Senior capt. of his regt. 1821. Not in the Army List for 1822.

[7] 4th son of Wm. Holbech, of Farnborough Hall, Banbury. Bn. 1785. Placed on h. p. 11th April, 1822. D. at Alveston 24th June, 1847.

[8] Eldest son (by his 2nd wife) of Archibald, Lord Douglas (extinct). Bn. 1785; d. 1821.

[9] Promoted capt. 14th Sept., 1815. Placed on h. p. 25th March, 1816. Living 1860.

[10] Afterwards lt.-col. North Devon Militia. Great-grandson of John Cleveland, M.P. for Barnstaple for seven Parliaments. Assumed the surname of Cleveland, in lieu of that of Willett, in 1817. M., in 1830, eldest dau. of John Chichester, of Arlington Court, Devon, and had issue. D. 5th July, 1849.

[11] Was maj. of his regt. from 1825 to 1830, when he was placed on h. p. as lt.-col. Living 1846.

[12] Son of the Hon. George Petre, by Maria, dau. of Philip Howard, of Corby. Placed on h. p. 1819. M., 17th Jan., 1818, Eliz., eldest dau. of Edmond Glynn, of Glynn, co. Cornwall. D., 26th Nov., 1852, leaving issue by a 2nd marriage.

[13] 4th son of Jason Hassard, of Gardenhill and Toam. Promoted capt. 17th June, 1819. Quitted the service before 1830. M., 1836, his cousin Eliz., dau. of Capt. Jason Hassard, and had issue. D. Sept., 1845.

[14] Younger son of Col. Black, H.E.I.C.S., by Margaret, eldest dau. of Maj. Jerome Noble. Joined the 6th Dgns., as cornet, in 1810. Placed on h. p. as capt. 1826. D., with the rank of maj., 2nd Nov., 1853.

[15] Placed on h. p. as capt. 1826. Living 1855.

[16] An Italian. Returned as "missing" in Siborne's Waterloo List. Lieut. 4th D. G. 15th Feb., 1816. Was afterwards Neapolitan Minister to England. His title was Prince Castelcicala, and at the last Waterloo banquet, June 18, 1852, he sat on Wellington's right hand. Lord Albemarle tells us, in his

autobiography, that the Duke proposed Prince Castelcicala's health, but stumbled over the name, which was happily supplied by Lord Sandys, who, as Lord Arthur Hill, had been senior A.D.C. to the veteran F. M. at Waterloo.

[17] Lieut. 24th Lt. Dns. 25th Sept., 1817.   Half-pay 15th Oct., 1820. Appointed barrack-master at Boyle in 1841.   D. in 1843.

[18] Serving with the regt. in 1830.

[19] Serving with the regt. in 1824.

[20] Surgeon to the 7th West India Regt. 19th Feb., 1824.   Half-pay same date.   Living in 1846.

[21] Surgeon to 35th Foot 7th Sept., 1815.   H. p. 25th June, 1817.

[22] H. p. 3rd Jan., 1828.   Living in 1830.

7TH (OR THE QUEEN'S OWN) REGIMENT OF LIGHT DRAGOONS (HUSSARS).

	COLONEL.	Regiment.	Rank in the Army.
	Henry, Earl of Uxbridge, w.	16 May, 1801	Lt.-Gen., 25 Apr. [1808
	LIEUT.-COLONEL.		
1	Sir Edward Kerrison, Kt.	4 Apr. 1805	Col., 4 June, 1813
	MAJORS.		
2	Edward Hodge, ĸ.	7 May, 1812	
	Wm. Thornhill, w.	8 Apr. 1813	
	CAPTAINS.		
3	Wm. Verner, w.	21 July, 1808	
4	Thos. Wm. Robbins, w.	25 May, 1809	
	Edward Keane	15 June, 1809	1..Dec. 1806
5	Peter Augustus Heyliger, w.	2 Aug. 1810	9 Mar. 1809
	Thomas Wildman, w.	18 Feb. 1813	
	James John Fraser, w.	17 June, 1813	
6	James D. Elphinstone	25 Sept. 1814	23 Dec. 1813
7	Edward Wildman, w.	23 Feb. 1815	7 Dec. 1814
	LIEUTENANTS.		
8	Arthur Myers, Adjt., ĸ.	24 May, 1810	
9	Standish O'Grady	6 Aug. 1812	
10	Wm. Shirley	7 Jan. 1813	19 Nov. 1812
11	Wm. Grenfell	11 Mar. 1813	
12	Robert Douglas, w.	17 June, 1813	
13	Robert Uniacke	15 July, 1813	
14	John Robert Gordon, w.	15 Sept. 1813	
15	John Daniel	21 Oct. 1813	
16	Edward James Peters, w.	10 Nov. 1813	
17	John Wildman	11 Nov. 1813	
18	Frederick Beattie, w.	16 Apr. 1815	
19	Stephen Rice	17 Apr. 1815	
20	Frederick Towers	18 Apr. 1815	

7TH (OR THE QUEEN'S OWN) REGIMENT OF LIGHT DRAGOONS (HUSSARS)—*continued*.

	Rank in the	
PAYMASTER.	Regiment.	Army.
[21] Thomas Felton	16 Apr. 1815	
QUARTERMASTER.		
[22] John Greenwood	25 Aug. 1809	
SURGEON.		
[23] David Irwin	22 July, 1795	
ASSISTANT SURGEONS.		
[24] Robert Alex. Chermside	16 Aug. 1810	
[25] James Moffat	24 Oct. 1811	
VETERINARY SURGEON.		
[26] Richard Dorville	13 Dec. 1810	

Blue.   Facings white.   Lace silver.

[1] Only son of Matthias Kerrison, of Breccles Hall, Norfolk. Bn. 1774. Distinguished himself in the Pa., and on the return of the 7th Light Dgns. to England, its officers presented Col. Kerrison with a piece of plate worth 200 guineas, in estimation of his conduct in Spain. Created a baronet in 1821, at the recommendation of Wellington. Was M.P. for Eye from 1824 to 1852. M. Mary, eldest dau. of Alex. Ellice, of Pittencrief, co. Fife, and had issue. K.C.B. and K.C.H. Col.-in-Chf. 14th Dgns. D. 9th March, 1853.

[2] Killed in the cavalry action at Genappe, 17th June, 1815. Pens. of £100 per ann. to his widow, who was younger dau. of Sir Edmund Bacon, Premier Bart. M.I. at Waterloo.

[3] Afterwards Sir Wm. Verner, Bart. Bn. 23rd Feb., 1782. Youngest son of James Verner, of Church Hill, co. Armagh, by Jane, dau. of Rev. Henry Clarke. Served in the Pa., and was present at Corunna. Promoted maj. for his distinguished gallantry at Waterloo. Retd. in 1826 as lt.-col. K.C.H. He was a staunch supporter of the Orange cause, and the Editor has heard his late father say that when quartered at Charlemont, in the north of Ireland, he partook of Sir William's princely hospitality at banquets, where the toasts were all to the honour and glory of the Orange cause, and the wine-glasses had stalks without bottoms, so as to ensure the toasts being fully honoured. Sir Wm. was once struck off the Commission of the Peace, by Lord Normanby, for giving the toast of "The Battle of the Diamond" at a public dinner in Ireland. D. 20th Jan., 1871.

[4] Placed on h. p. as lt.-col. 1821. Living 1842.

[5] Distinguished himself in charging with his troop the advanced French picquets on the morning of June 17th. Quitted the service 30th March, 1820.

[6] 4th son of Wm. Elphinstone, an East India director, by Eliz., eldest dau. of Wm. Fullerton, of Carstairs, co. Lanark. Bn. 1788. Lt.-Col. 3rd Foot Guards, 1823 ; h. p. 1828. Was twice m., and after his 2nd marriage with the only child of Sir Edward Buller, Bart., assumed the name of Buller before that of Drummond. D. 8th March, 1857, leaving issue by 2nd wife.

[7] Younger brother of Col. Thos. Wildman (see under Staff). Afterwards commanded 6th Dgn. Gds. K.H. M., 1818, Antonia, dau. of Lt.-Gen. Sir Hildebrand Oakes, G.C.B., and had issue. D. in Dec., 1846.

[8] M.I. at Waterloo.

[9] Afterwards Col. Viscount Guillamore, A.D.C. to the Queen. Bn. 26th Dec. 1792. Son of Standish O'Grady, 1st Viscount, by Katherine Waller. M., 16th Oct., 1828, Gertrude Paget, niece of the Marquis of Anglesey. D. 22nd July, 1848, leaving issue.

[10] Capt. 12th Sept., 1816. Major 17th June, 1824. Serving in 1830.

[11] Capt., 21st Lt. Dns., 24th Dec., 1818. H. p. 26th Oct., 1820. Living in 1846.

[12] Quitted the service in 1822.

[13] H. p. 24th July, 1817. Living in 1824.

[14] Son of J. Gordon, of Wincombe, Wilts. Promoted capt. 12th Dec, 1816. D. at Plymouth, 20th Sept., 1824.

[15] Capt. 5th June, 1824. Exchanged to 66th Foot, 8th June, 1826. D. at Bellevue, Meath, 1840.

[16] Serving in 1817. Out of regt. before 1824.

[17] Brother to Edward Wildman. Attained rank of col., h. p. list, 1854. M., 1824, Lady Margaret Charteris, dau. of 7th Earl of Wemyss. D. in 1878.

[18] H. p., 3rd April, 1817. Living in 1824.

[19] Left the regt. in 1816. Lt., Newfoundland Vet. Cy., 30th Sept., 1824. Serving in 1830.

[20] Capt., 18th July, 1820. H. p. 4th Sept., 1821. Major, 29th Aug., 1826. Lt.-Col., 23rd Nov., 1841. Living in 1846.

[21] Serving with the regt. in 1830.

[22] Retd. f. p. 1819. Living in 1830.

[23] D. in 1816.

[24] Surgeon on h. p. list in 1815. Living in 1824.

[25] Serving with the regt. in 1824. Attained rank of surgeon of 1st class, 23rd Jan., 1843. H. p. in 1849. D. at Devonport, 6th March, 1856.

[26] H. p. 17th Dec., 1829.

10TH (OR THE PRINCE OF WALES'S OWN ROYAL) REGIMENT OF LIGHT DRAGOONS (HUSSARS).

LIEUT.-COLONELS.	Rank in the Regiment.	Army.
[1] George Quentin, w.	13 Oct. 1808	Col., 4 June, 1814
[2] Lord Robert Manners	12 Nov. 1814	2 May, 1811

MAJOR.		
[3] Hon. Frederick Howard, K.	9 May, 1811	

CAPTAINS.		
[4] Thos. Wm. Taylor	12 Nov. 1814	Maj., 7 July, 1814
[5] H. C. Stapylton	12 Nov. 1814	3 Nov. 1808
[6] John Grey, w.	12 Nov. 1814	6 Apr. 1809
John Gurwood	12 Nov. 1814	6 Feb. 1812
[7] Charles Wood	12 Nov. 1814	Maj.,16 Mar.1815
[8] Henry Floyd	12 Nov. 1814	2 Dec. 1813.
[9] Arthur Shakespear	12 Nov. 1814	27 Jan. 1814

LIEUTENANTS.		
[10] John Whitehill Parsons	12 Nov. 1814	3 Dec. 1805
[11] Wm. Slayter Smith	12 Nov. 1814	17 Nov. 1808
[12] Robert Arnold	12 Nov. 1814	13 May, 1812
[13] Wm. Cartwright	12 Nov. 1814	6 Jan. 1814
[14] Samuel Hardman, Adjt.	15 Dec. 1814	9 Dec. 1813
[15] George Orlando Gunning	26 Dec. 1814	8 Apr. 1813
[16] J. C. Wallington	27 Dec. 1814	
[17] Ellis Hodgson	28 Dec. 1814	
[18] Wm. C. Hamilton	29 Dec. 1814	
[19] Anthony Bacon, w.	9 Feb. 1815	11 Mar. 1813
[20] W. H. Bingham Lindsey	15 June, 1815	

10TH (OR THE PRINCE OF WALES'S OWN ROYAL) REGIMENT OF LIGHT DRAGOONS (HUSSARS)—*contd.*

	Rank in the	
PAYMASTER.	Regiment.	Army.
21 James Tallon	15 Dec. 1813	

ASSISTANT-SURGEON.		
22 George Samuel Jenks	22 Oct. 1812	

VETERINARY SURGEON.		
Henry C. Sannerman	29 Mar. 1810	7 Dec. 1809

Blue. Facings scarlet. Lace silver.

[1] Eldest son of George Quentin, of Göttingen. Served five years in the Garde du Corps of Hanover. Joined the 10th Hussars as a cornet in 1793. Served with Sir John Moore in the Pa. C.B.; K.C.H.; A.D.C. to George IV., and Crown Equerry to Her Majesty. M., 1811, the dau. of James Lawrell, of Eastwick Park and Frimley, Surrey, and had issue. D. in London 7th Dec., 1851, aged 92.

[2] 3rd son of Charles, 4th Duke of Rutland, by Lady Mary Somerset, dau. of 4th Duke of Beaufort. Bn. 14th Dec., 1781. Afterwards Maj.-Gen., C.B., and Col.-in-Chf. 3rd Dgns. D. 15th Nov., 1835.

[3] 3rd son of Frederick, 5th Earl of Carlisle, by Lady Margaret Granville-Leveson, dau. of 1st Marquis of Stafford. Killed whilst gallantly leading the last charge. Bur. at Waterloo. M.I. Afterwards brought home and bur. at Streatham, 3rd Aug., 1815. Left issue by his marriage with Frances, only dau. of Wm. H. Lambton, of Lambton Hall, Durham, two sons. In 1879 Maj. Howard's remains were removed from Streatham, and re-interred in the family mausoleum at Castle Howard, Yorkshire.

[4] Afterwards Maj.-Gen. T. W. Taylor, Lt.-Gov. R.M.C., Sandhurst, and Col.-in-Chf. 17th Lancers. Served in the expedition to Java in 1811. Made brevet lt.-col. for Waterloo. D. at Haccombe, co. Devon, 8th Jan., 1854, aged 71.

[5] Henry Richard Chetwynd-Stapylton, eldest son of the Hon. Granville Chetwynd (youngest son of 4th Viscount Chetwynd), by Martha, dau. and heir of Henry Stapylton, of Wighill. Bn. 1789. Afterwards maj. of his regt. Retired 1822. M., 23rd Dec., 1820, Margaret, dau. of George Hammond, and had issue. D. 4th April, 1859.

[6] Afterwards Lt.-Col. of the Scots Greys. D. at Sidmouth, 21st Dec., 1843.

[7] 6th son of Thos. Wood, of Littleton, by Mary, only dau. and heir of Sir Edward Williams, 5th bart., of Eltham. Placed on h. p. 5th April, 1821.

[8] Eldest son of Gen. Sir John Floyd, Bart. Bn. 2nd Sept., 1793. Served in the Pa. Succeeded as 2nd bart., 1818. M., 1821, Mary, eldest dau. of Wm. Murray, of Jamaica, and had issue. D. 4th March, 1868.

[9] Son of John Shakespear, by Mary Drummond. A.D.C. to Lord Combermere. M. Sophia, dau. of Thos. S. D. Bucknall, and had issue. Placed on h. p. Oct., 1818. D. 1845.

[10] Afterwards Lt.-Col. Sir J. W. Parsons, K.C.M.G., the British Resident at Zante. Made lt.-col. 1841. D. at the Palace, Corfu, 1848, aged 68.

[11] Quitted the service about 1818. M., 30th April, 1818, Sarah, 3rd dau. of John Bockett, of Southcote Lodge, Berks. Adjt. to Yorkshire Yeomanry in 1822.

[12] Afterwards lt.-col. 16th Lt. Dgns. D. unm. 20th Aug., 1839.

[13] 2nd son of Ralph Cartwright, of Aynhoe (M.P. for Northampton), by the Hon. Emma Maude, dau. of 1st Viscount Hawarden. Served in the Pa. with the 61st. Regt. (medal and 5 clasps). Maj., unattached, 1825 ; lt.-gen., 1863. M., 6th Aug., 1822, Mary Anne, dau. and heir of Henry Jones, of Bloomsbury Square, London, and had issue. Living 1865.

[14] H. p. 6th June, 1816. D. 25th Nov., 1855.

[15] Bn. 18th Dec., 1796. 2nd son of Sir George Wm. Gunning, Bart., by Eliz., dau. of Henry, 1st Lord Bradford.

[16] John Clement Wallington became maj. in this regt. 1833. 2nd son of the Rev. Charles Wallington, by Frances, dau. of Hamlyn Harris, of Daventry. M. Alice, dau. of Wm. Charles Monk Mason. D. about 1865.

[17] Capt. 23rd Nov., 1820. H. p. 25th Oct., 1821.

[18] Capt. 21st. Nov., 1822. Only son of Wm. Hamilton, of Craighlaw, M.D. Promoted capt. in 1822. J.P. and D.L. for co. Wigtown. M. in 1825, Anne, dau. of Rev. A. Stewart, of Kirkcowan, and had issue. Took Holy Orders and resided many years in Guernsey. A correspondent writes under date of 22nd Feb., 1893 :—" Mr. Hamilton, who was an officer in the 10th Hussars at Waterloo, was a great favourite with all of us boys at Elizabeth College, and always on the 18th June the old chap came sailing down the Grange with the Waterloo medal on his clerical coat, just about our play hour, and we used to drag him into the playground, and cheer him till we made him cry and we were hoarse. He was living in 1867 and for some years afterwards."

[19] Afterwards Gen. Anthony Bacon, K.T.S. Served in the Pa. Was badly wnded. in the last charge, led by the gallant Maj. Howard, and lay all night on the field of battle. Appointed Capt. 13th Lt. Dgns., 1818 ; Maj. 17th Dgns., 1825. Served in the Portuguese Army 1832-3, and was Col. Commandant of their Cavalry. M. Lady Charlotte Harley, 2nd dau. of 5th Earl of Oxford. D. 2nd July, 1864

[20] 3rd son of Thos. Lindsey of Hollymount, co. Mayo, by Lady Margaret Bingham, dau. of 1st Earl of Lucan. D. in India in 1822.

[21] H. p. 25th Dec., 1818

[22] Serving in 1830.

11TH REGIMENT OF LIGHT DRAGOONS.

	Regiment.	Army.
LIEUT.-COLONEL.	Rank in the	
1 James Wallace Sleigh	14 Dec. 1809	
MAJOR.		
2 Archibald Money	14 Dec. 1809	Lt.-Col., 4 June, 1814
CAPTAINS.		
3 James Bouchier	20 Jan. 1803	Maj., 4 June, 1814
4 Benjamin Lutyens	4 Aug. 1804	Maj., 4 June, 1814
Michael Childers	14 June, 1805	Maj., 25 Aug. 1814
5 James Alfred Schreiber, w.	19 Nov. 1812	
6 John Jenkins	22 Dec. 1814	
7 Thomas Binney	26 Jan. 1815	
8 James Duberly	30 Mar. 1815	21 Oct. 1813
LIEUTENANTS.		
9 George Sicker, Adjt.	20 Feb. 1805	
10 Frederick Wood, w.	14 June, 1805	
11 Wm. Smith	21 Apr. 1808	
12 Richard Coles	29 June, 1811	
13 Benjamin Leigh Lye	30 June, 1811	
14 Edward Phelips, k.	3 July, 1811	
15 James Richard Rotton	9 Jan. 1812	
16 James S. Moore, w.	13 Oct. 1814	7 Apr. 1813
17 Robert Milligan, w.	22 Dec. 1814	
18 Wm. H. Stewart	30 Mar. 1815	
19 Benfield Des Vœux	30 Mar. 1815	
CORNETS.		
20 Barton Parker Browne	8 Apr. 1813	
21 Humphrey Orme	5 Aug. 1813	
22 George Schreiber	23 Dec. 1813	
23 Henry R. Bullock	30 Dec. 1813	
24 Philip Haughton James	29 Dec. 1814	
PAYMASTER.		
25 Daniel Lutyens	19 Oct. 1804	

11TH REGIMENT OF LIGHT DRAGOONS.—*continued.*

	Rank in the	
	Regiment.	Army.
QUARTERMASTER.		
²⁶ John Hall	29 Sept. 1814	
SURGEON.		
²⁷ James O'Malley	11 Mar. 1813	11 July, 1811
ASSISTANT-SURGEON.		
²⁸ Henry Steele	28 Apr. 1814	25 June, 1812

Blue. Facings buff. Lace silver.

[1] Afterwards Gen. Sir J. W. Sleigh, K.C.B., Col.-in-Chf. 9th Lancers. Was educated at Winchester. Cornet, 1795. Served in the campaign in Holland same year. With his regt. at Salamanca. Towards the close of Waterloo Day commanded the 4th Brigade. C.B. and K.M.B. Commanded the cavalry at siege of Bhurtpore. Was afterwards Military Sec. to Lord Wm. Bentinck. D. at Hanworth House, Middlesex, 5th Feb., 1865.

[2] Afterwards Lt.-Gen. Money, C.B. and K.C. Col.-in-Chf. 2nd Dgns. At the close of Waterloo Day he commanded the regt. D. at Crown Point, Trowse, Norfolk, 1858.

[3] Afterwards Lt. Gen. James Claud Bouchier, K.C. Had served in Egypt and in the Pa. Brevet lt.-col. for Waterloo. Col.-in-Chf. 3rd Dgn. Gds. D. 12th Feb., 1859, at Buxton Vicarage, Norfolk.

[4] Major Lutyens served under Abercromby in Egypt, and lived to be one of the last survivors of that campaign. He d. at The Terrace, Kensington, 23rd Dec., 1863.

[5] 4th son of Wm. Schreiber, by Mary, dau. and co-heir of James Sewell, of Alton Hall, co. Suffolk. Bn. at Wickham Market 21st Nov., 1789. Educated at Dalham Grammar School, Essex. Joined the 11th Lt. Dgns. about 1806, and was promoted lt. 1808. Served in the Pa. Was badly wnded. at Waterloo by a round shot, which broke his charger's back at same time. Placed on h. p. from 6th Dgn. Gds, with rank of Maj., 23rd June, 1825. M. Mary, dau. of Thos. Ware, of Woodfort, co. Cork, and had, with other male issue, a son, Brymer, now a maj.-gen. (retired) Royal Artillery, who communicated above information. J. A. Schreiber d. as a lt.-col., h. p., 1840.

[6] Born at Scotbury, co. Devon, 6th Jan., 1789. Raised men for a cornetcy, and entered the army as cornet in 11th Lt. Dgns. 29th Jan., 1807. Served in the Pa. In 1826 commanded two squadrons at Bhurtpore. M., 11th Nov., 1819, at Cawnpore, Stephena Isabella Patten, and had issue. D. as maj., 31st Oct., 1840.

[7] D. a capt. in this regt., at Berhampore, 26th Nov., 1821.

[8] Placed on h. p. from same regt., 12th Aug., 1819. Son of Sir James Duberly, Knt., of Gaynes Hall, co. Huntingdon, by his 1st wife, Rebecca Howard. Served in the Pa. M., 21st Sept., 1837, the 3rd dau. of the Hon. Wm. Grey, and had issue. D. 3rd March, 1864.

⁹ H. p. 30th July, 1818. Appointed a Knight of Windsor. D. 17th Jan., 1848.

¹⁰ H. p. 25th March, 1817. Living in 1846.

¹¹ Promoted capt. same regt. 30th Oct., 1817. 2nd son of Ferdinando Smith, of Halesowen Grange, co. Worcester, by Eliz., dau. of Humphrey Lyttelton. Bn. 24th June, 1785. D. unmarried in India, 4th May, 1824.

¹² H. p. 24th July, 1817. Living in 1836.

¹³ H. p. in 1817. Adjt. N. Somerset Y. C. in 1821. The Lyes are a Wiltshire family, and have served their country on many notable occasions. At Inkermann a son of Capt. Richard Leigh Lye, and a nephew of the above, met a soldier's death.

¹⁴ Son of Rev. Charles Phelips (4th son of Edward Phelips, of Montacute, co. Somerset), by Mary, dau. of Thos. Blackmore, of Briggins Park, Herts.

¹⁵ Afterwards Lt.-Col. J. R. Rotton, J.P. for Sussex. D. at Chichester, 13th Feb., 1855.

¹⁶ James Stewart-Moore, of Ballydivity, co. Antrim, J.P. and D.L. ; High Sheriff 1849. Eldest son of J. Stewart-Moore, by Margaret, dau. of Ven. Wm. Sturrock, Archdeacon of Armagh. Served in the Pa. and in India. Pierced in three places at Genappe by a Polish lancer. Bn. 1793. M., 1845, Frances Richardson, and had issue. Retired on h. p. as capt., 25th Dec., 1819. D. 1870.

¹⁷ Promoted capt. 24th April, 1816. Exchanged to 2nd Life Gds. 10th Oct., 1816. Quitted the service in 1822.

¹⁸ This officer's second name is omitted in the Army Lists. He appears to be the Wm. Henry Stewart who is described in Burke's *Peerage and Baronetage* as "Major 19th Lancers." 2nd son of Sir James Stewart, Bart., M.P. for Donegal in 1802. D., unmarried, 6th June, 1820, aged 27.

¹⁹ Afterwards Capt. 3rd Foot Gds. Retd. as lt.-col. h. p. 1829. 4th son of Sir Charles des Vœux, 1st Bart., by Mary Anne, dau. of Dean Champagné. M., firstly, 1833, Georgina, dau. of Richard Streatfield, and had issue. D. 30th Nov., 1864.

²⁰ Subsequently served in India, and was at the capture of Bhurtpore. Commissions dated : cornet, April 8th, 1813 ; lt., June 22nd, 1815 ; capt., May 5th, 1824 ; maj., June 28, 1838. Lt.-col., retd., 1851. D. 16th June, 1889.

²¹ The last of an ancient family. Son and heir of Walden Orme. Quitted the service as Capt. 6th Dgns., 1829. D. at Hale, near Stamford, 6th Oct., 1860.

²² 6th son of Wm. Schreiber and Mary his wife. Twin brother of Rev. Thos. Schreiber, Rector of Bradwell, in Essex. Bn. at Wickham Market 19th Oct., 1794. Educated at Dalham Grammar School. Had his horse shot under him at Waterloo. Afterwards A.D.C. to Sir John Cameron. Exchanged to 18th Lt. Dgns., and was placed on h. p., as capt., 1821. M. Anne, dau. of — Hume of Colchester. Lt.-col. h. p. 1851. Resided latterly at Cheltenham, where the Editor had the pleasure of knowing him in 1867.

[23] 4th son of Jonathan Watson (who assumed, in 1810, the surname of Bullock), of Faulkbourn Hall, Witham, Essex. Appointed capt. in 1st Life Gds. 26th Dec., 1821. Maj. h. p. 23rd July, 1831. M., 1825, Charlotte, 2nd dau. of John Hall, of Weston Colville, Cambridgeshire, and had issue. D. at Bury St. Edmunds, 9th July, 1855.

[24] Quitted the service in 1818.

[25] Afterwards in 3rd Dgn. Gds. D. at Broxbourne 6th June, 1841.

[26] H. p. 1819 from 6th West India Regt.

[27] 6th son of George O'Malley, of Gornsay, Castlebar, co. Mayo, by Eliz. Clarke. D. at Cawnpore, 11th Sept., 1821. See notes to 44th Foot for account of his brother George.

[28] D. at Meerut in 1825.

12TH (OR THE PRINCE OF WALES'S) REGIMENT OF LIGHT DRAGOONS.
[12TH LANCERS.]

Rank in the

	Regiment.	Army.
LIEUT.-COLONEL.		
1 Hon. F. C. Ponsonby, w.	11 June, 1811	Col., 4 June, 1814
MAJOR.		
2 James Paul Bridger	10 Dec. 1811	
CAPTAINS.		
3 Samson Stawell	29 Jan. 1806	28 Feb. 1805
4 George F. Erskine	19 May, 1808	
5 Edwin W. T. Sandys, w.	30 Mar. 1809	19 Aug. 1808
6 Houston Wallace	10 Jan. 1811	11 Jan. 1810
7 Alexander Barton	17 Jan. 1811	
8 Henry Andrews	9 July, 1812	
9 Alexander Charles Craufurd	(Volr.)	9 June, 1814
LIEUTENANTS.		
10 Wm. Heydon	13 June, 1805	
11 James Chatterton	6 June, 1811	
12 John Vandeleur	10 July, 1811	
13 Wm. Hay	11 July, 1811	
14 Wm. H. Dowbiggen, w.	31 Dec. 1811	8 Aug. 1811
15 Albert Goldsmid	20 Feb. 1812	
16 Abraham Laue	30 Mar. 1815	15 Oct. 1812
Lindsey James Bertie, k.	30 Mar. 1815	7 May, 1812
17 John Henry Slade	6 Apr. 1815	
18 Thomas Reed	2 May, 1815	
19 John Griffiths (sic) Adjt.	4 May, 1815	
CORNET.		
20 John Elliott(sic) Lockhart, k.	28 Apr. 1814	
PAYMASTER.		
21 Wm. [Loftus] Otway	14 Feb. 1811	
QUARTERMASTER.		
22 Richard Sidley	10 June, 1813	
SURGEON.		
23 Benjamin Robinson	15 Oct. 1803	2 Feb. 1795
ASSISTANT-SURGEON.		
24 John G. Smith	28 Oct. 1813	11 Mar. 1813
VETERINARY SURGEON.		
25 James Castley	17 Aug. 1809	18 June, 1807

Blue. Facings yellow. Lace silver.

[1] Aftds. Maj.-Gen. Sir Frederick Cavendish Ponsonby, K.C.B. and K.M.T., Gov. of Malta. 2nd son of Frederick, 3rd Earl of Bessborough, by Lady Henrietta, 2nd dau. of 1st Earl Spencer. Bn. 6th July, 1783. Cornet 10th Lt. Dgns. 1800. Maj. 23rd Lt. Dgns. 1807. At head of this regt. distinguished himself at Talavera, in 1809. Lt.-col. of the regt. 1810. At Barossa, with a squadron of German dragoons, he charged the French cavalry covering the retreat, overthrew them, and took two guns. Lt.-Col. 12th Lt. Dgns. 1811. Again signally distinguished himself at the battles of Salamanca and Vittoria. His experiences at Waterloo were almost unique, as when lying grievously wnded. on the field, after a most gallant charge, in the French lines, a lancer who was passing by and saw Ponsonby move, exclaimed : " *Tu n'est pas mort, coquin*," and struck his lance through the English officer's back. " My head dropped " (wrote Ponsonby in his subsequent narrative of his experiences), "the blood gushed into my mouth, a difficulty of breathing came on, and I thought all was over." But the bitterness of death was not yet past. Soon after, a tirailleur came up and roughly searched him all over, robbing Ponsonby of what money he had about him. He was hardly quit of this scoundrel before another appeared with the same intent. At last a good Samaritan appeared in the shape of a French officer, who administered brandy to the apparently dying English-man, and then passed on "to pursue the retreating British " ! What followed is best given in Ponsonby's own words : "Presently another tirailleur appeared, who came and knelt and fired over me, loading and firing many times, and conversing with great gaiety all the while. At last he ran off." The evening came, and with it the Prussians. " Two squadrons of Prussian cavalry, both of them two deep, passed over me in full trot, lifting me from the ground and tumbling me about cruelly. A German soldier, bent on plunder, came and pulled me about roughly before he left me." An English private next appeared, and on Ponsonby telling him who he was, the soldier picked up a sword and stood sentry over him. Next morning Ponsonby was removed in a cart to a farmhouse, and laid in a bed from which poor Sir A. Gordon had just been carried out dead. Col. Ponsonby had received seven wounds ; a surgeon slept in his room, and he was saved by continual bleeding—120 ounces in two days, besides the great loss of blood on the field.—*Narrative*. M., 1825, Emily, youngest dau. of 3rd Earl Bathurst, and had issue. D. 11th Jan., 1837.

[2] Bt.-lt. col. for Waterloo, and C.B. Retd. in 1821. M., 1831, Jane, 4th dau. of John Copeland. D. 17th May, 1841.

[3] Appears to have been a son of Sampson Stawell, of Kilbrittain, co. Cork. Lt.-col. of same regt. 1827. Present with his regt. at Queen Victoria's coronation, and received a special gold medal. D. 21st Aug. 1849.

[4] George Francis Erskine. Was 2nd son of Hon. Hy. Erskine (2nd son of 5th Earl of Buchan), the eminent Scotch advocate. Maj. same regt. 24th Oct., 1821. Retd. as lt.-col.

[5] Had served with distinction in the Pa. D. of his wounds soon after Waterloo. There have been generations of the name of Edwin Sandys, and this " Edwin W— T— Sandys " may have been a cadet of the noble house of Sandys, now extinct.

[6] Quitted the service in 1822.

[7] Promoted bt.-maj. 21st Jan., 1819, for distinguished conduct in the field while on service in the Pa. In 1826 a body of British troops was sent to Lisbon to aid the Portuguése Govt. Four troops of the 12th Lancers (so styled since 1817), commanded by Maj. Barton, embarked at Portsmouth in

December for Portugal, where they remained for two years. Living in 1830.

⁸ Retd. on h. p. as maj. 25th Jan., 1828. Restored to full pay as Maj. 3rd Lt. Dgns. D. in Bengal, 1838.

⁹ A volunteer from the 2nd Ceylon Regt. Was transferred to 12th Lancers as capt. 26th Oct., 1820, and received a bt. majority in Aug., 1821. His Waterloo medal was for long in the Seaforth collection. Only son of Sir James Craufurd, Bart., of Kilbirney, co. Stirling. M., 1818, Barbara, 4th dau. of 7th Earl of Coventry, and d. s. p. 1838.

¹⁰ This unfortunate officer was twenty years a lieut. in this regt. Promoted capt. 2nd June, 1825, and placed on h. p. 22nd Dec. same year. Living 1830.

¹¹ 2nd son of Sir Jas. Chatterton, Bart., by Rebecca, dau. of Abraham Lane, of Cork. Bn. 1792. Saw much service in the Pa. Aftds. held high commands. K.C.B. and K.H. M., 1825, Annetta, dau. of James Atkinson, of York. Succeeded to the baronetcy in 1855. On the occasion of the Queen's coronation, commanded the 4th Dgn. Gds., and received a special gold medal. At the Duke of Wellington's funeral carried the "Great Banner," by Her Majesty's request, "in consideration of his long, faithful, and distinguished services." Gen. and Col.-in-Chf. 5th Lancers, 1858. D. s. p. in London, Jan. 1868.

¹² Aftds. commanded the 10th Hussars, and received a special gold medal at the Queen's coronation. Elder son of John Ormsby Vandeleur, of Maddenstown, co. Kildare, by Frances Pakenham, dau. of Thos., 1st Lord Longford.

¹³ Served with 52nd L.I. in the Pa. Quitted the service before 1824, with rank of capt. Aftds. C.B. and Second Commissioner Metropolitan Police, 1839. D. 29th Aug., 1855.

¹⁴ Served in the Pa. with the 52nd L.I. Placed on h. p. as lieut., 1821. Living 1846. M. Lady Georgiana Maule, and had issue.

¹⁵ Served in the Pa. Aftds. maj.-gen., retd. list. D. in London 6th Jan., 1861.

¹⁶ Cousin to Sir James Chatterton, being grandson of Abraham Lane, of Cork. Capt. same regt. 6th Nov., 1823. Maj. 76th Foot, 1826. Lt.-col. unatt., 1830.

¹⁷ Eldest son of Gen. Sir John Slade, Bart., of Maunsell House, co. Somerset, by Anna, dau. of James Dawson. Maj. h. p. 1827. Predeceased his father. D. a lt.-col. h. p. 30th Aug., 1843, at Barnes. He had m.. 1st Feb., 1837, Frances McVeagh. She m., secondly, Adm. J. A. Paynter.

¹⁸ Aftds. Gen. Sir Thos. Reed, K.C.B., Col.-in Chf. 44th Foot. Served in India, and commanded a brigade of the Army of the Sutlej. Received the thanks of the Gov.-gen. in India for his valuable services during the mutiny. D. 1883.

¹⁹ *Griffith*. Had been appointed adjt. 29th July, 1813. Adjt. to 5th D.G. 10th Apr., 1823. Lieut. 28th Foot 15th Oct., 1829. Capt. 1st W.I.R. 28th June, 1839. Ret. f. p. before 1846. D. 15th Nov., 1859.

²⁰ Eldest son of Wm. *Eliott*, of Borthwickbrae, M.P. for co. Selkirk for twenty-four years, by Marianne, only child of Allan Lockhart, of Cleghorn, after which marriage W. Eliott assumed the additional surname of Lockhart.

²¹ H. p. as paymaster 1st W.I.R. 6th July, 1820. Living in 1830.

²² D. in Oct., 1823.

²³ H. p. 30th June, 1825. Living in 1846.

²⁴ Serving in 1817.

²⁵ Serving in 1830.

13TH REGIMENT OF LIGHT DRAGOONS.
[13TH HUSSARS.]

Rank in the

LIEUT.-COLONEL.	Regiment.	Army.
Patrick Doherty	4 June, 1813	Col., 4 June, 1814

MAJOR.

| 2 Shapland Boyse, w. | 4 June, 1813 | Lt.-Col., 4 June, [1814 |

CAPTAINS.

3 Brook Lawrence	3 Feb. 1804	Maj., 4 June,1814
4 Joseph Doherty, w.	19 Mar. 1807	Maj., 4 June,1814
5 James Macalester	25 June, 1807	12 Apr. 1814
6 Mansell Bowers	8 Mar. 1810	1 Mar. 1810
7 James Gubbins, k.	7 Feb. 1811	18 May, 1809
8 Charles Gregorie	20 June, 1811	4 Aug. 1808
9 Frederick Goulburn	18 Apr. 1815	12 July, 1810

LIEUTENANTS.

10 John Irving Moss	7 Mar. 1805	
11 George Doherty, w.¹	18 Sept. 1806	
12 John H. Drought	8 Sept. 1808	
13 Charles Robert Bowers, w.	18 Oct. 1810	
14 Allan T. Maclean	11 July, 1811	
John Geale, k.	25 July, 1811	
15 Robert Nisbett	26 Dec. 1811	
16 Wm. Turner	16 Apr. 1815	6 Feb. 1812
17 James Mill	17 Apr. 1815	7 Nov. 1811
18 George Hussey Packe, w.	21 Apr. 1815	6 Jan. 1814
19 Henry Acton	4 May, 1815	
20 John Wallace	17 May, 1815	
21 Jacob Æ. Irving, w.	18 May, 1815	
Geo. Lloyd Hodges	19 Jan. 1815	7 Jan. 1808
22 Geo. Pym, k.		

CORNET.

| 23 Joseph Wakefield | 26 May, 1814 | |

PAYMASTER.

| 24 Alexander Strange | 11 Apr. 1811 | |

13TH REGIMENT OF LIGHT DRAGOONS—*continued.*

Rank in the

	QUARTERMASTER.	Regiment.	Army.
25	Wm. Minchin	10 Sept. 1812	

SURGEON.

| 26 | Thos. Galbraith Logan | 9 Sept. 1813 | 24 Dec. 1812 |

ASSISTANT-SURGEON.

| 27 | Abraham Armstrong | 18 May, 1809 | |

VETERINARY SURGEON.

| 28 | John Constant | 3 Mar. 1814 | |

Blue.   Facings buff.   Lace gold.

[1] Col. Patrick Doherty belonged to a good old Irish family which has done good service to its country, both in the army and on the judicial bench. In the two great wars in which Great Britain played a leading part during the 19th century, the 13th Regt. of Lt. Dgns. (Hussars) has been commanded by a Doherty; and three generations of this family have been closely associated with this same regt. In 1796 Patrick Doherty embarked for the West Indies with his regt. on active service. It is on record that no less than twenty-two officers of the 13th Lt. Dgns. fell victims to "Yellow Jack" when serving in St. Domingo; and the skeleton of the regt., with two or three surviving officers, returned to England. This fatality brought rapid promotion to Doherty, and in 1813 he succeeded to the command of the 13th. For his services in the Pa. he was made bt.-col. The editor of the *Military Calendar* states that on Waterloo Day Col. Doherty was lying ill at Brussels, suffering from a most severe attack of West Indian fever and ague; but as it is probable that he took part in the operations of the 16th or 17th June, it does not debar him from being added to the roll of Waterloo officers. He undoubtedly received the medal for Waterloo, as well as the C.B. in 1816. Col. Doherty was subsequently made K.C.H. Quitted the service in Dec., 1818, and d. at Bath, 20th Jan., 1837. He was uncle to John Doherty, of Dublin, who held the high post of Chief Justice of Ireland, and dying, in 1850, left, with other male issue, the present Maj. H. Doherty, of the Artillery Militia, who formerly commanded a troop in the 3rd Hussars.

[2] Made C.B. for Waterloo. Served in the Pa. 2nd son of Samuel Boyse, of Barrow, New Ross, co. Wexford, by Dorothea, dau. of Shapland Carew, of Castleboro, same county. D., unm., 1833.

[3] There were three of this family in the regt. in 1815. Brook Lawrence served thirty-eight years in this regt., and was made bt.-lt.-col. for Waterloo. He d. at Brompton 11th Aug., 1823, aged 59.

[4] Son of Col. P. Doherty. Promoted maj. in this regt. 8th Dec., 1818. D. at Bangalore 12th June, 1819.

5 Served in the Pa. and in India. In the last charge made by his regt. at Waterloo was wounded in the ankle, which troubled him ever afterwards. Quitted the service in 1823. D. at Kames House, Millport, 17th Sept., 1852. The Clan Alester of Kintyre and the Isles is one of the oldest in Scotland.

6 Promoted maj. in same regt. 5th June, 1823. M. Eleanor, eldest dau. of Lt.-Gen. Sir Thos. Dallas, and had issue. D. 1831.

7 Fell by a cannon ball when charging with his regt. at Waterloo. "The moment of his death was that of victory." See flattering notice in the *Gentleman's Magazine* for 1815, II., p. 275.

8 Serving in 1817. Out of the regt. in 1818.

9 Youngest son of Munbee Goulburn, of Portland Place, by the Hon. Susanna Chetwynd, eldest dau. of Wm. 4th Visct. Chetwynd. Appointed maj. in 104th regt. 15th Feb., 1816. Placed on h. p. 25th July, 1817. D. in 1837.

10 Promoted capt. 31st Aug., 1815. Placed on h. p. 25th March, 1816. Capt. 48th Foot 26th Feb., 1828.

11 Son of Col. P. Doherty. Served in the Pa. "Was severely wounded in the head at Waterloo, and was struck by a ball which was stopped and flattened by the interposition of his watch. He had taken out his watch to remark the time, when the regt. was ordered to advance; and not being able to return it, he put it into the breast of his jacket, and thus providentially his life was saved." (Anecdote by T. Carter.) K.H. Attained the rank of maj., and d. at Dublin in Dec., 1835.

12 Eldest son of John Armstrong Drought, of Lettybrook, King's County, by Letitia Head, of Ashley Park, Tipperary. Bn. 20th Aug., 1790. Served throughout the Par. War. Placed on h. p. 1816. M., 20th July, 1853, Frances Spunner, and had issue. D. 29th April, 1876.

13 Brother to the above Capt. Bowers. Attained rank of lt.-gen. Living 1869.

14 2nd son of Archibald Maclean, of Pennycross and Carsaig, co. Argyll, by Alicia, dau. of Hector Maclean, of Torens, in same county. Served in the Pa. Bn. 1793. Attained the rank of lt.-gen. M., 1843, Agnes, dau. of Wm. Furlong, of Welshot, co. Lanark. Lt.-col. h. p. 1843.

15 Capt. h. p. 20th Dns. 19th Nov., 1818. Living in 1846.

16 Capt. 78th Foot 3rd Nov., 1819. H. p. 27th June, 1822. Living in 1846.

17 Promoted capt. 24th March, 1816. Placed on h. p. 25th May, 1816.

18 2nd son of Charles J. Packe, of Prestwold Hall, Loughborough, by Penelope, eldest dau. of Richard Dugdale. Capt. 21st Dgns. 27th June, 1816. M., 1st Sept., 1824, Mary Anne, eldest dau. of John Heathcote, of Connington Castle, co. Huntingdon, and had issue. M.P. for South Lincolnshire 1859 to 1868. D. 2nd July, 1874.

19 2nd son of Joseph Edward Acton, a lt.-gen. in the Neapolitan service and Gov. of Gaeta, by Eleanora, Countess Berg de Trips, of Dusseldorf. Exchanged to 12th Lt. Dgns. as lieut. 14th Nov., 1816. On h. p. 1817. M. Charlotte, only dau. of Dr. Clogston, of Bombay, and had issue.

20 Placed on h. p. 25th July, 1816. Living in 1830.

[21] Belonged, apparently, to the Dumfriesshire family (of Bonshaw Tower). Aftds. lt.-col. on retd. list. His second name was Æmilius, which came into the family by the marriage of Wm. Irving to Æmilia, dau. of Andrew Lord Rollo. H. p. 1818. D. at Niagara 7th Oct., 1856.

[22] 4th son of Francis Pym, of the Hasells, Beds., M.P., for Beds.

[23] Aftds. exchanged, as lieut., into the 19th Lt. Dgns. M., 1836, Anne, eldest dau. of George Wakefield. D. at Kamptee, Madras, 17th May, 1840, then Lt.-Col. of the 39th Foot.

[24] H. p. 62nd Foot, 1831. D., in Nov. 1840, a military Knight of Windsor.

[25] Qr.-Mr. 53rd Foot 7th Sept., 1826. Serving in 1830.

[26] Surgeon 5th D. G. 25th Nov., 1818. Serving in 1830.

[27] Surgeon 7th March, 1816. Surgeon 87th Foot 24th April, 1826. H. p. 1830. Living in 1846.

[28] Vet. Surgeon to 5th D. G. 30th March, 1826. H. p. in 1843. Living in 1846.

15TH (OR THE KING'S) REGIMENT OF LIGHT DRAGOONS (HUSSARS).

LIEUT.-COLONELS.	Rank in the Regiment.	Rank in the Army.
Sir Colquhoun Grant, K.C.B.	25 Aug. 1808	Maj.-Gen., 4 June, [1814
1 Leighton C. Dalrymple, w.	16 Dec. 1813	

MAJOR.

2 Edwin Griffith, к.	5 Nov. 1812	

CAPTAINS.

3 Joseph Thackwell, w.	9 Apr. 1807	
4 Skinner Hancox	11 May, 1809	
5 John Whiteford, w.	24 July, 1809	
6 Philip Wodehouse	26 Dec. 1809	14 June, 1811
7 Fred. Charles Philips	16 Apr. 1812	
8 Wm. Booth	17 Sept. 1812	
9 John Carr	20 Apr. 1815	3 Oct. 1809

LIEUTENANTS.

10 Edward Barrett	28 June, 1810	
Ralph Mansfield, w.	16 Aug. 1810	
11 Isaac Sherwood, к.	13 Sept. 1810	
12 Wm. Bellairs	7 May, 1812	
13 Henry Lane	3 Sept. 1812	
14 Wm. Byam, w.	17 Sept. 1812	
15 Edward Byam, w.	9 Apr. 1813	
16 George A. F. Dawkins, w.	3 June 1813	
17 Henry Dixon	25 Aug. 1813	
18 John James Douglas	26 Aug. 1813	
19 Wm. Stewart	6 Jan. 1814	
20 John Pennington	13 Jan. 1814	
21 Henry Buckley, к.	25 Aug. 1814	

CORNET.

22 Joseph Griffith, Adjt.	4 Aug. 1814	

15TH (OR THE KING'S) REGIMENT OF LIGHT DRAGOONS (HUSSARS)—*continued*.

	Rank in the	
PAYMASTER.	Regiment.	Army.
23 James Coppin Cocksedge	27 May, 1813	

SURGEON.

24 Thomas Cartan — 9 Sept. 1813

ASSISTANT-SURGEONS.

25 Samuel Jeyes — 28 Nov. 1811
26 Wm. Gibney — 28 Oct. 1813

VETERINARY SURGEON.

27 Conrad Dalwig — 29 Apr. 1813

Blue. Facings scarlet. Lace silver.

[1] Lt.-Col. Cathcart Dalrymple was 2nd son of Gen. Sir Hew Dalrymple, Bart., by Frances, youngest dau. and co-heir of Gen. Leighton. Made C.B. for Waterloo. D. unm. 1820.

[2] M.I. at Waterloo. The following touching verses to the memory of this gallant officer were published soon after his death :—

"Weep not ; he died as heroes die,
The death permitted to the brave ;
Mourn not ; he lies where soldiers lie,
And valour envies such a grave.

"His was the love of bold emprise,
Of soldier's hardships, soldier's fame !
And his the wish by arms to rise,
And gain a proud, a deathless name."

[3] Bn. 1st Feb., 1781. 4th son of John Thackwell, of Moreton Court, co. Worcester, and a direct descendant of Rev. Thos. Thackwell, rector of Waterperry, co. Oxford, in 1607. Served in Ireland during the rebellion. Joined the 15th Lt. Dgns. as a cornet in 1800, and served 32 years in that regt., during twelve of which he held the command. During the Par. war he boldly attacked and forced back at Granada 200 French dgns. with 50 men of his regt., making several prisoners, for which he was recommended for a bt. majority. At Waterloo, when charging with his regt., Thackwell was wounded in the fore-arm of his left arm, "but he instantly seized the bridle with his right hand, in which was his sword, and still dashed on at the head of his regt., the command of which had devolved upon him. Another shot took effect on same arm, but he immediately seized the bridle

G 2

with his teeth." At the close of the day his left arm was amputated close to the shoulder. Proceeded to India in 1837 as Col. of 3rd Lt. Dgns. Distinguished himself in the Afghan, Gwalior, and Sutlej campaigns. Made a K.C.B. for Ghuznee. Commanded the cavalry in the Punjaub campaign. He was a G.C.B. and K.H., Col.-in-Chf. 16th Lancers, and Inspector-General of Cavalry in 1854. M., 29th July, 1825, Maria, eldest dau. of Francis Roche, of Rochemount, co. Cork, and had issue. D. at Aghada Hall, co. Cork, 8th April, 1859.

[4] Commanded the regt. at the close of Waterloo day. Bt. maj. for Waterloo. Appointed Lt.-col. of 7th Dgn. Gds. 18th December, 1823. Commanded the latter regt. until June, 1830. M., 23rd Aug., 1843, Caroline, eldest dau. of Lancelot Rolleston, of Watnall Hall. Resided at Woodborough Hall, co. Notts. D. before 1849.

[5] Promoted maj. in same regt. 16th June, 1820. Quitted the service in 1822.

[6] Eldest son of the Rev. Philip Wodehouse (2nd son of Sir Armine Wodehouse, M.P. for Norfolk), by Apollonia, dau. and co-heir of John Nourse, of Woodeaton, co. Oxford. Lt.-col. unattached 1821, and Inspecting Field Officer of Militia same date. M., 13th June, 1832, Lydia, dau. of Joseph Lea, of The Hill, Stonebridge, and had issue.

[7] This officer had a curious and unpleasant experience at Cambray a few days after Waterloo. As he was riding through some gardens the ground suddenly gave way under his horse's feet. The captain threw himself off his charger's back, and the next moment the horse fell to the bottom of a well 80 or 100 feet deep, and was killed instantaneously. (*Records.*) Promoted maj. in same regt. 11th July, 1822. Retd. on h. p. as lt.-col. 14th Jan. 1826. Living in 1830.

[8] Of Beighton, Yorkshire. Promoted maj. in same regt. 18th Dec. 1823. Quitted the service before 1830. M., 1832, Harriet, dau. of Sir Wm. Cave Browne-Cave, Bart., of Stamford.

[9] Placed on h. p. 25th May, 1816. Restored to f. p., as capt. in 41st Foot, 3rd Jan., 1822. Living in 1824.

[10] Placed on h. p. 25th May, 1816.

[11] M.I. at Waterloo.

[12] Of Mulbarton Lodge, co. Norfolk. Was 4th son of Abel Walford Bellairs, High Sheriff for Rutland, who represented a very ancient Leicestershire family, which can be traced back to the 12th century. Served in the Pa. Received the honour of knighthood from George IV. M. Cassandra, dau. and heir of Edmund Hooke, of Mulbarton Lodge. Quitted the service as captain in 1820, and d. 2nd October, 1863, leaving issue. Henry Bellairs, elder brother to the above, entered the Rl. Navy, and was wounded at Trafalgar. He afterwards entered the 15th Hussars, and on leaving the army took Holy Orders and became Vicar of Hunsigore, Yorkshire.

[13] Retd. on h. p. with rank of lt.-col. 9th June, 1825. M., 8th Dec., 1825, Harriet Frances, 2nd dau. of Lawrence, 2nd Lord Dundas. Living in 1842.

[14] Eldest son of Edward Byam, of Cedar Hill, Antigua, by Christiana Matilda, dau. of Mathew Byam, of Dublin. Quitted the service in 1817. Inherited the family estates in Antigua, and became President of that island. Knighted in 1859. M., 8th Feb., 1815, Martha, dau. of Thos. Rogers, of Antigua, and had issue. Living in 1862.

[15] Promoted capt. same regt. 25th Aug., 1819. Lt.-col. unattached, 26th Sept., 1826. Col. 23rd Nov., 1841. Maj.-gen. 11th Nov., 1851. Served in the Pa., and was severely wounded by a grape shot while carrying the regimental colours of the 38th Foot at Salamanca. Col.-in-Chf. 18th Hussars 1858. Bn. 1794. Brother to Wm. Byam. M., 1829, Eliz. Augusta, sister of Sir Grenville Temple, Bart., and had issue. D. 9th Sept., 1864. For an account of this historical family see *Gentleman's Magazine* for 1848.

[16] Bn. 1791. Younger son of Jas. Dawkins (who assumed the surname of Colyear on succeeding to the estates of his uncle, Charles, Earl of Portmore), by Hannah, dau. of Thos. Phipps. M. Elizabeth, dau. of Rev. Sir Wm. Cooper, Bart., and d. s. p. 1821.

[17] Of Gledhow Hall, co. York, and Astle Hall, co. Chester Bn. 19th Nov., 1794. Eldest son of John Dixon, of Gledhow, by Lydia, dau. of Rev. John Parker, of Astle. Quitted the service as a capt. in above regt. M., 24th Dec., 1829, Emma, dau. of Rev. E. S. Wilmot, of Chaddesden, co. Derby, and d. s. p. 3rd Aug., 1838.

[18] Afterwards Sir John James Douglas, Bart., of Springwood Park, Kelso, son of Sir George Douglas, of co. Roxburgh, 2nd Bart. and M.P. for that county, by Lady Eliz. Boyle, dau. of John, 3rd Earl of Glasgow. Born 18th July, 1792. Served in the Pa. Capt. 16th Dec., 1819. H. p. 25th July, 1820. M., 1822, the only dau. and heir of Henry Scott, of Belford, co. Roxburgh, and assumed the surname of Scott in addition to that of Douglas. D. 23rd Jan., 1836, leaving issue.

[19] Promoted capt. 15th June, 1820. Placed on h p. 25th Oct., 1821 Living in 1830.

[20] Quitted the service in 1821.

[21] M.I at Waterloo.

[22] Called "Henry Griffiths" in *Army List* for 1829 and in subsequent *Lists*. Lieut. 24th May, 1815. H. p. as lieut. from Rl. Staff Corps 12th March, 1829. Appointed a Mil. Knight of Windsor and d. in Oct., 1852.

[23] Out of the regt. in Aug., 1819.

[24] Surgeon 8th Foot 25th Sept., 1818. Serving in 1824. Out of the regt. in Feb., 1826.

[25] Surgeon 2nd May, 1822. Serving with regt. in 1830. H. p. before 1846.

[26] H. p. 25th Dec., 1818. Living in 1830.

[27] Placed on h. p. from 2nd Lt. Dns. German Legion, 21st Aug., 1817.

16TH (OR THE QUEEN'S) REGIMENT OF LIGHT.
DRAGOONS.
[16TH LANCERS.]

	Rank in the	
LIEUT.-COLONEL.	Regiment.	Army.
[1] James Hay, w.	18 Feb. 1813	
MAJOR.		
[2] George Home Murray	18 Feb. 1813	
CAPTAINS.		
[3] John Henry Belli	29 Jan. 1807	Maj., 7 May, 1812
[4] Clement Swetenham	11 June, 1807	
[5] Richard Weyland, w.	5 Sept. 1811	18 July, 1811
John Phillips Buchanan, K.	28 May, 1812	
[6] Wm. Tomkinson	3 June, 1812	12 Mar. 1812
[7] Charles King	18 Feb. 1813	
LIEUTENANTS.		
[8] J. — Barra, Adjt.	4 Oct. 1808	
[9] Wm. Osten	17 Nov. 1808	
[10] Trevor Wheler	11 July, 1811	
[11] Francis Swinfen	1 Aug. 1811	
[12] George Baker	15 Aug. 1811	
[13] Richard Beauchamp	19 Feb. 1812	
[14] Nath. Day Crichton, w.	20 Feb. 1812	
[15] Edward B. Lloyd	12 Mar. 1812	
[16] Wm. Nepean	2 Apr. 1812	
[17] Jas. Arch. Richardson	12 Nov. 1814	1 Apr. 1813
[18] John Luard	2 Mar. 1815	30 May, 1811
[19] Wm. Harris	30 Mar. 1815	21 Jan. 1813
[20] Hon. C. Monckton	30 Mar. 1815	8 July, 1813
[21] Alexander Macdougall	30 Mar. 1815	30 Dec. 1813
CORNETS.		
[22] Wm. Beckwith	7 Jan. 1813	
[23] Wm. Po'hill	1 July, 1813	
[24] George Nugent	7 Oct. 1813	
[25] Alexander Hay	11 Nov. 1813	
PAYMASTER.		
[26] George Neyland	10 Sept. 1812	

16TH (OR THE QUEEN'S) REGIMENT OF LIGHT DRAGOONS.—*continued*.

	Rank in the Regiment.	Army
QUARTERMASTER.		
[27] John Harrison	25 Jan. 1810	
SURGEON.		
[28] Isaac Robinson	21 Apr. 1804	22 Dec. 1803
ASSISTANT SURGEONS.		
[29] John M'Gr. Mallock	16 Apr. 1812	
[30] Dennis Murray	22 June, 1815	
VETERINARY SURGEON.		
[31] John Jones	25 Nov. 1813	

Blue. Facings scarlet. Lace gold.

[1] Afterwards Lt.-Gen. James Hay, C.B., Col.-in-Chf. 79th Highlanders. Served in the Pa. with above regt., and as capt. commanded the regt. in an affair with the Lancers de Berg, at Espesia, in which the enemy was defeated, and an officer with 70 men taken prisoners. Honourably mentioned in Wellington's despatches. Had his right arm broken at Salamanca. Recd. the gold medal and clasp. Was so seriously wounded at Waterloo that he could not be moved from the field for eight days. Given a distinguished service pension. D. at his seat, near Kilburn, co. Longford, 25th Feb., 1854.

[2] Made bt.-lt.-col. and C.B. for Waterloo. Lt.-col. of above regt. 25th May, 1822. Served in the Pa., and recd. the gold medal for Salamanca. D. at Cawnpore 15th Dec., 1833, whilst in command of above regt. and holding the rank of brig.-gen. at that station.

[3] Maj. in same regt. 10th Oct., 1816. Bt.-lt.-col. 21st Jan., 1819. Unattached h. p. list 1826. Son of John Belli, whose widow's death is recorded in the *Gentleman's Magazine* for 1842.

[4] Eldest son of Roger Comberbach, who assumed the surname and arms of Swetenham. Bn. 7th Feb., 1787. Served in the Pa. with above regt. Quitted the service with rank of maj. in 1817. M., 1st May, 1817, Eleanor, dau. of John Buchanan, of Donelly, co. Donegal, and had issue. Owned the estate of Somerford Booths, co. Chester, which had been in possession of his ancestors since A.D. 1100. D. 17th Nov., 1852.

[5] 3rd son of John Weyland, of Woodeaton, co. Oxford, and Woodrising, co. Norfolk. Served in the Pa. Quitted the service as maj. in 1820. Bn. 25th March, 1780. M., 12th Sept., 1820, Charlotte, dau. of Charles Gordon, of Cluny, and widow of Sir J. L. Johnstone, Bart., and had issue. D. in Oct., 1864.

[6] Bn. 18th Jan., 1790. 4th son of Henry Tomkinson, of Dorfold, Nantwich, by Anne, dau. of John Darlington, of Aston, co. Chester. Attained rank of lt.-col., h. p. 10th Jan., 1837. Served in the Pa., and was severely wounded at the passage of the Douro. Purchased the estate of Willington Hall, co. Chester, from Lord Alvanley in 1828. M., 9th Feb. 1836, Susan, dau. of Thos. Tarleton, and had issue. D. 1872.

[7] Was made brig.-maj. to the 4th Brigade after the battle of Waterloo. Ten years later, at siege of Bhurtpore, assisted by Capt. Luard and two orderlies of 16th Lancers, captured a Rajah. K.H. Lost an arm at El Bodon in the Par. War, when lieut. in 11th Lt. Dgns. D. at Dublin, 5th July, 1844.

[8] Joseph Barra was a gallant Par. veteran, where he won his spurs. Promoted capt. 29th July 1815. Placed on h. p. 25th March, 1816. Appointed Adjt. of the "Chester Yeomanry," which post he held until his death, 13th July, 1839. Bd. at Knutsford with military honours. At his funeral a sword was placed on his coffin, which bore this inscription :—" To Lieut. and Adjt. Barra, 16th or Queen's Lt. Dgns., this sword was presented by the officers of his regt. as a token of their high esteem and approbation of his services both at home and abroad, 30th March, 1815."

[9] Wilhelm Baron Osten, K.H., had previously served in the K. G. L., and had smelt powder in the Par.War. Member of the family of Van der Osten in Hanover, "of high military and judicial fame." Retd. from British service in 1834. Afterwards gen. in Hanoverian army. D. at Rufford Abbey 24th Jan., 1852.

[10] Afterwards Sir Trevor Wheler, Bart. Maj. 5th Dgn. Gds. 1829. Bn. 20th Dec., 1797. Eldest son of Sir Trevor Wheler, 8th Bart., by Harriet, dau. of Richard Beresford, of Ashbourne, co. Derby. Was twice m., and left issue by 1st wife. D. 6th Sept., 1869.

[11] Eldest son of John Swinfen by his second wife, Anne Ford. Placed on h. p. as lieut. 25th May, 1817. D. at Lapley Hall, co. Stafford, 20th Aug., 1839, leaving issue by his mge. with Mary Anne Yonge.

[12] 7th son of Wm. Baker, M.P., of Bayfordbury, Herts. Col. on retd. h. p. list 1846. D. 22nd Dec., 1859.

[13] 5th son of Sir Thos. Beauchamp, Bart., by Mary, 2nd dau. of Robert Palmer, of Sunning, Berks. Bn. 30th Jan., 1793. Afterwards lt.-col. Grenadier Guards. M., 4th October, 1828, Sophia, youngest dau. of Benjamin Ball, of Fort Fergus, co. Clare, and had issue Ret. as col. 9th March, 1832. D. 1850.

[14] Appointed capt. 5th Dgn. Gds. 17th Jan., 1822. Maj. in same regt. 6th April, 1826. D. 6th May, 1833, in London.

[15] Eldest son of Bell Lloyd, of Crogen yr Edeirnion, co. Merioneth, by Anne, dau. of George Anson, of Orgrave, co. Stafford. Placed on h. p. as lieut. 5th Aug., 1819. M., 1819, Lowry, dau. of Robert Morris, and had issue. D. 8th May, 1864.

[16] 3rd son of Sir Evan Nepean, 1st bart., Under Sec. of State for Ireland. Bn. 1795. Attained the rank of maj.-gen. M., in 1820, Emilia, dau of Col. Yorke, and had issue. D. 8th Dec., 1864.

[17] H. p. 25th Jan., 1816.

[18] 4th son of Peter John Luard, of Blyborough, capt. 4th Lt. Dgns., by Louisa Dalbiac. Afterwards maj. and bt.-lt.-col. 21st Foot. Served in the

Rl. Navy, 1802-7. Entered 4th Lt. Dgns. 1809. Served in the Pa. Captured a Rajah at the siege of Bhurtpore. An eminent draughtsman. Bn. 5th May, 1790. D. 1875.

[19] Capt. 2nd June, 1825. H. p. 8th June, 1830. Living in 1846.

[20] 2nd son of 4th Viscount Galway, by Eliz., dau. of Dan. Matthew, of Felix Hall, Essex. Captain in Cape Corps, 1823. Exchanged to 24th Foot 1824. D. 11th May 1830.

[21] Serving in 1824. Out of the regt. before 1830.

[22] Bn. 20th Aug., 1795. Eldest son of Wm. Beckwith, of Trimdon, co. Durham, by Caroline, dau. of John Nesham, of Houghton-le-Spring. Served in the Pa. with 16th Lt. Dgns. In 1831, as maj. of the 14th Lt. Dgns., greatly distinguished himself by the presence of mind and determination he showed in suppressing the Bristol riots. These riots were not suppressed until many of the ringleaders and their followers had perished, some being cut down by the cavalry when charging through the streets, but by far the greater number being burnt to death, when intoxicated, in the conflagration that devastated part of the city. Before the arrival of the squadron of the 14th Lt. Dgns. at Bristol the only available military force was a troop of the 3rd Dgn. Gds., which was ordered to protect the city gaol. The captain of this troop remained in his quarters, and allowed a cornet of only sixteen months' service to command the troop on this special service. It is recorded of this young officer, Cornet Charles Kelson, that when riding with his troop through the slums of Bristol a burly blacksmith rushed out of his shop, sledge-hammer in hand, and aimed a blow at the officer's head. As the smith bent his head with the weight of the hammer the subaltern's sword flashed through the air, and the Goliath's head rolled on the ground. Beckwith was a K.H., and at his death a Gen. and Col.-in-Chf. 14th Hussars. He m., 5th April, 1821, Priscilla Maria, dau. and heiress of Thos. Hopper, of Silksworth House, co. Durham, but d. s. p. 23rd Feb., 1871.

[23] 2nd son of Edward Polhill, of Clapham, by Sarah, dau. of John Spooner, of Barbadoes. Lieut. in same regt. 13th Dec., 1815. Exchanged to 1st Life Gds. 26th Oct., 1816. On h. p. 23rd Lt. Dgns. 23rd Jan., 1819. Living in 1860.

[24] Lieut. 14th Dec., 1815. Lieut. 7th D. G. 14th Dec., 1821. Capt. 22nd July, 1824. Serving in 1830.

[25] Of Nunraw. Bn. 6th Sept., 1796. M.I. at Waterloo. 3rd son of Robert Hay of Drumelzier, by Janet, eldest dau. of James Erskine, of Cardross.

[26] Left the regt. 2nd Sept., 1824.

[27] Lieut. 25th Jan., 1816. H. p. 25th March same year.

[28] Serving with the regt. in 1830. Dep. Inspector-Genl. 22nd July, 1830. H. p. before 1846.

[29] Surgeon 46th Foot 2nd Feb., 1826. Serving in 1830.

[30] Surgeon 23rd Nov., 1832. Appointed surgeon to 10th Lt. Dns., 14th Dec., 1841. Out of said regt. 30th June, 1848.

[31] Out of the regt. in 1822.

18TH REGIMENT OF LIGHT DRAGOONS (HUSSARS).*

	Rank in the Regiment.	Army.
LIEUT.-COLONEL.		
1 Hon. Henry Murray	2 Jan. 1812	
CAPTAINS.		
2 Richard Croker	9 July, 1812	
3 James Grant	17 Dec. 1812	
4 George Luard	21 July, 1813	
5 Jas. Rich. Llewis Lloyd	12 Nov. 1814	25 Aug. 1809
LIEUTENANTS.		
6 Charles Hesse, w.	4 May, 1809	
7 James Henry Waldie	13 Feb. 1812	
8 George Woodberry	10 Dec. 1812	
9 Hon. Lionel C. Dawson	24 June, 1813	10 Nov. 1807
10 Martin French	14 Oct. 1813	29 Oct. 1812
11 Thomas Prior	6 Jan. 1814	
12 Robert Coote	22 Feb. 1814	
13 Henry Duperier, Adjt., w.	23 Feb. 1814	
14 John Thos. Machell	24 Feb. 1814	
15 Donald M'Duffie	29 Sept. 1814	10 Mar. 1814
Henry Somerset	12 Nov. 1814	
Horace Seymour	12 Nov. 1814	29 Dec. 1812
16 Wm. Henry Rowlls	22 Dec. 1814	
17 John Rolfe Gordon	9 Feb. 1815	15 Oct. 1812
18 William Monins	20 Apr. 1815	
PAYMASTER.		
19 Wm. Deane	13 Aug. 1802	
SURGEON.		
20 Wm. Chambers	25 Feb. 1804	9 July, 1803
ASSISTANT-SURGEON.		
21 John Quincey	5 Mar. 1812	
VETERINARY SURGEON.		
22 Daniel Pilcher	13 June, 1811	

Blue.   Facings white.   Lace silver.

* Known as the "Drogheda Light Horse." Raised in Ireland by the Marquis of Drogheda, in 1759, and numbered as the 19th Lt. Dragoons. Was re-numbered in 1763 as the 18th Lt. Dragoons; became Hussars in 1807, and was disbanded in 1821.

[1] Afterwards Gen. the Hon. Sir H. Murray, K.C.B., Col.-in-Chf. 14th Lt. Dgns. 4th son of David, 2nd Earl of Mansfield, by his 2nd wife, the Hon. Louisa Cathcart, dau. of Charles, 9th Lord Cathcart. Bn. 6th Aug., 1784. Commanded the above regt. in the Pa., and was present at the battle of Morales, although then suffering from a severe wound in the knee. "Two days after, inflammation set in in the knee, yet he followed the regt. in a spring waggon in rear, till upon the representation of the surgeon that if he went on with the troops he must die, he was sent back to the hospital station at Palencia, where, with abscess and acute rheumatism, he nearly died" (Col. Malet's *Records 18th Hus.*). At Waterloo he led the regt. in Sir H. Vivian's brilliant charge at the' conclusion of the battle. M., 28th June, 1810, Emily, dau. of Gerard de Visme, and had issue. Resided during the latter part of his life at Wimbledon Lodge, and d. there 29th July, 1850. M.I. St. Mary's Church, Wimbledon.

[2] Richard Hare Croker was 2nd son of Richard Croker, of Ballynagarde, co. Limerick, by Margaret Anne, sister of 1st Earl of Listowel, and dau. of Richard Hare. Bt.-maj. for Waterloo. H. p. 16th Nov., 1820. Afterwards col. retd. list. M. Amelia, dau. of John Haigh, of Whitwell Hall, co. York, and had issue. D. 15th Jan., 1854 at Leamington.

[3] Afterwards Maj.-gen. James Grant, C.B., Gov. of Scarborough Castle Served at Seringapatam and in Sicily. Also served in India with 17th Lt. Dgns. and in the Pa. with above regt. Bt.-lt.-col. for Waterloo. D. at Hillingdon, Mdx., 5th April, 1852.

[4] 3rd son of Peter John Luard, of Blyborough, capt. 4th Lt. Dgns., by Louisa, dau. of Charles Dalbiac, of Hungerford Park. Bn. 1788. Served in the Pa. Placed on h. p. as maj. 8th April, 1826. D. unm. in Dec., 1847.

[5] Quitted the service in 1818.

[6] Capt. in the Staff Corps 22nd Feb., 1816. Placed on h. p. 1819. Afterwards killed in a duel with Count Leon, a natural son of the Emperor Napoleon.

[7] Commanded his troop at Waterloo. Placed on h. p. as lieut. 7th Sept., 1820. Living in 1846.

[8] Serving in 1817. Out of the regt. when it was disbanded.

[9] "On baggage guard, marched with the regt. 16th, ordered to the rear 17th June, 1815." 4th son of John, 2nd Visct. and 1st Earl of Portarlington. Bn. 7th May, 1790. M., 15th Sept., 1820, Lady Eliz. Nugent, 2nd dau. of 7th Earl of Westmeath, and had issue. D. 25th Feb., 1842.

[10] The family of French claims to be one of the 14 ancient "tribes" of Galway. Certain it is that it is a very ancient one, and has left many branches in the sister kingdom. There seem to have been several bearing the Christian name of "Martin," including an "Hon. Martin Ffrench" (son of 2nd Baron Ffrench). Bn. 1790, and d. 1871.

[11] Eldest son of Thos. Prior, of Rathdowney, Queen's Co., by Catherine, dau. of Joseph Palmer, of Cuffboro' in same county. Placed on h. p. 23rd April, 1817. Capt. h. p. 28th Nov., 1834. Living 1846.

[12] Robert Carr Coote was promoted capt. 26th Nov., 1818. Placed on h. p. 11th Nov., 1821. 2nd son of Chidley Coote, of Ash Hill, co. Limerick, by Eliz., dau. of the Rev. Ralph Carr, of Bath. M. Margaret Grier, and had issue. His elder brother succeeded to the Coote baronetcy on the death of Lord Mountrath. D. 5th Nov., 1834.

[13] H. p. in Nov. 1821. Living in 1846.

[14] 4th son of Lt.-Col. Christopher Machell, of Beverley, by Anne, dau. of Col. Christopher Scott, of Aldbro'. Placed on h. p. 10th Nov., 1821. D. 13th Oct., 1853, at Beverley.

[15] Left the regt. in April, 1817. H. p. as lieut. 40th Foot 27th April, 1820. Living in 1846.

[16] Commanded his troop at Waterloo. Placed on h. p. 23rd April, 1817.

[17] Quitted the service in 1816.

[18] Served in the Pa. with the 52nd L. I. Placed on h. p. 25th March, 1817. Afterwards lt.-col. of the East Kent Militia. Bn. 20th Feb., 1792. Eldest son of John Monins (late 43rd L. I.), of The Palace, Canterbury. M., 7th Oct., 1812, Miss Jull, and had issue. D. 1857.

[19] "Marched with the regt. 16th, ordered to the rear the 17th June." Ret. f. p. 1842. D. 1852.

[20] Surgeon to 22nd Foot 13th Dec., 1821. H. p. 3rd Sept., 1825. Living in 1830.

[21] Assistant-surgeon to 15th Hussars 6th June, 1822. D. or left the regt. in 1827.

[22] H. p. 10th Nov., 1821. Living in 1830.

23RD REGIMENT OF LIGHT DRAGOONS.*

	Rank in the	
LIEUT.-COLONEL.	Regiment.	Army.
1 John, Earl of Portarlington	6 Apr. 1809	Col., 4 June, 1814

MAJORS.

2 John Mervin Cutcliffe, w.	2 Sept. 1813	
3 Peter Augustus Lautour	6 Jan. 1814	20 May, 1813

CAPTAINS.

4 Charles Webb Dance, w.	9 Apr. 1807	
5 Philip Zachariah Cox	15 Mar. 1810	
6 John Martin	8 Feb. 1813	
7 Thomas Gerrard, w.	1 July, 1813	Maj., 1 Jan. 1812
8 Roderick M'Neil	19 Jan. 1815	1 Dec. 1814
9 Henry Grove	19 Apr. 1815	Maj., 1 Jan. 1812
10 James Maxwell Wallace	20 Apr. 1815	22 Oct. 1807

LIEUTENANTS.

11 George Dodwell	25 Apr. 1805	
12 Ant. Bolton	16 Oct. 1806	19 Dec. 1805
13 Stephen Coxens, K.	17 Nov. 1808	
14 Charles Tudor	14 Mar. 1810	26 Oct. 1808
15 John Banner	15 Mar. 1810	
16 John Lewes	4 Mar. 1813	
17 Cæsar Bacon	14 Oct. 1813	
18 Brabazon Disney, w.	15 Sept. 1814	5 Aug. 1813
19 Robert Johnson	20 Oct. 1814	
20 Thomas B. Wall, w.	9 Feb. 1815	
21 H. Hill, Adjt.	5 Apr. 1815	
22 George Wm. Blathwayt	4 May, 1815	

CORNET.

23 Wm. Hemmings	6 Apr. 1815	

PAYMASTER.

24 Thomas Dillow	31 Jan. 1809	

23RD REGIMENT OF LIGHT DRAGOONS.—*continued*.

	Rank in the	
QUARTERMASTER.	Regiment.	Army.
²⁵ Joseph Crouchley	15 Feb. 1810	
SURGEON.		
²⁶ Samuel L. Steele	20 Apr. 1809	12 Nov. 1803
ASSISTANT-SURGEON.		
²⁷ H. Cowen	4 Aug. 1808	
VETERINARY SURGEON.		
²⁸ John Ship	3 Apr. 1806	

Blue. Facings crimson. Lace silver.

* Raised in 1794 as the 26th Lt. Dragoons. Re-numbered "23rd" in 1802. Made Lancers in 1816. Disbanded in Jan. 1818.

[1] The star of the Dawsons was not propitious on the morning of the 18th June, 1815. Whilst one brother had been sent to the rear on the evening of 17th June as officer in charge of the baggage guard of 18th Hussars, the eldest brother, John Dawson, 2nd Earl of Portarlington, had betaken himself that same evening to Brussels or elsewhere. The consequence of this step was that "on the morning of Waterloo, by an unfortunate mistake, he was prevented from joining his regiment in time to command it in the brilliant exploits it performed on that memorable day." His anguish was extreme. He joined the 18th Hussars, and served with Sir H. Vivian's brigade in the destructive and successful charge made by that corps towards the close of the battle. In this charge Lord Portarlington had a horse shot under him. No one who knew this nobleman doubted his courage for a moment, but his absence from duty on such an occasion necessitated his retirement from the 23rd Dgns. in Sept., 1815. The Prince Regent showed much kind feeling for Portarlington, and did his best to uphold the unfortunate officer in the eyes of the world. Lord Portarlington purchased a half-pay ensigncy in 86th Foot 21st Oct., 1821. Became lieut. on h. p. 10th Sept., 1825. Capt. h. p. 9th Aug., 1831. This rank was a curious anomaly, as his lordship's name had been retained in the *Army List* as a "colonel" ever since Waterloo, and he was also awarded the Waterloo medal. But the one misfortune of his life was ever before him, and the remorse from knowing that he alone was the author of it weighed upon him to such an extent that he took to dissipation, lost a large fortune, and d. at a humble lodging in an obscure London slum, 28th Dec., 1845. In early life he had served in the Pa., and was present at the battle of Talavera. He d. unm.

² Commanded the regt. at Waterloo in the absence of Lord Portarlington, and was severely wounded early in the day. Bt.-lt.-col. and C.B. Promoted lt.-col. of this regt. 28th Sept., 1815. Placed on h. p. in 1818 on the reduction of his regt. D. in 1822. He belonged to the Devonshire family of this name (Cutcliffe, of Damage), the head of which bears the Christian name of "Mervyn." *Also K H.p Order of Crescent (Egypt) D. 1822.*

³ Younger son of Joseph François Louis de Lautour, who came of an old Alsatian family, for many years a banker at Madras. Served in the Pa. with the 11th Lt. Dgns., and specially distinguished himself at El Bodon. On 7th Sept., 1812, when in command of a squadron of 11th Dgns., he attacked and took prisoners a company of French artillery near Valladolid. At Waterloo he succeeded to the command of the above regt. early in the day, and later on, same day, to the command of the brigade. C.B., and K.H., and bt. of lt.-col. Placed on h. p. 25th Jan., 1818. Afterwards Gen. and Col.-in-Chf. 3rd Lt. Dgns. M. Cameron, dau. of John Innes, of Cowie, and had issue. D. at Bromley 11th Jan., 1856.

⁴ Promoted capt. 20th June, 1816, and appointed maj. 2nd Life Gds. 24th July, 1816. Bt.-lt.-col. 27th March, 1817. Exchanged to h. p. with Maj. Roderick M'Neil, 19th July, 1822. Had been knighted by George IV. in the previous August. D. 13th Nov., 1844.

⁵ On h. p. 1817. M., 17th Feb., 1817, Louise, youngest dau. of Adm. Sir Albemarle Bertie, Bart. D. 24th Jan., 1811.

⁶ Afterwards lieut.-col. unattached. Living 1842.

⁷ 3rd son of Thos. Gerrard, of Gibbstown, co. Meath. Bn. 9th Dec., 1779. H. p. 1818. Lt.-col. h. p. 1821. M., 18th March, 1831, Letitia, dau. of Rev. George Garnett, of Williamston, co. Meath, and had issue. D. 7th April 1836.

⁸ Afterwards maj. 2nd Life Gds. Bt.-lt.-col. 17th Jan., 1822. Lt.-col. 91st Foot 16th July 1841-1842. D. as gen. in Oct., 1863.

⁹ On h. p. 1818. Bt.-lt.-col. 1821.

¹⁰ Afterwards Sir James Maxwell Wallace, K.H., Col.-in-Chf. 17th Lancers. Son of John Wallace, of Greenock, N.B., by a dau. of Robert Colquhoun. Bn. 1785. Served at the Cape of Good Hope as cornet 21st Lt. Dgns., and saw much service in Caffraria, 1812. On the 16th June, 1815, was appointed orderly officer, by Wellington's permission, to Gen. Count Dornberg, and following day acting brig.-maj. Was twice m. His 2nd wife (in 1836) was the widow of Sir Alexander Don, Bart., of Newton Don, N.B. D. 3rd Feb., 1867, aged 82.

¹¹ H. p. 30th May, 1816. Living in 1846.

¹² Lieut. 3rd D. G. 3rd Aug., 1818. Adjt. 6th Nov., 1823. Capt. 11th Foot 3rd Aug., 1826. Serving in 1830.

¹³ Son of Ebenezer and Anne Coxens, to whom a pension of £80 per annum was granted in 1815.

¹⁴ H. p. 25th Jan., 1818. Living in 1846.

¹⁵ Capt. 93rd Highlanders 21st Nov., 1828. In 1836 he wrote a reply in *The United Service Magazine* to Col. Gawler's *Crisis of Waterloo*, of which more hereafter. D. 24th Dec., 1837.

¹⁶ H. p. 25th Jan. 1818. Living in 1830.

[17] H. p. 25th Jan. 1818. Major, unattached, 10th Jan., 1837. Living in 1860. Served previously in 11th Lt. Dns.

[18] Son of Thos. Disney, of Rock Lodge, co. Meath. Capt. 67th Foot 8th Apr., 1816. H. p. 25th July, 1817. Exchanged to Rl. Fusiliers 22nd Apr., 1819. Major 3rd March, 1825. Lt.-col. 31st Aug., 1830, unattached. D. in Dublin 15th March, 1833.

[19] H. p. 25th Jan., 1818. Living in 1830. Called "Johnston" in *Army List* for 1830.

[20] Capt. h. p. 81st Foot 16th May, 1822. Appointed Sub-Inspector of Militia in the Ionian Islands, 30th May, 1829.

[21] Reduced with the regt. in Jan., 1818.

[22] The representative of Wm. Blathwayt, Secretary at War to King William III., and Clerk of the Privy Council to no less than four English Sovereigns. G. W. Blathwayt, of Dyrham Park, Chippenham, was bn. 25th Feb., 1797. M. 21st Jan., 1822, Mary Anne, dau. of the Rev. T. Agmondisham Vesey, and had issue. In 1851 he was a lieut.-col. on the retd. list. D. 14th May, 1871.

[23] Lieut. 17th Aug., 1815. H. p. 93rd Highlanders 25th Mar., 1817. Capt. 25th Borderers 19th Sept., 1826. Serving in 1830.

[24] Reduced with the regt. in Jan., 1818.

[25] Reduced with the regt. in Jan., 1818. Living in 1830.

[26] D. or left the regt. in 1816.

[27] Surgeon to 41st Foot 8th June, 1820. Serving in 1824. Out of the regt. in 1825.

[28] H. p. Jan. 1818. D. at Hackney, 1834.

1st REGIMENT OF FOOT GUARDS.*

(2nd and 3rd Battalions.)

	Rank in the Regiment.	Army.
SECOND MAJOR.		
[1] Henry Askew, w.	25 July, 1814	Col., 4 June, 1814
THIRD MAJOR.		
[2] Hon. Wm. Stuart, w.	25 July, 1814	Col., 4 June, 1814
CAPTAINS AND LIEUT.-COLONELS.		
[3] Hon. H. T. P. Townshend, w.	26 Oct. 1809	
[4] Richard Harvey Cooke, w.	7 Nov. 1811	
[5] Edward Stables, κ.	4 June, 1812	
[6] Sir Francis d'Oyly, K.C.B., κ.	23 Sept. 1812	
[7] Henry d'Oyly, w.	27 May, 1813	
John George Woodford	1 July, 1813	
[8] George Fead, w.	13 Dec. 1813	
[9] Charles Thomas, κ.	25 Dec. 1813	
[10] Alexander, Lord Saltoun	25 Dec. 1813	
[11] John Reeve	25 Dec. 1813	
[12] Wm. Miller, κ.	3 Mar. 1814	
[13] Hon. James Stanhope	25 July, 1814	17 Mar. 1814
[14] Goodwin Colquitt	25 July, 1814	
[15] Wm. Henry Milnes, κ.	25 July, 1814	
Sir Henry H. Bradford, K.C.B., w.	25 July, 1814	28 Dec. 1809
[16] Sir Henry Hardinge, K.C.B.	25 July, 1814	30 May, 1811
Sir Thos. Noel Hill, Kt., K.C.B.	25 July, 1814	3 Oct. 1811
Delancey Barclay	25 July, 1814	28 Feb. 1812
Lord Fitzroy Somerset, K.C.B., w.	25 July, 1814	27 Apr. 1812
LIEUTENANTS AND CAPTAINS.		
[17] Robert Adair, w.	26 Oct. 1809	
[18] Thos. Streatfield, w.	23 Nov. 1809	
[19] J. H. Davies	7 Dec. 1809	4 Feb. 1804
[20] Charles Allix, Adjt.	13 Dec. 1810	
Lord James Hay	27 June, 1811	8 Feb. 1810
[21] Edward Grose, κ.	26 Sept. 1811	

1st REGIMENT OF FOOT GUARDS—*continued.*

		Rank in the	
		Regiment.	Army.
LIEUTENANTS AND CAPTAINS—*continued.*			
James Gunthorpe, Adjt.		7 Nov. 1811	
Chath. Hor. Churchill		27 Aug. 1812	Maj., 22 Nov. 1813
22 Hon. Robert Clements, w.		23 Sept. 1812	
Lord Charles Fitzroy		23 Sept. 1812	
23 Robert Ellison		20 Dec. 1812	
24 Harry Weyland Powell		22 Jan. 1813	
Newton Chambers, ĸ.		7 Apr. 1813	
George Disbrowe		8 Apr. 1813	
Wm. Gordon Cameron		10 June, 1813	
25 Lonsdale Boldero		20 Oct. 1813	
26 Robert Wm. Phillimore		13 Dec. 1813	
Hon. Orlando Bridgeman, w.		8 Jan. 1814	
27 Charles Parker Ellis, w.		10 Jan. 1814	
28 James Simpson, w.		11 Jan. 1814	
Augustus, Viscount Bury		12 Jan. 1814	
29 Edward Clive		13 Jan. 1814	
30 Wm. Fred. Johnstone		16 Mar. 1814	
31 Francis Fownes Luttrell, w.		17 Mar. 1814	
32 Thomas Brown, ĸ.		22 Mar. 1814	
33 Edward Pery Buckley		23 Mar. 1814	
Francis Dawkins		28 Apr. 1814	
34 James Nixon		12 May, 1814	
35 Charles F. R. Lascelles, w.		9 June, 1814	
Wm. George Moore		30 Sept. 1814	14 Apr. 1814
36 Samuel W. Burgess, w.		20 Oct. 1814	
ENSIGNS.			
37 Rees Howell Gronow		24 Dec. 1812	
38 Robert Batty, w.		14 Jan. 1813	
39 Richard Master		21 Jan. 1813	
40 Wm. Barton, w.		4 Feb. 1813	9 May, 1811
41 Hon. H. S. V. Vernon		8 Apr. 1813	
42 Edward Pardoe, ĸ.		29 Apr. 1813	
43 Courtney Chambers		10 June, 1813	
44 James Butler		23 June, 1813	17 June, 1812
45 Thos. Robert Swinburne		24 June, 1813	
46 Charles James Vyner		2 Sept. 1813	
47 Fred. Dashwood Swann		20 Oct. 1813	

1st REGIMENT OF FOOT GUARDS—*continued.*

	ENSIGNS—*continued.*	Regiment.	Rank in the Army.
	James, Lord Hay, K.	21 Oct. 1813	
48	John Pasley Dirom	18 Nov. 1813	Lt., 2 Sept. 1813
49	John F. M. Erskine	1 Dec. 1813	
50	Robert Bruce, w.	9 Dec. 1813	
51	Hon. T. Seymour Bathurst	11 Jan. 1814	
52	Hon. Ern. A. Edgcombe	12 Jan. 1814	
53	George Fludyer, w.	13 Jan. 1814	
54	Wm. Fred. Tinling	27 Jan. 1814	
55	Algernon Greville	1 Feb. 1814	
56	George Thomson Jacob	3 Feb. 1814	
57	Donald Cameron	17 Feb. 1814	
58	Samuel Hurd	3 Mar. 1814	
59	Fletcher Norton	17 Mar. 1814	
60	Henry Lascelles, w.	7 Apr. 1814	
61	George Mure	14 Apr. 1814	
62	George Allen	21 Apr. 1814	
63	Thos. Elmsley Croft, w.	28 Apr. 1814	
64	Hon. S. S. Barrington, K.	24 Nov. 1814	7 Sept. 1814
65	Joseph St. John	25 Nov. 1814	
66	Daniel Tighe	26 Nov. 1814	
67	James Talbot	16 Feb. 1815	
	QUARTERMASTER.		
68	Robert Colquhoun	25 Nov. 1812	21 Aug. 1806
	SURGEONS.		
69	Wm. Curtis	5 Oct. 1809	21 Aug. 1806
70	Sam. Wm. Watson	25 Dec. 1813	14 July, 1809
	ASSISTANT-SURGEONS.		
71	John Harrison	29 June, 1809	
72	Andrew Armstrong	18 July, 1811	
73	John Gardner	25 Dec. 1813	
74	Fred. Gilder	9 June, 1814	

Facings blue. Lace gold.

* By a General Order, dated 29th July, 1815, H.R.H. the Prince Regent was pleased to approve of the 1st Regt. of Foot Guards being made a regt. of Grenadiers, and styled " The 1st, or Grenadier, Regt. of Foot Guards ' in commemoration of their having defeated the Grenadiers of the French Imperial Guards at Waterloo.

[1] Bn. 7th May, 1775. 3rd son of John Askew, of Pallinsburn, co. Northumberland. C.B. Knighted by George IV. Lt.-gen. D. s. p. 25th June, 1847, at Cologne.

[2] 3rd son of Alexander, 10th Baron Blantyre, by Catherine, dau. and heir of Patrick Lindsay, of Eaglescairnie. Bn. 1778. C.B. for Waterloo. Attained rank of lt.-gen., and d. unm. 15th Feb., 1837.

[3] Lt.-col. of the Grenadier Guards 25th July, 1821. Bt.-col. 12th August, 1819. Aftds. K.C.H. and Lt.-Gov. of Windsor Castle. 2nd son of 1st Viscount Sydney, by Elizabeth, eldest dau. and co-heir of Richard Powys, of Hintlesham, co. Suffolk. D. unm. 24th May, 1843.

[4] Second in the Pa., and commanded a detachment of Guards at St. Sebastian, for which he received the gold medal. C.B. for Waterloo. Quitted the service as bt.-col. 25th March, 1818. D., in London, 8th Oct., 1856.

[5] M. I. at Waterloo. He was of Great Ormead, Herts.

[6] 3rd son of the Rev. Matthias d'Oyly, Rector of Buxted, Sussex, and Archdeacon of Lewes, by his marriage with Miss Poughfer. Had served in this regt. since 1794. In the expedition to the Helder, in 1799, he acted as A.D.C. to his uncle, Gen. d'Oyly. Served in Sicily, also in the Pa.; and was made K.C.B. for his valuable services in Spain and France. Fell by a musket ball towards the close of Waterloo.

[7] Brother to the above. Bn. 21st April, 1780. Promoted maj.-gen. 28th June, 1838, and was made Col.-in-Chf. of 33rd Foot, 28th Sept., 1847. Lt.-Gen. 1851. Had served in Holland and the Pa. Was A.D.C. to Gen. Cooke at the siege of Cadiz, and was sent home with despatches announcing the raising of the siege in 1812. Severely wounded at Waterloo. M. 1836, Caroline, youngest dau. of Colonel Gore-Langton, M.P. D. 26th Sept., 1855.

[8] Made C.B. for Waterloo. Son of Lt.-Gen. George Fead, Col. Comdt. R.A., who d. at Woolwich in 1815. Retd. 1828, and d. at Lewisham, 13th Sept,. 1847. By his will, dated 16th Dec., 1844, he bequeathed all his property to his wife, Caroline Fead, who was sole executrix to his will.

[9] Began his military career as ensign in the East Middlesex Militia, from which he volunteered to accompany the expedition to Holland in 1799, and received promotion for his gallantry in that campaign from the Duke of Gloucester. Served in the Pa., and distinguished himself at Salamanca. In the autumn of 1814 he married Sarah Garcy Brandon, niece of Mr. Serjeant Shepherd. A pens. of £200 per ann. was granted to his widow, who was left in distressed circumstances.

[10] Son of Alexander Fraser, 15th Lord Saltoun, by Margaret, only dau. and heir of Simon Fraser, of Ness Castle. Saw much service in the Pa. Had four horses shot under him whilst defending Hougomont without (Col. M'Donell defending within). "Towards the close of Waterloo day he returned to his place in the line with about but one-third of the men with whom he had gone into action. He then took a prominent part in the last celebrated charge of the Guards." K.T.; K.C.B.; G.C.H.; K.M.T.; K.St.G. Lt.-Gen. and Col.-in-Chf. 2nd Foot. Commanded a brigade in the war with China, 1842. Was justly described by Wellington, on one occasion, as a "pattern to the army both as man and soldier." M. a natural dau. of Lord Chancellor Thurlow, and d. s. p. 18th August, 1853, near Rothes.

[11] Eldest son of Wm. Reeve, of Leadenham House, Grantham, by Millicent, dau. of Capt. John King, of 1st Foot Guards. Attained the rank of Gen. and

Col.-in-Chf. 61st Regt. Had served in the Pa., and at Walcheren. M., 11th July, 1821, Lady Susan Sherard, dau. of Philip, 5th Earl of Harborough, and had issue. D. 3rd Oct., 1864.

[12] D. at Brussels on 19th June, 1815, of wounds received at Quatre Bras. On being wounded he sent for his friend, Col. C. Thomas, and said, " I feel I am mortally wounded, but I am pleased to think it is my fate rather than yours, whose life is involved in that of your young wife." After a pause, he said : " I should like to see the colours of the regt. before I quit them for ever." They were brought and waved round his wounded body. " His countenance brightened, he smiled, declared himself well satisfied, and was carried from the field." M.I. at Waterloo. Was 2nd son of Sir William Miller, Bart. (a lord of session by title of Lord Glenlee), by Grizel, dau. of George Chalmers, of co. Fife.

[13] 3rd son of Charles, 3rd Earl Stanhope, by his 2nd wife, Louisa, dau. and sole heir of the Hon. Henry Grenville, Gov. of Barbados. Bn. 7th Sept., 1788. M. 9th July, 1820, the Hon. Frederica Murray, dau. of 3rd Earl of Mansfield, and had issue. Placed on h. p. 28th Feb., 1822. D. 5th March, 1825.

[14] C.B. for Waterloo. Quitted the service in 1820. Brother to the John Colquit who, as capt. in this regt. highly distinguished himself at the taking of Seville in 1812, and d. of his wounds soon after. Goodwin Colquit m. Miss Wallace, of Kelly, N.B., and had issue.

[15] 2nd son of Sir Robert Milnes, Bart., by Charlotte, 3rd dau. of Capt. J. A. Bentinck, R.N. D. from his wounds, 20th June, 1815. M.I. at Waterloo.

[16] Afterwards Viscount Hardinge, G.C.B., and K.T.S. 3rd son of Rev. Henry Hardinge, Rector of Stanhope, co. Durham, by Frances, dau. of James Best, of Park House, Boxley, Kent. Served throughout the Par. War, most of the time being D.Q.M.G. of the Portuguese army. Received the gold medal and five clasps. In 1815 was attached to the Prussian army, being so employed by Wellington, whom he kept *au fait* of what was passing. Was present at the battle of Ligny, where he was sev. wnded. in the left hand. " On the night of the 16th June, 1815, he lay in a wretched hut with his amputated left hand lying by his side." Wellington's despatch to Earl Bathurst, of 30th June, 1815, did full justice to Hardinge's services with Prince Blucher's army. In 1846 was created a viscount in acknowledgment of his valuable services as Gov.-Gen. in the East Indies. (Medal and two clasps for the Sutlej campaign.) Col.-in-Chf. 57th Regt., 1843. Com.-in-Chf. at home, 1852, and F.-M. 1855. M. 10th Dec., 1821, Lady Emily Stewart, 7th dau. of Robert, 1st Marquis of Londonderry, and had issue. D. 24th Sept., 1856.

[17] D. at Brussels on 23rd June, 1815, of wounds received at Quatre Bras ; son of Robert Adair, to whom administration of his son's effects and personalty was granted, 29th March, 1816. P.C.C.

[18] 2nd son of Henry Streatfield, of Chillingstone, Edenbridge, Kent, by Elizabeth, dau. of Dr. Ogle, Dean of Winchester. Promoted capt. and lt.-col. 2nd July, 1815. Quitted the service, 26th Dec, 1821. D. at Penshurst, 26 Sept., 1852.

[19] This officer's proper name was " Thomas Henry Hastings Davies." He was of Elmley Castle, co. Worcester, and M.P. for Worcester. 2nd son of Thomas Davies, Advocate-General, Calcutta. Retd. on h. p. as lt.-col. 1818. M., 21st Jan., 1824, Augusta, only child of Thomas de Crespigny, and d. s. p. 11th Dec., 1846.

[20] 2nd son of John Peter Allix, of Swaffham House, Cambridge, by Sarah, dau. of Rev. Wm. Collyer. Bn. 24 April, 1787. M. 10th April, 1841, Mary, dau. of Charles Allix, of Willoughby Hall, co. Lincoln, and had issue. Capt. and lt.-col. 4th July, 1815. Col. 10th Jan., 1837. D. 24th April, 1862.

[21] This officer's name appears on the tablet erected by the Grenadier Guards, in the church at Waterloo, in memory of the officers of that regt. who fell in the Waterloo campaign. His parentage cannot be traced, and he seems to have left no will. The name of Grose is familiar to all from being that of the author of *Military Antiquities.*

[22] 2nd son of the 1st Earl of Leitrim by Eliz., dau. of 1st Earl of Massareene. Bt.-maj. for Waterloo. D. in July, 1828, as capt. and lt.-col. same regt.

[23] 2nd son of Henry Ellison, of Hebburn, co. Durham, by Henrietta, dau. of John Isaacson. Bt.-maj. for Waterloo. Maj. and bt.-col. in same regt. 9th Jan.,1838. D. 3rd July, 1843, leaving issue by his wife, who was a dau. of 4th Lord Rokeby.

[21] Served at Walcheren and in the Pa. Son of Thomas Powell and Clarissa his wife. M., in 1816, Eliza Buckworth, and had issue. Quitted the service in 1821. D. 17th July, 1840. M.I. in Lyndhurst Church, Hants.

[25] Afterwards adjt. to his battalion, and maj. same regt. 1845. His name is not given in the pedigree of "Boldero, of co. Suffolk," but as there is a "Lonsdale" Boldero in the Suffolk family at this present time, the above, doubtless, belonged to this ancient family. Retd. in Oct., 1846.

[26] This officer's name was Wm. Robert, and not as given in the 1815 *Army List*. Retd. on h. p. 22nd July, 1824, as capt. Eldest son of W. R. Phillimore, of Kendalls, co. Herts, by the Hon. Sarah Ongley, dau. of 1st Lord Ongley. Bn. 1793. M. Anna, dau. of W. A. West, and had issue. D. at Brighton, 30th Nov., 1846.

[27] 2nd son of John Ellis, by Antonetta, dau. of Sir P. Parker, Bart. Dangerously wounded at Waterloo. Lt.-col. h. p. 1831. Col. 1841. M. 5th May, 1817, Julia, dau. of Vice.-Adm. Christopher Parker. D. at Clevedon, 6th Aug., 1850.

[28] Afterwards Gen. Sir James Simpson, G.C.B. Com.-in-Chf. in the Crimea after the death of F.-M. Lord Raglan. Served in the Pa. from May, 1812, to May, 1813. In 1815 was a student in the "first," or as it was called later, the "senior" department of the R.M. College (which dept. was the forerunner of the "Staff College"), but joined his battn. (the 2nd) in Flanders in the spring of this year. Was sev. wnded. at Quatre Bras. Served as 2nd in command to Sir Charles Napier during the campaign against the mountain and desert tribes situated on the right bank of the Indus in 1845. Was Chief of the Staff in the Crimea, for which he was well qualified by his long experience of staff work. Much against his will he was chosen to succeed Lord Raglan as C.-in-C. After two unsuccessful attacks on the Redan had taken place, Gen. Simpson was subjected to severe criticisms, and although he was upheld by the Home Government, and made G.C.B. with rank of full gen., he soon after resigned his command, and was succeeded by Sir Wm. Codrington. Simpson returned to England. He was son of David Simpson, of Teviot-bank, N.B., by Margaret, dau. of John Eliot. of Borthwick-brae. M., 1839, Eliz., dau. of Sir Robert Dundas, Bart. (she d. 1840) and d. at Horringer, near Bury St. Edmunds, 18th July, 1868.

[29] Eldest son of Edward Bolton Clive, of Whitfield, co. Hereford, by the Hon. Harriet Archer, dau. and co.-heir of Andrew, last Baron Archer, Capt. and lt.-col. 1826. Col. 1840. D. unm. 14th April. 1845.

[30] Attained the rank of capt. and lt.-col. and quitted the service in 1840. Living in 1874.

[31] 3rd son of John Fownes-Luttrell, of Dunster Castle. M.P. for Minehead, by Mary, eldest dau. of Francis Drewe, of Grange, Devon. Bn. 1792. Lt.-col Grenadier Guards. Quitted the service 28th April, 1825. Of Kilve Court, and Wootton House, Somerset. M., 1824, his cousin Emma Drewe. D. Jan., 1862, leaving issue.

[32] Belonged to the family of "Brown of Kingston Blount, co. Oxford." Was killed at Quatre Bras. M.I. at Waterloo. His brother, Henry Alexander Brown, lived for many years at St. Leonard's, where he was long remembered as "a fine old gentleman of the old school."

[33] Afterwards Gen. E. P. Buckley, M.P., of New Hall, Salisbury. M., 13th May, 1828, Lady Catherine Bouverie, dau. of 3rd Lord Radnor, and had issue. Son of Col. Edward P. Buckley, of Woolcombe Hall, co. Dorset, by Lady Georgina West. D. 1873.

[34] Exchanged to 60th Foot 15th June, 1820, and retd. on h. p. three weeks later. Living in 1846.

[35] Son of Rowley Lascelles by Eliz., younger dau. of Sir Charles Gould, Bart. (who assumed the name of Morgan), by Jane, eldest dau. of Thomas Morgan, of Ruperra, co. Glamorgan. Maj. in this regt. 4th July, 1843, and lt.-col. comg. 10th April, 1849. Retd. on f. p. before 1855. D. 8th Nov. 1860.

[36] There were two officers of this name in the army in 1815. The other Samuel was a capt. on retd. list of 10th Veteran Battn. The above Samuel quitted the service before 1824.

[37] Son of Wm. Gronow, of Court Herbert, co. Glamorgan, the representative of a very old Welsh family. Quitted the service 24th Oct., 1821. Lt. Gronow belonged to the 1st Batt., which was not at Waterloo. Sir T. Picton took him out to Flanders as an "honorary" A.D.C., but finding no employment for him, he was advised to join the 3rd batt. of his regt. which was at Waterloo. This he did, and took part in the great battle as a guardsman. His experiences of that memorable day have been given to the world in an interesting little book entitled *Reminiscences of Capt. Gronow*. He was aftds. M.P. for Stafford, and d. in Paris 22nd Nov., 1865.

[38] Son of Dr. Robert Batty, of Hastings (who was born at Kirby Lonsdale in co. Westmoreland). Educated at Caius College, Cambridge. An eminent amateur draughtsman. F.R.S. Wrote a short account of the campaign in the Netherlands, 1815, illustrated with plates of the battle of Waterloo drawn by himself. M. Johanna, eldest dau. of Sir John Barrow, 1st Bart., of Ulverstone, co. Lancaster. D. 20th Nov., 1848, as lt.-col. on h. p. list.

[39] Bn. 24th March, 1795. 4th son of Richard Master, by Isabella, dau. of Lt.-col. Wm. Egerton, of the 1st Foot Guards. Promoted lt. and capt. 1st July, 1815. H. p. 25th Feb., 1819. M. Anna Catherine Frederica von Puckpock, of Wasserburg, in Bavaria. Served in the Netherlands in the campaigns of 1813, 1814, and 1815. Served also in Corsica (1812), North America, and the West Indies. He received a reward from the Patriotic Fund. Living in 1860.

[40] Had served previously in the 87th Foot. Promoted lt. and capt. 3rd July, 1815. On h. p. 4th Oct., 1827.

[41] The Hon. Henry Sedley Venables Vernon was eldest son of the 3rd Lord Vernon, by his 2nd wife, Alice, dau. of Sir John Whiteford, Bart.

Promoted lt. and capt. 5th July, 1815. Quitted the service 28th March. 1822. M., 29th August, 1822, Eliza, dau. of Edward Coke, of Longford Court, co. Derby, and had issue. D. 12th Dec., 1845.

[42] 4th son of John Pardoe, M.P., for Plympton, Camelford, and Westlowe, by Jane, dau. of Thomas Oliver, of the Great House, Leyton, Essex. Bn. 4th April, 1796. Sev. wnded. at the siege of Bergen-op Zoom, 1814, and especially mentioned in despatches.

[43] Promoted lt. and capt. 6th July, 1815. Aftds. capt. in 57th Foot. Maj. in 25th Foot 1825. Commanded the latter regt. for eighteen years. D. in June, 1848.

[44] James Arthur Butler had formerly served in the 2nd Foot. Exchanged to 80th Foot as capt. in 1823. On h. p. as maj. unattached 19th Nov., 1825. Bt.-lt.-col. 1838. Attained rank of gen. 5th Dec., 1871. He carried the colours of his battn. at Waterloo, and was present at the storming of Peronne, that virgin fortress which had never before surrendered to an enemy. Living in 1874.

[45] Eldest son of Thomas Swinburne, of Pontop Hall, co. Durham, by Charlotte, dau. and co-heir of Robert Spearman. Attained rank of maj.-gen., and was F.R.S. He was at the taking of Peronne in 1815, and in 1823 exchanged as capt. to 3rd Dgn. Gds. Was twice married, and left issue by both wives. D. 28th Feb., 1864.

[46] 2nd son of Robert Vyner, of Grantby Hall, co. Lincoln, by Lady Theodosia Ashburnham, dau. of 2nd Earl of Ashburnham. Bn. 1797. Promoted lⁱ. and capt. in 1817. Went on h. p. in 1822. D. unm. in 1837.

[47] Promoted lt. and capt. 16th July, 1818. Placed on h. p. 25th Dec., 1818. Retd. 15th Sept., 1839.

[48] Eldest son of Lt.-gen. Alexander Dirom of Mount Annan, co. Dumfries, by Magdalen, dau. of Robert Pasley. Bn. 6th Nov., 1794. Left the service as lt.-col. in 1836. D. s. p. 2nd June, 1857.

[49] John Francis Miller Erskine succeeded as 9th Earl of Mar, and 14th Lord Erskine, on the death of his father, the 8th Earl of Mar, in 1828. Aftds. inherited as 11th Earl of Kellie. Quitted the service in 1821. M. 24th April, 1827, Philadelphia, dau. of Sir Granville Menteth, Bart. D. s. p. 19th June, 1866.

[50] Eldest son of Alexander Bruce, of Kennet, N.B., by Hugh (sic), dau. of Hugh Blackburn, of Glasgow. Established his claim to the attainted barony of "Balfour of Burleigh," and succeeded in 1869 as 6th Lord. Quitted the service in 1824. M., 2ndly, 1848, Jane Dalrymple Hamilton, dau. of Sir James Fergusson, Bart., and had issue, a son and successor to the title. D. 13th Aug., 1864.

[51] 3rd son of Henry, 3rd Earl Bathurst, by Georgina, dau. of Lord George Lennox. Appointed to Cape Corps as capt. in 1823. Lt.-col. 9th June, 1825. Retd. on h. p. (unattached list) in 1828. M., 6th October, 1829, Julia, dau. of John Peter Hankey, and d. in 1834 leaving issue.

[52] Eldest son of 2nd Earl of Mount-Edgcombe, by Lady Sophia Hobart, dau. of 2nd Earl of Buckinghamshire. Quitted the service in 1819. Aftds. Col. of the Cornwall Militia, and A.D.C. to the Queen. M. 6th Dec., 1831, Caroline, eldest dau. of Rear-Adm. Fielding, and had issue. Succeeded as 3rd Earl in 1839. D. 3rd Sept., 1861.

[53] Eldest son of George Fludyer, of Ayston, co. Rutland, by Lady Mary Fane, dau of 9th Earl of Westmoreland. Quitted the service in 1834. D. in Feb., 1856. His youngest brother (John Henry) succeeded to the Fludyer baronetcy in 1876.

[54] Promoted maj. on unattached list 10th Dec., 1825. D. in London 7th Apr., 1850.

[55] There were several " Algernon Grevilles " in the younger branches of the noble house of Warwick. The above appears to be the son of Capt. W. Fulke Greville, R.N. Bn. 1791. D. 23rd Nov., 1857, having m. in Dec., 1813, Caroline, 2nd dau. of Sir Bellingham Graham, and left issue.

[56] Exchanged to 3rd Dgn. Gds. as cornet in 1818. H. p. 24th Sept., 1818. Restored to f. p. as lt. 4th Dgn. Gds., 1839. Col. Dorset Militia, 1846. D. at Rayrigg, Windermere, 13th May, 1885.

[57] Of Lochiel. Eldest son of Donald Cameron, by Anne, dau. of Sir Ralph Abercromby. Quitted the service in 1832. M., same year, Lady Vere Catherine Hobart, sister of 5th Earl of Buckinghamshire, and had issue. " Lochiel " d. 2nd Dec., 1858.

[58] On h. p. 60th Foot as capt. 24th July, 1817. Retd. in Sep., 1825.

[59] Afterwards Baron Grantley. Eldest son of Fletcher Norton, by Caroline, dau. of James Balmain. Succeeded as 3rd Baron in 1822. Quitted the service in 1821. M., 26th July, 1825, Charlotte, 2nd dau. of Sir Wm. Beechey, Knt. D. s. p. 28th Aug., 1875.

[60] Afterwards 3rd Earl of Harewood. 2nd son of Henry, 2nd Earl, by Henrietta, eldest dau. of Lt.-Gen. Sir John Sebright, Bart. Retd. on h. p. as lt., 24th Aug., 1820. M., 5th July, 1823, Lady Louisa Thynne, dau. of 2nd Marquis of Bath, and had issue. D. 22nd Feb., 1857.

[61] Eldest son of Thomas Mure, of Warriston. by Helen, eldest dau. of the Hon. Patrick Boyle, of Shewalton. co. Ayr. His grandfather served with the Scots Greys at Fontenoy. H. p. June, 1820. M., 17th Sept., 1835, Fanny, only dau. of Wright Squire, of Bridge House, Peterboro', and d. s. p. 16th March, 1868.

[62] Quitted the service in 1826. D. at Sidmouth, 9th May, 1826.

[63] Bn. 2nd Sept., 1798. Eldest son of Sir Richard Croft, Bart., by Margaret, dau. of Dr. Denman. Educated at Westminster School. F.S.A. Succeeded as 2nd bart. in 1818. Quitted the service in 1820, and m. in 1824 only child of Richard Lateward, and had issue a dau. D. 29th Oct., 1835.

[64] Killed at Quatre Bras. 3rd son of the Right Hon. and Rev. Lord Viscount Barrington, Prebendary of Durham, by Elizabeth, 2nd dau. of Robert Adair.

[65] Placed on h. p. as lt. in 19th Lt. Dgns. in 1822. Living in 1830.

[66] 2nd son of Wm. Tighe, of Woodstock, co. Kilkenny, by Marianne, dau. and co-heir of Daniel Gahan, of Coolquill, co. Tipperary. Of Rosanna, co. Wicklow. High Sheriff, 1827. H. p. 15th Feb., 1821. M., 1st March, 1825, the Hon. Frances Crofton, and had issue. D. 20th Dec., 1881.

[67] 4th son of Matthew Talbot, of Castle Talbot. co. Wexford, by his 2nd wife, who was a dau. of John D'Arcy of Kiltullagh. Of Knockmullen, co. Wexford. On h. p. 2nd Dgn. Gds., 1822. M., 1824, Mary, dau. of Edward Sutton, of Summer Hill, Wexford, and had issue. D. 1852.

[68] D. 1st Aug., 1844.

[69] D. in London, 1824.

[70] Surgeon-major 11th Nov., 1824. H. p. 17th March, 1837. D. 3rd Nov., 1849.

[71] Surgeon-major 17th March, 1837. H. p. 17th Apr., 1840. Living in 1846.

[72] Died in Edinburgh, Feb. 1828.

[73] Surgeon to the Wilts Yeomanry, in 1840.

[74] Appointed Assist.-Surg. Coldstream Guards, 20th June, 1822. Surgeon 16th March, 1838. Retd. on h. p. 14th April, 1843. Living in 1874.

COLDSTREAM REGIMENT OF FOOT GUARDS.
(*2nd Battalion.*)

	Rank in the Regiment.	Army.
SECOND MAJOR.		
1 Alexander Geo. Woodford	25 July, 1814	Col., 4 June, 1814
CAPTAINS AND LIEUT.-COLONELS.		
2 James Macdonell, w.	8 Aug. 1811	7 Sept. 1809
3 Daniel M'Kinnon, w.	25 July, 1814	
4 Henry Dawkins	25 July, 1814	
Hon. Alex. Abercromby, w.	25 July, 1814	Col., 4 June, 1814
Sir Colin Campbell, K.C.B.	25 July, 1814	Col., 4 June, 1814
5 Hon. Edward Acheson	25 July, 1814	6 Mar. 1811
Sir Wm. M. Gomm, K.C.B.	25 July, 1814	17 Aug. 1812
6 Henry Wyndham, w.	25 July, 1814	20 Jan. 1814
LIEUTENANTS AND CAPTAINS.		
7 George Bowles	1 Feb. 1810	
8 Thos. Sowerby	27 June, 1810	
John Fremantle	2 Aug. 1810	Lt. Col., 21 Mar. [1814
9 Wm. Lovelace Walton, Acting Adjt.	7 Mar. 1811	
Charles A. F. Bentinck	24 Sept. 1812	
10 John Stepney Cowell	9 Sept. 1813	
11 Edward Sumner, w.	23 Sept. 1813	24 Sept. 1812
12 John Lucie Blackman, к.	11 Jan. 1814	
13 Beaumont, Lord Hotham	13 Jan. 1814	
14 Hon. Robert Moore, w.	2 June, 1814	
ENSIGNS.		
15 Hon. James Forbes	13 Feb. 1812	
16 Henry Gooch	23 July, 1812	
Augustus Cuyler	15 Oct. 1812	9 June, 1812
17 Mark Beaufoy	12 Nov. 1812	
18 Hen. Fred. Griffiths, w.	25 Jan. 1814	
19 Hon. John Montagu, w.	27 Jan. 1814	
20 George Rich. Buckley	17 Feb. 1814	
21 James Hervey	16 Mar. 1814	
22 Henry Vane, w.	15 Mar. 1814	
23 Francis Jas. Douglas	17 Mar. 1814	
24 Robert Bowen	24 Mar. 1814	
25 Alexander Gordon	19 May, 1814	
26 Hon. Walter Forbes	2 June, 1814	
27 Charles Short	13 Oct. 1814	

108   THE WATERLOO ROLL CALL.

COLDSTREAM REGIMENT OF FOOT GUARDS.—*cont.*
(*2nd Battalion.*)

Rank in the

QUARTERMASTER.	Regiment.	Army.
[28] Benjamin Selway	26 Nov. 1812	
SURGEON.		
[29] Wm. Whymper	25 Dec. 1813	
ASSISTANT-SURGEONS.		
[30] George Smith	17 Dec. 1812	
[31] Wm. Hunter	10 Feb. 1814	

Facings blue. Lace gold.

Afterwards F.-M. Sir Alexander Woodford, G.C.B. and G.C.M.G. Elder brother to Col. John G. Woodford (see Staff). On the death of Sir Ralph Woodford, Bart., Governor of Trinidad, Alexander Woodford became the head of this ancient family. His father was descended maternally from the Brideokes, of classical memory, of whom Dr. Brideoke, the "sometime" chaplain to James, the 4th Earl of Derby, in the reign of Charles I., was a good specimen of the "fighting parson" of olden days. This same Dr. Brideoke became Dean of Salisbury, and, by his extraordinary presence of mind and address, saved the heroic Countess of Derby, and her house at Latham, from being stormed by the Cromwellian army. In like manner did his descendant, Alexander Woodford, defend the farm of Hougomont in the early part of the afternoon of Waterloo Day against the repeated and vigorous attacks of the French. C.B. for Waterloo. Had previously served in the Pa. and received the gold cross and one clasp. Was also K.M.T., and K. St. G. of Russia. Filled high commands in the Ionian Islands and elsewhere. Col.-in-Chf. 40th Foot, 1842. Transferred to the Scots Fusilier Guards 15th Dec., 1861. D. 26th Aug., 1870.

[2] Afterwards Gen. Sir James Macdonell, G.C.B. and K.C.H., Col.-in-Chf. 71st Highland L.I. Was 3rd son of Duncan Macdonell, of Glengarry, and bn. at the family seat in Inverness-shire. Served in the Pa. and also at Maida, for which he recd. the gold medal. Macdonell's gallant defence of Hougomont is a matter of history. More than once was the place nearly taken by the French. "The French, however," says Siborne, in his graphic account of the battle of Waterloo, "succeeded in forcing the gate; but the defenders betook themselves to the nearest cover, whence they poured a fire upon the intruders, and then rushing forward a struggle ensued which was distinguished by the most intrepid courage on both sides. At length Lt.-col. Macdonell, Capt. Wyndham, Ensigns Gooch and Hervey, and Sergt. Graham, of the Coldstream Guards, by dint of great personal strength and exertions, combined with extraordinary bravery and perseverance, succeeded in closing the gate against their intruders." The struggle for the possession of Hougomont went on the whole day until the French retreat set in late in the evening. C.B. and K.M.T. for Waterloo. D. 15th May, 1859.

³ The historian of the Coldstream Guards, 2nd son of Wm. M'Kinnon, who was a direct descendant of Lachlan M'Kinnon, of the Isle of Skye, who was made a Knight Banneret by Charles II. on the field of Worcester. Maj. in above regt. 22nd June, 1826, bt.-col. same date. M. a dau. of John Dent, and d. s. p. 22nd June, 1836.

⁴ Eldest son of Henry Dawkins, of Over-Norton, co. Oxford. His mother was daughter of the late Gen. Sir H. Clinton, Commander-in-Chief of the British forces in America. Served with his regt. in the Pa. from 1809 to the close of the war, and was badly wounded before Bayonne when the French made a sortie from that town. Bn. 1788. M., 1821, eldest dau. of Thos. Duncombe, of Copgrove, co. York, and had issue. D. in Nov., 1864.

⁵ 2nd son of Arthur, 1st Visct. Gosford, by Millicent, dau. of Lt.-gen. Edward Pole. Col. Acheson was ordered to defend a certain part of the wood at Hougomont on Waterloo Day. "The enemy made a tremendous attack, and, at the first charge, the colonel's horse was shot dead. He fell under his horse, and was considerably stunned by the fall, in which situation he must have lain some time, as the enemy had passed and repassed, regarding him as dead. When he had recovered he found himself a prisoner by the weight of his horse. He extricated himself with difficulty by drawing his leg out of his boot." D. unm. 24th July, 1828.

⁶ Afterwards Gen. Sir H. Wyndham, K.C.B., M.P. for Cumberland and Col.-in-Chf. 11th Hussars. Natural son of 3rd Earl of Egremont. Was in eight general engagements in the Pa. "Seeing the carriage of Jerome Bonaparte in the wake of the general retreat of the French at Waterloo, he made a dashing attempt to capture Napoleon's brother, but Jerome leaped out by one door while Wyndham opened the other." Succeeded, in 1845, to the Egremont estates. D. s. p. at Cockermouth Castle, 2nd Aug. 1860, aged 70.

⁷ Afterwards Gen. Sir George Bowles, K.C.B., Col.-in-Chf. 1st West India Regt. and Lieut. of the Tower of London. 2nd son of Wm. Bowles, of Heale House, Wilts. Served in North Germany in 1805–1806, under Lord Cathcart. Present at the siege and capture of Copenhagen in 1807. Served in the Pa., and was present at most of the general actions. Bt.-maj. for Waterloo. Master of the Household to the Queen 1845–1851. D. in London 21st May, 1876.

⁸ Quitted the service in 1823. It appears from Plantagenet Harrison's *History of Yorkshire*, that the family of "Sowerby" dates back to the reign of Henry I., when one "Sueni" was "Lord of Sowerby" in Cumberland. Some interesting particulars regarding the Sowerby family are to be found in Mr. Harrison's book, but unfortunately they are particulars of the far-away Norman times.

⁹ Afterwards Gen. W. L. Walton, Col.-in-Chf. 5th Fusiliers. Son of the Dowager Lady Strachan. Served forty years in the Coldstream Guards, six of which were in command of the regt. Served at Copenhagen in 1807 and during the early part of the Par. War. Served also in Belgium, Holland, and France from Nov., 1813, to Nov., 1818. Was appointed Bde.-maj. to the 2nd Bde. of Guards (having been selected for that post by Sir John Byng) on the march from Waterloo to Paris, in place of Capt. Stothert, killed in action. M., 15th Aug., 1832, Harriet, dau. of P. H. Lovell, of Cole Park, Wilts. D., 11th Jan., 1865.

¹⁰ Has barely a title to appear in this list, as he was taken ill the evening of 17th of June, 1815, and sent to Brussels. But as the Coldstreams were

under fire on 16th June, 1815, having arrived at Quatre Bras at 4 P.M. that day, after a march of twenty-five miles from Enghien, it would be scarcely fair to omit this officer, who appears to have received the Waterloo medal. Was son of Gen. Andrew Cowell, Lt.-col. Coldstream Guards, of Coleshill, Bucks, by Martha Justine, younger dau. of Sir T. Stepney, Bart., of Llanelly (widow of Sir F. Head, Bart.). Took the additional surname of Stepney by royal licence. Created a baronet in 1871. M., 1820, Lady Mary Annesley, who d. 1821. 2ndly, in 1823, Euphemia, dau. of Gen. John Murray, of Castle Murray, co. Donegal, and had issue. Lt.-col., ret., 1830. K.H. for his services in the Pa. D. 15th May, 1877.

[11] Had previously served in the Rl. Fusiliers. D. at Brussels, 26th June, 1815, from his wounds.

[12] Youngest son of Sir George Blackman, Bart., by Mary, eldest surviving dau. of Lt.-col. Henry Harnage, of Belleswardine, Salop. Buried in the orchard at Hougomont, in the defence of which place he lost his life.

[13] The family of Hotham has furnished some distinguished officers to both our army and navy—especially to the latter service. But the most notable member of this ancient family was John de Hotham, Bishop of Ely, Lord Chancellor of England from 1316-1320. He was a great favourite with the young King Edward III., and had the choosing of a wife for that monarch. The story goes that he selected Philippa of Hainault " on account of the largeness of her hips," which he prognosticated meant a large family, and the shrewd chancellor-bishop was not far wrong, as Queen Philippa had seven sons. Lord Hotham, who served in the Pa., and was wounded at Salamanca, was eldest son of Col. Beaumont Hotham, of the Coldstreams, by Philadelphia, dau. of Sir John Dyke, Bart. Bn. 9th Aug., 1794. Lt.-col. unattached, 24th Dec., 1825. Gen. on retired list 1865. D. unm., 12th Dec., 1870.

[14] 2nd son of Stephen, 2nd Earl of Mountcashel, by Margaret, eldest dau. of 2nd Earl of Kingston. Bn. 11th July, 1793. Promoted capt. and lt.-col. h. p. April, 1824. D. unm. 2nd Nov., 1856.

[15] Eldest son of Gen. Lord Forbes (premier Baron of Scotland), by Eliz., eldest dau. of Walter Hunter, of Polmood, co. Peebles. D. as capt. and lt.-col. in this regt. 25th Feb., 1835.

[16] Promoted lt. and capt. 28th Oct., 1819. Quitted the service as lt.-col. 11th June, 1841.

[17] Quitted the service 9th Feb., 1825. D. at Bowness, 31st May, 1854

[18] D. at the Tower of London 19th Jan., 1821.

[19] 2nd son of 4th Lord Rokeby, by Eliz., dau. and heir of Francis Charlton. Lt. 64th Foot, 8th Apr., 1819. Quitted the service as lt.-col. 1832. D. unm. 12th Dec., 1843.

[20] 2nd son of Edward Pery Buckley, of Woolcombe Hall, Dorset. D. 1815, at Paris, with the Army of Occupation, of fatigue.

[21] Quitted the service in Oct., 1837.

[22] Promoted capt. 1st Aug. 1822. D. at Sidmouth, 9th Aug., 1829.

[23] Was thrown from his horse in St. James's Park, and d. from the injuries 29th May, 1821.

[24] Promoted capt. 55th Foot in Jan., 1823. Exchanged back to the Coldstreams the following month. Capt. and lt.-col. 1832.

[25] Killed at Cambray in a duel with a French officer 1st April, 1816.

26 2nd son of Lord Forbes. Bn. 29th May, 1798. Quitted the service in 1825 as capt. Succeeded as 18th baron in 1843. Was twice m., and left issue. D. 2nd May, 1868.

27 Promoted lieut. and capt. 17th April, 1823. Quitted the service before 1842 with rank of lt.-col. M., 4th June, 1828, Emily Sophia, eld. dau. of Richard Barwell, of Stanstead, Sussex. D. at Odiham, Hants, 19th Jan., 1857.

28 Serving with the regt. in 1830.

29 Placed on h. p. as surgeon-major 29th Apr., 1836. Living in 1846.

30 Surgeon-major 4th Sept., 1836. Aftds. took the surname of " Chenevix " in lieu of that of Smith. Accompanied the Coldstreams to Holland in Nov., 1813, and served in the Netherlands and France until 1818. Was at the bombardment of Antwerp ; the storming of Bergen-op-Zoom ; Quatre Bras and Waterloo ; capture of Paris. H. p. 16th Mar., 1838. D. at his residence in Sussex Gardens, Hyde Park, Apr., 1852.

31 Surgeon-major 16th Mar., 1838. H. p. 1836. Living in 1846.

3RD REGIMENT OF FOOT GUARDS.
(*2nd Battalion.*)

	Rank in the	
SECOND MAJOR.	Regiment.	Army.
1 Francis Hepburn	25 July, 1814	Col., 4 June, 1814

CAPTAINS AND LIEUT.-COLONELS.

H. Willoughby Rooke	28 Feb. 1812	
2 Douglas Mercer	20 Dec. 1813	
Hon. Sir Alex. Gordon,		
K.C.B., K.	25 Dec. 1813	6 Feb. 1812
3 Charles Dashwood, w.	25 Dec. 1813	
4 Francis Home	15 Mar. 1814	
Charles Fox Canning, K.	31 Mar. 1814	19 Aug. 1813
5 Edward Bowater, w.	25 July, 1814	
6 Charles West, w.	25 July, 1814	

LIEUTENANTS AND CAPTAINS.

Wm. Stothert, K.	4 Apr. 1811	
7 Wm. Drummond	24 Oct. 1811	
8 Robert B. Hesketh, w.	31 Oct. 1811	
9 Henry Hawkins	12 Dec. 1811	
10 R. H. Wigston	19 Dec. 1811	
11 Charles John Barnet	16 Apr. 1812	
12 Joseph Wm. Moorhouse	23 Apr. 1812	
13 Edward B. Fairfield	24 Mar. 1814	
14 George Evelyn, w.	31 Mar. 1814	
15 Hon. Hastings Forbes, K.	5 May, 1814	
16 John Elrington	19 May, 1814	
17 Hugh B. Montgomerie, w.	9 June, 1814	
18 Thomas Craufurd (*sic*), K.	1 Sept. 1814	
19 John Ashton, K.	2 Sept. 1814	

ENSIGNS.

20 Charles Lake, w.	31 Oct. 1811	
21 Hon. Edward Stopford	7 Nov. 1811	
22 Barclay Drummond, Acting		
Adjt.	5 Mar. 1811	
23 George Douglas Standen	19 Mar. 1811	
24 David Baird, w.	18 June, 1811	
25 Wm. James	4 Mar. 1813	
26 Wm. Fred. Hamilton	1 Apr. 1813	
27 Hon. Geo. Anson	8 Jan. 1814	

3RD REGIMENT OF FOOT GUARDS—*continued.*

Rank in the

ENSIGNS—*continued.*	Regiment.	Army.
[28] Thos. Wedgwood	11 Jan. 1814	
[29] Whitwell Butler	12 Jan. 1814	
[30] Andrew Contts Cochrane	13 Jan. 1814	
[31] Jeffery Prendergast	2 Feb. 1814	
C. Simpson, K.	3 Feb. 1814	
[32] Hugh Seymour Blane	31 Mar. 1814	
[33] Henry Montagu	21 Apr. 1814	
QUARTERMASTER.		
[34] John Skuce	22 Mar. 1810	
SURGEON.		
[35] Samuel Good	25 Dec. 1813	
ASSISTANT-SURGEONS.		
[36] J. R. Warde	27 Apr. 1809	21 Aug. 1806
[37] Fran. Gashry Hanrott	10 Dec. 1812	

Facings blue. Lace gold.

[1] Served in the Pa., and received the gold medal for Vittoria. Distinguished for the share he took in the defence of Hougomont. C.B. 2nd son of Col. David Hepburn, by Bethia, dau. and heiress of Graham, of Damside. M., July, 1820, Henrietta, dau. and heir of Sir Henry Poole, 5th and last bart., of Poole, co. Chester, and had issue. Attained rank of maj.-general, and d. 7th June, 1835.

[2] Afterwards assumed the surname of Henderson in addition to that of Mercer. 3rd son of Lt.-col. George Mercer, by Jean, eldest dau. of Sir Robert Henderson, Bart. Served in the Pa. C.B. for Waterloo. Attained rank of Lt.-gen. and Col.-in-Chf. 68th Foot. M., 2nd Nov., 1820, Susan, 3rd dau. of Sir Wm. Rowley, Bart., and had issue. D. at Naples 21st March, 1854.

[3] 2nd son of Sir Henry Walter Dashwood, Bart., by Ellen, dau. of John Graham, of Kernock, Bart. Retd. before 1830. M., 1822, Caroline, 4th dau. of Sir Robert Barlow, Bart. D. 20th April, 1832.

[4] Gained distinction in the defence of Hougomont, and succeeded Col. Macdonell (who was wounded) in the command *within* the building late .n the afternoon of Waterloo Day.

[5] Only son of Admiral Bowater. Served in the Pa. Groom in Waiting to Queen Victoria. K.C.B. Col.-in-Chf. of 49th Foot, 1846. Gen. D. at Cannes 14th Dec., 1861.

[6] Son of Col. West of same regiment. Appointed ensign in his regt. 8th Nov., 1804. Served in Hanover, Denmark, Spain, and Portugal. Was severely wounded in the sortie from Bayonne and again at Waterloo. Quitted the service as col. 1829. D. in 1872.

[7] Made bt.-maj. for Waterloo. Served in the Pa. from 1809–12 and in the campaign in Holland, 1814, and was present at the bombardment of Antwerp, and storming of Bergen-op-Zoom. Attained rank of col. in 1837. Living in 1855.

[8] 2nd son of Robert Bamford Hesketh, of Bamford and Upton, co. Chester, by Frances, dau. and heir of Rev. John Lloyd, of Gwyrch Castle, co. Denbigh. Bt.-maj. 4th Dec., 1815. D. unm. before 1820 of a wound received at Waterloo.

[9] In 1830 this officer was still a lt. and capt., and many of his juniors had purchased over his head.

[10] "On baggage guard" at the village of Waterloo on 18th June, 1815. Out of the list in 1824.

[11] Promoted capt. and lt.-col. 26th Oct., 1821. Out of the list in 1830.

[12] Capt. 65th Foot, 18th Nov., 1819.

[13] Out of the list in 1830.

[14] 3rd son of John Evelyn, of Wotton, by Anne, dau. of Anthony Shee, of Castlebar. Quitted the service before 1824. M. Mary, dau. of J. H. Massey Dawson, M.P., of Ballynacourte, Ireland, and had issue. D. 15th Feb., 1829.

[15] 3rd son of George, 6th Earl of Granard, by Selina, dau. of John, 1st Earl of Moira. Bn. 5th Dec., 1793.

[16] Promoted capt. and lt.-col. 16th Nov., 1826. D. in London in Nov., 1843. There were several of this family in the army. One of them, Capt. J. H. Elrington, held the appointment of "Major of the Tower," being so appointed in 1816.

[17] Descended from a branch of the noble and historic house of Eglinton. 2nd son of the Rev. Hugh Montgomerie, of Grey Abbey, by the Hon. Emilia Ward, youngest dau. of 1st Visct. Bangor. D. 2nd May, 1817, from the after effects of a wound received at Waterloo. A collateral ancestor, Sir Hugh Montgomerie, fell at the battle of Otterburne as far back as 1388. His death is thus recorded in the old ballad of Chevy Chase :

> "He had a bow bent in his hand,
>   Made of a trusty tree ;
> An arrow of a cloth-yeard long
>   Unto the head drew he.
>
> "Against Sir Hugh Montgomerie
>   So right his shaft he set,
> The grey goose wing that was therein
>   In his heart-blood was set."

[18] This officer's name is given as *Crawford* on the memorial tablet at Waterloo.

[19] The following *in memoriam* verses were written soon after Waterloo.

> "Hail, youthful Ashton, in thy field of blood !
> Thou bloom of honour gathered in the bud !
> Thy prime career of martial life began
> With spirit fit to shine in glory's van ;
> Comrades who groan'd to see thee yield thy breath,
> Yet almost envied thy heroic death.
> Accept thy country's praise ! thy mother's tears !
> Whose heavenly sorrow Heaven itself reveres !
> Kissing in agony affliction's rod,
> She yields her pride unmurm'ring to her God."

[20] Promoted lt. and capt. 2nd July, 1815. Out of the list before 1824

21 Acted as A. D.C. to Maj.-gen. Sir John Byng, at Waterloo. His name does not appear in the list of "staff officers in Flanders" in the *Army List* for June, 1815. 2nd son of the 3rd Earl of Courtown by Lady Mary Scott, eldest dau. of 3rd Duke of Buccleuch. Capt. 3rd July, 1815. Adjt. 4th July, 1822. Capt. and lt.-col. 1826. M., 5th July, 1830, Horatia, only dau. of Thos. Lockwood, and widow of Richard Tibbits. D. 5th July, 1840, leaving issue.

22 3rd son of Charles Drummond (banker) by Frances, 2nd dau. of Rev. Edward Lockwood, of Portman Square. Attained the rank of gen. Groom in Waiting to the Queen. M., 5th April, 1832, Maria, dau. of Wm. Crosbie. D. s. p. 3rd May, 1860.

23 D. as lt.-col. 16th Dec., 1840.

24 Quitted the service as capt. before 1824. Afterwards Sir David Baird, 2nd Bart. Succeeded his uncle, the famous general, in 1829. Severely wounded whilst defending Hougomont with his company. M., 10th August, 1821, Mary Anne Kennedy, eldest dau. of Archibald, Marquis of Ailsa, and had issue. D. whilst hunting 20th Dec., 1851.

25 H. p. 1819. D. at Lillebourne Rectory, Kent, 13th Oct., 1854.

26 Lt. and capt. 17th April, 1817. H. p. as lieut. 47th Foot, 1st Feb., 1821.

27 Afterwards maj.-gen. and M.P. for Staffordshire. 2nd son of 1st Visct. Anson, by Anne, dau. of Thos. Coke, of Holkham Hall, Norfolk. M., 30th Nov., 1830, Isabella, 3rd dau. of 1st Lord Forester, and had issue. D. 27th May, 1857, at Kurnand, as Comr.-in-Chief in India.

28 Afterwards lt.-col. D. at Tenby, 7th Nov., 1860.

29 Placed on h. p. 25th Feb., 1819. 4th son of the Rev. Richard Butler, D.D., vicar of Burnchurch, co. Kilkenny. Bn. 1799. M., 1833, Elizabeth, 2nd dau. of John Payne Garnet, of Arch Hall, co. Meath, and had issue.

30 2nd son of Adm. the Hon. Sir Alexander Cochrane, G.C.B., by Maria, dau. of David Shaw, and widow of Sir Jacob Wheate, Bart. Bn. 5th April, 1799. Placed on h. p. 14th Sept., 1820. M., 1835, the eldest dau. of Baron de Strack, col. in the Austrian service, and had issue. D. 22nd June, 1870.

31 Lieut. and capt. 9th Aug., 1821. Out of the regt. before 1830.

32 Afterwards Sir H. S. Blane, Bart., of Blanefield, co. Ayr. Son of Sir Gilbert Blane, M.D., by Eliz., only dau. of A. Gardiner. Lt. and capt. 15th March, 1821. Retd. as lt.-col. M., 23rd Jan., 1832, Eliza, dau. of John Armit, of Dublin, and had issue. Succeeded as 2nd bart. in 1834. D. 1869.

33 The prefix of "Honourable" has been omitted before this officer's name in the 1815 *Army List*. The Hon. Henry Robinson Montague was youngest son of Matthew, 4th Lord Rokeby. Fought at Quatre Bras and Waterloo. Attained the rank of gen. Commanded the 1st Division in the Crimea, and served at the siege of Sebastopol. Col.-in-Chf. Scots Gds. 1875. Succeeded his brother as 6th baron, 7th April, 1847. M., 18th Dec., 1826, Magdalen eld. dau. of Lt.-col. Huxley and widow of F. Croft. Left surviving female issue. D. 25th May, 1883.

34 Out of the regt. in May, 1819.

35 H. p. in 1845.

36 Serving with the regt. in 1824.

37 Retd. before 1st Jan., 1816.

I 2

1st (or the ROYAL SCOTS) REGIMENT OF FOOT.*

(*3rd Battalion.*)

	Regiment.	Rank in the Army.
MAJOR.		
1 Colin Campbell, w.	27 Sept. 1810	Lt.-Col., 17 Aug. [1812
CAPTAINS.		
2 Lawrence Arguimbau, w.	9 Mar. 1809	Maj.,11 Aug.1814
3 Robert Macdonald, w.	8 Feb. 1810	Maj.,21 Sept.1813
4 Wm. Buckley, k.	11 Oct. 1810	
5 Hugh Massey, w.	9 May 1811	Maj.,4 June, 1811
6 Wm. Gordon	16 Jan. 1812	
7 Robert Dudgeon, w.	30 July, 1812	
LIEUTENANTS.		
8 Archibald Morrison, w.	27 Oct. 1808	3 Dec. 1806
John Armstrong, k.	27 Apr. 1809	
John E. O'Neil, k.	8 June,1809	21 Apr. 1808
9 Wm. Jas. Rea, w.	22 June,1809	30 July, 1807
10 John Ingram, w.	12 July, 1809	18 Oct. 1808
11 Wm. Clarke, w.	21 June,1810	
12 Thomas Gordon	18 Feb. 1813	2 July, 1812
13 Allen Cameron, Adjt., w.	1 July,1813	26 June, 1812
14 John Stoyte, w.	4 July,1813	
15 Robt. Horsman Scott, w.	8 July,1813	
16 George Lane, w.	26 July,1813	
17 Joseph Symes, w.	23 Sept.1813	
18 James Alstone, w.	23 Sept. 1813	
Wm. Young, k.	4 Nov. 1813	
19 James Mann	18 Aug. 1814	
20 Wm. Dobbs, w.	29 Sept. 1814	
21 John Fitzwilliam Miller, w.	6 Oct. 1814	
22 George Stewart, w.	2 Dec. 1814	
23 J. L. Black, w.	23 Feb. 1815	10 Mar. 1814
ENSIGNS.		
24 Alexander Glen	21 Oct. 1813	
25 Charles Mudie	4 Nov. 1813	
26 Jas. Grant Kennedy, k.	12 Apr. 1814	
27 Charles Graham, w.	28 Sept. 1814	9 June, 1813

1st (or the ROYAL SCOTS) REGIMENT OF FOOT—*contd.*

	Rank in the	
ENSIGNS—*continued.*	Regiment.	Army.
28 Thomas Stevens, w.	29 Sept. 1814	
29 Joseph M'Kay, w.	6 Oct. 1814	
30 Alexander Robertson, K.	20 Oct. 1814	
Wm. Anderson, K.	27 Oct. 1814	14 July, 1814
31 Leon M. Cooper, w.	14 Dec. 1814	
32 Wm. Thomas	15 Dec. 1814	
33 Richard Blacklin (Volunteer), w.		
PAYMASTER.		
34 James Crooke Thomson	4 May, 1815	31 Jan. 1811
QUARTERMASTER.		
35 Thomas Griffith, w.	4 Aug. 1814	
SURGEON.		
36 Wm. Galliers	20 Apr. 1809	10 Sept. 1807
ASSISTANT-SURGEONS.		
37 Wm. Finnie	12 Nov. 1812	
Thos. Bolton	9 Dec. 1813	5 Mar. 1812

Facings blue. Lace gold.

* The 3rd Batt. of the Royal Scots, which was reduced in 1817, distinguished itself in a particular manner at Quatre Bras. " Being removed from the centre of the 5th Division, it charged and routed a column of the enemy. It was then formed in a square to receive the cavalry, and though repeated attacks were made, not the slightest impression was produced. Wherever the lancers and cuirassiers presented themselves they found a stern and undismayed front which they vainly endeavoured to penetrate." Mudford's *Historical Account of the Campaign in the Netherlands, in* 1815.

1 Served throughout the Par. War and recd. the gold medal and one clasp for commanding his battalion at the battles of Vittoria and Salamanca. Severely wounded at Quatre Bras. Made C.B. for Waterloo. Appointed to a h. p. lt.-colonelcy under the War Office Regulations of 25th April, 1826. D. at Inverary 1st Feb., 1833.

2 A protégé of H.R.H. the Duke of Kent, the Col.-in-Chf. of the regt. Attained the rank of Lt.-gen. and Col.-in-Chf. 80th Foot. D. 18th Aug., 1854, at Port Mahon.

3 Brother to Gen. Sir John Macdonald, Adjt.-Gen. of the British Army, and cousin to Etienne Macdonald, Duke of Tarentum and Marshal of France, whose father fought at Culloden in 1746. Robert Macdonald did good service in the Pa., and was present at five general actions. Was severely

wounded at the assault on the Convent of St. Sebastian, " and, although
suffering from the effects of his wounds, was present, and engaged, at the
assault on town of St. Sebastian, where he commanded two companies
ordered to the breach in advance of the 1st Bde. of the 5th Division, and was
at the surrender of the castle. Commanded the above regt. at Waterloo
until disabled by wounds. C.B. and K.St.A. of Russia, Lt.-col. 44th Foot,
29th Aug., 1829. For many years was British Consul at Belize, Central
America, where he was much esteemed. At his death, which occurred
14th Nov., 1860, a very eulogistic paragraph appeared in a Belize newspaper
containing these words : " Col. Macdonald's conversation was like reading a
page of history."

⁴ Killed at Quatre Bras. Left a widow with four young children, the
youngest of whom was born at Blackheath, three weeks after her husband's
death. A pension of £60 per annum was granted to Mrs. Mary Buckley.

⁵ There have been " Hugh Masseys " for generations both in the noble
Irish families of " Massey, Lord Clarina," and " Massy, Lord Massy."   The
above Hugh Massey was doubtless a cadet of the Limerick Masseys. He
was promoted bt.-lt.-col., h. p. list 12th Aug., 1819. M. Mary, sister of
Cornelius Rodes, of Barlboro', co. Derby, and d. before 1855.

⁶ Served with the Portuguese army in the Par. War, and was in command
of the 24th Portuguese regt. at the siege of St. Sebastian, for which he recd.
the British gold medal. Placed on h. p. 25th Dec., 1816. Living in 1830.

⁷ Severely wounded at Quatre Bras. D. whilst serving in the island of
Antigua, 28th Sept., 1827.

⁸ Capt., 21st Sept., 1815.   H. p. from York. Light Infantry 25th July,
1816. Living in 1824.

⁹ Capt. 60th Foot 22nd June, 1815. Out of said regt. before 1824.

¹⁰ John Nelson Ingram served previously in the 15th Foot. Capt. 1st Foot
7th April, 1825. Serving in 1830.

¹¹ H. p. 11th March, 1819.

¹² Capt. in 1831. Out of the regt. before 1842.

¹³ Reduced with the battalion.

¹⁴ Fought at Badajoz and Salamanca. Capt. 24th Foot 19th May, 1825.
Major, 8th Jan., 1841. Lt.-col. 17th Foot, 3rd April, 1846. D. at Bath,
13th Dec., 1854.

¹⁵ Reduced with the battalion.

¹⁶ Reduced with the battalion.

¹⁷ Reduced with the battalion.

¹⁸ Reduced with the battalion. D. 9th Nov., 1854.

¹⁹ Reduced with the battalion.

²⁰ Reduced with the battalion.

²¹ H. p. 17th Apr., 1817. M., 27th Sept., 1817, at Limerick, Prudence,
dau. of Edward Ferreter, R.N.

²² H. p. 25th March, 1816.

²³ Afterwards Lt.-Col. John Lewis Black. Had previously served in the
49th Foot, and was brought in from the h. p. list in Feb., 1815. Became

maj. in the 53rd Foot in 1844 and served in the Sutlej campaign with that regiment. He d. 3rd Feb., 1859.

[24] Lieut. 41st Foot 17th Aug., 1826. Serving in 1830. The " W " is omitted before this officer's name in several *Army Lists*.

[25] Lieut. 48th Foot 4th Oct., 1815. H. p. 25th March, 1817.

[26] Killed at Quatre Bras whilst carrying the colours. Age 16. 3rd son of Dr. Wm. Kennedy, physician at Inverness.

[27] Returned as "killed" in the *London Gazette* of 3rd July, 1815. Placed on h. p., 27th Feb., 1817. Out of the list 1830.

[28] Lieut. 22nd Foot 3rd Feb., 1820. H. p. 7th Apr. same year. D. 19th Sept., 1849, as barrack-master, Sheerness.

[29] H. p. 1st Aug., 1816.

[30] Brother to Lieut. John Robertson, of the 9th Foot, who died of wounds recd. at St. Sebastian. Pens. granted to his mother and two sisters in consideration of their distressed circumstances.

[31] Afterwards Lt.-col. Leonard Morse-Cooper, J.P. for Berks. Joined the Royal Scots in 1814 as a volunteer from the Rl. Military College. Was wounded in the sortie from Bayonne, and at Waterloo recd. five wounds. Promoted lieut. 23rd Jan., 1817. Exchanged to the 11th Lt. Dgns., and served with that regiment at the siege of Bhurtpore, in 1825 6, where he volunteered for the dismounted cavalry storming party. Maj. on the unattached h. p. list 10th Jan., 1840. Lt.-col. 1851. D. in Paris 24th March, 1862.

[32] Lieut. 5th Apr., 1820. Serving in 1830.

[33] A volunteer. Appointed ensign in this regt. 18th July, 1815. Lieut. 13th July, 1820. Capt. 8th Aug., 1833. H. p. unattached 6th Feb., 1846. Col. 1st Nov., 1858. Living in 1860.

[34] H. p. 1816.

[35] Left the regt. in 1824.

[36] Surgeon 7th Sept., 1815. H. p. before 1824.

[37] Surgeon 25th March, 1836. H. p. D. at Glasgow, Jan., 1863.

4TH (OR THE KING'S OWN) REGIMENT OF FOOT.*
(1st Battalion.)

	Regiment.	Rank in the Army.
LIEUT.-COLONEL.		
1 Francis Brooke	14 Feb. 1811	
CAPTAINS.		
2 Geo. David Wilson, w.	7 Aug. 1804	Maj.,21 Sept.1813
3 Euseby Stratford Kirwan	11 Jan. 1810	
4 Charles James Edgell, w.	5 Sept. 1805	
5 John Browne, w.	25 May, 1815	
LIEUTENANTS.		
6 Benjamin Martin	30 Oct. 1806	3 June, 1802
7 G. Richardson, w.	26 May, 1809	
8 Peter Bowlby	31 May, 1809	
9 Hygatt Boyd, w.	16 Aug. 1810	
10 Geo. Henry Hearne	29 Oct. 1810	
11 Benj. Marshall Collins, w.	1 Nov. 1810	
12 Wm. Squire, w.	14 Feb. 1811	
13 John Bushell	12 May, 1812	
14 Richard Mulholland	14 May, 1812	
15 Wm. Lonsdale	15 May, 1812	
16 Edward Bowlby	25 Feb. 1813	
17 Wm. [Henry] Clarke	28 July, 1813	
18 Wm. Richardson, Adjt.	20 Oct. 1813	
Fred. Feilde	17 Nov. 1813	
19 Arthur Gerard, w.	16 Mar. 1815	
20 John L. Fernandez	3 May, 1815	
ENSIGNS.		
21 Charles Levinge	18 Nov. 1813	
22 Wm. Taylor	9 Dec. 1813	22 July, 1813
23 Wm. M'Donald Matthews, w.	9 Dec. 1813	
24 Thos. E. H. Holland	9 Dec. 1813	
PAYMASTER.		
25 James Lonsdale	20 Dec. 1798	
SURGEON.		
26 Francis Burton	9 Sept. 1813	
ASSISTANT-SURGEON.		
27 Wm. Morragh	25 Jan. 1810	

Facings blue. Lace gold.

* This regt had just returned from active service in America and landed at Ostend a few days before Waterloo was fought.   In fact, Gen. Lambert's brigade only reached Waterloo by a forced march just as the battle was commencing.   Several captains of the 1st Batt. 4th Foot had been killed in the attack on New Orleans – hence the small number of captains present at Waterloo.   Siborne gives the names of six additional captains as present with this regt. at Waterloo, but as the official *Army List* for 1817 does not credit them with having the Waterloo medal, the Editor has been reluctantly compelled to omit their names.

¹ Served throughout the Par. War and recd. the gold cross for the battles of Badajoz, Salamanca, Vittoria, and siege of St. Sebastian.   C.B. for Waterloo.   2nd son of Francis Brooke, of Colebrooke, by Hannah, dau. of Henry Prittie, of Dunally, co. Tipperary.   M. Jane, dau. of George Burdett, M.P., and d. s. p.

² Served with the above regt. on the expedition to the Helder, in 1799. At siege of Copenhagen in 1807.   Wounded in the retreat from Corunna. With his regiment in the Walcheren expedition, 1809.   Returned to the Pa. and was severely wounded at the storming of Badajoz in leading the advance of the storming party of the 5th Division to the escalade of the St. Vicante bastion, for which he recd. the gold medal, although not a field officer.   A.D.C. to Gen. Sir W. Pringle in 1812.   C.B. for Waterloo and bt. of lt.-col.   Placed on h. p. 21st March, 1822.   Lt.-col. unattached list in Dec., 1828.   M., 1st July, 1828, Frances, eldest dau. of E. Jud, of Eastbury Lodge, Essex.   D. at Romford, Essex, 11th Jan., 1863.   His proper name was " George Davis Willson."

³ 2nd son of John Kirwan, K.C., by Anne, only child of Euseby Stratford, elder brother of 1st Earl of Aldborough.   Entered the Army in 1804 and joined 4th Foot, 1st Batt. ; served in the Pa. and was engaged in the Battles of Corunna, the disastrous Walcheren Expedition, Ciudad Rodrigo, Badajoz, Salamanca, St. Sebastian, Nive, Bladensburg, New Orleans, and Waterloo. After the Peace was appointed to the West India Rangers, but never joined the regt.   Received the Par. and Waterloo medals.   Md. twice ; d. in 1852, leaving issue.

⁴ D. in 1821 on passage to Barbados.

⁵ Badly wounded at the assault of Badajoz.   "At Waterloo, whilst at the head of his company, Capt. Browne received a fearful wound from a bullet, just over the ear, and fell senseless.   He was left on the field for dead and was reported killed.   His family in Ireland went into mourning for him.   However, he recovered by trepanning, and was made Maj. 92nd Highlanders.   Received two pensions for wounds, and d. 21st Nov., 1849."

⁶ H. p. 35th Foot 11th Nov., 1818.

⁷ Serving in 1817.

⁸ Serving in 1824.

⁹ H. p. 22nd Aug., 1816.

¹⁰ H. p. 29th Aug., 1816.

¹¹ H. p. 30th Dec., 1818.   D. Dec., 1854.

¹² D. before 1st Jan., 1816.

¹³ H. p. from 5th West India Regt. 31st Dec., 1818

¹⁴ H. p. 25th March, 1817.

[15] H. p. 25th March, 1817.

[16] H. p. 25th March, 1823.

[17] Capt. 3rd Aug., 1830.

[18] Ret. f. p. 10th Rl. Garrison Bat. before 1824.

[19] H. p. 25th Feb., 1816.

[20] H. p. 25th Feb., 1816.

[21] 2nd son of Sir Charles Levinge, Bart., by Eliz., only dau. of Nicholas Reynell, of Reynella, co. Westmeath.   Bn. 20th March, 1796.   Promoted capt. 24th Oct., 1821.   Exchanged to 52nd L.I., 1823.   Maj. 71st Highland L.I. 15th Jan., 1829.   Quitted the service before 1842.   M., 2nd June, 1825, Barbara, dau. of Hugh Johnstone, of St. John's, New Brunswick, and had issue.   K.H.   D. 1843.

[22] Afterwards Lieut. in 37th Foot.   Quitted the service before 1824.

[23] H. p. 62nd Foot 1826.   D. Jan., 1856.

[24] H. p. 83rd Foot, 14th Jan., 1819.

[25] H. p. 25th Jan., 1819.

[26] Surgeon 66th Foot 16th Dec., 1819.   Out of said regt. in 1826.

[27] Reduced in 1818.

14TH (OR THE BUCKINGHAMSHIRE) REGIMENT OF FOOT.*

(3rd Battalion.)

		Rank in the Regiment.	Army.
	MAJORS.		
1	Francis Skelly Tidy	10 Sept. 1807	Lt.-Col., 4 June,
2	John Keightley	13 Jan. 1814	[1813
	CAPTAINS.		
3	George Marlay	14 June, 1810	Maj.,21June,1813
4	Thos. Ramsay	18 Oct. 1810	17 May, 1810
5	Wm. Turnor	15 Aug. 1811	
6	Wm. Ross	24 Dec. 1813	16 Dec. 1813
7	Richard Adams	13 Jan. 1814	
8	Christian Wilson	4 Nov. 1814	
9	J. L. White	5 Nov. 1814	
10	Wm. Hewett	13 Apr. 1815	24 Nov. 1814
	LIEUTENANTS.		
11	Wm. Akenside	6 Aug. 1807	2 Jan. 1807
12	Charles Myler Brannan	3 Dec. 1807	
13	Samuel Beachcroft	28 Nov. 1811	
14	Wm. Buckle, Adjt.	3 Nov. 1812	
15	George Baldwin	9 Nov. 1814	
16	John Nickelson	5 Apr. 1815	
17	Lyttleton Westwood	6 Apr. 1815	
18	Henry Boldero	13 Apr. 1815	
19	Jas. Campbell Hartley	24 May, 1815	
	ENSIGNS.		
20	Wm. Reed	13 Jan. 1814	
21	George Mackenzie	22 Jan. 1814	
22	Robert B. Newenham	27 Jan. 1814	
23	C. Fraser	10 Feb. 1814	
24	Aug. Fred. F. Adamson	3 Mar. 1814	
25	Wm. Keowen	21 Apr. 1814	
26	John Manley Wood	19 May, 1814	
27	Arthur Ormsby	2 June, 1814	
28	James Ramsay Smith	13 Oct. 1814	
29	Alfred Cooper, w.	1 Nov. 1814	
30	Joseph Bowlby	2 Nov. 1814	

14TH (OR THE BUCKINGHAMSHIRE) REGIMENT OF FOOT—*continued.*

	ENSIGNS—*continued.*	Regiment.	Rank in the Army.
31	John Powell Matthews	3 Nov. 1814	
32	Richard John Stacpoole	8 Nov. 1814	
33	Richard Birt Holmes	10 Nov. 1814	
34	Hon. George Thos. Keppel	4 Apr. 1815	

PAYMASTER.

| 35 | Robert Mitton | 17 Feb. 1814 | |

QUARTERMASTER.

| 36 | Alexander Ross | 20 Jan. 1814 | |

VOLUNTEER.

| 37 | Montague Burrows | | |

ASSISTANT-SURGEONS.

| 38 | Alexander Shannon | 27 Jan. 1814 | |
| 39 | Henry Terry | 21 Mar. 1814 | |

Facings buff.   Lace silver.

* At the close of the Par. War the British Army was reduced to a peace footing. The 3rd Batt. of the 14th Foot survived this general reduction until the spring of 1815, when the dreaded order for its disbanding arrived. Before this became an accomplished fact the escape of Napoleon from Elba, and the consequent war with France, put a stop to further reductions. The 3rd Batt. 14th was ordered to Belgium. Being composed chiefly of very young recruits, the 14th were ordered to Antwerp to join the garrison there, but through their colonel's personal application to Gen. Lord Hill, this order was countermanded by Wellington himself, who inspected the regt. from the window of his hotel at Brussels. "They are a very pretty little battalion," said he to Lord Hill; "tell them they may join the grand division as they wish." And so it came to pass that the "peasants," as the battalion of *young bucks* were waggishly styled, took part in the "combat of giants."

¹ Youngest son of the Rev. Thomas Holmes Tidy, chaplain to H.M. 26th Foot, and afterwards rector of Red Marshall, co. Durham, by Henrietta Augusta, dau. of the Rev. Wm. Skelly, by Lady Betty Gordon, dau. of Alexander, Duke of Gordon. If "fighting blood" is hereditary, then must "Frank Tidy," as he was always called, have had a good share, for he was maternally descended from Charles Mordaunt, the "fighting" Earl of Peterborough, and had for his uncle the gallant Francis Skelly, maj. in the 71st Highlanders, who gained renown at the siege of Seringapatam. Joined the 43rd Regt. in Ireland as a volunteer at the age of 16, and was soon gazetted an ensign. When serving with his regt. in the West Indies "a

mortality of from ten to thirteen men a day reduced the 43rd to 96 rank and file, and Guadaloupe being disputed inch by inch, the 43rd, at the time of its capture at Berville, did not contain more than two officers and twenty men fit for duty." Tidy was confined for 15 months on board a hulk, subject to the tyranny and cruelty of Victor Hughes, thence sent to France, and eventually allowed to return to England on parole. Appointed adjt. of the 43rd. Promoted capt. 1st West India Regt. 1798 ; in 1799 exchanged to the Royal Scots. A.D.C. to Sir George Beckwith in the West Indies. Maj. 8th W.I. Regt., and transferred to the 14th Foot 1807. Served in Spain in 1808 ; Walcheren expedition 1809. Horse shot at Waterloo. C.B. Served in Burmese War with 1st Batt. Lt.-col. 44th Regt. 1825. D. at Kingston, Canada, while in command of the 24th Regt., 9th October, 1835, leaving issue, several sons and daughters. An interesting memoir of Col. Tidy was published in 1849 (written by his dau., Mrs. Ward) entitled : *Recollections of an Old Soldier.*

² Bt.-lt.-col. for Waterloo. Was at the taking of St. Lucia in 1796 and served at Walcheren in 1809. Appointed maj. 23rd Fusiliers 25th July, 1816, and lt.-col. of 11th Foot 2nd June, 1825. Afterwards lt.-col. of 35th Foot and Resdt. Gov. of Santa Maura and Zante. D. at Pickhill Hall, near Wrexham, 6th Sept. 1852, aged 74.

³ Son of maj. George Marlay, of Twickenham, Mdx., by Lady Catherine Butler, dau. of the Earl of Lanesborough. Bn. 1791. Served in the Pa. as A.A.G., and recd. the gold cross for Nivelle, Nive, Orthes, and Toulouse. C.B. for Waterloo. Placed on h. p. 25th March, 1816. M., 1828, Catherine, dau. of Jas. Tisdall, of Bawn, co. Louth, and had issue. D. 8th June, 1830.

⁴ Served with the 52nd at the siege of Copenhagen and battle of Kioge. In the Pa. from 1808-9 and again from 1810-11 with 47th Regt. Placed on h. p. 25th March, 1816. Living 1855.

⁵ Afterwards Maj.-Gen. Wm. Turnor. Served in Hanover with the 14th in 1805-6 and in the Pa., including battle of Corunna. Was also in the Walcheren expedition. D. 12th Dec., 1860.

⁶ Afterwards maj. 23rd Fusiliers. Lt.-col. unattached 1837. Living 1846.

⁷ Placed on h. p. 25th March, 1816. Bn. 1780. Served in Egypt. At capture of Copenhagen, 1807. Eldest son of Samuel Adams, by Eliz., dau. of Alex. Leslie. M., 1805, Louisa, dau. of N. Peers, and had issue. D. 11th Feb. 1836.

⁸ Exchanged as capt. to 38th Foot, in 1822. Out of the army before 1829.

⁹ Placed on h. p. 5th April, 1816. Afterwards Capt. J. L. White, late of the Ionian Islands Militia, a Military Knight of Windsor (Royal Foundation). Served with the expedition to the Elbe and Weser, under Lord Cathcart, and in numerous battles in the Pa., including Almeida, Ciudad Ridrigo, storming of Badajoz, Salamanca, capture of Madrid. Also served in Flanders and France ; was present at the attack on Merxem, the bombardment of Antwerp, and the siege of Bergen-op-Zoom, the storming of Cambray, and capture of Paris. Living 1874.

¹⁰ 3rd son of the Rt. Hon. Sir George Hewett, Bart., of Nethersall, co. Leicester, by Julia, dau. of the late John Johnson, of Blackheath, Kent. Bn. 1791. Exchanged as capt. to Rifle Brigade 14th Aug., 1823. Retd. as maj. from latter regt. 19th Aug., 1828. Lt.-col. unattached list same date. M. in June, 1826, Sarah, 2nd dau. of Gen. Sir James Duff. D. at his resi-

dence, Southampton, in Oct., 1891.   He was the last of the Waterloo commissioned officers.

[11] Capt. 6th Sept., 1821.   Serving in 1830.

[12] Reduced with the battalion in 1816.

[13] Reduced with the battalion in 1816.

[14] Reduced with the battalion in 1816.

[15] Lieut. 31st Foot 18th March, 1822.   Capt. 14th June, 1833.   Major 23rd Dec., 1842.   Out of the regt. before 1850.

[16] Lieut. John *Nicholson* was placed on h. p. 25th March, 1816.   Living 1846.

[17] H. p. 25th March, 1816.

[18] H. p. from 27th Foot 25th June, 1818.   Living 1846.

[19] H. p. 25th March, 1816.

[20] Lieut. 26th June, 1815.   Lieut. 48th Foot 18th July, 1816.   Capt. 8th June, 1825.   Serving in 1830.

[21] H. p. 25th March, 1816.

[22] Robert Burton Newenham quitted the service before 1823.   He appears to have been a grandson of Sir Edward Newenham, knt., who m. Grace, dau. of Sir Charles Burton, Bart.

[23] A certain Charles Fraser, who had served at Waterloo, was appointed Ens. and Lieut. in 3rd Foot Guards, 3rd July, 1815, and was promoted Lieut. and Capt. 25th Feb., 1819.

[24] Ret. before 1st Jan. 1816.

[25] Serving in 1817.   Out of the regt. before 1824.

[26] Capt. h. p. 67th Foot 10th Sept., 1825.   Bt.-major 28th June, 1838. Major 14th Foot 28th Aug., 1840.   H. p. 3rd Apr. 1846.   Living 1855.

[27] Wounded at the taking of Cambray.   Lieut. 27th Jan., 1823.   Capt. h. p. 1838.   D. in 1851.

[28] Living in 1874 as Lt. J. R. Smith, h. p. 38th Foot.   Entered the army in 1814.   Was present at the storming of Cambray, and afterwards at the capture of Hattras, in the East Indies.   Also served in the Deccan campaign of 1817-18.   His commissions are dated : Ensign, Oct. 13th, 1814 ; lt., March 20th, 1824.

[29] The only officer of the 14th Foot wounded at Waterloo, and he, strange to say, " was the shortest man in the regiment " (Lord Albemarle's account of the battle.)   A brother ensign, Arthur Ormsby, was wounded at Cambray six days later.

[30] Capt. 90th Foot 26th Dec., 1826.   Serving in 1830.

[31] 1st Lieut. Rl. Welsh Fusiliers 7th Apr. 1825.   Ret. h. p. 10th Foot 31st Dec., 1830.   Living 1846.

[32] H. p. 24th Feb., 1818.

[33] H. p. 9th May, 1818.

[34] The 6th Earl of Albemarle, gen. in the army, unattached.   Bn. 13th June, 1799.   2nd son of Wm. Charles 4th Earl of Albemarle, by his first wife, the hon. Eliz. Southwell, dau. of Edward Lord de Clifford.

England may thank Wm. III. for having given us the Keppels 200 years ago. It was this monarch who brought over Arnold Joost Van Keppel (descended from Walter Van Keppel, Lord of Keppel, 1179) as a page in 1688, and who raised him from one high post to another until he became Earl of Albemarle, a Knight of the Garter, and gen. of the Dutch forces in 1702. This nobleman fought under Marlborough in the wars of Queen Anne, and our last Stuart monarch stood sponsor to Lord Albemarle's eldest son, who succeeded his father as William Anne 2nd Earl—a general officer and British ambassador to Paris. The two eldest sons of the 2nd earl were equally distinguished in their respective professions—the army and navy. Viscount Bury was A.D.C. to the Duke of Cumberland at Fontenoy and Culloden. He subsequently attained the rank of lt.-gen. and was com.-in-chf. at the reduction of the Havannah, which brought him much renown. His brother Augustus became famous as Adm. Keppel, and for his eminent services was created Visct. Keppel, of Elvedon, Suffolk (extinct). Gen. Visct. Bury succeeded as 3rd Earl, and it was his grandson, the sixth earl, who joined the 3rd Batt. 14th Foot six weeks before Waterloo. The following Waterloo anecdote is given by Mrs. Ward in her memoir of Col. Tidy (already referred to), and is corroborated by Lord Albemarle himself in his interesting autobiography published in 1876 :—

"Mr. Keppel was sitting on a drum just in front of my father's mare when she was shot—he was even stroking the poor thing's face at the time that the ball struck her down, broke the bit of the bridle and knocked him head over heels, drum and all. The animal plunging in her agony, threw the square into great confusion, and her misery was speedily put an end to by the soldiers' bayonets." On the 25th May, 1820, Ensign Keppel (then in 22nd Foot) was promoted lieut. Exchanged to 20th Foot, 1821 ; Capt. 62nd Foot, 1825 ; and in 1827 was promoted to an unattached majority. Lt.-Col., 1841; Col., 1854; M.-Gen., 1858; Lieut.-Gen., 1866; and Gen. 1874. M. 4th Aug., 1831, Susan, dau. of Sir Coutts Trotter, Bart., and by her (who d. 3rd Aug., 1885) had issue. D. 21st Feb., 1891.

[35] Paymaster 47th Foot 2nd May, 1816. Serving in 1824.

[36] " For some time after the firing had begun," writes Lord Albemarle in his account of Waterloo, " Mrs. Ross, our quartermaster's wife, remained with the regt. She was no stranger to a battle-field, and had received a severe wound in Whitelock's disastrous retreat from Buenos Ayres (1807) at the time her husband was a sergt. in the 95th. She was at length persuaded to withdraw, and retired to the belfry of Waterloo Church."

[37] Commissioned ensign 14th Foot 27th June, 1815. Out of the regt. before 1st Jan., 1817.

[38] Out of the regt. in 1816.

[39] H. p. 25th March, 1816.

23RD REGIMENT OF FOOT (OR ROYAL WELSH FUSILIERS).

		Rank in the	
LIEUT.-COLONEL.		Regiment.	Army
[1] Sir Henry Walton Ellis, K.C.B., w.		23 Apr. 1807	Col., 4 June, 1814
MAJORS.			[1812
[2] Thomas Dalmer		10 Dec. 1807	Lt.-Col., 17 Aug.,
[3] J. Humph. Edw. Hill, w.		12 Mar. 1812	Lt.-Col., 21 Sept., [1813
CAPTAINS.			
Joseph Hawtyn, κ.		11 Sept. 1806	Maj., 17 Aug. 1812
[4] Francis Dalmer		10 Dec. 1807	Maj., 26 Aug. 1813
[5] Thomas Strangeways		6 Apr. 1809	
Wm. Campbell		15 June, 1809	Maj., 12 Apr. 1814
[6] Charles Jolliffe, κ.		18 June, 1811	
Thos. Farmer, κ.		16 Apr. 1812	
[7] Henry Johnson, w.		14 May, 1812	
Henry S. Blanckley		6 Apr. 1815	21 May, 1812
FIRST LIEUTENANTS.			
[8] Francis O'Flaherty		6 Aug. 1807	
[9] James Milne		21 Oct. 1807	
[10] Wm. Walley		10 Dec. 1807	
[11] Evan M. Brown		20 Apr. 1809	
G. Fensham, κ.		4 Jan. 1810	
[12] Ralph Smith		22 Mar. 1810	
[13] Harry Palmer		11 Apr. 1811	
[14] Isaac Watkins Harris		20 June, 1811	
[15] J. Enoch, Adjt.		15 Aug. 1811	
[16] Gismond Phillips (*sic*)		5 Sept. 1811	
[17] John Macdonald		11 Oct. 1811	
[18] George Fielding		7 Nov. 1811	
[19] Robt. Pattison Holmes		12 Dec. 1811	
[20] Charles Fryer		7 May, 1812	
[21] W. A. Griffiths, w.		13 May, 1812	
[22] John Clyde, w.		14 May, 1812	
[23] Alexander A. Brice		21 May, 1812	
[24] Anthony G. Sidley		16 July, 1812	
[25] Alexander Clayhills		17 Sept. 1812	
[26] Edward Methold		23 Mar. 1815	

23RD REGIMENT OF FOOT (OR ROYAL WELSH FUSILIERS)—*continued*.

	Rank in the	
SECOND LIEUTENANTS.	Regiment.	Army.
²⁷ Thomas Lilly	1 Oct. 1812	
²⁸ George Dunn	15 Apr. 1813	
²⁹ George Stainforth	29 July, 1813	
³⁰ Gerald FitzGibbon	26 Aug. 1813	
Wm. Leebody, K.	9 Sept. 1813	
³¹ Edward Thomas Ellis (Volunteer)		
QUARTERMASTER.		
³² George Sidley	14 Apr. 1808	
SURGEON.		
³³ John Dunn	10 Sept. 1803	9 July, 1803
ASSISTANT-SURGEONS.		
³⁴ Thomas Smith	2 July, 1812	
³⁵ John Williams	13 May, 1813	
³⁶ John Monro	26 May, 1814	

Facings blue.   Lace gold.

¹ Was sev. wnded. at Waterloo, in the breast, by a shot from a carbine, On his way to the rear he was thrown from his horse, whilst attempting to jump a ditch, and one of his men carried him to a small outhouse, where his wound was dressed. On the night of 19th June the hovel took fire, and he was with difficulty rescued by Assistant-Surgeon Munro, of above regt. He d. next day. This gallant and universally lamented officer was son of Maj.-Gen. John Joyner Ellis, and was a native of Worcester. He had served in Holland, Egypt, America, the West Indies, Spain, Portugal, and France. M.I. in Worcester Cathedral. Bd. at Braine l'Alleud, within a few hundred yards of the place where he fell.

² Afterwards Lt.-Gen. T. Dalmer, C.B., Col-in-Chf. 47th Foot. Horse shot under him at Waterloo. D. 25th Aug., 1854.

³ Commanded a Portuguese regt. during the Par. War, and received the gold cross for four general actions. C.B. for Waterloo. Exchanged as maj. to 49th Regt., 2nd Oct., 1823. Out of the list 1829.

⁴ Brother to above T. Dalmer. Bt. lt.-col. for Waterloo. Attained rank of col. and d. 2nd Oct., 1855.

⁵ Retd. on f. p. as capt. in 9th Rl. Veteran Battalion. D 15th Jan., 1838, at Richmond Place, Dublin. Bro. of Col. Strangeways, of Shapwick, Somerset.

⁶ Youngest son of T. S. Jolliffe, of Ammerdown, co. Somerset, formerly M.P. for the borough of Petersfield, by his 2nd wife, Mary, dau. and heir of

Samuel Holden. Served at Copenhagen, in North America, and the West Indies. Served several campaigns in the Pa. Sev. wnded at Orthes. Had not entirely recovered from this wound when the tocsin of war once more summoned him to the field of battle.

[7] Afterwards Maj. H. Cavendish Johnson. Served at Copenhagen in 1807 ; the West Indies, and the Pa. At the siege of Badajoz, Johnson fell from the breach pierced with gunshot wounds, which prevented his doing any regimental duty until 1815, when he served at Waterloo and was again wounded. D. in Ireland, 19th Feb., 1853, aged 78.

[8] Capt. 17th July, 1815. H. p., 15th Foot 3rd Aug., 1820.

[9] Capt. 18th July, 1815. Out of the regt. before 1824.

[10] Capt. 19th July, 1815. H. p. 14th Foot, 6th Apr., 1820.

[11] Capt. 20th July, 1815. Paymaster to his regt. 23rd Oct., 1817. H. p. 16th Oct., 1828.

[12] H. p. 53rd Foot, 8th May, 1823.

[13] Out of the regt. before 1824.

[14] Capt. 7th Apr., 1825. H. p. 9th Apr., 1826. Living 1846.

[15] Capt. 22nd July, 1830. Maj. 14th Apr., 1846 Lt.-col. unattached 1st Feb., 1851. A.Q.M.G. same date. Col. 28th Nov., 1854. D. in London, 13th July, 1855. He had the Par. medal with four clasps—Badajoz, Ciudad Rodrigo, Albuera, Salamanca.

[16] *Grismond Philipps.* 3rd son of George Philipps, of Cwmgaili, Caermarthenshire, who was M.P. for the borough. Served at Albuera, Nivelle, Nive, Orthes, and Toulouse (medal with five clasps). Bn. 1792. M. Catherine, dau. of — Warlow, Esq., and niece of Sir Thos. Picton. H. p. 26th Aug., 1819. D. in 1850. His elder bro., John George, was a midshipman on board H.M.S. *Minotaur* at the battle of the Nile. Communicated by Lieut. Griffith Philipps, R.N.

[17] Capt. 28th Aug., 1827. Paymaster 16th Oct., 1828. Out of the regt. in March, 1831.

[18] Capt. 6th June, 1822. Serving in 1830.

[19] Capt. 4th Sept., 1823. Maj. 17th Dec., 1830. D. at Quebec, 23rd July, 1849, as col. comg. reserve batt. Rl. Welsh Fusiliers.

[20] H. p. 17th July, 1817.

[21] Serving in 1830.

[22] D. from his wounds.

[23] H. p. 5th Oct., 1820.

[24] Lt. Anthony Gardiner Sidley (or Sedley), aftds. of 3rd W. I. Regt. Entered the service in 1811. Served in the Pa. and in the Burmese War. Lt.-col. 63rd Foot 16th Sept., 1845. Living in 1874 as a lt.-col. retd. list and a military Knight of Windsor.

[25] Placed on h. p. as lt. 67th Regt., 30th May, 1822. 2nd son of James Menzies-Clayhills, of Invergowrie, co. Forfar. M. Elizabeth, dau. of Gen. Hunter, of Burnside, and d. s. p. 18th June, 1865.

[26] Afterwards capt. on h. p. list of 3rd D. G.

[27] Capt. in Ceylon Rifles 1839. Distinguished himself in the Kandian Insurrection of 1848, and commanded the only European troops employed

on this occasion. Received the special thanks of Lord Torrington, Gov. of Ceylon, for his gallantry. D. as lt.-col. April, 1862.

[28] H. p. 16th Apr., 1817.

[29] Placed on h. p. as 1st lt. 25th March, 1817. Of Hutton, co. York. D. at Nivelle, Belgium, 27th April, 1860.

[30] Afterwards sub-inspector of the Constabulary in Ireland. D. at Plymouth, 7th Sept., 1844.

[31] Nephew to Sir Henry Walton Ellis, col. of this regt., who fell at Waterloo. Mentioned in Lord Albemarle's autobiography. In the regt. in 1830.

[32] Retd. f. p. 1827. D. 1839.

[33] Out of the regt. 13th July, 1826.

[34] Afterwards Surgeon-Major Thomas Smith, M.D., h. p. Joined the service in 1812 ; served in the campaigns of 1813, 1814, and 1815 ; was present at Vittoria, the Pyrenees, Nivelle, Orthes, and Toulouse. His commissions are dated : Hospital Assistant, March 29, 1812 ; Assist.-Surgeon, July 2, 1812 ; Surgeon, July 13, 1826 ; Surgeon-Major, Jan. 4, 1839. Living in 1874.

[35] H. p. 1816.

[36] D. in Apr., 1841, at Glasgow, as Surgeon 58th Foot.

27TH (OR INNISKILLING) REGIMENT OF FOOT.*

(1st Battalion.)

	Rank in the	
CAPTAINS.	Regiment.	Army.
[1] John Hare, w.	9 Sept. 1805	Maj.,17June,1813
George Holmes, k.	30 Apr. 1807	
[2] John Tucker, w.	3 Mar. 1808	
LIEUTENANTS.		
[3] George M'Donnell (*sic*) w.	25 July, 1806	
[4] Wm. Henderson, w.	8 Oct. 1806	
[5] Richard Handcock, w.	5 Nov. 1806	
[6] Wm. Faithful Fortescue, w.	4 Dec. 1806	
[7] Thomas Craddock, w.	7 May, 1807	
[8] Wm. Talbot	7 Feb. 1808	
[9] E. W. Drewe, w.	9 Feb. 1808	
[10] Charles Manley, w.	28 July, 1808	
[11] John Millar, w.	11 Sept. 1808	
[12] John Betty	7 Mar. 1810	
[13] Andrew Gardner	30 Sept. 1813	
ENSIGNS.		
[14] Wm. Kater, w.	22 Apr. 1813	
[15] John Ditmas, w.	3 June, 1813	
[16] Thos. Smith, w.	24 June, 1813	
Samuel Ireland, k.	25 Aug. 1815	
[17] Tobias Handcock, w.	4 May, 1815	
QUARTERMASTER.		
[18] Thomas Taylor	26 Sept. 1805	
ASSISTANT-SURGEONS.		
[19] Gerald Fitzgerald	25 Apr. 1811	
[20] Thomas Mostyn	19 Dec. 1811	

Facings buff. Lace gold.

* This regt. had just returned from active service in America. Out of 698 men, this regt. lost 480 at Waterloo, having been almost blown to pieces when standing in square above the sandpit on the Charleroi road.

[1] Afterwards Maj.-Gen. Hare, C.B. and K.H., Gov. of the Eastern District of the Cape of Good Hope. Began his military career as ensign in the Tarbet Fencibles, when he volunteered with 300 men into the regulars, and joined 69th Regt. Embarked for the Helder, and served in that campaign under the Duke of York. Served under Abercromby in Egypt. Also in Naples, Sicily, Calabria, and the Pa. Bt. lt.-col. for Waterloo. Lt.-col. of this regt. 31st March, 1825. D. on his passage home from the Cape in March, 1847.

[2] His full name was John Montmorency Tucker. Exchanged as capt. to 8th Foot, 23rd May, 1816. Quitted the service before 1824. D. at Huggens's Military Asylum, Northfleet, Kent, 22nd Feb., 1852.

[3] Afterwards Gen. George *Macdonald*, Col.-in-Chf. 16th Foot, who lived to be "Father of the British Army." Entered the army in 1805 ; joined the Expedition to Hanover in 1805 ; the Army in Sicily in 1806 ; the Expedition to Naples in 1810, and was present at the capture of Ischia and Procida ; returned to Sicily in 1811 ; was subsequently employed in Spain, and was present at the battle of Castalla and siege of Tarragona ; afterwards served in Canada. He was wounded no less than three times at Waterloo. Commissions dated : Ensign, Sept. 5, 1805 ; Lt., July 25, 1806 ; Capt., August 17, 1815 ; Maj., 31st Aug., 1830 ; Lt.-Col., 1837 ; Col., 1851 ; Maj.-Gen., 1855 ; Lt.-Gen., 1863 ; Gen., 1871.

[4] Placed on h. p. 25th April, 1816. Living 1830.

[5] Capt. 46th Foot, 17th Feb., 1837. Bt.-major same year. Living 1846.

[6] D. from wounds received at Waterloo. 2nd son of John Fortescue, of 24th Foot, who was at the taking of Quebec. The above m., 1798, Honoria Oliver, and had issue.

[7] 7th son of Wm. Cradock, of Loughborough, co. Leicester. Bn. 6th Oct., 1786. Served throughout the Par. War with the 27th Foot. At siege of Badajoz Lt. Cradock entered the town in command of his regt. Served at the attack on New Orleans in 1815. At Waterloo a bullet passed right through his cheeks carrying away the roof of his mouth. Appointed a Knight of Windsor in 1842. Retd. as major 73rd Foot. D. 5th April, 1851.

[8] The "W" is omitted before this officer's name in the *Army List* for 1824.

[9] Capt. 7th Jan., 1824. Capt. 95th Foot 19th May, 1825. Serving in 1830.

[10] Had a bullet through his thigh at Waterloo. Had served in the Pa. Capt. same regt. 10th Sept., 1829. D. in an apoplectic fit, 5th Nov., 1839, on board the ss. *Barretta, jun.*, when 17 days' sail from Cape of Good Hope.

[11] Adjt. 25th Foot 6th November, 1823. H. p. capt. 13th March, 1827. D. about 1840.

[12] Serving in 1817. Out of the regt. before 1824.

[13] Living in 1874 as lt. half pay 27th Foot. Entered the Army in 1811. His commissions are dated : Ensign, 14th Nov., 1811 ; Lt., 30th Sept., 1813.

[14] Lieut. 17th Aug., 1815.   Out of the regt. before 1st Jan., 1817.

[15] Lieut. 9th Nov., 1815.   Lieut. 25th Foot 21st May, 1818.   Son of Lt.-Col. Harry Ditmas, of the Garrison Batt. of Invalids.

[16] Thos. Charlton Smith.   Entered the Army in 1813.   Served in the Pa., and was present at the affair of Ordal.   He was sev. wnded. at Waterloo. Previously to entering the Army he served for a brief period in the Navy, and was three times wounded.   His commissions are dated : Ensign, 24th June, 1813 ; Lt., 5th Aug., 1819 ; Capt., 27th March, 1835 ; Maj., 30th Sept., 1842 ; Lt.-col., 15th Sept., 1848 ; Col., 28th Nov.. 1854 ; Maj.-gen., 21st Dec., 1862 ; Lt.-gen., 25th Oct., 1871.

[17] H. p. 26th March, 1816.

[18] Left the regt. in 1816.

[19] Surgeon 69th Foot 7th Sept., 1815.

[20] Hospital assistant 9th Nov., 1810.   Surgeon 6th Oct., 1825.   Serving in 1855.   This veteran had the Par. medal with eight clasps, and had also served at the battle of Plattsburg, in America.

28TH (OR THE NORTH GLOUCESTERSHIRE) REGIMENT OF FOOT.*

	Rank in the	
LIEUT.-COLONEL.	Regiment.	Army.
1 Sir Charles P. Belson, K.C.B.	23 Nov. 1804	Col., 4 June, 1812
MAJOR.		
2 Robert Nixon, w.	15 Dec. 1804	Lt.-Col., 30 May, [1811
CAPTAINS.		
3 Wm. Prescott Meacham, K.	9 July, 1803	Maj., 4 June, 1814
4 Wm. Irving, w.	9 July, 1803	Maj., 4 June, 1814
5 Richard Llewellyn, w.	28 Feb. 1805	Maj.,23 Apr. 1812
6 Charles Caddell	9 Mar. 1809	
7 Richard Kelly, w.	13 Apr. 1809	
8 John Bowles, w.	28 July, 1809	
9 Thomas English, w.	31 Jan. 1810	
10 Charles Teulon, w.	27 Sept. 1810	
LIEUTENANTS.		
11 Jas. Henry Crummer	2 July, 1807	
12 John Fred. Wilkinson, w.	8 Sept. 1808	
13 Matthew Semple	6 Oct. 1808	
14 Roger P. Gilbert, w.	27 Apr. 1809	
15 Robert Prescott Eason, w.	17 May, 1809	
16 Wm. Irwin, w.	20 July, 1809	
17 Henry Hilliard, w.	16 Nov. 1809	
18 Samuel Moore	28 Jan. 1810	
19 John Coen, w.	29 Jan. 1810	
20 Charles B. Carruthers	30 Jan. 1810	
21 J. P. Clarke, K.	1 Mar. 1810	
22 J. Wm. Shelton, w.	22 Mar. 1810	
23 James Deares	25 Apr. 1811	
24 George Ingram, K.	6 Aug. 1812	
25 T. Bridgeland, Adjt., w.	15 Apr. 1813	
26 Edward Embury Hill	9 Sept. 1813	
27 Thos. Wm. Colleton	25 Nov. 1813	
28 James Parry	27 Jan. 1814	

28TH (OR THE NORTH GLOUCESTERSHIRE) REGIMENT OF FOOT—*continued*.

	Rank in the	
ENSIGNS.	Regiment.	Army.
29 Robert Thomson Stuart	5 Aug. 1813	
30 Wm. Serjeantson	26 Aug. 1813	
31 Richard Martin	8 Sept. 1813	
32 James Simkins	9 Sept. 1813	
33 Wm. Mountsteven, w.	25 Nov. 1813	
34 W. Lynam	31 Mar. 1814	
PAYMASTER.		
35 John Dewes	20 June, 1799	
QUARTERMASTER.		
36 Richard Reynolds	9 Mar. 1809	
ASSISTANT-SURGEON.		
37 Patrick H. Lavens	24 Oct. 1811	

Facings yellow.   Lace silver.

* This regt. was for many years known as the " Slashers."   This name is said to have been first given in the early part of the American War, when the regt. had swords, which they used to some purpose.   The 28th might have been appropriately called "Prescott's Own," as the Col.-in-Chf., Gen. Robert Prescott, had been closely associated with this regt. for 50 years or longer, and was lt.-col. commanding for about 12 years.   From 1789 until his death in Dec., 1815, he was col.-in-chf., and took the deepest interest in all that concerned his old corps.   He had more than one godson in the regt., whose fathers had fought under him in America, whom he advanced in their military career by his own personal interest.   And the 28th were equally attached to their old colonel, who had seen much service in America and the West Indies, where he held high commands.   Like many others, before and since, who have filled responsible situations in countries where the native or "barbarian" element is largely represented, Gen. Prescott was fully imbued with the idea of his own great importance.   An amusing instance of this is found in an order issued by him when commanding the troops in Canada :—

LIEUT.-GENERAL PRESCOTT'S ORDERS.

" St. Pierres, 16th *June*, 1794.

"Whereas Vice-Adm. Sir John Jervis has given orders, I am told, frequently here on shore, and particularly by note dated off Point Petre, June 11th, 1794, which must have arisen from great ignorance or great presumption and arrogance.

" If from ignorance, poor man ! he is to be pitied, but if from presumption and arrogance, he is to be checked.

" It is, therefore, Lt.-General Prescott's orders that in future no attention whatever is to be given to such notes or orders, and his signature to such to be as little regarded as that of John Oakes or Peter Styles."

A martinet he lived and a martinet he died. His last whisper on his death-bed was an inquiry as to whether there was a Hessian sentry at his door. Although he did not die in harness the veteran " Slasher " died under the colours of the 28th, as on the death of the late Robert Prescott (grandson of the above) the old colours of the 28th were found among his effects and returned to the regt. They had doubtless been worked by the fair fingers of the old general's wife.

[1] Succeeded to the command of the 8th Brigade after Quatre Bras. Lt.-Col. 56th Regt. 9th May, 1816. Had served throughout the Par. War with above regt., and received the gold cross with two clasps. Maj.-Gen. 1819. D. at Blackheath 5th Nov., 1830, aged 57.

[2] 7th son of Alexander Nixon, of Mullynesker, High Sheriff of Fermanagh 1761, by Mary, dau. of Alex. Montgomery. Served in Egypt and in the Pa. C.B. for Waterloo. Quitted the service 1816. D. s. p.

[3] This officer had fought in Egypt and in the Pa. His father had been regimental paymaster.

[4] Distinguished himself in the Pa., and had a musket-ball through his right arm at Quatre Bras. Bt. lt.-col. for Waterloo. Quitted the service in 1826. Both his arms had been nearly disabled by wounds. D. 14th Jan., 1834.

[5] Afterwards Gen. Sir Richard Lluellyn, K.C.B., Col.-in-Chf. 39th Regt. Entered the army wit 1 temporary rank as capt. in the 52nd, and served in the Mediterranean. In 1801 was placed on h. p. but when the war recommenced he re-entered the army and purchased a company in the 28th Foot in 1805. Fought at Busaco and Albuera, and other actions in the Pa. Was an excellent horseman, and on one occasion in the Pa., when employed on staff duty, he was galloping after the retreating French when he came on an open portmanteau, in which he espied some silver spoons and forks of an antique pattern. As he galloped past he bent in the saddle and made a grab with his right hand at the glittering contents. His dexterity was rewarded with several specimens of old French plate. This anecdote is given on the authority of a relative of the Editor, who used to meet the old general in society, who told the story himself. Made bt. lt.-col. and C.B. for his gallantry at Waterloo. He was son of Richard Lluellyn, of South Witham, co. Lincoln, by a dau. of Warren Maude, of Sunnyside, Northumberland. M., 1831, Eliz., dau. of Lt.-Gen. Raymond. D. 7th Dec., 1867.

[6] 5th son of John Cadell, of Cockenzie and Tranent, co. Haddington. Bn. 1786. M., 1829, Isabella, dau. of Macdonald of Boisdale. K.H. Promoted major 28th Foot, 1826. Author of *Narrative of the Campaigns of the 28th Regiment since their Return from Egypt*, from which book the Editor has culled several notes. Served throughout the Par. War. At the close of Waterloo Day commanded the 28th. D. s. p. as lt. col. on retd. list, 1866.

[7] Quitted the service before 1830, after being a capt. in this regt. for about 20 years.

[8] Wounded at Quatre Bras. Placed on h. p. in 1817.

[9] Served in the Pa., and was wounded at Waterloo. Quitted the service before 1824. Believed to have belonged to an Armagh family of this surname.

[10] Maj. in this regt. 7th Oct., 1819. H. p. 4th Aug., 1825.

[11] Was severely wounded in the left leg at Albuera. In 1832, when serving as senior capt. in this regt., the old wound broke out afresh and caused much suffering. Applied for a pension for wounds to which he had been entitled, but it was refused on the ground of the lapse of years since the said wound was received.

[12] Out of the regt. before 1824.

[13] Capt. 38th Foot, 24th Oct., 1823. Serving in 1830.

[14] Distinguished himself at the passage of the Douro, 12th May, 1807, in the brigade under the command of Sir Edward Paget. 5th son of the Rev. Edmund Gilbert, vicar of Constantine, co. Cornwall, by Anne, dau. of Henry Garnett, of Bristol. Bn. 1790. Attained rank of maj. unattached 19th Sept. 1826. Living in 1830.

[15] Distinguished himself at the passage of the Douro. Capt. same regt. 1825. Living 1830.

[16] "The strongest man in the regt." Several anecdotes of this officer's prowess are given in Col. Cadell's book, referred to above. Wounded at Quatre Bras. Promoted capt. 9th May, 1816. In the regt. 1840, in which year he retd., and d. at Sydney, N.S.W. in 1841.

[17] Afterwards Paymaster H. Hilliard, h. p., late lt. 68th Foot. Entered the army 1808, served in the Pa., and was present at several engagements, including Busaco, Albuera, and the 1st siege of Badajoz; was also at Quatre Bras. His commissions are dated : Ensign, Feb. 25th, 1808 ; lt., Nov. 16th, 1809 ; paymaster, March 22nd, 1821. Living in 1874.

[18] Capt. 14th Dec., 1826. Serving in 1830.

[19] Serving as lieut. in 1824. Out of the regt. before 1830.

[20] Serving as lieut. in 1830.

[21] Had served in the Pa.

[22] John Willington Shelton was son and heir of John Shelton, of Rossmore House, Limerick. Served in the Pa. Was four times wounded at Waterloo. Placed on h.p. 1817. M., 14th Aug., 1817, Mary, dau. of John Richards, of Blackdown House, Southampton, and had issue. D. 19th July, 1847.

[23] Called "Deans" in Col. Cadell's book. This zealous officer accompanied the cavalry on foot in the pursuit of the enemy, and attacked every Frenchman who came in his way. He was taken prisoner and stripped of all his clothes except his shirt, in which state he joined the regt. next day, severely wounded into the bargain. Quitted the service before 1824.

[24] Distinguished himself at the battle of Albuera. Had his leg amputated after Waterloo; the tourniquet shifted in the night, and he bled to death. M.I. at Waterloo.

[25] Had served in the ranks, and was promoted from sergt.-maj. to be adjt. and ensign.

[26] Capt. 7th March, 1822. H. p. 17th Aug., 1822.

[27] 2nd son of Sir James Nassau Colleton, 6th Bart., of Ash Park, co. Herts, by Susanna, dau. of William Nixon, of Lincoln. Afterwards lt. in Rl. Staff Corps.

[28] Living in 1874 as a lt. h. p. 28th Foot.

[29] Lieut. 18th July, 1815. H. p. 25th March, 1817. Living in 1846.

[30] Afterwards lt. 40th Foot. Capt. 17th Dec., 1829. Of Hanlith, Tasmania. Eldest son of Robert Serjeantson (a blood relative of Gen. Prescott's wife), by Isabella, dau. of Wm. Dorman, of Harbour Hill, Kinsale. M. Marion, dau. of Richard Willis. Was murdered at Hobart Town, Tasmania, 30th Nov., 1835.

[31] Lieut. 4th Oct., 1815. H. p. 25th March, 1817.

[32] Serving in 1817.

[33] Lieut. 25th Oct., 1820 ; capt. 25th June, 1835. Paymaster 79th Highlanders 10th June, 1836. H. p. 1847. Attained rank of major-general retd. list. His full name was Thos. Wm. Blewett Mountsteven.

[34] Serving in 1817. H. p. 2nd April, 1818.

[35] H. p. 22nd Aug., 1816.

[36] Placed on h. p as 2nd lt. from 1st W.I.R. 12th Feb., 1824.

[37] Surgeon 14th Lt. Dragoons 13th Nov. 1828. Serving in 1842. Out of said regt. 21st July, 1843.

30TH (OR THE CAMBRIDGESHIRE) REGIMENT OF FOOT.

(*2nd Battalion.*)

	Rank in the	
LIEUT.-COLONEL.	Regiment.	Army.
[1] Alexander Hamilton, w.	25 July, 1811	4 June, 1811
MAJORS.		[1814
[2] Morris Wm. Bailey, w.	26 Dec. 1808	Lt.-Col., 4 June,
[3] Charles A. Vigoreux (*sic*), w.	4 June, 1813	Lt.-Col., 21 June,
		[1813
CAPTAINS.		
Thos. Walker Chambers, к.	2 Apr. 1807	Maj.,16 Feb. 1815
[4] Alex. M'Nabb, к.	11 May, 1809	
[5] Robert Howard	1 Sept. 1813	
[6] Arthur Gore, w.	11 Feb. 1814	14 July, 1808
[7] Matthew Ryan	26 May, 1814	Maj., 4 June, 1813
[8] Donald Sinclair	7 July, 1814	
[9] James Finucane	2 Mar. 1815	15 Aug. 1811
[10] Richard Heaviside	15 June, 1815	
LIEUTENANTS.		
[11] Benj. Walter Nicholson	15 Apr. 1806	
[12] John Gowan	8 May, 1806	
[13] Richard Mayne, w.	8 June, 1809	
[14] Matthias Andrews, Adjt., w.	19 Sept. 1809	
[15] Richard Chas. Elliott, w.	23 June, 1811	
[16] A. W. Freear	24 June, 1811	
[17] John Rumley, w.	25 June, 1811	
[18] Andrew Baillie	27 June, 1811	
[19] Robert Daniel, w.	15 July, 1811	
[20] Parke Percy Neville	17 July, 1811	
[21] John Roe, w.	18 July, 1811	
[22] Theophilus O'Halloran	8 Aug. 1811	
[23] Richard Harrison, w.	11 Sept. 1811	
[24] Robert Hughes, w.	29 Oct. 1812	
[25] Purefoy Lockwood, w.	22 Apr. 1813	
[26] John Pratt, w.	6 May, 1813	
Henry Beere, к.	7 Sept. 1814	
[27] Francis Tincombe	8 Sept. 1814	

30TH (OR THE CAMBRIDGESHIRE) REGIMENT OF FOOT—*continued.*

LIEUTENANTS—*continued.*	Rank in the Regiment.	Army.
Edmund Prendergast, K.	23 Nov. 1814	
[28] Wm. Ouseley Warren, w.	24 Nov. 1814	
[29] Thomas Moneypenny (*sic*),W.	23 Mar. 1815	
[30] David Latouche	25 May, 1815	
[31] Robert Naylor Rogers	14 June, 1815	
[32] Edward Drake	15 June, 1815	

ENSIGNS.

John James, K.	2 Sept. 1813	
[33] Edw. Nevil Macready	8 Sept. 1814	
James Bullen, K.	23 Nov. 1814	

PAYMASTER.

[34] Hugh Boyd Wray	9 Aug. 1806	

QUARTERMASTER.

[35] John Williamson	27 Oct. 1814	

SURGEON.

[36] J. G. Elkington	11 Mar. 1813	

ASSISTANT-SURGEONS.

[37] John Evans	22 Aug. 1811	
[38] Patrick Clarke	25 June, 1812	

Facings pale yellow. Lace silver.

[1] This gallant officer received the thanks of Sir Thomas Picton for his services at Quatre Bras where he (Hamilton) was sev. wnded. After the battle it was thought necessary to amputate his leg; and three times had the tourniquet encircled his limb, preparatory to amputation, when each time the surgeon was called elsewhere. It was then decided to let the leg take its chance, and Hamilton eventually recovered. C.B. for Waterloo. Quitted the service in 1829 with rank of Col. All his service had been spent in "the old three tens," as the 30th were called, and he had fought with them in Egypt and in the Pa. Had the gold medal for Salamanca. D. at Woolwich, 4th June, 1838. In his obituary notice, given in the *United Service Journal*, it is stated that he was nearly related to the noble house of Lothian. Whatever family he may have belonged to, he did it credit. He left a widow and two sons.

² C.B. for Waterloo. Aftds. lt.-col. of 64th Regt. Retd. before 1824. D. at Bath, 28th Nov., 1845.

³ Lt.-Col. *Vigoureux* was sev. wnded. at Waterloo. C.B. Lt.-Col. of the 45th Regt., 20th Dec., 1826. D. as col. on retd. list, 24th Dec., 1841.

⁴ It appears that this officer acted as an additional A.D.C. to Gen. Sir T. Picton, at Waterloo. At the second funeral of Picton in St. Paul's Cathedral one of the mourners was the Rev. Dr. M'Nabb, from Canada, nephew of the above. The antiquity of the M'Nabb is delightfully illustrated by the well-known remark of one of their clan that "at the flood they did not need to take refuge in Noah's Ark, as the M'Nabbs had a boat of their own !"

⁵ Made bt.-maj. for Waterloo. Promoted maj. on unattached list, 1826, Lt.-col. 1837. D. at Wigfair, St. Asaph, 22nd Sept., 1856.

⁶ Afterwards Lt.-Gen. Arthur Gore, K.H. Son of the Hon. Richard Gore, M.P. for Donegal. D. 23rd June, 1869.

⁷ H. p. 1817.

⁸ H. p. 1817.

⁹ H. p. 1817.

¹⁰ H. p. 1817.

¹¹ H. p. 1817.

¹² H. p. 1818.

¹³ D. in 1827.

¹⁴ Capt. 16th Sept., 1827. Serving in 1830.

¹⁵ H. p. 1817. Capt. unattached 28th Aug., 1827. Living in 1874.

¹⁶ H. p. 1817.

¹⁷ D. 1819.

¹⁸ H. p. 1817.

¹⁹ H. p. 1819, 59th Foot.

²⁰ Served in the Pa., and was twice wounded, when leading the ladder party in the escalade of the St. Vincent Bastion, at the siege of Badajoz. Sev. wnded. at the siege of Burgos, when acting as Assistant Engineer in the storm of the first line of the Castle, 4th Oct., 1812. At the bombardment of Antwerp, and assault on Bergen-op-Zoom. Served in the Mahratta War of 1817-18, and was present at battle of Maheidpore and siege of Asserghur. Commanded the left wing of the 63rd Regt. in India for some years as maj. and bt. lt.-col. Received the Legion of Honour for services rendered on board the French ship *Benguile*, on passage from India to Europe in August, 1831. He was also presented with the Freedom of the City of Dublin. Joined the corps of Gentlemen-at-Arms, 1st Aug., 1847, and was subsequently made a Knight of Windsor. D. at Windsor Castle, 6th Feb., 1865, aged 72.

²¹ H. p. 1823.

²² H. p. 1818.

²³ D. 1819

²⁴ Maj., 1st West India Regt., 3rd March, 1843, and lt.-col. of same regt., 1st March, 1848. Col. 1854. Received the Par. War medal with 4 clasps. D. in Sept., 1855.

[25] Belonged to the Grenadier company. Ensign (aftds. Major) Macready in his interesting journal of the campaign of 1815 (printed in *Historical Records of the XXX Regt.*, says : "Lockwood of ours had gone home with a silver plate in his skull, on which was engraved 'bomb proof.'" H. p. 25th Aug., 1816. Living in 1846.

[26] Exchanged to 28th Foot, 9th Dec., 1819. Major 27th Foot 22nd March, 1827. Serving in 1830.

[27] H. p. 1817.

[28] H. p. 1817.

[29] Thomas Gybbon-*Monypenny* was descended from the ancient Scotch family of Monypenny, of Pitmillie, co. Fife ; but his ancestor, Capt. James Monypenny, R.N., settled in Kent about 1714, since which date this branch of the family has chiefly resided in Kent. His father was Thos. Monypenny, of Rye, Sussex. Placed on h. p. 1817. M., 8th Jan., 1818, Silvestra Rose, eldest dau. of Robert Monypenny, of Merrington Place, Rolvenden, Kent, and had issue. Lt.-col. of the West Kent Militia. M.P. for Rye, 1837–41. D. 16th Jan., 1854.

[30] H. p. 1816.

[31] H. p. 19th Feb., 1818. Staff officer of pensioners at Amherstburg, Canada West, before 1836. Drowned while fishing in the Detroit river 5th May, 1854.

[32] H. p. 1816 from 28th Foot.

[33] Brother to the great tragedian. Joined the 2nd Batt. 30th Foot, as a volunteer, in 1814, at the age of 16. Served under Lord Lynedoch in Holland. At Waterloo, when only an ensign, commanded the light company towards the close of the battle. His private journal, in which he gives his experiences at Waterloo, is quoted from in Sir H. Havelock's military work, entitled *Three Main Questions of the Day* (published in 1867) in order to show how the bravest cavalry failed again and again, at Waterloo, in breaking through the infantry squares when those squares were well provided with ammunition in addition to their bayonets. "Here come these fools again," growled the 30th rank and file as they prepared to pour a destructive fire on the advancing French cuirassiers, which invariably emptied many saddles and sent the remainder from whence they came. Served at the siege of Asseerghur, and was aftds. milit. sec. to Sir John Wilson in Ceylon. Was promoted maj. h. p. unattached, 22nd Nov., 1839. Wrote the *Life of Marshal Suvarow*, which was published after his death. D. at Clevedon, 4th Nov., 1848.

[34] H. p. 1831.

[35] An amusing anecdote relative to this officer is given in the *United Service Journal* for 1838. Col. A. Hamilton of this regt., had a very valuable charger at Waterloo, and knowing that if it was shot in the battle he would only get the Government price of £20 for another charger, he exchanged horses, before going into action at Quatre Bras, with his steady old quartermaster, who, being a non-combatant, was to remain in the rear. The quartermaster's horse was what is called a "safe convenience," but the colonel's charger was very high-spirited and fresh. Unaccustomed to the quietude of his position in the rear of the army, he fretted and fumed at being kept back from the excitement going on in front. His rider had a bad time of it, and was a source of much amusement to the idlers and

"non-effectives" in the rearward.   The narrator of this incident says that
on the evening of the 16th June, 1815, Sir W. Ponsonby sent his A.D.C. to
offer to buy Hamilton's fine charger (his owner being wounded), but the
bargain hung fire in some way, and the gallant Ponsonby lost his life on the
18th June, as we have seen, from being badly mounted.

   [36] Appointed assistant-surgeon 24th July, 1808.   Taken prisoner at Talavera
and sent to France.   Exchanged.   Rejoined in Portugal, after Busaco.
Served at Fuentes d'Onor, Ciudad Rodrigo, Badajoz, Salamanca, and capture
of Madrid.   Taken prisoner after siege of Burgos when in charge of the
wounded.   H. p. 1817.   Surgeon 1st Batt. 1st Royals in July, 1821.   Transferred to 17th Lancers in Sept., 1828.   Surgeon R.H.M.S. Dublin, 1814.
D. there in 1853.   Interred at Arbour Hill, Dublin.

   [37] Out of the regt. in 1821.

   [38] H. p. 82nd Foot 12th Jan., 1816.

32ND (OR THE CORNWALL) REGIMENT OF FOOT.

	MAJORS.	Rank in the Regiment.	Army.
1	John Hicks	3 Aug. 1804	Lt.-Col., 4 June,
2	Felix Calvert	11 May, 1815	[1811

	CAPTAINS.		
3	Charles Hames	25 May, 1803	Maj., 1 Jan. 1812
4	Henry Ross-Lewin	6 Aug. 1804	Maj., 4 June, 1814
5	Wm. H. Toole, w.	7 Sept. 1804	Maj., 4 June, 1814
6	John Crowe, w.	30 May, 1805	
	Jaques Boyse, к.	17 Mar. 1808	7 Aug. 1806
7	Thos. Cassan, к.	14 Sept. 1809	16 Apr. 1807
8	Edward Whitty, к.	17 May, 1810	
9	Hugh Harrison, w.	19 Jan. 1815	11 June, 1812
10	Charles Wallett, w.	23 Mar. 1815	

	LIEUTENANTS.		
11	Henry Wm. Brookes, w.	14 May, 1807	
12	David Davies, Adjt.	6 Nov. 1807	18 June, 1807
13	George Barr, w.	7 Nov. 1807	
14	Michael Wm. Meighan, w.	9 Nov. 1807	
15	Sam. Hill Lawrence, w.	10 Nov. 1807	
16	Theobald Butler	28 Apr. 1808	
17	John Boase, w.	9 June, 1808	
18	Thos. Ross-Lewin, w.	15 Dec. 1808	
19	John Shaw M'Cullock	10 Aug. 1809	
20	Jas. Robt. Colthurst, w.	13 Oct. 1809	
21	James Robinson, w.	17 May, 1810	
22	Robt. Tresilian Belcher	17 Jan. 1811	
23	James Fitzgerald, w.	11 July, 1811	
24	Thos. J. Horan, w.	11 June, 1812	
25	Edward Stephens, w.	10 Sept. 1812	
26	Henry Quill, w.	17 Dec. 1812	
27	Jonathan Jagoe, w.	9 Feb. 1815	10 June, 1813
28	George Small	23 Mar. 1815	

S 5473.

L

32ND (OR THE CORNWALL) REGIMENT OF FOOT
—continued.

| | Rank in the | |
ENSIGNS.	Regiment.	Army.
[29] Jasper Lucas	6 Jan. 1813	
[30] James M'Couchy	7 Jan. 1813	
[31] Henry Metcalfe, w.	18 Mar. 1813	
[32] John Birtwhistle, w.	14 Apr. 1813	
[33] Alexander Stewart, w.	15 Apr. 1813	
[34] George Brown	10 June, 1813	
[35] Wm. Bennett, w.	16 Mar. 1815	14 Jan. 1813
[36] Chas. R. K. Dallas, w.	23 Mar. 1815	18 Nov. 1813

PAYMASTER.

Thomas Hart	26 July, 1810	

QUARTERMASTER.

Wm. Stevens	19 Sept. 1804	

SURGEON.

Wm. Buchanan	17 Mar. 1804	9 July, 1803

ASSISTANT-SURGEONS.

Rynd Lawder	25 May, 1809	
Hugh M'Clintock	5 Nov. 1812	

Facings white.   Lace gold.

[1] C.B., and K.St.A. for Waterloo. Served in the Pa., and received the gold cross for four general actions. Quitted the service 1828 as col. D. 18th May, 1838.

[2] Made bt. lt.-col. for Waterloo. Son of Nicholson Calvert, of Hunsdon, by Frances, dau. of Edmund Sexton Pery, Viscount Pery. Attained rank of lt.-gen., and d. in 1862.

[3] Quitted the service before 1824. D. at Brighton, 23rd Feb., 1860.

[4] Of Ross Hill, Kildysart, co. Clare. Son of George Ross-Lewin, of Ross Hill, by Anne, dau. of Thomas Lewin, of Cloghans, co. Mayo. Bn. 1778. Served in the Pa., and was wounded in the last charge at Salamanca. M. Anne, dau. of Wm. Burnett, of Eyrescourt, and had issue. Quitted the service before 1824. D. 27th April, 1843. Wrote his autobiography, which gives a good account of Waterloo.

⁵ Afterwards on f. p., retd. list, 4th Rl. Veteran Batt. D. 17th Aug., 1831.

⁶ Afterwards lt.-col. and K.H. D. at Fairlea Villa, Bideford, in March, 1860.

⁷ Son of Capt. John Cassan, 56th Foot. Killed at Quatre Bras. A pension was granted to his widow.

⁸ Killed at Quatre Bras.

⁹ Retd. on h. p. 16th May, 1822. Living 1855.

¹⁰ Exchanged to the 61st Regt. in 1828. Retd. as capt. and bt.-maj. from the Ceylon Rifles. Living 1846.

¹¹ H. p. 3rd Dec., 1818.

¹² Capt. 19th July, 1815. H. p. 1828. D. at Walworth, 6th Oct., 1854.

¹³ Capt. 20th July, 1815. Serving in 1817.

¹⁴ Capt. 30th Sept., 1819. H. p. 25th Oct., 1822.

¹⁵ Adjt. 27th July, 1815. Capt. 7th Apr., 1825. H. p. 15th Dec., 1825.

¹⁶ H. p. 14th Foot 22nd June, 1820.

¹⁷ H. p. 94th Foot 19th June, 1817. D. 11th Sept., 1854, at Pendennis Castle, where he was barrack-master.

¹⁸ Younger brother to above Maj. H. Ross-Lewin. Served in the Pa., and in 1848 recd. the silver war medal with eight clasps. Quitted the service as lieut. M. Frances, dau. of Daniel O'Grady, and d. s. p. 1857.

¹⁹ Serving in 1817. Out of the regt. before 1824.

²⁰ Afterwards appointed Sub-inspector of Militia in North America. Retd. on h. p. as capt. in 1830. Bt.-maj. 21st July, 1854. Out of the *Army List* 1855.

²¹ H. p. 20th March, 1823.

²² Siborne makes the following mention of this officer in his history :— "The ensign carrying the regimental colour of the 32nd was sev. wnded. Lt. Belcher, who commanded the left centre sub-division, took it from him. In the next moment it was seized by a French officer whose horse had just been shot under him. A struggle ensued between him and Lt. Belcher; but while the former was attempting to draw his sword, the covering colour-sergt. (named Switzer) gave him a thrust in the breast with his halbert, and the right-hand man of the sub-division (named Lacy) shot him."

²³ H. p. 1817.

²⁴ H. p. 1817.

²⁵ Serving in 1817. Out of the regt. before 1824.

²⁶ Retd. f. p., 9th Rl. Veteran Batt., before 1824.

²⁷ H. p. 1817.

²⁸ H. p. 1817.

²⁹ H. p. 1817.

³⁰ Lieut. 20th July, 1815. Lieut. 48th Foot 26th March, 1824. Serving in 1830.

³¹ 3rd son of the Rev. Francis Metcalfe, Rector of Kirkbride, Cumberland, and Vicar of Rudston, co. York, by Harriet dau. of John Clough, of York.

Sev. wnded. at Waterloo. Promoted lieut. 27th July, 1815. Placed on h. p. 25th March, 1817. D. 1828.

[32] Carried the regtal. colour at Waterloo until sev. wnded. Attained the rank of maj.-gen. D. at Cheltenham, 6th Oct., 1867.

[33] Serving in 1817. Out of the regt. before 1824.

[34] Lieut. 30th Sept., 1819. Capt. 10th Feb., 1832. Bt.-major 15th June, 1838. Serving in same regt. in 1846.

[35] Ensign 68th Foot 30th Dec., 1819. Serving in 1824.

[36] 2nd son of Charles Stuart Dallas, by Susan King. Was sev. wnded. at Waterloo. Placed on h. p. as ensign in 1820. Quitted the service some years after, and entered the Church, and in 1842 was curate of Micheldever, Whitchurch, Hants. M. his cousin, Julia Maria Dallas, and had issue. D. 1860.

33RD (OR THE 1ST YORKSHIRE WEST RIDING) REGIMENT OF FOOT.*

		Rank in the	
LIEUT.-COLONEL.	Regiment.	Army.
1 Wm. Keith Elphinstone	30 Sept. 1813	

MAJOR.

2 Edward Parkinson, w.	17 Mar. 1813	

CAPTAINS.

3 Wm. M'Intyre, w.	3 Dec. 1810	
4 Charles Knight, w.	26 Dec. 1811	30 Aug. 1810
John Haigh, к.	6 Aug. 1812	
5 J. M. Harty, w.	11 Mar. 1813	
6 Ralph Gore	28 July, 1814	
7 John Longden	8 Sept. 1814	

LIEUTENANTS.

8 Thomas Reid, w.	20 July, 1806	
Peter Barailler	7 Sept. 1809	21 Mar. 1807
9 George Barrs	14 Nov. 1809	
Henry Rishton Buck, к.	16 Nov. 1809	
10 Arthur Hill Trevor	1 Jan. 1810	
John Boyce, к.	1 Jan. 1811	
J. Hart, к.	25 Apr. 1811	
11 James Murkland, w.	1 June, 1811	
12 Fred. Hope Pattison	24 Sept. 1812	
13 Arthur Gore, к.	11 Mar. 1813	
14 Richard Westmore, w.	1 Apr. 1813	
Thos. D. Haigh, к.	29 July, 1813	28 Jan. 1813
15 Jas. Gordon Ogle, w.	17 Mar. 1814	
16 Sam. Alex. Pagan, w.	7 Apr. 1814	
17 Edward Clabon	18 Aug. 1814	
18 Joseph Lynam	8 Sept. 1814	
19 John Archbold	27 Oct. 1814	
John Cameron, к.	9 Feb. 1815	

33RD (OR THE 1ST YORKSHIRE WEST RIDING) REGIMENT OF FOOT—*continued.*

		Rank in the	
ENSIGNS.	Regiment.		Army.
20 Henry Bain, w.	15 Oct. 1812		
21 James Forlong, w.	11 Mar. 1813		
22 John Alderson, w.	21 Apr. 1813		
23 Wm. Bain	22 Apr. 1813		
24 Jas. Arnot Howard	6 May, 1813		
25 Wm. Thain, Adjt., w.	13 May, 1813		
26 Andrew Watson	10 June, 1813		
27 Charles Smith	24 June, 1813		
28 Wm. Hodgson	21 Apr. 1814		
29 Gerald Blackall	12 May, 1814		
30 George Drury, w.	9 Feb. 1815		

PAYMASTER.

31 Edward Stoddart	2 Apr. 1807

QUARTERMASTER.

32 James Fazarckerley (*sic*)	25 Sept. 1808

SURGEON.

Robert Leaver	31 Mar. 1814

ASSISTANT-SURGEONS.

Wm. D. Fry	12 Nov. 1812
D. Finlayson	31 Mar. 1814

Facings red. Lace silver.

* In 1793 the Hon. Arthur Wellesley was appointed lt.-col. of this regt. and commanded it for nearly ten eventful years. Wellington never forgot his old regiment, and it is recorded that he honoured Sir Colin Halkett's brigade with several visits on Waterloo Day. In one visit late in the afternoon of that eventful day, he inquired "How they were?" The answer was that two-thirds of their number were down, and that the rest were so exhausted that leave to retire, even for a short time, was most desirable, some of the foreign corps, who had not suffered, to take their place. Gen. Halkett was told that the issue of the battle depended on the unflinching

front of the British troops, and that even a change of place was hazardous in
the extreme.   Halkett impressively said, " Enough, my lord ; we stand here
until the last man falls."

[1] Afterwards Maj.-Gen. W. Keith Elphinstone, C.B., Com.-in-Chf. in
Bengal.   3rd son of the Hon. Wm. Fullerton Elphinstone, and grandson of
the 10th Baron Elphinstone.   C.B. and K.S.A. for Waterloo.   Served in
Afghanistan, and in the retreat from Cabul was taken captive by Akhbar
Khan, and fell a sacrifice to bodily fatigue, 23rd April, 1842.

[2] Made bt. lt.-col. for Waterloo.   Served with the 33rd in India, and was
on the staff of the expedition which captured the island of Bourbon.   Served
in the campaign in Holland in 1814.   Was severely wounded at Quatre Bras.
Attained rank of lt.-gen. and col.-in-chf. 93rd Highlanders.   C.B.   D. 14th
Jan., 1858.

[3] Promoted maj. 30th Dec., 1818.   Exchanged to 1st W. I. Regt. 15th Feb.,
1821.   D. 23rd April, 1828.

[4] A native of Charleville.   Succeeded to the command of the above regt.
after 1830, and d. 21st July, 1841, on board the ss. *Pandora* at St. Thomas's,
on his way home from Barbados.

[5] Afterwards Col. Joseph M. Harty, K. H., retired f. p.   Entered the army
in 1807.   He served at the capture of Bourbon and the Isle of France (1810),
the campaigns in Germany and Holland, including the attacks on Merxem
and the assault of Bergen-op-Zoom (1813-14).   His commissions are dated ;
Ensign, April 23rd, 1807 ; Lt., May 1st, 1807 ; Capt., March 11th, 1813 ;
Maj., Dec. 20th, 1827 ; Lt.-Col., July 22nd, 1841 ; Col., Nov. 28th, 1854.
Living 1874.

[6] Quitted the service as capt. in this regt.

[7] Bt.-major 1st Nov., 1821.   H. p. unattached, 1st May, 1827.

[8] Capt. 16th June, 1815.   Retd. f. p. 10th Jan., 1837.   Living in 1846.

[9] Capt. 7th April, 1825.   H. p. 25th May, 1826.

[10] Afterwards K.H. and lt.-col. of 59th Regt.   Inspecting Field Officer
Recruiting Staff, 1855.   Maj.-Gen. 1858.   Living 1860.

[11] Left the regt. in 1817.

[12] Placed on h. p. as lt. 18th May, 1821.   Fifty years later he published
for private circulation a short account of his Waterloo experiences, which
the Editor had the pleasure of perusing a few years ago when staying at
Oban, N.B., where the Veteran's son resided on his own property.

[13] Eldest son of Lt.-Col. Ralph Gore, of the 33rd, by Sarah, dau. of George
Wynne, Mayor of Plymouth, 1791.

[14] Became major in this regt. 1840, and retired on f. p. in 1842 with rank
of lt.-col.   Living in 1865.

[15] Belonged to an Irish family.   D. as lt. in the regt., at Hull, 12th Sept.,
1817, aged 26, and was buried with military honours in Trinity Church,
Hull.

[16] H. p. 55th Foot, 14th Feb., 1822.

[17] Capt. 19th Sept., 1821.   Exchanged to 58th Foot, 30th Jan., 1823.   Out
of the regt. before 1830.

[18] Lieut. 54th Foot 27th Nov. 1822.   Out of the regt. before 1830.

[19] H. p. 1817.

[20] This officer's Waterloo medal was many years in the Editor's collection of war-medals.   Lieut. 11th Aug., 1815.   H. p. 1817.

[21] Major 43rd L. I. 1st July, 1828.   Lt.-col. 7th May, 1841.   Retd. 17th Oct. 1851.   K.H.   D. at Toronto.

[22] Lieut. 13th Aug., 1815.   H. p. 1817.

[23] Lieut. 14th Aug., 1815.   H. p. 1817.   D. in Feb., 1860.

[24] Lieut. 10th Aug., 1815.   H. p. 1817.

[25] Capt. 17th Nov., 1825.   Exchanged to 21st Foot, and was promoted bt.-major in 1838.   Serving in 1842.

[26] Lieut. 24th Foot, 18th June, 1818.   H. p. 1823.   Living in 1879.

[27] Lieut. 14th Aug., 1815.   H. p. 1817.

[28] Lieut. 19th Aug., 1815.   H. p. 1817.

[29] D. or left the regt. in 1816.

[30] Lieut. 23rd Nov., 1815.   H. p. 1817.

[31] H. p. 1817.

[32] *Fazackerley.*   Lieut. 1st Rl. Veteran Batt. 19th Oct., 1815.   Retd. f. p. 1816.

40TH (OR 2ND SOMERSETSHIRE) REGIMENT OF FOOT.

(1st Battalion.)

| | | Rank in the | |
MAJORS.	Regiment.	Army.
1 Arthur Rowley Heyland, K.	10 Nov. 1814	26 Aug. 1813
2 Fielding Browne	19 Jan. 1815	

CAPTAINS.		
3 Sempronius Stretton	11 Sept. 1806	Maj.,22 Nov. 1813
4 Conyngham Ellis, w.	30 Nov. 1809	
5 John Henry Barnett, w.	13 June, 1811	
6 Robert Phillips	25 July, 1811	
7 Wm. Fisher, K.	19 Sept. 1811	
8 Edward Cole Bowen	7 Nov. 1811	
9 Peter Bishop	12 Mar. 1812	
10 Thos. Decimus Franklyn	10 Nov. 1814	

LIEUTENANTS.		
11 John Thoreau	28 May, 1807	
12 Robert Moore, w.	14 Apr. 1808	
13 Wm. Oliver Sandwith	25 May, 1809	2 Oct. 1805
14 Wm. Manning, Adjt.	14 Sept. 1809	
15 Henry Millar	5 Sept. 1810	
16 John Richardson	6 Sept. 1810	
17 James Anthony, w.	16 May, 1811	
18 James Mill, w.	18 Sept. 1811	
19 Andrew Eugene Glynne, w.	19 Sept. 1811	
20 Wm. Neilly	26 Sept. 1811	
21 Richard Hudson	7 Nov. 1811	
22 Henry Wilkinson	12 May, 1812	
23 John Foulkes	14 May, 1812	
24 Thos. Campbell, w.	3 Sept. 1812	
25 Hugh Boyd Wray	10 Sept. 1812	
26 Richard Jones	8 Oct. 1812	
27 Hon. Michael Browne, w.	10 Dec. 1812	
28 Illay Robb, w.	23 Dec. 1812	
29 Donald Macdonald	7 June, 1815	
30 Frederick Ford, K.		
31 George Hibbert	14 June, 1815	
32 Richard Rudd	15 June, 1815	

40TH (OR 2ND SOMERSETSHIRE) REGIMENT OF FOOT—
continued.

| | Rank in the | |
ENSIGNS.	Regiment.	Army.
³³ Henry Hemsley, w.	25 Apr. 1813	
³⁴ J. L. Wall	25 Aug. 1813	
³⁵ Pharaoh Harley	26 Aug. 1813	
³⁶ Henry Glyn	25 Nov. 1813	
³⁷ Wm. Aldworth Clarke, w.	6 Jan. 1814	
³⁸ Richard Thornhill, w.	7 June, 1815	
³⁹ James Murphy	8 June, 1815	
PAYMASTER.		
Fred. Holland Durand	10 Mar. 1814	
SURGEON.		
⁴⁰ Wm. Jones	3 Sept. 1812	
ASSISTANT-SURGEONS.		
Wm. Barry	4 Jan. 1810	
George Scott	9 Sept. 1813	

Facings buff.   Lace gold.

¹ Eldest son of Rowland Heyland, of Castle Roe, co. Derry, by his 2nd wife (*née* MacDonald). M. Mary Kyffin, and had issue. His eldest son distinguished himself in the Crimea, and the youngest lost an arm at the battle of the Alma.

² C.B. and bt. lt.-col. for Waterloo, where he commanded his regt. during the latter part of the battle. Promoted major in Rifle Brigade. Placed on h. p. 1837. Col. 1820. Served throughout the Par. War, and commanded the regt. at the assault of Badajoz, for which he received the gold medal. In 1848 he received the silver war medal with 7 clasps. Served also at New Orleans. For some years he held the appointment of barrack-master at the Regent's Park Barracks, and d. in London 22nd July, 1864.

³ Afterwards Lt.-Col. S. Stretton, C.B., of Lenton Priory, Notts. Lt.-col. 21st June, 1817. Retired on h. p. 1824. M., 3rd March, 1821, the Hon. Catherine Massey, dau. of Nathaniel, 2nd Baron Clarina. (She d. 3rd July same year.) D. 6th Feb., 1842. M.I. in Athlone parish church. The tablet gives Col. Stretton's services in the Pa. as follows :—" He was present in the following battles, in several of which he had the honour to command the above distinguished corps, viz., Vittoria, Pampeluna, Roncevalles, the several actions in the Pyrenees [gold medal] heights of St. Antonio, the passage of the Bidassoa, and heights above Vera in Spain. The battle of Sara and

passage of the Nivelle, Bayonne, and passage of the Nive, Orthes, and Toulouse."

⁴ Made bt.-major for Waterloo.   D. 1817.

⁵ Serving as senio. capt. in 1830.

⁶ Serving in 1817.   Out of the regt. before 1824.

⁷ This officer had his head taken off by a cannon ball in the afternoon of Waterloo Day, when standing near the colours.   "There goes my best friend," exclaimed a private of Capt. Fisher's company. " I will be as good a friend to you," said the subaltern, who immediately took the deceased's place in the square.   This produced a grim laugh among the men, as they knew what the subaltern did not—that the private had spoken ironically, for he was an old offender, and had constantly been punished by Capt. Fisher. —(*Autobiography of Sergt. W. Lawrence.*)

⁸ Retd. in 1823.

⁹ Of Bishop's Court, Waterford.   Major 7th Sept., 1828.   Unattached list 1829.   K.H.   M., 7th Sept., 1815, Julia, dau. of Wm. Talbot, of Castle Talbot, and had issue.   Living 1830.

¹⁰ Retired on h. p. 19th Sept., 1823.   Served at Monte Video, Buenos Ayres, and in the Pa.   D. at Thorpe-le-Soken 3rd Nov., 1857.

¹¹ Capt. 19th July 1815.   Exchanged to 37th Foot 3rd May, 1821.   Bt.-major in 1837.   Serving in 1842.

¹² Capt. 20th July, 1815.   Paymaster 10th June, 1824.   D. in 1845.

¹³ H. p., 27th Foot, 28th June, 1821.

¹⁴ H. p., 21st Foot, 30th May, 1822.

¹⁵ Capt. 25th June, 1827.   Serving in 1830.

¹⁶ Capt. 17th Nov., 1831.   Exchanged to 83rd Foot in 1833.   Retd. in 1840.

¹⁷ H. p. 18th Nov., 1819.

¹⁸ Was struck by a spent ball in his right eye, which was seriously impaired for life.   (Pension.)   Major 8th Apr., 1826.   H. p. 7th May, 1829.

¹⁹ H. p. 1816.   This officer lived to receive the Par. medal with nine clasps in 1849.

²⁰ Capt. 63rd Foot 16th Aug., 1831.   Sold out 1833.   D. 1864.   He recd. the Par. medal with nine clasps.

²¹ H. p., 22nd Foot, 21st March, 1822.   D. in 1827.

²² H. p. 1818.   D. in 1861.

²³ H. p., 58th Foot, 26th Oct., 1820.

²⁴ H. p. 1817.

²⁵ H. p. 1817.   D. 10th Feb., 1854.

²⁶ H. p. 1817.

²⁷ H. p. 1816.   4th son of Valentine, 5th Visct. Kenmare.   D. 1825.

²⁸ Superseded soon after Waterloo.

²⁹ H. p. 25th Feb., 1816.

³⁰ Shot through the spine, but lived a few hours.

[31] Capt. 6th March. 1823.   Major 13th Nov., 1835.   C.O. during first Afghan War.   (C.B., bt. lt.-col. and medal).   Lt.-col. 22nd July, 1845.   D. 12th Nov., 1847.

[32] H. p. 25th Feb., 1816.

[33] H. p. 28th Foot, 1822.   D. at Chapel House, Ealing, 6th March, 1855.

[34] H. p. 1816.

[35] H. p. 1816.

[36] H. p. 1816.

[37] Lieut 1st March, 1821.   H. p. 25th Oct., 1821.

[38] Served as a volunteer at Waterloo.   Lieut. 15th Aug., 1822.   Serving in 1825.

[39] Served as a volunteer at Waterloo.   Ens. 47th Foot 26th July, 1820. Lieut. 60th Rifles 1827.

[40] D. in Aug., 1862, at Burton on Trent.

42ND (OR THE ROYAL HIGHLAND) REGIMENT OF FOOT.

Rank in the

LIEUT.-COLONEL.	Regiment.	Army.
1 Sir Robert Macara, K.C.B., K.	16 Apr. 1812	1 Jan. 1812

MAJOR.

2 Robert Henry Dick, w.	14 July, 1808	Lt.-Col., 8 Oct., [1812

CAPTAINS.

3 Archibald Menzies, w.	5 June, 1805	
4 George Davidson, w.	25 Sept. 1807	Maj., 4 June, 1813
5 John Campbell	3 Dec. 1807	Maj., 12 Apr. 1814
6 Mungo Macpherson, w.	9 Feb. 1809	
7 Donald McDonald, w.	25 Jan. 1810	
8 Daniel McIntosh, w.	2 May, 1811	
9 Robert Boyle, w.	11 July, 1811	

LIEUTENANTS.

10 Donald Chisholm, w.	10 Oct. 1805	
11 Duncan Stewart, w.	1 Jan. 1807	
12 Donald McKenzie, w.	23 July, 1807	3 Dec. 1806
13 James Young, Adjt., w.	25 May, 1808	
14 Hugh Andrew Fraser, w.	8 Feb. 1809	
15 John Malcolm	14 Dec. 1809	
16 Alexander Dunbar, w.	25 Jan. 1810	
17 James Brander, w.	2 May, 1811	
18 Roger Stewart	11 July, 1811	
19 Robert Gordon, K.	29 Aug. 1811	
20 James Robertson	10 Oct. 1811	
21 Kenneth McDougall	12 Feb. 1812	
22 Donald McKay	28 May, 1812	
23 Alexander Innes	15 Oct. 1812	
24 John Grant	18 Feb. 1813	
25 John Orr, w.	29 Apr. 1813	
26 George Gunn Munro, w.	10 June, 1813	

ENSIGNS.

27 George Gerard, K.	29 Apr. 1813	
28 Wm. Fraser, w.	10 June, 1813	
29 A. L. Fraser, w.	23 Sept. 1813	16 Sept. 1813
30 Alexander Brown	25 Dec. 1813	
31 Alexander Cumming	17 Feb. 1814	

42ND (OR THE ROYAL HIGHLAND) REGIMENT OF FOOT—*continued.*

Rank in the

	Regiment.	Army.
QUARTERMASTER.		
[32] Donald McIntosh, w.	9 July, 1803	
SURGEON.		
[33] Swinton McLeod	9 July, 1803	
ASSISTANT-SURGEONS.		
[34] Donald Macpherson	1 June, 1809	
[35] John Stewart	20 July, 1809	4 May, 1809

Facings blue.   Lace gold.

[1] The death of Sir R. Macara at Quatre Bras was inexpressibly sad. "He was wounded about the middle of the engagement, and was in the act of being carried off the field by four of his men, when a party of French unexpectedly surrounded and made them prisoners. Perceiving by the colonel's decorations that he was an officer of rank they immediately cut him down with his attendants." His relations obtained Macara's Waterloo medal, which was for long in the Tancred Collection. A touching poem to Robert Macara's memory is to be found in the *Waterloo Memoirs;* the following are the last three verses of a pæan of praise sung by the Goddess of Fame :—

> "Here the Goddess ceased her lay ;
> Weak, her wings refused to fly ;
> Faint, her voice forbore to say
> How Macara dared to die.

> "Be it, then, to friendship giv'n
> Such a warrior's name to save,
> While 'tis borne on breeze of heav'n
> That he found a soldier's grave.

> By unequal hosts oppos'd,
> Still he proved his valour true ;
> For his bright career was clos'd
> On the plains of Waterloo ! "

[2] Succeeded to the command after Macara's death. C.B. for Waterloo. Had served in the Pa., and received the gold medal and one clasp for Fuentes d'Onor and Salamanca. A.D.C. to George IV., 1825. H. p. unattached list, 1825 ; maj.-gen., 1837. K.C.B. and K.C.H. Col.-in-Chf. 73rd Regt. 1845. Killed at the battle of Sobraon, 10th Feb., 1846, at the moment of victory. He had m., 11th April, 1818, Eliza., dau. of J. Macnabb, of Arthurstone, Perth.

[3] In Capt. George Jones's *Waterloo Memoirs* is to be found an interesting letter regarding Major Menzies of the 42nd, who was dangerously wounded at Quatre Bras. The major's name is omitted in this letter :—"On the 16th June, Major ——, of the 42nd, preferring to fight on foot, in front of his men, had given his horse to hold to a little drummer-boy. After severe fighting he fell wounded near a brave private, Donald Mackintosh. The

drummer left the horse to assist his friend Donald. A French lancer attempted to seize the horse, on which the prostrate Donald exclaimed, 'Hoot
man, ye mauna tak that beast, 't belangs to our captain here !' The lancer,
little heeding, seized the horse. Donald, with a last expiring effort, loaded
his musket and shot the lancer dead. A French cavalry officer, seeing the
major bestirring himself, rode up and attempted to dispatch him with his
sword. As he stooped from his saddle, the major seized his leg, and managed
to pull him off his horse upon him. Another lancer, observing this struggle,
galloped up and tried to spear the major and relieve his officer; but the
former, by a sudden jerk and desperate exertion, placed the French officer
uppermost, who received the mortal thrust below his cuirass and continued
lying upon the major's body for near ten minutes, sword in hand. A pause
in the battle permitted some men of the 42nd to carry their officer into the
square of the 92nd, where he was found to have received sixteen wounds."
Acted as major after Sir R. Macara's death at Quatre Bras until wounded
himself. Promoted maj. 18th June, 1815. Left the regt. in 1828. D. in
1854. This gallant officer's claymore (an Andrea Ferrara) is in the possession of his grand-daughters, the Misses Murray Menzies.

[4] D. from his wounds at Brussels. Pension of £100 per ann. to his
widow.

[5] Brother of Sir Guy Campbell, Bart. Made C.B. and bt. lt.-col. after
Waterloo. Had the gold medal for Orthes. M., 10th March, 1831, Louise,
Gabrielle Clementine Bernie, of Paris, and had issue. D. 31st March, 1841,
at Marseilles.

[6] Retd. as major 1826. D. at Hastings in Nov., 1844.

[7] H. p. 1819. D. at Musselburgh, 1865.

[8] Retd. 1821. D. at Hamilton, 13th March, 1830.

[9] H. p. 1821. D. in London, 11th July, same year.

[10] Capt. Rl. Vet. Batt. 1815. Retd. f. p. 1821. D. at Edinburgh in 1853.

[11] H. p. 25th March 1817.

[12] Retd. 1821. D. at Edinburgh, 5th Dec., 1838.

[13] H. p. 1819. D. at Edinburgh, 15th June, 1846.

[14] Capt. 12th Dec., 1822. Maj. 3rd Dec., 1829. H. p. 4th May, 1832.
D. at Maidstone, as bt. lt.-col., in Jan., 1855.

[15] Afterwards capt. and bt.-maj. same regt. D. 1829.

[16] Quitted the service as lieut. in 1825, and d. at Inverness, 15th Feb.,
1832.

[17] Afterwards maj. in same regt. Promoted lt.-col. on unattached list
15th Aug., 1826. Eldest son of John Brander, of Pitgavenny House, Elgin,
by Margaret, dau. of Alexander Brander, Provost of Elgin. M., Jan., 1834,
Margaret Browne. J.P. and D.L. for co. Elgin. D. s. p., 1854, at Pitgavenny.

[18] Capt. h. p. 1827. D. in 1833, while serving with the Rl. African Corps.

[19] Killed at Quatre Bras. Son of the Rev. John Gordon, of Duffus, N.B.

[20] Adjt. 14th Sept., 1815. Capt. h. p. 13th Feb., 1827. D. as capt. 48th
Foot, at Chatham, Apr., 1833.

[21] Retd. 1826. D. in Skye, 1827.

[22] Capt. 3rd Dec., 1829. D. at Sterling 13th Feb., 1832.

[23] D. as lieut. h. p. unattached, 1875, as a military Knight of Windsor.

[24] Retired on h. p. 25th Oct., 1821. D. at Stratford, Essex, 13th June, 1827.

[25] Bn. 3rd April, 1790, at Greenock. His father was a merchant, and his mother, Margaret MacGregor, a descendant of the Glengyle family. Entered the army from the militia. Accompanied the 1st Batt. 42nd Highlanders to the Pa.; was present at Salamanca, the siege of Burgos, storming of St. Michael, the retreat to Portugal, and at all the actions in the Pyrenees. Was wounded at Burgos, and again severely at Waterloo. On the reduction of the army after Waterloo, he joined the 94th (the old Scots Brigade), and, on a further reduction, was appointed to the 8th Rl. Veteran Batt. Capt. Orr was Superintendent of the late Scottish Naval and Military Academy for thirty years. M. in 1816, Jane, 2nd dau. of Alex. Rollock, of Glasgow, and had issue. D. 7th Dec., 1879.

[26] H. p. 25th March, 1817.

[27] Killed at Quatre Bras. Eldest son of George Gerard, jun., of Midstrath, N.B.

[28] Of Balmakewan. Attained rank of lt.-col. h. p., and d. in Oct., 1851.

[29] H. p. 1825. D. at Edinburgh, 1835.

[30] H. p. 25th March, 1817.

[31] H. p. 26th Aug., 1819. D. 1852.

[32] Left the regt. in 1818. D. at Perth in July, 1829.

[33] H. p. 1829. D. in London, 27th Dec., 1847.

[34] H. p. 1835. D. at Chatham, 1839.

[35] H. p. 1818. D. at Perth, 2nd Jan., 1837.

44TH (OR THE EAST ESSEX) REGIMENT OF FOOT.

(*2nd Battalion.*)

	Rank in the	
LIEUT.-COLONEL.	Regiment.	Army.
[1] John M. Hamerton, w.	31 Mar. 1814	4 June, 1811
MAJOR.		
[2] George O'Malley	27 Apr. 1815	Lt.-Col., 4 June. [1813
CAPTAINS.		
John Jessop	15 June, 1804	Maj., 4 June, 1814
[3] Adam Brugh, w.	11 June, 1807	
[4] David Power, w.	31 Dec. 1807	
[5] Wm. Burney, w.	2 June, 1814	
[6] Mildmay Fane, w.	30 Mar. 1815	28 July, 1814
LIEUTENANTS.		
[7] Robert Russell, w.	14 July, 1808	
[8] Ralph J. Twinberrow	30 Mar. 1809	
[9] Robert Grier	13 May, 1812	
Wm. Tomkins, k.	20 May, 1813	
[10] W. B. Strong	16 Dec. 1813	
[11] John Campbell, w.	28 Mar. 1814	
[12] Nich. Toler Kingsley	29 Mar. 1814	
[13] James Burke	30 Mar. 1814	
[14] Henry Martin	31 Mar. 1814	
[15] Wm. Marcus Hearn	7 July, 1814	
[16] Alexander Reddock	2 Feb. 1815	
ENSIGNS.		
[17] James Christie, w.	26 Nov. 1812	
[18] Benjamin Whitney, w.	25 Feb. 1813	
[19] Gillespie Dunlevie	20 May, 1813	
[20] Peter Cooke, k.	18 Nov. 1813	
[21] Thomas McCann, Adjt., w.	31 Mar. 1814	
[22] James Carnegie Webster, w.	21 Apr. 1814	
[23] Alexander Wilson, w.	19 May, 1814	
[24] Thos. Aubrey Sinclair	4 May, 1815	

44TH (OR THE EAST ESSEX) REGIMENT OF FOOT
—continued.

Rank in the

	Regiment.	Army.
PAYMASTER.		
25 James Williams	4 Oct. 1810	
QUARTERMASTER.		
26 Henry Jones	9 July, 1803	
SURGEON.		
Oliver Halpin	29 Apr. 1813	11 Apr. 1811
ASSISTANT-SURGEONS.		
John Collins	1 Dec. 1808	
Wm. Newton	27 Dec. 1810	

Facings yellow.   Lace silver.

¹ Afterwards Gen. John Millett Hamerton, C.B., Col.-in-Chf. 55th Regt. The following obituary notice appeared in the *Illustrated London News* in Feb., 1855 :—"This highly-distinguished officer died on the 27th ult., at Orchardstown, his country residence in Tipperary, after a short illness. He was a soldier from his youth, and obtained his first commission of cornet at the early age of fifteen, in 1792. In 1794 he served under the Duke of York ; in 1795 embarked for the West Indies ; in 1796 assisted at the capture of St. Lucia ; and, in 1801, fought with distinction in Egypt. Subsequently he took part in the Pa. campaigns, in command of the 1st Batt. of the 44th. At Waterloo he bravely led on the 2nd Batt. of the same gallant regiment, and was left for dead on that bloody field, having received several severe wounds in the head and thigh. Owing to the attachment of a faithful non-commissioned officer, Sergeant Ryan, who brought his wounded and insensible commander under the care of skilful medical treatment, he slowly recovered, and with his devoted follower returned home. A chivalric soldier, an honourable and most amiable gentleman, General Hamerton is deeply lamented by all who came within the influence of his high and endearing qualities." He m. Mrs. Hennessy (*née* Sullivan), and had issue.

² Was twice wounded at Waterloo and had two horses shot under him. C.B. Previous to entering the army had served as a volunteer with the militia, and did good service during the Irish Rebellion. In 1825 succeeded to the command of the Connaught Rangers. He was 5th son of George O'Malley, of Gornsay, Castlebar, co. Mayo. D. in London, 16th May, 1843. M.I. at Castlebar.

³ Bt.-maj. for Waterloo. D. 1825.

⁴ Serving in 1817.

⁵ Afterwards Col. W. Burney, K.H., retired full pay. Entered the army in 1808. He served at the capture of Ischia and Procida in 1809 ; defence of Cadiz (1810) ; Sabugal, Fuentes d'Onor, and the retreat from Burgos ; sub-

sequently in the campaign in Holland (1814) ; Quatre Bras, where he was twice wounded ; and the Burmese war. Commissions dated : Ensign, April 28th, 1808 ; Lieut. May 1st, 1810 ; Capt. June 2nd, 1814 ; Maj. Sept. 6th, 1827 ; Lt.-col. Nov. 23rd, 1841 ; Col. Nov. 28th, 1854. Living in 1876.

[6] 5th son of the Hon. Henry Fane, M.P., by Anne, dau. of Edward Buckley Batson. Served in the Pa., and was present at Vittoria, capture of San Sebastian, and Nive. Severely wounded at Quatre Bras. Attained rank of Gen. and Col.-in-Chf. 54th Regt. D. 12th March, 1868.

[7] Retd. as lieut. f. p. 10th Rl. Veteran Batt. in 1821.

[8] D. 1823 as lieut.

[9] H. p. 25th March, 1817.

[10] H. p. 25th March, 1817.

[11] Serving in 1816. Out of the regt. in Jan., 1817.

[12] Serving in 1816. Out of the regt. in Jan., 1817.

[13] H. p. 25th March, 1816.

[14] H. p. 25th March, 1816.

[15] H. p. 25th March, 1816.

[16] H. p. 25th March, 1816.

[17] Siborne immortalises the name of this officer, in his history of the battle of Quatre Bras, as follows :—" A French lancer gallantly charged at the colours of the 44th, and severely wounded Ensign Christie, who carried one of them, by a thrust of his lance, which, entering the left eye, penetrated to the lower jaw. The Frenchman then endeavoured to seize the standard, but the brave Christie, notwithstanding the agony of his wound, with a presence of mind almost unequalled, flung himself upon it—not to save himself, but to preserve the honour of his regiment. As the colour fluttered in its fall, the Frenchman tore off a portion of the silk with the point of his lance ; but he was not permitted to bear the fragment beyond the ranks. Both shot and bayoneted by the nearest of the soldiers of the 44th, he was borne to the earth, paying with the sacrifice of his life for his display of unavailing bravery." Promoted lieut. 26th Oct., 1815. Placed on h. p. 25th March, 1816. Living 1827.

[18] Capt. 28th Apr., 1825. Exchanged to 14th Foot 16th Sept., 1826. Retd. as major 1840. D. 1862.

[19] H. p. 65th Foot 13th March, 1823.

[20] Killed at Quatre Bras whilst carrying the King's colours. Bn. 17th May, 1789. 4th son of Richard Cooke, of Stourbridge, co. Tipperary, by Mary, dau. of Jeremiah Laylor, of Barnagrotty, King's county.

[21] H. p. 24th Feb., 1816.

[22] Aftds. Lt.-Col. Jas. Carnegie Webster, h. p. unattached. Severely wounded at Quatre Bras. Living in 1876.

[23] Lieut. 31st May, 1821. Serving 1830.

[24] H. p. 25th March, 1816.

[25] H. p. 25th Apr., 1816. D. Dec., 1853.

[26] Qr.-Mr. 92nd Highrs. 3rd Sept., 1830.

M 2

51st (or the 2nd YORKSHIRE WEST RIDING) REGIMENT OF FOOT (LIGHT INFANTRY).*

	Rank in the Regiment.	Army.
LIEUT.-COLONEL.		
1 Hugh Henry Mitchell	13 June, 1811	4 June, 1813
MAJOR.		
2 Samuel Rice	13 July, 1809	Lt.-Col., 22 Nov. [1813
CAPTAINS.		
3 John Thos. Keyt	24 June, 1804	Maj., 4 June, 1814
4 James Campbell	1 Aug. 1805	
5 William Thwaites	2 Jan. 1807	Maj., 4 June, 1814
6 Richard Storer	13 July, 1809	
7 Jas Henry Phelps	21 Sept. 1809	
8 James Ross	12 Dec. 1811	
9 John Ross	15 Apr. 1813	
10 Sam. Beardsley, w.	16 Sept. 1813	
11 Edward Frederick	28 Apr. 1814	
LIEUTENANTS.		
12 Benjamin B. Hawley	10 May, 1809	
13 Thos. Brook	18 May, 1809	
14 Francis Minchin	12 July, 1809	
15 Walter George Mahon	13 July, 1809	
16 Wm. Henry Hare	20 July, 1809	
17 Oliver Ainsworth	26 July, 1810	
18 Henry Read	20 Feb. 1811	
19 Francis Kennedy	21 Feb. 1811	
20 Joseph Dyas	11 July, 1811	
21 John Flamanck	12 Dec. 1811	
22 Wm. Henry Elliott	13 Aug. 1812	
23 Wm. Davidson Simpson	3 Dec. 1812	
24 Frederick Mainwaring	15 Apr. 1813	
25 Wm. Jones, Adjt.	16 Apr. 1813	
26 Chas. Wm. Tyndale, w.	3 June, 1813	
27 Henry Martin	21 Oct. 1813	
28 Harry Hervis Roberts	7 Jan. 1814	
29 Egerton C. H. Isaacson	14 July, 1814	
30 Thos. Troward	29 Sept. 1814	
31 John Lintott	25 Dec. 1814	22 Apr. 1813

51ST (OR THE 2ND YORKSHIRE WEST RIDING) REGIMENT OF FOOT (LIGHT INFANTRY)—*continued.*

		Rank in the	
ENSIGNS		Regiment.	Army.
32 G. F. Berkeley St. John		3 June, 1813	
33 Wm. Henry Krause		21 Oct. 1813	
34 W. Johnstone		6 Jan. 1814	25 Oct. 1813
35 Alexander Fraser		21 Apr. 1814	
36 John Blair		14 July, 1814	18 May, 1814
37 Henry Lock		13 Oct. 1814	

PAYMASTER.

38 John Gibbs   15 Feb. 1810

QUARTERMASTER.

39 Thos. Askey   18 Mar. 1813

SURGEON.

40 Richard Webster   14 July, 1808   26 Oct. 1804

ASSISTANT-SURGEONS.

41 John F. Clarke   25 June, 1812
42 Percy FitzPatrick   11 Mar. 1813

Facings grass green. Lace gold.

---

* On the morning of 18th June, 1815, the 51st was composed of 2 field officers, 9 captains, 26 subalterns, 6 staff officers, 39 sergts., 18 drummers, and 521 privates.

[1] Served under Sir Eyre Coote in Egypt, and was present at the taking of Alexandria. Commanded the 4th British Brigade at Waterloo. C.B. and K. St. Vladimir. M. in 1804, Lady Harriet Somerset, youngest dau. of the 5th Duke of Beaufort, and had issue. D. in London, 20th April, 1817, aged 45.

[2] Served in the Pa., and had the gold medal for Nivelle. Commanded the 51st at Waterloo. C.B. Lt.-col. of this regt. 1817. D. 7th March, 1840. He belonged to an old family in Carmarthenshire, and was brother to Ralph Rice, Judge at Bombay, who d. 1850.

[3] At Waterloo, Maj. Keyt was appointed by Col. Mitchell to command the light companies of the 51st, 14th, and 23rd regts. (which three regts. were under Col. Mitchell's command), and for this command he was made bt. lt.-col. and C.B., after Waterloo. Was appointed Lt.-col. of the 84th Regt. in 1828, and d. in Jamaica in 1835.

⁴ Promoted maj. in this regt., 17th May, 1821 ; lt.-col. in 1831 ; and retired on h. p. 1838. K.H. M.-Gen. 1854. Served in the Pa., and in 1848 received the silver war medal with five clasps. D. at Breslington, 8th May, 1856.

⁵ Major 22nd June, 1815. Quitted the service before 1824.

⁶ Retd. as capt. 1823. D. at Egham, 1844.

⁷ Lt.-col. 1837. D. at Sydney, 1842.

⁸ Retd. 1824.

⁹ Maj. in this regt., 5th Nov., 1825. Lt.-col. on unattached list 1836, served in the Pa. and in the Walcheren expedition. Was severely wounded at Waterloo, and is said, "to have lost five brothers in this battle." D. at Hardway, Herts, 16th Sept., 1851, aged 61.

¹⁰ Retd. 1820 as capt.

¹¹ Edward Henry Frederick was 5th son of Sir John Frederick, Bart., by Mary, youngest dau. and co-heir of Richard Garth, of Morden, Surrey. Bn. 6th Aug., 1788. Retired on h. p. as capt. 7th April, 1826. D. 1846.

¹² Capt. 7th Apr. 1825. Retd. 1835.

¹³ H. p. 1825. D. 21st Dec., 1845 at Askham Bryan, Yorkshire.

¹⁴ Capt. 22nd June, 1815. Out of the regt. before 1824. Barrack-master at Sheffield, 1854. D. a military Knight of Windsor, 1865.

¹⁵ Capt. 91st Foot 1830. Retd. same year.

¹⁶ Capt. 18th Nov., 1819. H. p. 25th July, 1822. Living 1846.

¹⁷ Capt. 14th Aug., 1828. Retd. 1843 D. 3rd Dec., 1859, at Launceston, Australia.

¹⁸ Paymaster 68th Foot 8th Oct., 1818. Out of the army, 1836.

¹⁹ H. p. 1824. D. at Lincoln, 1857.

²⁰ One of the greatest heroes of the Par. War. Led the Forlorn Hope on two successive occasions during the siege of Badajoz, in 1811, when Fort San Christoval was assaulted by the British. The second assault, on the night of 9th June, is graphically described in *Reminiscences of a Subaltern* :— "At ten o'clock at night, 200 men moved forward to the assault, Dyas leading the advance. He made a circuit until he came exactly opposite to the breach instead of entering the ditch as before ; a sheep-path, which he remembered in the evening while he and Major MacGeechy made their observations, served to guide them to the part of the glacis in front of the breach. Arrived at this spot, the detachment descended the ditch, and found themselves at the foot of the breach ; but here an unlooked-for event stopped their further progress, and would have been in itself sufficient to have caused the failure of the attack. The ladders were entrusted to a party composed of a foreign corps in our pay, called 'the Chasseurs Britanniques' ; these men, the moment they reached the glacis, glad to rid themselves of their load, flung the ladders into the ditch, instead of sliding them between the palisadoes ; they fell across them, and so stuck fast, and being made of heavy green wood, it was next to impossible to *move*, much less place them upright against the breach, and almost all the storming party were massacred in the attempt. Placed in a situation so frightful, it required a man of the most determined character to continue the attack. Every officer of the detachment had fallen, Major MacGeechy one of the first ; and at this moment Dyas and about five-and-twenty men were all that remained of the 200,

Undismayed by these circumstances, the soldiers persevered, and Dyas, although wounded and bleeding, succeeded in disentangling one ladder, and placing it against what was considered to be the breach, it was speedily mounted, but upon arriving at the top of the ladder, instead of the *breach*, it was found to be a *stone wall* that had been constructed in the night, and which completely cut off all communication between the ditch and the bastion, so that when the men reached the top of this wall, they were, in effect, as far from the breach as if they had been in their own batteries. From this faithful detail it is evident that the soldiers did as much as possible to ensure success, and that failure was owing to a combination of untoward circumstances over which the troops had no control. Nineteen men were all that escaped." The gallantry of Ensign Joseph Dyas was proclaimed to the world in Wellington's account of the two assaults of San Christoval, but for all that a grateful War Office allowed him to remain a subaltern for ten years longer !

" I know a man of whom 'tis truly said
He bravely twice a storming party led,
And volunteered both times ; now here's the rub,
The gallant fellow still remains a sub."

In Dec. 1820, owing to the representations of Col. Gurwood and Sir H. Torrens, the Duke of York promoted Dyas a capt. in the 2nd Ceylon Regt., but impaired health obliged him to retire on h. p. 9th Aug., 1821. D. 28th Apr., 1850 at Ballymuir, Ireland.

21 Major 16th Dec., 1836. H. p. 30th June, 1837. Retd. 1849 as bt.-col. unattached.

22 Commanded the above regiment for many years. Was son of Capt. John Elliott, R.N., one of Capt. Cook's circumnavigators. Attained the rank of Gen. and Col.-in-Chf. 51st Regt. G.C.B. and K.H. M. in 1831 a dau. of W. Adams, of Ipswich. D. in London, 27th Feb., 1874.

23 Retd. 1821. D. April, 1855.

24 Afterwards maj. in same regt. Promoted lt.-col. unattached list 1849. Served in the Pa. with the 51st. M. Mary, dau. of Lt.-Col. Popham, and had issue. D. in Jersey, 25th Sept., 1858. He was 4th son of Edward Mainwaring, and grandson of Edward Mainwaring, of Whitmore Hall, co. Stafford—a family co-existent with the Norman Conquest.

25 H. p. 60th Rifles 25th Feb., 1819.

26 Son of Col. Tyndale of 1st Life Guards. He represented the younger branch of an ancient Gloucestershire family which resided at Stanchcombe in that county. Retired on h. p. as capt. in 1837, and was aftds. maj. on unattached list. For a short time held the post of military sec. to Gen. Sir A. Woodford at Gibraltar. M. in 1845 his cousin, a dau. of Samuel Phelps. D. s. p. at Gosport, 23rd Dec., 1854.

27 H. p. 1818. D. 1840.

28 H. p. 1818. Retd. 1840.

29 Served in the Pa. Retired on h. p. as lieut. 1823. For some years previous to that date he was lieut. to the garrison company in the Bahamas. Was subsequently adjt. to the Brecknock Militia. D. at his residence, Upper Nutwell, co. Devon, 29th Dec., 1860.

30 H. p. 1818. Retd. 1829. D. 17th June, 1859.

31 Capt. 29th May, 1817. Exchanged to 13th Foot, 9 Apr., 1825. D. at Dinapore, 9th Aug., 1829.

[32] Second son (by a second wife) of Gen. the Hon. Frederick St. John (son of 3rd Visct. Bolingbroke). Acted as orderly officer to Sir H. Clinton at Waterloo. Aftds. maj. in the 52nd L.I. Retd. 1840. M. in Jan., 1836, Henrietta, third dau. of the Rev. John Jephson, and had issue. A Knight of Windsor. D. 24th July, 1866.

[33] H. p. 1818. Retd. 1825. Took Holy Orders and settled in Dublin.

[34] Eldest son of the Rev. H. Johnston, of Malherry, co. Dublin. H. p. 25th Dec., 1818. M. 2nd July, 1831, Sarah, dau. of Wm. Mills, of Cordoxtown, co. Kildare, and granddaughter of Sir John Dillon, Bart. D. 1836 at Dublin.

[35] Lieut. 47th Foot, 14th Sept., 1820. Capt. 1833. Retd. 1839.

[36] Lieut. 15th Foot, 8th Apr., 1825. D. at Montreal, 25th May, 1833.

[37] H. p. 60th Foot, 30th Sept., 1819. D. at Mominabad, East Indies, 16th May, 1824.

[38] H. p. 1846. D. same year.

[39] H. p. 97th Foot 18th Feb., 1819. Retd. 1830.

[40] Surgeon 4th D. G. 3rd Aug., 1826. D. at Piershill Barracks, Edinburgh, 14th Feb., 1831.

[41] Inspector-Gen. of Hospitals, 1843. H. p. 1847. D. 29th Oct., 1848.

[42] H. p. 1818.

52ND (OR THE OXFORDSHIRE) REGIMENT OF FOOT (LIGHT INFANTRY).

(1st Battalion.)

LIEUT.-COLONEL.	Regiment.	Rank in the Army.
1 Sir John Colborne, K.C.B.	18 July, 1811	Col., 4 June, 1814
MAJOR.		
2 Charles Rowan, w.	9 May, 1811	Lt.-Col., 27 Apr. [1812
CAPTAINS.		
3 Patrick Campbell	16 Aug. 1804	Maj.,21June,1813
4 Wm. Chalmers	27 Aug. 1807	Maj.,26 Aug.1813
5 Wm. Rowan, w.	19 Oct. 1808	Maj., 3 Mar. 1814
6 Charles Diggle, w.	24 May, 1810	
7 John Shedden	9 May, 1811	
8 James Fred. Love, w.	11 July, 1811	Maj.,16 Mar. 1815
9 James McNair	11 May, 1812	
10 Edward Langton	12 May, 1812	
11 John Cross	31 Dec. 1812	
Charles, Earl of March	8 Apr. 1813	9 July, 1812
Charles Yorke	24 Dec. 1813	
LIEUTENANTS.		
12 John Winterbottom, Adjt., w.	28 Feb. 1810	
13 Charles Dawson, w.	21 June, 1810	
14 Mathew Anderson, w.	19 July, 1810	12 Oct. 1809
15 Charles Kenny	13 Sept. 1810	
16 George Harley Love	18 Apr. 1811	
17 Wm. Ripley	2 May, 1811	
18 J. C. Barrett	9 May, 1811	
19 Wm. Henry Clerke	19 Sept. 1811	29 July, 1811
20 George Hall	9 May, 1812	
21 Wm. Richmond Nixon	11 May, 1812	
22 George Gawler	12 May, 1812	
23 George Whichcote	8 July, 1812	
24 Wm. Ogilvy	17 Sept. 1812	
25 Edward Richard Northey	1 Oct. 1812	
26 Hon. Wm. Browne	26 Nov. 1812	
27 Edward Scoones	24 Dec. 1812	
28 George Campbell, w.	25 Feb. 1813	
29 Wm. Austin	6 Apr. 1813	

52ND (OR THE OXFORDSHIRE) REGIMENT OF FOOT
(LIGHT INFANTRY)—*continued.*

Rank in the

LIEUTENANTS—*continued.* Regiment.   Army.

30 John J. Snodgrass   7 Apr. 1813
31 Jas. Stewart Cargill   8 Apr. 1813
32 Wm. Crawley Yonge   29 Apr. 1813
33 Thos. Cottingham, w.   5 Aug. 1813
34 Charles Holman   11 Nov. 1813
35 George Moore   6 Dec. 1813
36 Edward Mitchell   8 Dec. 1813
37 Charles Shaw   9 Dec. 1813
38 John Hart   20 Jan. 1814
39 Geo. Ewing Scott   10 Feb. 1814
40 Henry Thos. Oakes   11 Feb. 1814
41 John Rogers Griffiths   12 Apr. 1815
42 John Burnet   8 May, 1815
43 Ronald Stewart   9 May, 1815
44 George Robson   10 May, 1815
45 Fred. Wm. Love   11 May, 1815

ENSIGNS.

46 Joseph Jackson   7 Dec. 1813
47 Thos. Massie   8 Dec. 1813
48 Wm. Nettles, K.   9 Dec. 1813
49 Duncan Macnab   16 Dec. 1813
50 John Montague   10 Feb. 1814
51 James Frere May   28 Apr. 1814
52 Eaton Monins   1 Dec. 1814
53 Wm. Leeke   4 May, 1815

PAYMASTER.

James Clark   17 Apr. 1814

QUARTERMASTER.

Benjamin Sweeten   22 Apr. 1813

SURGEON.

J. B. Gibson   20 Dec. 1810 | 7 Dec. 1809

ASSISTANT-SURGEONS.

Pryce Jones   20 Apr. 1809
Wm. Macartney   3 Sept. 1812
54 Thos. Brisbane   3 June, 1813

Facings buff. Lace silver.

[1] Afterwards F.-M. Lord Seaton, G.C.B., G.C.H., &c., and Col.-in-Chf. 2nd Life Guards. Only son of Samuel Colborne, of Lyndhurst, Hants, by Cordelia, dau. of John Garstin, of Castle Leiragh, co. Westmeath. Bn. 16th Feb., 1778. Educated at Christ's Hospital and Winchester College. Ensign 20th Foot, 1794. Served in Egypt and at the battle of Maida. Was military sec. to Sir John Moore. Commanded a brigade in Portugal, Spain, and France (gold cross and three clasps). "Of his own accord he led the forward movement at Waterloo which determined the fortune of the day. When the column of the Imperial Guard was gaining the summit of the British position, and was forcing back one of the companies of the 95th, Colborne, seeing his left endangered, started the 52nd on its advance. Wellington saw the movement, and instantly sent to desire him to continue it." Col. Chesney, the able author of *Waterloo Lectures* in commenting on the steadfast manner in which the British Guards faced the advancing Imperial Guards on the summit of the hill, says : "While on their left, Colborne, peerless among all the brave men who led Wellington's battalions, coolly formed in line the 52nd, and without other prompting than that of his own genius for battle, advanced against their flank." Created Baron Seaton, of Seaton, Devon, 14th Dec., 1839. F.-M. in 1860. M. 21st June, 1814, Eliz., eld. dau. of Rev. James Yonge, rector of Newton Ferrers, and had issue. D. 17th April, 1863.

[2] Afterwards Sir Charles Rowan, K.C.B. Chief Commissioner of the Metropolitan Police. Served as A.A.G. to the Light Division in the Pa. (gold medal and two clasps). 5th son of Robert Rowan, of Mullans, co. Antrim, by Eliza, dau. of Hill Wilson, of Purdysburn, co. Down. C.B. for Waterloo. Retired as bt. lt.-col. D. s. p. 8th May, 1852.

[3] Commanded the 52nd at Nive (gold medal). Placed on h. p. 4th May 1818 ; lt.-col. h. p. 1830. C.B. Living 1842.

[4] Afterwards Gen. Sir W. Chalmers. C.B. and K.C.H. Col.-in-Chf. 78th Highlanders. Served in Sicily, in the Walcheren expedition, and throughout the Par. War ; being present at seventeen engagements. Commanded a wing of the 52nd at Waterloo and had three horses shot under him. Bt. lt.-col., 18th June, 1815. Eldest son of Wm. Chalmers, of Glenericht, Perthshire. Bn. 1787. D. at Dundee, 2nd June, 1860.

[5] Younger brother to Sir Charles Rowan. Aftds. F.-M. Sir Wm. Rowan, G.C.B., and Col.-in-Chf. 52nd L. I. Saw much active service all over Europe, and was a highly distinguished officer. M., 1811, Martha, dau. of John Spong, of Mill Hall, Kent, and d. s. p. at Bath, 26th Sept., 1879

[6] Saw much service in the Pa. Severely wounded at Waterloo. Bt. maj. Aftds. maj.-gen., and K.H. D. at Cheltenham, 18th Sept., 1862.

[7] Probably son. of Lt.-Col. John Shedden, h. p. 114th Regt. Quitted the service before 1824 as bt. maj.

[8] Afterwards Gen. Sir James Love. K.C.B. and K.H. Inspector-Gen. of Infantry and Col.-in-Chf. 57th Regt. Served in Sweden, Spain, Portugal, and America, and received four severe wounds at Waterloo. Aftds. British Resident at Zante, and Lt.-Gov. of Jersey. Bn. 1789. Son of James Love by Mary Wyse. M., 1825, Mary, dau. of Thos. Heavyside. D. 13th Jan., 1866.

[9] Maj. in same regt. 1822. Lt.-Col. of 73rd Regt., 1830. K.H. Of Greenfield, near Glasgow. D. there, 15th April, 1836.

[10] Elder son of Wm. Gore Langton, of Combe Hay, by Jacintha, only child of Henry Powell Collins. Bn. 1789. Served at Corunna, H. p. 1817. D, 3rd March, 1860, at Stapleton Park, Bristol,

THE WATERLOO ROLL CALL.

[11] Bn. 1787, son of Wm. Cross, of Dartan, co. Armagh, by Mrs. Mary Stratford (*née* Irwin). Served with the 52nd in Sweden, Spain, and Portugal (medal with ten clasps). Subsequently commanded the 68th Regt., and retired as col. in 1843. K.H. Lt.-Gov. comg. forces in Jamaica. D. 27th Sept. 1850.

[12] Bn. in the parish of Saddleworth, Yorkshire, in 1781. Previous to enlisting in the 52nd, in 1799, worked as a cloth weaver. Corporal, 1801; sergt., 1803; sergt.-major, 1805; ensign and adjt., 1808; lieut. and adjt., 1810; paymaster, 1821. D. of yellow fever at St. Anne's, Barbados, 26th Nov., 1838. Served all through the Par. War, and was wounded on several occasions.

[13] Serving in 1817. Out of the regt. before 1824.

[14] Retd. 1821.

[15] Capt. 19th Foot 10th Jan., 1834. Out of the said regt. before 1842.

[16] Adjt. 29th May, 1823. Out of said regt. in 1829.

[17] H. p. 1st Aug., 1816.

[18] H. p. 18th Feb., 1819.

[19] Eldest son of the Rev. Sir W. H. Clerke, Bart., rector of Bury, in Lancashire, by Byzantia, eldest dau. of Thos. Cartwright, of Aynho, co. Northampton. Succeeded 1818. M., 1820, Mary, dau. of Geo. Kenrick, of Mertyn, co. Flint, and had issue. D. 1861.

[20] Afterwards Maj. 72nd Regt. Living 1830.

[21] H. p 1819.

[22] Son. of Capt. Samuel Gawler, 73rd Regt., who was killed at the storming of Fort Muggerall, 24th Dec., 1804. Bn. 21st July, 1795. Educated at R. M. College, Great Marlow. A commission was given to him in 1810 in recognition of his father's services. Served in the Pa., and led the ladder party of the stormers of the 52nd at Badajoz. An extract from his journal is given in Moorsom's *Records of the 52nd Regiment*, and graphically describes the crisis of Waterloo. If Col. Gawler claims the whole credit for the 52nd, he is at one with the rest of the officers of that gallant regt. The truth seems to be that there were two distinct columns of Napoleon's Guards launched against our troops at the close of Waterloo, and that whilst one was met and routed by our Guards in the centre, the other was attacked in flank by the 52nd and hurled back. Promoted from the 52nd to an unattached lt.-colonelcy, 12th Aug, 1834. K.H. Col. 1846. Appointed Governor and Resident Commissioner of South Australia, April, 1838. Superseded, 15th May, 1841. M., 21st Sept., 1820, Maria, eldest dau. of John Cox, of Derby, and had issue. D. 7th May, 1869. Bd. at Southsea, Portsmouth. Miss Gawler (daughter of Col. Gawler) supplied part of the above information.

[23] Ensign 10th Jan., 1811. Bn. 21st Dec., 1794. 4th son of Sir Thos. Whichcote, Bart., by Diana, dau. of Edward Turnor, of Stoke Rochford, co. Lincoln. Whichcote joined the 52nd as a volunteer in Dec., 1810, and served with the regt. in the Pa., France, and Flanders, and was present in the actions of Sabugal, El Bodon, and Alfayetes, siege and storm of Ciudad Rodrigo and of Badajoz, battle of Salamanca, retreat from Burgos, battle of Vittoria, action at Vera, battles of the Pyrenees, Nivel'e, the Nive, Orthes, Tarbes, and Toulouse (medal with nine clasps). Capt. 22nd June, 1818. Exchanged to 4th D.G. 25th July, 1822. Attained the rank of General 5th Dec., 1871. At the time of his death, which occurred 26th Aug., 1891, he was "Father of the British Army."

[24] Afterwards the Hon. Wm. Ogilvy, of Loyal, Perthshire. 4th son of Walter Ogilvy, *de jure* Earl of Airlie, by Jane, dau. of John Ogilvy, of Murkle. Saw much service in the Pa. Previous to entering the army served in the navy. Capt. 5th Oct., 1815. Exchanged to the Cape Corps. H. p. 1816. His eldest brother, in 1826, was, by Act of Parliament, recognised as Earl of Airlie with the other dignities appertaining to that title. M.P. for St. Andrews and the eastern burghs. D. in April, 1871.

[25] Afterwards in the 3rd Foot Guards. Served in the Pa. and the South of France. Of Woodcote House, Epsom, Surrey. Bn. 8th Feb., 1795. Eldest son of the Rev. Edward Northey, Canon of Windsor, by Charlotte Taylor (sister of Gen. Sir Herbert Taylor). High Sheriff for Surrey, 1856. Was twice md., and by his wife (Charlotte, dau. of Gen. Sir George Anson, G.C.B.) had issue. D. in Dec., 1878.

[26] 3rd son of Valentine, 5th Viscount Kenmare. M., 26th April, 1826, Anne, dau. of Thos. Segrave. H. p. 1817.

[27] Afterwards Maj. 81st Regt. Quitted the service with that rank. Living 1876.

[28] H. p. 49th Foot 7th Aug., 1823.

[29] Served at the siege of Ciudad Rodrigo. Lieut. 97th Foot 25th March, 1824. Capt. 51st Foot 26th Sept., 1834. Retd. on h. p. as major 42nd Highlanders 25th July, 1845.

[30] Afterwards Lt.-Col. Snodgrass. M. Maria, dau. of Maj.-Gen. Sir Archibald Campbell, Bart. D. in Nova Scotia, April, 1841, whilst holding the appointment of D.Q.M.G. in that colony.

[31] H. p. 25th July, 1816.

[32] Afterwards Colonial Sec. at Cape of Good Hope. Son of the Rev. Duke Yonge. Served in the Pa. Retired on h. p. as lieut. in 1823. D. 26th Feb., 1854.

[33] Placed on h. p. 1818. Served in the Pa., and in 1848 received the war medal with eight clasps. D. in Apr., 1861.

[34] H. p. 25th Dec., 1818.

[35] Lieut. 32nd Foot 29th Sept., 1817. Paymaster, 19th Oct., 1826. Serving in 1846.

[36] H. p. 1816. Lieut. 47th Foot, 10th Apr., 1818.

[37] Afterwards Sir Charles Shaw, K.T.S. Served in the Pa. In 1831 joined the Liberation Army of Portugal, in the Azores, as Col. of Marines on board the fleet of Sir George Sartorius, and commanded a regt. throughout the civil war in Portugal. Served in the Spanish Legion from 1835. 3rd son of Charles Shaw, of Ayr, North Berwick. M. Louisa, only dau. of Major Martin Curry, 67th Regt. D. at Homburg in 1871, and was buried there with military honours.

[38] Lieut. 4th Lt. Dns., 5th July, 1821. Capt. 16th June, 1825. H. p. 1827.

[39] Lieut. 25th Foot 13th Dec., 1821. Serving 1824.

[40] Placed on h. p. 1817. Eldest son of Sir Henry Oakes, Bart., by Dorothea, dau. of George Bowles, of Mount Prospect, co. Cork. M., 1st May, 1817, Frances, 5th dau. of Wm. Douglas, of Teddington, Middlesex, and had issue. Succeeded his father in 1827. D. 30th Sept., 1850.

[41] Adjt. to the 52nd after the battle of Waterloo, *vice* Winterbottom wounded. H. p. 1816. Living 1830.

[42] H. p. 1816.

[43] H. p. 1816.

[44] H. p. 1816.

[45] H. p. 1816.   D. 1829.

[46] Retd. before 1st Jan., 1816.

[47] Lieut. 28th Sept., 1815.   Retd. before 1st Jan., 1817.

[48] One of the five sons of Capt. Robert Nettles, of Nettleville, co. Cork, by Esther, dau. of John Conran, of Dublin.   Killed whilst carrying the King's colours, which were aftds. found under his body on the field of battle.

[49] Lieut. 17th July, 1817.   H. p. 25th Dec., 1818.

[50] The following creditable conduct of this young officer is narrated by Capt. Moorsom in the *History of the* 52*nd* :—"Ensign John Montague was ordered to the rear with a detachment of invalids a few days before Waterloo, and had gone back a day's march, when he met a party proceeding to the front to join the 52nd.   As an engagement was daily expected he asked the date of commission of the young officer proceeding to Waterloo, and, finding himself the senior, assumed command of the whole—directed the junior to proceed with the invalids, while he (Montague) returned to his regt. By so doing he was able to be present at the great conflict."   Capt. in 40th Regt. 7th Aug., 1823.   Living 1830.

[51] Younger bro. of Sir John May, R.A.   Bn. 31st March, 1898.   Lieut. 29th Jan., 1818.   Capt. 57th Foot, 1st Aug., 1826.   Exchanged to 41st Foot 10th Aug. same year.   Major of last-named regt. at time of his death, which occurred on board the *Orontes*, near the Cape of Good Hope, 2nd June, 1837.

[52] Afterwards Maj.-Gen. Eaton Monins, younger brother to Wm. Monins of 18th Hussars.   D. at Walmer 16th June, 1861.

[53] Son of Samuel Leeke, of Havant, Hants.   Promoted lieut. 20th Nov., 1823.   Quitted the service 1824.   Entered as fellow commoner at Queen's College, Cambridge, 1825.   Ordained Jan., 1829, to curacy of West Ham, Pevensey.   Curate of Brailsford, Derby, 1831.   Incumbent of Holbrooke, co. Derby, 1840.   M., in Oct., 1828, to Mary Anne, dau. of John Cox, of Derby.   D. at Holbrooke 6th June, 1879.   (Communicated by Miss Gawler.) Mr. Leeke wrote and published *Lord Seaton's Regiment at Waterloo*, a book that attracted considerable attention at the time.

[54] H. p. 1830.   D. 1855.

69TH (OR THE SOUTH LINCOLNSHIRE) REGIMENT OF FOOT.

(*2nd Battalion.*)

	Rank in the	
LIEUT.-COLONEL.	Regiment.	Army.
[1] Charles Morice, K.	4 June, 1813	Col. 4 June, 1814

MAJOR.

[2] George Muttlebury	28 Nov. 1811	Lt.-Col., 17 Mar. [1814

CAPTAINS.

[3] J. Lewis Watson	9 July, 1803	Maj., 4 June, 1813
[4] Henry Lindsay, w.	9 July, 1803	Maj., 4 June, 1814
Hon. Wm. Curzon, K.	17 Dec. 1812	
[5] Geo. Sackville Cotter	3 June, 1813	
[6] Charles Cuyler	10 June, 1813	
[7] Benjamin Hobhouse, K.	12 Aug. 1813	
[8] George Ulrick Barlow	30 Dec. 1813	
[9] Robert Blackwood, K.		8 Nov. 1813

LIEUTENANTS.

[10] Wm. Harrison	27 Jan. 1808	
[11] Roger Franklyn	18 Apr. 1810	
[12] Stephen Parker	11 Apr. 1811	
[13] Brooke Pigot, w.	9 May, 1811	
[14] Christopher Busteed, w.	25 Jan. 1813	15 Jan. 1813
[15] Neil Roy	1 July, 1813	
[16] Chas. Wm. Ingle	1 Feb. 1814	
[17] Joseph Hill	2 Feb. 1814	
[18] Henry Oldershaw, Adjt.	3 Feb. 1814	
[19] Charles Lenox Dickson	21 Apr. 1814	
[20] Edm. Martin Wightwick, K.	5 May, 1814	
[21] John Stewart, w.	10 Nov. 1814	
[22] Henry Anderson, w.	15 June, 1815	

69TH (OR THE SOUTH LINCOLNSHIRE) REGIMENT OF FOOT—*continued.*

	Rank in the	
ENSIGNS.	Regiment.	Army.
[23] Edward Hodder, w.	29 July, 1813	
[24] Wm. Bartlett	3 Feb. 1814	
[25] Charles Seward	24 Feb. 1814	
[26] Henry Duncan Keith	21 Apr. 1814	
[27] Geo. S. H. Ainslie	10 Nov. 1814	
[28] Christopher Clarke, w. (Volunteer).		

PAYMASTER.

[29] Philip Vyvian   28 Jan. 1813

QUARTERMASTER.

[30] Matthew Stevens   6 Dec. 1810

SURGEON.

Clement Banks   5 June, 1806

ASSISTANT-SURGEON.

James Bartlett   16 July, 1812

Facings green.   Lace gold.

[1] Had been wounded in the previous year in the night attack on Bergen-op-Zoom. Killed at Quatre Bras. His death, and that of many of the men of the 69th, was entirely due to the inexperience of the Prince of Orange, who stopped Col. Morice from forming square, and ordered him to re-form column.

[2] C.B. for Waterloo. "Section after section of the 69th was swept off by the enemy's artillery at Waterloo, whilst the French cavalry repeatedly surrounded the devoted regt. ; but whenever the smoke cleared off, there it stood firm and undaunted." Lt.-Col. of this regt. in July, 1817. M., 31st October, 1828, Mrs. Brown, of Cavendish Place, Bath. D. 11th Jan., 1854.

[3] Bt. lt.-col. for Waterloo. Maj. 71st Highlanders, 1819. Retd. on h. p., 1829. D. at Leasingham Hall, Lincoln, 12th April, 1842.

[4] Severely wounded at Quatre Bras in defending the colours. H. p. 16th Dec., 1819. His name disappeared from the *Army List* after 1827.

[5] 2nd son of the Rev. George Sackville Cotter, by Margaret, dau. of Bayly Rogers, of Cork. Placed on h. p. 1st Dec., 1816. Aftds. settled in

Canada, where he held the rank of col. in the volunteers. His experiences at Quatre Bras and Waterloo are given in Capt. (aftds. Gen. Sir Wm.) Butler's *Historical Events Connected with the 69th Regiment.* D. in Canada, 9th April, 1869, leaving issue by his wife, Jane, dau. and co-heir of Wm. Crofts, of Danesfort, co. Cork.

[6] Afterwards Sir Charles Cuyler, Bart. Eldest son of Gen. Sir Cornelius Cuyler, Bart., by Anne, dau. of Maj. Grant. M., 6th Feb., 1823, Catherine, dau. of the Rev. Fitzwilliam Halifax, and had issue. Lt.-Col. 69th Regt., 1826. D. 23rd July, 1862.

[7] 2nd son of Sir Benjamin Hobhouse, Bart., by his first wife, Charlotte, dau. and heir of Samuel Cam, of Chantry House, Wilts. Acted as orderly officer to Sir Colin Halkett at Waterloo, and being a conspicuous figure on a fine horse, was a mark for the enemy's bullets.

[8] Eldest son of Sir George Barlow, Bart., of Fort William, Bengal, by Eliz., dau. of Burton Smith. Bn. 8th Oct., 1791. Exchanged to the 4th Lt. Dns., 5th April, 1821. M., 27th Feb., 1817, Hilare, 3rd dau. of Capt. Sir R. Barlow, R.N., K.C.B. D. s. p. in India, 1824. His widow remarried, 1829, Wm., Earl Nelson.

[9] Eldest son of the Hon. and Rev. Hans Blackwood, who succeeded his brother, in 1836, as Baron Dufferin. Bn. 13th July, 1788. Buried in the orchard at Hougomont.

[10] Capt. 13th Aug., 1815. H. p. 25th Nov., 1816.

[11] H. p. 25th March, 1826.

[12] Capt. 62nd Foot, 25th June, 1830. D. at Pau in May, 1853.

[13] Capt. 29th Aug., 1826. Retd. f. p. Nov., 1840.

[14] D. at Mullingar as lieut. in above regt., 4th Nov., 1828. His Waterloo medal was formerly in the Tancred collection.

[15] Serving in 1824. Out of the regt. before 1830.

[16] H. p. 25th April, 1826.

[17] Retd. 1835 as capt.

[18] Qr.-mr. 33rd Foot 3rd Aug., 1832. Serving 1842.

[19] H. p. 7th Sept., 1826. D. May, 1860.

[20] D. 17th June, 1815, from wounds received at Quatre Bras; 5th son of Wm. Wightwick, of New Romney, Kent.

[21] H. p. 1816.

[22] "Bn. in co. Kilkenny. Obtained his ensigncy through the interest of the Marquis of Ormonde. Served at the bombardment of Antwerp and at Bergen-op-Zoom. Slightly wounded at Quatre Bras by a ricochetting bullet; served as a lieut. of the light company at Waterloo, and near the close of the battle was shot through the left lung, the ball making its exit at the back, breaking the scapula. He aftds. served in the 75th Foot. Was for 26 years commandant of the Invalid Depôt at Chatham, and d. in 1860, having attained the rank of colonel." Communicated by above officer's son Major-Gen. E. A. Anderson.

[23] 7th son of Geo. Hodder, of Fountainstown, co. Cork. H. p. lieut., 1826. Living in 1855.

[24] Lieut. 10th Aug., 1815. H. p. 25th April, 1826.

S 5473.

[25] Lieut. 11th Aug., 1815. H. p. 25th Nov., 1816.

[26] Lieut. 14th Aug., 1815. Exchanged to 2nd Foot, 25th Jan., 1825. Serving 1830.

[27] Afterwards served in the 1st Dragoons. Assumed the surname of Harcourt. Placed on h. p. as cornet, 1822.   D. at Bedford, 29th Dec., 1867, aged 72.

[28] A cadet from the Military College. Greatly distinguished himself at Quatre Bras, where the 69th was badly cut up by Kellermann's Cuirassiers. He killed three cuirassiers before he himself fell covered with 22 sabre cuts. Recovered from his wounds, and was rewarded with an ensigncy in the 42nd Highlanders. He d in 1831 as a subaltern in 33rd Foot. Sir W. Butler's *Records of* 69*th Regt.* (London, 1870).

[29] Assumed the surname of Robinson. H. p. 88th Foot, 28th June, 1827.

[30] This was " the same man who, eighteen years before, at St. Vincent, had broken the stern galley window of the *San Nicholas,* and led the way for Nelson to the quarter-deck of the Spanish vessel."   He appears to have been a Scotchman, with a keen sense of humour, as, when a man was killed by his side, by a long shot from the enemy, on the morning of Waterloo Day, he quietly remarked, " Aweel, it is time for a respectable non-combatant to gang awa' ! "—Sir W. Butler's *Records of* 69*th Regt.*   D. as Qr.-mr. 69th Foot, at Cannanore, India, 1821.

71st (HIGHLAND) REGIMENT OF FOOT (LIGHT INFANTRY).

	Rank in the	
LIEUT.-COLONEL.	Regiment.	Army.
1 Thomas Reynell, w.	5 Aug. 1813	Col., 4 June, 1813
MAJORS.		
2 Arthur Jones, w.	22 June, 1809	Lt.-Col., 4 June,
3 Leslie Walker	2 Sept. 1813	[1814
CAPTAINS.		
4 Samuel Reed	29 Sept. 1808	29 Nov. 1806
5 Joseph T. Pidgeon	1 Dec. 1808	
6 Archibald Armstrong	10 May, 1809	
7 Donald Campbell, w.	22 June, 1809	
Edmund L'Estrange, k.	6 July, 1809	Maj., 12 Apr. 1814
8 Wm. Alex. Grant, w.	12 Oct. 1809	
9 James Henderson, w.	19 Oct. 1809	
10 Augustus J. M'Intyre	17 May, 1810	
11 Charles Johnstone, w.	10 Dec. 1812	Maj., 4 June, 1814
12 Alexander Grant	15 Apr. 1813	
LIEUTENANTS.		
13 Joseph Barailler, w.	7 Feb. 1808	
14 Loftus Richards	21 Apr. 1808	
15 John Raleigh Elwes, w.	12 May, 1808	
16 Charles Stewart	29 Dec. 1808	
17 Robert Baldwin	11 May, 1809	
18 Wm. Crosbie Hanson	6 July, 1809	
19 Robert Lind, w.	10 Oct. 1809	
20 John Roberts, w.	12 Oct. 1809	
21 James Coates, w.	13 Oct. 1809	
22 John Fraser	17 Oct. 1809	
23 Edward Gilborne	18 Oct. 1809	
24 John Witney	19 Oct. 1809	
25 William Long	14 June, 1810	
26 Robert Law, w.	27 May, 1811	
27 Charles T. Cox	29 May, 1811	
28 Carique Lewin, w.	27 June, 1811	

71st (HIGHLAND) REGIMENT OF FOOT (LIGHT INFANTRY)—*continued.*

	LIEUTENANTS—*continued.*	Rank in the Regiment.	Army.
29	Wm. Woolcombe	9 Sept. 1811	
30	Wm. Torriano	12 Dec. 1811	
31	George Wm. Horton	23 Jan. 1812	25 July, 1811
32	John Coote, w.	27 May, 1812	
33	Wm. Anderson, Adjt., w.	7 Aug. 1812	
34	Chas. Moorhead	3 Sept. 1812	
35	David Soutar	24 Sept. 1812	
36	Norman Campbell	14 Apr. 1814	

ENSIGNS.

37	Abraham Moffatt	5 Aug. 1813
38	Wm. Smith	1 Sept. 1813
39	Henry Walker Thompson	16 Sept. 1813
	John Todd, K.	18 Nov. 1813
40	John Barnett	25 Nov. 1813
41	Archibald M. Henderson	25 Dec. 1813
42	John Spalding	28 Jan. 1814
43	John Impett	14 Apr. 1814
44	Anthony R. L'Estrange	7 Dec. 1814
45	Rob. Copley (Volunteer)	

PAYMASTER.

46	Hugh Mackenzie	8 Nov. 1798

QUARTERMASTER.

Wm. Gavin	2 Apr. 1812

SURGEON.

47	Arthur Stewart	3 Sept. 1812

ASSISTANT-SURGEONS.

John Winterscale	8 Feb. 1810
Samuel Hill	22 Mar. 1810

*Facings **buff**.   Lace silver.*

[1] Afterwards Gen. Sir T. Reynell, Bart., K.C.B., Col.-in-Chf. 71st L.I. 3rd son of Thomas Reynell (who was killed at the battle of Saratoga, in America, in 1777), by Anne, dau. of Samuel Coutty, of Kinsale. Served in Egypt in 1801. Recd. the orders of St. George of Russia and Maria Theresa of Austria for his services at Waterloo, in addition to the C.B. Commanded a division at the siege of Bhurtpore, and received the thanks of both Houses of Parliament. M., 12th Feb., 1831, Lady Eliz. Pack, widow of Maj.-Gen. Sir Denis Pack, and d. s. p.

[2] The following memoir of Col. Jones's services appeared in the *United Service Journal* for 1837 :—" Nov. 12th, on Lake Erie, Upper Canada, Lt.-Col. Arthur Jones, C.B., late of the 71st Highland L.I. This officer was appointed Ensign 36th Foot, 1st Jan., 1795 ; Lt. 71st Foot 5th Oct., 1795 ; Capt., 24th March, 1803 ; Maj., 22nd June, 1809 ; and Bt. Lt.-Col., 4th June, 1814. He served at Madras from his first appointment to October, 1797, when his regiment embarked for Europe. In August, 1805, he sailed, with the expedition under Lt. Gen. Sir D. Baird, for the Cape of Good Hope ; he was present with the regt. at the action on the 8th Jan., 1806 ; and also at the surrender of the town and castle of Cape Town on the 10th. He em barked at the Cape in April following, with his regt., on the expedition to South America, under Gen. Beresford. On the 25th June, the landing of this small force was effected at the point of Quilmes, up the River Plate, without opposition. He was present in the affairs of the 26th and 27th, which terminated in the surrender of the city of Buenos Ayres to the British ; and was with the troops employed in dispersing the enemy from the vicinity of the city, on the 1st August ; at the defending of the city on the 10th, 11th, and 12th, when the British were obliged to capitulate, and become prisoners of war ; and was marched, as such, a considerable distance into the interior of the country. He next served with the army in Portugal, and was present at the action of Roleia, and battle of Vimiero. He served under the late Sir John Moore in Spain ; was present the whole of that campaign, and at the battle of Corunna. He embarked in July, 1809, on the expedition to the Scheldt, and was present at the siege of Flushing ; he returned with his regt. to England in December, and in May, 1810, was ordered to join the 2nd batt. in Scotland ; and shortly after the command of the batt. devolved on him. In Jan., 1814, he proceeded to join the 1st batt. in Spain, landed at St. Sebastian, and marched in charge of a detachment for the 2nd division of the army, which he joined in Aire on the 10th of March, and served with it in the different operations that took place against the enemy from that period until a short time after the battle of Toulouse, 10th April, 1814. In Feb., 1815, he embarked with the 71st Light Infantry for North America, but was countermanded, and they pro-ceeded in April to Belgium, and he was present with it at the battle of Waterloo. He remained with the regt., which formed part of the Army of Occupation, until October, 1818, when he embarked with it for England, and for Ireland in May, 1822. The command of the regt. devolved on him in May, 1824, when he embarked with it for North America, and was promoted lt.-col., 2nd June, 1825 ; he remained in command of the regt. till June, 1831. Lt.-Col. Jones was wounded when capt. at the battle of Vimiero ; and wounded severely when bt. lt.-col. at the battle of Waterloo, late in the evening. For his services, and particularly for his conduct at Waterloo, stated by Maj.-Gen. Sir F. Adam (then Commander of the 3rd British Light Brigade) in a letter to the Duke of Wellington, and from his Grace's recommendation in consequence, Lt.-Col. Jones was appointed a Companion of the Bath."

[3] C.B. for Waterloo.   Exchanged in 1819 to 54th Regt. Bt. lt.-col., 31st Aug., 1815. Lt.-col., unattached, 1st July, 1828. Living 1830.

[4] Bt.-maj. for Waterloo.   Retd. on h. p. 1821.   Lt.-col., h. p. 1837. D. 13th July, 1842.

[5] Retd. as lt.-col. in 1841 by the sale of his commission. He held the Par. medal with 8 clasps. D. in Oct., 1850.

[6] Serving in 1817. Out of the regt. before 1824.

[7] Retd. f. p. 2nd Rl. Veteran Batt., 1821.

[8] Serving in 1817. Out of the regt. before 1824.

[9] Serving as senior capt. in 1830. Out of the regt. before 1842.

[10] H. p. 56th Foot 31st Dec., 1818.

[11] Capt. and bt.-major h. p. Rifle Brigade, 6th Apr., 1820.

[12] Serving in 1830. Out of the regt. before 1842.

[13] Capt. in 37th Foot in 1820. Living 1825.

[14] Belonged to the family of "Richards of Macmine," co. Wexford. Placed on h. p. 25th Feb., 1816. Living 1825.

[15] D. a few days after Waterloo from his wounds. Youngest son of Col. Elwes, and brother of Sir W. Elwes, Bart. He had been only ten months married to a dau. of Col. Aird, Rl. Waggon Train.

[16] Capt. 27th July, 1820. Major 24th May, 1836. H. p. 24th Apr., 1838. D. 24th Dec., 1851, as lt.-col.

[17] H. p. 7th Fusiliers, 6th June, 1816.

[18] Capt. 16th May, 1822. Serving 1830.

[19] Belonged to a respectable family in the county of Antrim. "He received a grape shot at Waterloo, weighing 10 oz., which he kept as a relic, hooped in silver. The shot entered at the breast, and was cut out at the shoulder three days after." D. at Waterloo Cottage, Cookstown, co. Antrim, 3rd July, 1851, aged 70.

[20] Capt. 7th Apr., 1825. H. p. 6th June, 1827. D. as bt.-major 16th Jan., 1854.

[21] Was fifteen years a lt. in this regt. M. the only dau. of John Wilson town clerk of Lanark ; she d. at Lanark in Dec., 1815.

[22] Joined the 71st Regt. as a private when sixteen years of age. Eight years after he received an ensign's commission for distinguished gallantry. At the taking of the Cape of Good Hope was one of a party of thirty who volunteered to storm a battery. John Fraser was the only man of this Forlorn Hope who lived to return, and he was not unwounded. At Buenos Ayres he was publicly complimented by Sir Denis Pack for his conspicuous gallantry. Placed on h. p. before 1820, and d. at Edinburgh, 20th June, 1824.

[23] H. p. 1818.

[24] Serving in 1817. Out of the regt. before 1824.

[25] Capt. 31st Oct., 1822. Retd. as h. p. maj. 9th Foot, 1838. D. in March, 1860.

[26] Capt. 18th Oct., 1821. Exchanged to 33rd Foot 20th March, 1823. Capt. Ceylon Rifles 25th Sept., 1824. Serving 1830.

[27] Afterwards Lt. C. T. Cox, h. p. 71st Highland Light Infantry. Entered the Army in 1809. Was engaged in numerous battles during the campaigns from 1810 to 1815, including the retreat to and the occupation of the lines of Torres Vedras, Vittoria, Pyrenees, Nivelle, Nive, Orthes, Tarbes, and Toulouse. At Vittoria he was sev. wnded, a musket ball having passed through the lungs and lodged in the body. He was taken prisoner, but the enemy being hard pressed, he was left on the field. He was present at the capture of Paris. Commissions dated: Ensign, June 29, 1809 ; Lt., May 29, 1811. D. 1875.

[28] 3rd son of James Lewin, of Cloghans, co. Mayo. Retd. on h. p. as a lt. from 19th Lt. Dns. in 1822. D. s. p. 1844.

[29] H. p. 25th Oct., 1821.

[30] Son of Capt. Torriano, 30th Foot, who was killed in action at Toulon, 15th Oct., 1793, and grandson of Capt. C. Torriano, R.A., wounded and disabled for life at the battle of Laffeldt, 1st July, 1747. Lieut. Wm. Torriano joined the 1st Batt. 71st in 1811 and proceeded to Portugal. Promoted lieut. into 2nd Batt. at home, but remained with 1st Batt. in the field until the return of the army from France. Was present at Arroyos des Molinos, Almaraz, with covering army before Badajoz ; severely wounded at Vittoria and taken prisoner,but shortly after retaken at Nive; Bayonne (twice wounded); Orthes, and Toulouse, besides many minor affairs. A French reserve battery was captured by the 71st towards the close of the battle of Waterloo, and Siborne (Vol. II., p. 234) narrates how "some men of the right flank company of the 71st, under Lieut. Torriano, immediately turned round one of the guns, which was then discharged into the retiring columns of the Imperial Guard by Capt. Campbell, A.D.C. to Major-General Adam, and was, there is reason to believe, the last French gun fired on that day." Adjt. 18th Oct., 1821. Retd. 1824 by the sale of his commission. D. at Budleigh Salterton, Devonshire, 1862. Above information communicated by Col. C. Torriano, late R.A.

[31] 2nd son of Thomas Horton, of Howroyde, co. York, by Lady Mary Gordon, dau. of George, 3rd Earl of Aberdeen. Served in the Pa. Capt. 81st Regt. 1820 ; Bt.-maj. 1821 ; Lt.-col., unattached, 1826 ; Col. 1842. M., 1826, Frances, dau. of Rev. Wm. Garnier, rector of Rookesbury, Hants, and had issue. Living 1876.

[32] Retd. f. p. 1821. D. at Halifax, N.S., 1st Oct., 1852.

[33] H. p. 25th Dec., 1818.

[34] H. p. 25th Dec., 1818.

[35] Lieut. Connaught Rangers 7th Jan., 1819. Capt. 2nd Feb., 1830. Paymaster 71st Foot 1843. D. 16th Dec., 1849.

[36] H. p. 25th Dec., 1818.

[37] H. p. 1816.

[38] H. p. 1816. D. in Apr., 1860.

[39] Lieut. h. p. 74th Foot, 1822.

[40] Lieut. 23rd Nov., 1815. H. p. 61st Foot 12th Sept., 1822. D. as lt.-col. 3rd West York Militia, at Dublin, 24th Feb., 1855.

[41] H. p. 27th Foot 22nd May, 1817.

[42] Lieut. 25th Foot 30th March, 1826. Serving 1830.

[43] Capt. 6th Feb., 1835.   H. p. Jan., 1841.

[44] Afterwards maj. in this regt., and retired on f. p. in 1852.   Youngest brother to Maj. L'Estrange, of same regt., who fell at Waterloo.   D. at Edinburgh, 1873.

[45] Commissioned ensign in above regt. 22nd June, 1815.   H. p. 1816. Living 1830.

[46] H. p. 1824.   D. 25th June, 1854.

[47] Inspector-Gen. of Hospitals 1845.   H. p. same year.   D. 1854.

73rd (HIGHLAND) REGIMENT OF FOOT.

(2nd Battalion.)

	Rank in the	
LIEUT.-COLONEL.	Regiment.	Army.
1 Wm. George Harris, w.	29 Dec. 1806	Col., 4 June, 1814

MAJORS.

Dawson Kelly	31 Oct. 1811	
2 Arch. John Maclean, w.	28 May, 1812	

CAPTAINS.

3 Henry Coane, w.	8 Mar. 1810	8 Feb. 1810
Alexander Robertson, k.	21 Nov. 1810	
4 Wm. Wharton, w.	13 Aug. 1812	
John M. Kennedy, k.	8 Oct. 1812	
5 John Garland, w.	26 Nov. 1813	

LIEUTENANTS.

6 Richard Leyne	2 Feb. 1809	
7 Jos. Wm. H. Strachan, k.	11 Oct. 1810	26 Oct. 1809
John R. McConnell, w.	8 Aug. 1811	
John Acres, k.	20 Nov. 1811	
Matthew Hollis, k.	12 Dec. 1811	
8 Joseph Dowling	13 Aug. 1812	
9 Thos. Reynolds, w.	10 Mar. 1814	
10 Donald Browne, w.	24 Mar. 1814	
11 John Y. Lloyd, w.	4 Aug. 1814	
12 Robert Stewart (*sic*)	11 Aug. 1814	

ENSIGNS.

13 Robert Greville Hesilrige, w.	17 Sept. 1810	
14 Wm. MacBean, w.	1 Apr. 1813	
15 Thomas Deacon, w.	5 Apr. 1813	
16 Chas. Bedford Eastwood, w.	6 Apr. 1813	
17 George Dandridge Bridge, w.	7 Apr. 1813	
18 George Hughes	29 Apr. 1813	
Wm. Lawson Lowe, k.	19 Aug. 1813	
19 Aldworth Blennerhassett	23 Mar. 1814	
20 Charles Page, k.	10 Aug. 1814	
21 Patrick Hay, Adjt., w.	19 Jan. 1815	

73RD (HIGHLAND) REGIMENT OF FOOT—*continued.*

PAYMASTER.	Rank in the Regiment.	Army.
John Williams	31 May, 1810	

SURGEON.

[22] Duncan McDearmid	5 Sept. 1811	24 Jan. 1811

ASSISTANT-SURGEONS.

[23] John Rioch	2 July, 1812	
[24] Frederick B. White	23 Mar. 1815	

Facings dark green.   Lace gold.

[1] Afterwards Lt.-Gen. Lord Harris, K.C.H. and C.B., Col.-in-Chf., 73rd Regt. Son of the famous Gen. Sir George Harris, of Seringapatam renown, who was created a baron in Aug., 1815. Bn. 17th Jan., 1782. Served under his father in India, and was one of the first to enter the breach at Seringapatam. At Waterloo the 73rd were literally cut to pieces, and at the close of the battle only fifty unwounded men were left out of a total of from 500 to 600 men. " Once, and once only, during the dreadful carnage at Waterloo did the stern 73rd hesitate to fill up a gap which the relentless iron had torn in their square. Their Colonel, at once pushing his horse lengthwise across the space, said, with a smile, 'Well, my lads, if you won't, I must.' Immediately his horse was led back to his proper place and the ranks closed up by men still more devoted than before." C.B. and K.W. for Waterloo. Was twice md., and left issue by both wives. D. 30th May, 1845.

[2] D. from his wounds at Brussels. Bn. 16th June, 1778. 4th son of Gilbert Maclaine, of Scalasdale, in the island of Mull.

[3] There were two capts. of this name in the 73rd in 1815, Anthony and Henry. The former d. at Kandy, Ceylon, as maj., 5th Jan., 1819. The latter quitted the service in 1820. The Coanes are Irish, but a branch was settled at Bath in 1815.

[4] Served in the Pa., and was present at Fuentes d'Onor and siege of Badajoz. Was with the 85th in the Walcheren expedition, and with the 73rd during the campaigns of 1813 and 1814 in Swedish Pomerania, Hanover, and the Netherlands. Severely wounded at Waterloo, being shot through both thighs by a musket ball. Retired on h. p. 1st June, 1820. D. in 1855.

[5] Son of John Garland, of Dorchester. Was desperately wounded at Waterloo. After the battle he was carried to Brussels, and after months of suffering was able to return to Dorchester. He was not then expected to recover, and by some error his death was reported in the papers in the autumn of 1816. Here is the *first* obituary notice in the *Gentleman's Magazine* :—" At his father's, Dorchester, Capt. John Garland, 73rd Foot. He was in most of the Peninsular battles, and was desperately wounded at Waterloo at the close of the action, only two men of his company being then left, and was confined at Brussels until his recent return to England."

But John Garland did *not* die in 1816, and lived to become a bt. maj. on unattached list in 1825, and a bt. lt.-col. in 1838. His *second* obituary notice is given in the *Annual Register* for 1851 :—"Jan. 17. At Lille, Lt.-Col. John Garland, K.H., late of Quatre Bras Cottage, Dorchester, who was severely wounded at Waterloo."

6 Capt. 2nd Aug., 1815. Eldest son of Dr. Maurice Leyne, of Tralee, by Agnes, dau. of Cornelius the McGillicuddy of the Reeks. Bn. 1790. Served first in the Kerry Militia comded. by Col. Crosbie. Joined the 73rd with 400 volunteers from his militia regt., the latter being induced to join the regular army by Leyne. His zeal was rewarded with a lieutenancy in the 73rd. At Waterloo succeeded to the command of the regt. and kept it as long as the regt. was in France. Placed on h. p. 5th July, 1817. Subsequently joined the 58th Foot for a few years and served in New South Wales. Md. in 1817, Eliz., dau. of James Connor, of Tralee, Clerk of the Peace for Kerry. Capt. Leyne was for some years a stipendiary magistrate. Above information communicated by Mr. Leyne, son of Capt. R. Leyne.

7 Serving in 1817. Out of the regt. before 1824.

8 Lieut. 1st Rl. Veteran Batt. 27th Nov., 1823. Barrack-master at Coventry in 1830.

9 H. p. 12th Foot 1824.

10 Had his left arm amputated after the battle, and d. shortly after.

11 Capt. 3rd Feb. 1820. Major 20th March, 1828. Serving in 1830.

12 Eldest son of Robt. Steuart, of Brownlee, Lanarkshire. H. p. 25th Dec., 1818. Restored to full pay 1819. Capt. 91st Foot, 3rd March, 1825. H. p. unat. 19th June, 1826. D. 5th Nov., 1849. Above information was communicated by Capt. Alex. Steuart, Queensland Defence Force, great nephew to Capt. Robt. Steuart.

13 3rd son of Col. Grey Haselrigge, by Bridget, dau. of Rev. Richard Buckley, and a direct descendant of Col. Sir Arthur Haselrigge, Bart., the Parliamentary commander, whose regt. of cuirassiers, known as the " Lobsters," performed some signal service during the Civil Wars. Bn. 23rd Oct., 1796 Quitted the service as lieut. D. unm.

14 D. as lieut. in 1819.

15 Lieut. 3rd Aug., 1815. Lieut. 16th Foot 6th Feb., 1822. 1st Lieut. Ceylon Rifles 12th Jan., 1824. Capt. 29th Apr., 1836. H. p. 7th Sept., 1836. Living 1846. Sergt. Thos. Morris, of the 73rd, in his *Recollections of Military Service*, records that Ensign Deacon was shot through an arm at Quatre Bras and conveyed by the baggage-train to Brussels. "The officer's wife, who with her three children had been left with the baggage guard, passed the whole night in searching for her husband among the wounded. At length she was informed he had been conveyed to Brussels. . . . Conveyances there were none to be had, and she was in the last state of pregnancy. She made the best of her way on foot with her children, exposed to the terrific storm of thunder, lightning, and rain, which continued without intermission for about ten hours. Faint, exhausted, and wet to the skin, having no other clothes but a black silk dress and light shawl, she yet happily surmounted all these difficulties, reached Brussels on the morning of the 18th, and found her husband in very comfortable quarters, where she also was accommodated, the next day giving birth to a fine girl, who was afterwards christened ' Waterloo Deacon.' "

[16] Lieut. 4th Aug., 1815. Exchanged to 3rd Ceylon Regt.. and was placed on h. p. 11th June, 1818.

[17] Lieut. 3rd Oct., 1815. H. p. 1817.

[18] Lieut. 4th Oct., 1815. H. p. 3rd Aug.. 1822.

[19] Lieut. 5th Oct., 1815. Lieut. 38th Foot 1st Dec.. 1823. Capt. 26th Aug., 1834. H. p. 1838. Living 1846.

[20] Son of Mr. Wm. Page, of Fitzroy Square, London. An autograph letter from aforesaid gentleman, written in Nov., 1815, addressed to " Capt. Leyne, commanding H.B.M. 73rd Regt., Camp near Boulogne, France," is still in possession of the Leyne family, and bears testimony to the writer's appreciation of Capt. Leyne's expressions of deep sympathy with the bereaved father on the death of his brave son.

[21] Lieut. 13th Feb., 1816. Capt. 7th Feb., 1822. Serv ng 1824.

[22] D. in Oct., 1830.

[23] Retd. as surgeon h. p. 67th Foot in 1841. Living 1846.

[24] H. p. 25th June, 1817. Living 1830

79TH REGIMENT OF FOOT (OR CAMERON HIGH-LANDERS).*

Rank in the

LIEUT.-COLONEL.	Regiment.	Army.
1 Neil Douglas, w.	3 Dec. 1812	

MAJORS.		[1813
2 Andrew Brown, w.	15 Oct. 1812	Lt.-Col., 26 Aug.
3 Duncan Cameron, w.	29 Oct. 1812	Lt.-Col., 12 Apr.
		[1814

CAPTAINS.		
4 Thomas Mylne, w.	24 Apr. 1805	
5 Peter Innes	4 Sept. 1805	
6 James Campbell, w.	5 Sept. 1805	
7 Neil Campbell, w.	8 Apr. 1806	
8 William Marshall, w.	19 July, 1806	
9 Malcolm Fraser, w.	29 Nov. 1806	
10 Wm. Bruce, w.	14 Mar. 1811	
11 John Sinclair, w.	4 May, 1811	
Robert Mackay, κ.	2 Apr. 1812	
12 John Cameron, w.	26 May, 1814	

LIEUTENANTS.		
13 Alexander Cameron, w.	12 May, 1807	
Donald Cameron, κ.	13 May, 1807	
14 Thomas Brown, w.	15 Dec. 1807	
15 Wm. Maddocks, w.	21 Apr. 1808	25 July, 1801
16 Wm. Leaper, w.	15 Dec. 1808	
17 James Fraser, w.	16 Mar. 1809	
Duncan M'Pherson, κ.	19 July, 1810	
18 Donald M'Phee, w.	29 Nov. 1810	
19 Fulton Robertson	21 Feb. 1811	
20 Ewen Cameron, w.	29 May, 1811	
John Kynock, Adjt., κ.	13 June, 1811	
21 Alexander Forbes, w.	8 Aug. 1811	
22 Charles McArthur, w.	17 Oct. 1811	
23 Kewan Izod Leslie	1 Apr. 1812	
24 John Powling, w.	15 Oct. 1812	
25 James Cameron	25 Jan. 1813	11 July, 1811

79TH REGIMENT OF FOOT (OR CAMERON HIGH-LANDERS)—*continued.*

		Rank in the Regiment.	Army.
LIEUTENANTS—*continued.*			
	Ewen Kennedy, ᴋ.	25 Feb. 1813	
26	W. A. Riach, w.	17 June, 1813	
27	John Thompson	18 Nov. 1813	
28	George Harrison	2 Mar. 1815	
ENSIGNS.			
29	John Mackenzie	24 Dec. 1812	
30	Chas. Jas. McLean	17 June, 1813	
31	John Nash, w.	18 Nov. 1813	
32	James Robertson, w.	6 Jan. 1814	
33	Archibald Cameron	13 Jan. 1814	
34	Alex. Spiers Crawford, w.	18 May, 1814	
35	James Campbell	19 May, 1814	
36	Alex. Cameron (Volr.), w.		
PAYMASTER.			
37	John McArthur	21 Nov. 1811	
QUARTERMASTER.			
38	Angus Cameron	13 Feb. 1812	
SURGEON.			
	George Ridesdale	9 Sept. 1813	
ASSISTANT-SURGEONS.			
	Wm. G. Burrell	14 Dec. 1809	13 July, 1809
	David Perston	18 Oct. 1810	1 Feb. 1810

Facings dark green.   Lace gold.

* The Cameron Highlanders were raised in Jan., 1794, by Lt.-Gen. Sir Alan Cameron, K.C.B. (then Maj. Cameron), who was their first colonel. The officers were mostly selected from the half-pay list, and had served, like their colonel, in the American war. The regt. served during the campaign in Holland, and the mortality was so great that, in 1799, this Scotch regt. had to be again raised. The call for officers and men was nobly responded to by the Clan Cameron :—

> "And wild and high the Cameron's gathering rose,
> The war-note of Lochiel, which Albyn's hills have heard,
> And heard, too, have her Saxon foes."

How the "Cameron men" fought at Waterloo is testified to by the number of their killed and wounded in that battle, and it is also recorded that, when all the field officers and captains of this regt. had been disabled, the regt. was led on to victory by Lieut. Cameron, a nephew of Sir Alan Cameron, the col.-in-chf.; but which of the *four* lieutenants of this name cannot now be traced. On the evening of 18th June, 1815, 9 officers, 21 sergts., 7 drummers and 260 rank and file remained unwounded out of a total of 41 combatant officers, 40 sergts., 11 drummers, and 684 rank and file—the effective strength of the regt. at Quatre Bras.

[1] Afterwards Lt.-Gen. Sir Neil Douglas, K.C.B. and K.C.H. Col.-in.-Chf., 78th Highlanders. 5th son of John Douglas, of Glasgow, and a descendant of the Earls of Angus. Wounded in the knee at Quatre Bras. C.B. for Waterloo. Had served with the 79th at the siege of Copenhagen, in Sweden, in the Walcheren expedition, and in the Pa. Received the gold cross for the Pyrenees, Nivelle, Nive, and Toulouse. Also the silver war medal with two clasps for Corunna and Busaco. D. in Sept., 1853.

[2] C.B. for Waterloo. Retd. in 1831. D. 1835.

[3] C.B. for Waterloo. Quitted the service in 1819. D. at Toronto, Oct. 1842.

[4] Bt.-maj. for Waterloo. Quitted the service in 1821. D. at Edinburgh, 1832.

[5] H. p. 20th Nov., 1816. D. at Tunnach, near Wick, 1822.

[6] Maj. unattached 1826. Retd. same year.

[7] D. from his wounds. A pension of £50 per ann. was granted to his mother, Catherine Campbell.

[8] Maj. 1824. Bt. lt.-col. and inspecting f. o. of militia, Nova Scotia, 1830. Retd. as lt.-col. 17th Sept., 1839.

[9] D. in Ireland, 1822.

[10] Exchanged to 82nd Foot 10th July, 1817. Maj. 31st Dec. 1827. H. p. 27th Nov., 1828. Retd. as bt.-col. 1849. D. 1868.

[11] D. from his wounds.

[12] D. from his wounds.

[13] Capt. 19th July, 1815. Bt.-maj. Jan., 1819. D. at Tobago, in Oct., 1820.

[14] Capt. 20th July, 1815. H. p. 1816.

[15] Capt. 12th Oct., 1815. H. p. 1816. D. 1844.

[16] Capt. 12th Dec., 1822. H. p. 6th Oct., 1825.

[17] Capt. 3rd June, 1819. Retd. 1830. D. 1849.

[18] H. p. 2nd June, 1819.

[19] Lieut. 36th Foot 27th Aug., 1829. Retd. 1835.

[20] D. in Ireland in 1822, of brain fever, through the effects of a blow from a stone thrown by a peasant.

[21] Attained rank of major 7th Aug., 1835. H. p. 25th May, 1838. D. 1851 at Kingston, Canada.

[22] Retd. 1821. D., Inverness, 1846.

[23] Capt. 60th Rifles 18th Oct., 1815. H. p. 1817.

[24] D. from his wounds 23rd Oct., 1815.

25 D. at Blandecque, France, 1818.

26 Capt. 7th Apr., 1825.   Retd. 1842.   D. 1843.

27 H. p. 1820.

28 H. p. 1817.   Lost on passage to South America in 1819.

29 Lieut. 16th July, 1815.   H. p. 1817.

30 3rd son of Archibald McLean, of Pennycross, co. Argyll, and bro. to Allan T. McLean, of 13th Lt. Dragoons.   Lieut. 18th July, 1815.   H. p. 1816.

31 H. p. 1817.

32 H. p. 1816.

33 H. p. 1821.   D. 1824.

34 Lieut. h. p. 67th Foot 1825.   D. 1853.

35 Out of the regt. before 1st Jan., 1816.

36 Ensign 17th July, 1815.   Lieut. 7th March, 1822.   H. p. 1827.   D. in France in Jan., 1832.

37 Superseded 1821.

38 Paymaster Canadian Rifles 29th Oct., 1841.   D. in Canada, Sept., 1845.

92ND REGIMENT OF FOOT (GORDON HIGHLANDERS).

	Rank in the	
LIEUT-COLONEL.	Regiment.	Army.
1 John Cameron, K.	23 June, 1808	Col., 4 June, 1814
MAJORS.		
2 James Mitchell, w.	30 Mar. 1809	Lt.-Col., 3 Mar.,
3 Donald Macdonald	26 Nov. 1812	[1814
CAPTAINS.		
4 George W. Holmes, w.	28 Mar. 1805	
5 Dugald Campbell, w.	13 June, 1805	
6 Peter Wilkie, w.	21 May, 1806	
7 Wm. Charles Grant, K.	28 July, 1808	
8 Wm. Little, K.	7 Jan. 1813	
9 Archibald Ferrier, w.	4 Mar. 1813	
LIEUTENANTS.		
10 Claude Alexander, Adjt.	19 Sept. 1805	
James John Chisholm, K.	4 Feb. 1808	
11 Robert Winchester, w.	6 Feb. 1808	
12 Thos. Hobbs, w.	7 Feb. 1808	
13 Thos. Macintosh, w.	9 Feb. 1808	
14 Donald Macdonald	10 Feb. 1808	
15 Andrew Will	18 Feb. 1808	
16 Alexander Gordon	3 Mar. 1808	
17 James Kerr Ross, w.	4 May, 1808	
18 Ronald Macdonald, w.	5 May, 1808	
19 Thos. Gordon	28 July, 1808	
20 Hector Innes, w.	13 Apr. 1809	
21 George Logan, w.	5 Oct. 1809	
22 Ewen Campbell	30 Oct. 1809	
23 Richard M'Donell	1 Nov. 1809	
24 John M'Kinlay, w.	2 Nov. 1809	
25 Richard Josiah Peat	12 Apr. 1810	
26 George Mackie, w.	8 Oct. 1812	
27 Alexander McPherson, w.	22 Oct. 1812	
28 Ewen Ross, w.	26 Nov. 1812	
29 James Hope, w.	7 Jan. 1813	

S 5473.

O

92ND REGIMENT OF FOOT (GORDON HIGHLANDERS)
—continued.

ENSIGNS.	Rank in the Regiment.	Army.
[30] John Bramwell, w.	29 July, 1813	
[31] Robert Logan, w.	5 Aug. 1813	
[32] John Clarke	26 Aug. 1813	
[33] Angus McDonald	15 Sept. 1813	
Abel Becher, K.	16 Sept. 1813	
[34] Robert Hewitt	21 Oct. 1813	
John M. R. McPherson, K.	22 Oct. 1813	
[35] Duncan McPherson	23 Dec. 1813	

PAYMASTER.

[36] James Gordon	16 Apr. 1807	

SURGEON.

George Hicks	22 Aug. 1811	

ASSISTANT-SURGEON.

John Stewart, w.	5 Nov. 1812	

Facings yellow.   Lace silver.

[1] The heroic Fassifern, great-grandson of John Cameron, 18th of Lochiel, and one of the six children of Ewen Cameron of Inverscadale, on Loch Linnhe, by his first wife, Lucy Campbell, of Balmadine. In early life was articled to a Writer to the Signet at Edinburgh ; but when war broke out, in 1793, his military tastes inclined him to forsake the pen for a sword. Obtained a commission in the 26th Cameronians in 1793. His chief services were in the Pa. with above regt., and the honourable augmentation to his family arms, by the Prince Regent, 20th May, 1815, tells the true story of his exploits at "Almaraz" and the "Pass of Maya." K.T.S. He met his death at Quatre Bras whilst leading the 92nd against a large body of French troops. Never was a commanding officer more universally lamented. He was buried on the 17th June during the height of the storm which raged that day. His grave was dug in a quiet lane by his devoted foster-brother, Ewen McMillan, a private in the 92nd, who had accompanied his master through all his campaigns. By desire of his family, Cameron's body was aftds. disinterred and removed to Scotland, where it was re-interred in Kilmallie churchyard, where a tall obelisk, with an inscription by Sir Walter Scott, marks his grave. His aged father, Ewen Cameron, was created a bart. in consideration of his gallant son's services. The title is now extinct.

[2] Succeeded to the command of the regt. when Cameron was wounded, but was himself soon disabled. C.B. Served in the Pa. and had the gold medal for Orthes. Commanded the regt. until 1819, when he quitted the service.

[3] Does not appear to have been present at Quatre Bras, but commanded the regt. at Waterloo. C.B. and bt.-lt.-col. 5th son of John Macdonald, of Dalchosine, co. Perth, by Mary, dau. of Robert Menzies, of Glassie, co. Perth. Retired on h. p. 26th Nov., 1818. Living in 1830.

[4] Succeeded to the command at Quatre Bras when Maj. Mitchell was wounded. Promoted maj. 18th June, 1815. Quitted the service in 1818.

[5] Bt.-maj. 11th Jan., 1816. Out of the *Army List* in 1819.

[6] Maj. in this regt. 21st Jan., 1819. Quitted the service in 1823. Had served in Egypt and the Pa. Aftds. held the appointment of barrack-master, and d. at Horsfield, Bristol, 4th Nov., 1852.

[7] Killed at Quatre Bras. A pension of £60 per annum was granted to his widow, Susan Grant. The late Gen. Sir Thornton Grant, who distinguished himself in the Crimea with the 49th Regt., was son of the above.

[8] The obituary notice of this officer in the *Scots Magazine* describes him as " son of Mr. Little, a farmer at Burnfoot (?)."

[9] Probably belonged to the military family of "Ferrier, of Belsyde," co. Linlithgow. Maj. in 92nd, 22nd Oct., 1818. Quitted the service before 1824.

[10] Promoted capt. 18th July, 1815. Quitted the service in 1821. This officer may be the "Claud Alexander, of Ballochmyle," described in Burke's *Landed Gentry* as of the 1st Regt. of Guards (?).

[11] Afterwards Lt.-Col. Robert Winchester, K.H. Retd. as bt.-col. Nov., 1842. Served in the Pa. and was wounded both at Quatre Bras and Waterloo. Son of Charles Winchester, of Aberdeen. D. 23rd July, 1846, at Edinburgh.

[12] Promoted capt. 20th July, 1815. Retired on h. p. 25th May, 1820. Living 1842. This officer's widow attained the great age of 102 on 18th June, 1896. Her five sons all served in the Army, and she had one son and seven grandsons serving in June, 1896. H.M. Queen Victoria sent her congratulations to Mrs. Hobbs on the occasion of the 102nd anniversary of latter's birthday.

[13] Capt. 4th Nov., 1819. H. p. 25th Oct., 1821.

[14] H. p. 2nd July, 1818.

[15] Served in the Pa. D. a lieut. in this regt., from yellow fever, 7th Oct. 1819, at Snow Hill Camp, Jamaica.

[16] H. p. 25th Oct., 1816.

[17] Afterwards Maj.-Gen. J. Kerr Ross, K.H. Served through the Par. War (medal and six clasps), where he was A.D.C. to Gen. Sir John Buchan. 3rd son of Col. Andrew Ross, by Isabella Macdonnell, of Aberhallader. M., 1827, Margaret, 2nd dau. of James McInroy, of Lude, co. Perth. D. at Edinburgh, 26th April, 1872.

[18] His proper name was "Reginald Ranald Macdonald." Aftds. Maj. and Bt. Lt.-Col. 4th Foot. Severely wounded at Waterloo. Served on the staff in India, and d. at Bombay 31st May, 1845. He was a C.B. and K.H.

[19] Served all through the Par. War. D. a lieut. in this regt., of yellow fever, at Kingston, Jamaica, 17th Sept., 1819.

[20] Employed on recruiting service in 1817. Out of the regt. before 1824.

o 2

[21] Son of Wm. Logan, merchant, Aberdeen.   D. a lieut. in this regt., from yellow fever, at Up Park Camp, Jamaica, 4th Oct., 1819. He had served over ten years in the regt.

[22] D. as lieut. in 1822.

[23] Serving in 1817.   Out of the regt. before 1824.

[24] H. p. 1817.

[25] Serving in 1824.   Out of the regt. before 1830.

[26] Adjt. 24th Aug., 1815.   Out of the regt. before 28th Oct., 1821.

[27] H. p. 25th March, 1817.   D. 1855.

[28] H. p. 25th March, 1817.

[29] H. p. 25th March, 1817.   H. p. as adjt. to a recruiting district Dec., 1842. Had the Par. medal with three clasps.   D. in Kensington, 18th March, 1860.

[30] Was severely wounded at Quatre Bras (right leg amputated).   Lieut. 18th July, 1815.   H. p. 1817.   Living 1876.

[31] Lieut. 19th July, 1815.   H. p. 31st Foot 12th Aug., 1824.

[32] Lieut. 20th July, 1815.   Placed on h. p. 1817, but restored as lieut. in same regt. 15th March, 1821.   Out of the regt. before 1830.

[33] Held the colours of the 92nd at Waterloo until disabled by wounds. Lieut. 24th Aug., 1815.   H. p. 25th March, 1817.   D. at Whinnyhall, Fifeshire, 3rd Feb., 1832.

[34] Lieut. 61st Foot 3rd Nov., 1819.   H. p. 16th Dec., 1819.   Appointed barrack-master at Clonmel in 1854.

[35] Lieut. 22nd Oct., 1818.   Capt. 22nd Sept., 1825.   H. p. April, 1826.

[36] A close and personal friend of Col. Cameron, whose funeral he attended on 17th June, 1815.   H. p. 2nd March, 1820.   Had the Par. medal with seven clasps.   Living 1855.

95th REGIMENT OF FOOT (RIFLEMEN).

(1st Battalion.)

LIEUT.-COLONEL.	Rank in the Regiment.	Army.
1 Sir Andrew F. Barnard, K.C.B., w.	29 Mar., 1810	Col., 4 June, 1813
MAJOR.		
2 Alexander Cameron, w.	14 May, 1812	Lt.-Col., 27 Apr., [1812
CAPTAINS.		
3 Jonathan Leach, w.	1 May, 1806	Maj.,21 June,1813
Charles Beckwith, w.	28 July, 1808	Maj., 3 Mar. 1814
Charles Smyth, k.	4 Oct. 1809	16 June, 1808
4 Henry Lee	20 Sept. 1810	
Henry George Smith	28 Feb. 1812	Maj.,29Sept.,1814
5 Edward Chawner, w.	14 May, 1812	
6 Wm. Johnstone, w.	22 Oct. 1812	
FIRST LIEUTENANTS.		
7 Jonathan Layton	3 June, 1809	
8 John Molloy, w.	5 June, 1809	
9 John Cox	8 June, 1809	
10 Archibald Stewart	2 Oct. 1809	
11 Wm. Chapman	26 Apr. 1810	
12 Richard B. Frere	21 Aug. 1810	
13 Wm. Lister, k.	23 Aug. 1810	
14 John Gardiner, w.	30 Aug. 1810	
15 John Kincaid, Adjt.	23 May, 1811	
16 George Simmons, w.	25 July, 1811	
John Stilwell, k.	26 Sept. 1811	
17 J. P. Gairdner, w.	12 May, 1812	
18 Wm. Haggup	13 May, 1812	
19 John G. Fitzmaurice, w.	14 Jan. 1813	
20 George Drummond	28 Jan. 1813	
21 Elliott Dunkin Johnston, k.	7 Dec. 1813	
22 Orlando Felix, w.	4 May, 1815	10 Nov, 1814

95TH REGIMENT OF FOOT (RIFLEMEN)—*continued.*

Rank in the

SECOND LIEUTENANTS.	Regiment.	Army.
[23] Allen Stewart, w.	10 Dec. 1812	
[24] Wm. Wright, w.	11 Mar. 1813	
[25] James Church, w.	26 Aug. 1813	30 July, 1813
[26] Wm. Shenley, w.	21 Apr. 1814	

PAYMASTER.

John Mackenzie	27 June, 1805

QUARTERMASTER.

— Bagshaw	13 Oct. 1814

SURGEON.

Joseph Burke	29 June, 1809

ASSISTANT-SURGEONS.

James Robson	21 Nov. 1811	22 Feb. 1810
Robert Heyt	3 Sept. 1812	

VOLUNTEER.

[27] Charles Smith.

Regimentals green.   Facings black.

[1] Bn. at Fahan, co. Donegal, in 1773. Son of Rev. Henry Barnard, D.D., and grandson of the Bishop of Derry. He received the Russian order of St. George for Waterloo; also the Austrian order of Maria Theresa. Was made commandant of the British division occupying Paris after the capitulation. D. Lt.-Governor of Rl. Hospital, Chelsea, 17th Jan., 1855.

[2] "A pupil of Sir John Moore." Bn. 1781. Younger son of Alexander Cameron, of Inverallert, co. Argyll. Served in Holland in 1799 and in Egypt in 1801. Was severely wounded in the arm and side at the battle of Alexandria. Served through most of the Par. War, until severely wounded at the battle of Vittoria. Severely wounded in the throat at Waterloo. Received a gold medal for Egypt and a gold medal with two clasps for Ciudad Rodrigo, Badajoz, and Salamanca. C.B. for Waterloo. Maj.-Gen. 1838. Col.-in-Chf. 74th Regt. 1846. D. 26th July, 1850.

[3] At Waterloo the command of the battalion devolved upon Leach when his two senior officers were wounded. C.B. and bt. lt.-col. In 1831 published *Rough Recollections of an Old Soldier.* D. as lt.-col. 14th Jan., 1855, at Worthing, aged 70.

[4] According to the *Army List* of 1st Jan., 1820, this officer was "superseded." His name appears, however, in the h. p. list of this regt. n 1821 and for some years after.

[5] Afterwards capt. retired f. p. 4th Rl. Vet. Batt. D. 1826.

[6] An interesting memoir of this gallant soldier appeared in the *United Service Journal* for 1837. He was a native of Dumfriesshire, where his father had a small property of his own. In 1805 he joined the 52nd L. I. as an ensign, and in the year following was appointed to a lieutenancy in the Rifle Brigade (as the old 95th is now styled). As a lieut. he had the good fortune to command one of the four companies of the Rifles which, under Sir S. Beckwith, at the Pass of Barba del Puerco, on 19th March, 1810, so gallantly repulsed 600 chosen French troops who attempted to surprise them at midnight. I extract the following from the above memoir :—" On the 19th Jan., 1812, he was one of the officers who volunteered and led the stormers at the taking of Ciudad Rodrigo, and was fortunate enough to come out unscathed, although one of the first to enter that deadly pass. At the storming of Badajoz on the 6th April, 1812, his name again stood on the list of volunteers for the Forlorn Hope, but as it was claimed by a senior officer of the division, he was obliged to limit his expectations to one of the posts of honour with the storming party. Sir Andrew Barnard, however, who commanded the Light Division, knowing how peculiarly well qualified he was for desperate enterprise, assigned him a post in front of the Forlorn Hope, in the command of a party carrying ropes prepared with nooses to throw over the sword-blades which formed the chevaux-de-frise, in the hope of being able to displace it by dragging it down the breach, but Johnstone and all his party were stricken down before they got within throwing distance. His appearance next morning is thus described by a brother officer, Capt. Kincaid, in *Random Shots from a Rifleman*, page 287 :—'The first tent that I entered was Johnstone's. With his shattered arm bandaged, he was lying fast asleep, and coupling his appearance with the daring duty he had been called on to perform but a few hours before in front of the Forlorn Hope, I thought that I had never set my eyes upon a nobler picture of a soldier ! His whole appearance, even in sleep, showed exactly as it had been in the execution of that duty ; his splendid figure was so disposed as if he was taking the first step in the breach—his eyebrows were elevated—his nostrils still distended, and altogether he looked as if he would clutch the castle in his remaining hand ! No one could have seen him at that moment without saying—There lies a hero ! ' " Johnstone was wounded both at Quatre Bras and Waterloo. Promoted maj. 24th Dec., 1829. Quitted the service in 1831. Was Colonial Sec. at Cape of Good Hope, and d. at sea 6th April, 1836.

[7] H. p. 21st May, 1818.

[8] Capt. 5th Aug., 1824. H. p. 28th May, 1829. Lt.-col. unatt. 11th May, 1851. Had the Par. medal with 8 clasps. See account of this officer in the *Cornhill Magazine* for Dec., 1897.

[9] Afterwards Maj.-Gen. John Cox, K.H. Was present at eleven general actions in the Pa. Had a compound fracture of his left arm at the storming of Ciudad Rodrigo. Defended a battery with his company at Waterloo. D. at Cheltenham, 7th Feb., 1863. There were two officers of this name in the Rifles in 1815, who appear to have been brothers, and of the same family as Sir Richard Cox, Bart., Lord Chancellor of Ireland.

[10] Attained the rank of major 17th Dec., 1829. Retd. 1835.

[11] H. p. 1819. D. at Leamington 12th Feb., 1854.

[12] Appointed barrack-master at Tobago, 1830. D. there 1832.

[13] Wounded at Quatre Bras and d. in a house there next day.

[14] Afterwards Capt. and Bt.-Maj. 82nd Regt.   D. at Jock's House, Kinnoull, 18th June, 1852—"On the anniversary, and at the same hour, on which he was carried severely wounded from the field of Waterloo."

[15] Bn. at Dalbeath, near Falkirk, in Jan., 1787. Served in the Pa. and was one of the leaders of the storming party of the Light Division at Ciudad Rodrigo. Received the silver war medal in 1848, with nine clasps. Had his horse shot under him at Waterloo. Was aftds. knighted and appointed an exon in the Yeomen of the Guard. D. at Hastings 22nd April, 1862. Author of *Adventures in the Rifle Brigade.*

[16] Served through the Par. War. Was shot through the liver at Waterloo ; likewise had two ribs broken and a bullet in his chest. Wrote a narrative of the Waterloo campaign. Quitted the service as bt. maj., and d. in Jersey, 5th March, 1858.

[17] H. p. 1819. Retd. 1827.

[18] Adjt. at Waterloo. Exchanged as lieut. to 11th Foot 3rd Aug., 1820. H. p. 14th Feb., 1828.

[19] Aftds. major-general and K.H. D. 24th Dec., 1865.

[20] H. p. 1826, 3rd Vet. Batt. D. 1827.

[21] Killed by a cannon ball. 3rd son of Lt.-Gen. Johnston, H.E.I.C.S.

[22] Wounded at Quatre Bras. Attained rank of maj. gen. "He was the first to decipher the names and titles of the Pharaohs, and an epitome he drew up was translated into French and Italian." D. at Geneva, 5th April, 1860.

[23] A chivalrous and daring Highlander. Singled out a French officer at Waterloo and had a duel with him. When Stewart's sword broke off at the hilt he instantly closed with the Frenchman, "whom he finished in an instant." In later *Army Lists* his name is spelled "Stuart." Aftds. Capt. in the 3rd Buffs. H. p. 1836. D. in the Norwich Military Lunatic Asylum 6th July, 1847.

[24] Entered the army in 1813. Served in Holland in 1813 and 1814, and was present at the attack on Merxem and bombardment of the French fleet at Antwerp. H. p. 1st lieut. 1818. Living 1876.

[25] H. p. 1816. D. 1824.

[26] H. p. 31st Jan., 1828.

[27] 2nd Lieut. 19th July, 1815. H. p. 25th Dec., 1817. Col. of the Whittlesea Yeomanry Cavalry 1831. Retd. 1837. Younger bro. of Henry George (aftds. Sir Henry) Smith and of Thos. Smith, both of the 95th. D. at Whittlesea 24th Dec., 1854. Bd. in St. Mary's Church. Communicated by Mr. George Moore Smith.

95TH REGIMENT OF FOOT (RIFLEMEN).
(2nd Battalion.)

	MAJORS.	Rank in the Regiment.	Rank in the Army.
1	Amos Godsill Norcott, w.	22 Dec. 1808	Lt.-Col., 25 July, 1810. [1814
2	George Wilkins, w.	10 May, 1809	Lt.-Col., 4 June,

	CAPTAINS.		
3	George Miller, w.	21 Jan. 1808	Maj., 3 Mar. 1814
4	Joseph Logan	2 Feb. 1809	
5	Thos. MacNamara	26 Aug. 1813	
6	John Garlies McCullock, w.	21 Oct. 1813	
7	Charles Eaton	21 Apr. 1814	
8	Francis le Blanc	1 Dec. 1814	

	FIRST LIEUTENANTS.		
9	Wm. Humbley, w.	13 Oct. 1808	
10	John Charles Hope	2 Feb. 1809	
11	Thos. Cochrane	22 Feb. 1809	
12	John Robert Budgen	4 May, 1809	
13	Thomas Smith, Adjt.	7 June, 1809	
14	Francis Bennett	1 Oct. 1809	
15	Francis Dixon	4 Jan. 1810	
16	Edward Coxen, w.	28 June, 1810	
17	Dugald Cameron, w.	1 May, 1811	
18	Robert Cochrane, w.	8 May, 1812	
19	John Allen Ridgeway, w.	9 May, 1812	
20	John Fry, w	10 May, 1812	
21	Edward Madden	13 July, 1812	
22	Vere Webb, w.	9 Dec. 1813	
23	Chas. Gordon Urquhart	27 Oct. 1814	
24	J. Lynam, w.	22 Mar. 1815	
25	Charles Rochfort	15 June, 1815	

	SECOND LIEUTENANTS.		
26	Wm. Shaw	25 Apr. 1813	
27	Richard Fowler	22 Oct. 1813	22 Feb. 1813
28	Thos. Bowen Sheean	25 Dec. 1813	
29	Richard Cocks Eyre, w.	22 Apr. 1814	
30	John Prendergast Walsh, w.	5 May, 1814	
31	R. J. N. Kellett (Volunteer)		

95TH REGIMENT OF FOOT (RIFLEMEN)—*continued.*

	Rank in the	
PAYMASTER.	Regiment.	Army.
Angus McDonald	15 Feb. 1810	
QUARTERMASTER.		
Donald Ross	3 Apr. 1806	
SURGEON.		
Francis Scott	25 Jan. 1810	
ASSISTANT SURGEONS.		
John Armstrong	11 Mar. 1813	
Robert Scott	15 Sept. 1814	5 Nov. 1812

[1] Afterwards Maj.-Gen. Norcott, C.B. Served in the Pa., and had the gold medal for Corunna. K. St. A. for Waterloo. D. at Cork in 1838 whilst commanding the southern district.

[2] C.B. for Waterloo. Served in the Pa., and had the gold medal for Salamanca. Retd. as bt. lt.-col. in 1817. K.H. D. at Shirley, Southampton, 8th Nov., 1862.

[3] C.B. and bt. lt.-col. for Waterloo. Served in the Pa., and had the gold medal for Nivelle. Lt.-Col. unattached list, 25th May, 1826. D. 1843.

[4] Appointed lt.-col. of 63rd Foot in 1829, and d. at Dover, 1st Sept., 1844, when in command of that regt.

[5] Quitted the service as capt. Served in the Pa., and in the Buenos Ayres expedition. Was a J.P. for the counties of Cork, Waterford, and Limerick. D. at Cork, 7th Jan. 1832.

[6] " M'Culloch had been wounded in the shoulder on Massena's retreat from Portugal in March, 1811, and this wound deprived him of the use of the arm. At Waterloo, by a shot fired very late in the day, he lost the other arm. He was promoted, 'having no longer an arm to wield for his country,' as he told the Duke of Wellington, ' but being anxious to serve it,' to a majority in the 2nd Garrison Battalion in Dec., 1815, and d. in London in 1818." Sir W. Cope's *History of the Rifle Brigade.*

[7] Retired on h. p. as capt., 14th Aug., 1823. Served through the Par. War, and had the silver medal with seven clasps. Living in 1860.

[8] Afterwards Lt.-Col. 46th Regt. M., 10th April, 1828, Eliz., 2nd dau. of Thomas Porter, of Rockbeare House, Devon. Col. 23rd Nov., 1841. Retd. in 1845. Living 1879.

[9] This officer had been present at almost every battle and action in the Pa., and when the long-looked-for silver war medal was given, in 1848, he received one with thirteen clasps. Sev. wnded. at Waterloo. Attained the rank of lt.-col. unattached, 1851, and d. 26th Oct., 1857, at Eyresbury.

[10] Recommended for promotion by Gen. Sir H. Clinton for gallantry at Waterloo. Capt. 9th Nov., 1820. Eventually succeeded to the command of the 1st batt, D, 12th Oct., 1842,

[11] D. as lt. in this regt. 1823 at Kinsale.

[12] Born 1st Dec., 1791. Eldest son of Thomas Budgen (of the family of Budgen, of Ballindoney, co. Wexford). J.P. and D.L. for Surrey, and J.P. for co. Wexford. M., 13th Jan., 1823, Williamza Caroline Mary, 3rd dau. of Col. Lorenzo Moore, of the "Battle-axe Guards," by Henrietta, only dau. of Sir S. T. Janssen, Bart. Had the Par. War medal with eight clasps. H. p. 1818. D. 1866.

[13] Brother to Gen. Sir Harry Smith (see under Staff). His full name was Thos. Lawrence Smith. Served through the Par. War, for which in 1848 he received the silver medal and ten clasps. Recommended for promotion for gallantry at Waterloo, by Sir H. Clinton. H. p. 1819.

It is stated in Cope's *History of the Rifle Brigade:* "On July 7th, 1815, the army marched into Paris, and the 2nd Batt. had the honour of being the first corps which entered, Lieut. and Adjt. Thos. Smith riding in front of the Battalion, being the first British officer who entered Paris on that famous day." Was aftds. principal barrack-master at Aldershot. Recd. a special pension and was made a C.B. D. 6th Apr., 1877. Bd. in the military cemetery, Aldershot.

[14] D. in May, 1817.

[15] H. p. 80th Foot 11th Dec., 1817. D. in Jersey, 1832.

[16] Capt. 8th Apr., 1825. Paymaster 60th Rifles 9th Feb., 1826. Served in last-named regt. 31 years. Served in the Punjaub campaign. Had the Par. medal with 10 clasps.

[17] H. p. 1817 89th Foot. D. in Aug., 1846.

[18] Capt. 22nd May, 1828. Major retd. f. p. 1841. Knight of Windsor. D. at the Lower Ward, Windsor Castle, and was buried in the catacombs there, with military honours, all the naval and military knights attending, in May, 1864.

[19] Afterwards Lt.-Col. Ridgeway. Adjt. N. Devon Militia, 1831. D. 11th June, 1856, at Newton St. Cyres, Exeter.

[20] Capt. Rifle Bde., 22nd July, 1830. D. 1840.

[21] H. p. 1818. D. at Chichester, 1819.

[22] H. p. 1831.

[23] Probably one of the Urquharts of Meldrum, Perthshire. Adam Urquhart, of this family, married Lady Mary Gordon, sister of 1st Duke of Gordon. Retd. on h. p. 30th Jan., 1823. D. 1827.

[24] H. p. 1818. D. 1821.

[25] 7th son of Gustavus Rochfort, M.P. for Westmeath, by Frances, dau. of John Bloomfield, of Redwood. Retd. on h. p. 25th Aug., 1821. M., 1832, Hannah, eldest dau. of Col. Pratt, of Cabra Castle, and had issue. Of Rochfort Lodge, co. Donegal. D. 1844.

[26] D. as lt. on h. p. in 1829.

[27] Assumed the surname of Butler on succeeding to the Barton estate, co. Stafford. 2nd son and eventual heir of Thomas Fowler, of Pendeford Hall, by Harriet Fowler. Served in the Pa. Placed on h. p. 25th Dec., 1818. Was thrice married, and had issue. D. 14th March, 1864.

[28] Retd. 1830.

[29] H. p. 1817.

[30] Lost right leg at Waterloo. Retd. 1833 as lieut. h. p. 6th Foot. Took Holy Orders.

[31] 2nd Lieut. 18th July, 1815. Retd. as capt. in 1838. D. at Florence in Nov. 1853.

95TH REGIMENT OF FOOT (RIFLEMEN).

(*Two companies of the 3rd Battalion.*)

| | Rank in the | |
MAJOR.	Regiment.	Army.
¹ John Ross, w.	11 May, 1809	Lt.-Col., 6 Mar. [1811

CAPTAINS.

Charles Geo. Gray	6 May, 1809	
² James Fullerton, w.	7 May, 1809	Maj., 7 Apr. 1814
³ Wm. Eeles	7 Dec. 1813	
Charles Eeles, K.	20 July, 1814	

FIRST LIEUTENANTS.

⁴ Gentle Vickers	14 May, 1812
⁵ Thos. Taylor Worsley, Adjt., w.	2 Oct. 1812
⁶ Godfrey H. Shenley, w.	17 Mar. 1814

SECOND LIEUTENANTS.

⁷ Alexander Milligan	25 Nov. 1813
⁸ Charles Probart	25 Nov. 1813

ASSISTANT-SURGEON.

⁹ Thos. P. McCabe	19 Aug. 1813

¹ Afterwards Maj.-Gen. Sir John Ross, K.C.B. Lt.-Col. Cape Corps (1824). Served in the Pa., and received the gold cross for Barossa, Vittoria, Orthes, and Toulouse. D. 21 April, 1835.

² Son of Lewis Fullarton, of Kilmichael, Isle of Arran. C.B. and bt. lt.-col. for Waterloo. M., 7th Aug., 1817, Jane, dau. of Colin M'Cleverty, M.D., of Chestervale, Jamaica. Lt.-col. 96th Regt. 1827. K.H. D. at Halifax, N.S., 8th March, 1834.

³ Afterwards lt.-col. 1st Batt. (*see* under Capt. Charles Eeles, of Staff). H. p. 1850.

⁴ D. in South America, 1823.

⁵ Belonged to the old Yorkshire family of Worsley, of Hovingham. Served through the Par. War, and in 1848 received the silver medal with nine clasps. "He was wounded, at the siege of Badajoz, under one of his ears. The ball made the circuit of his neck, and was taken out on the opposite side. He was

THE WATERLOO ROLL CALL. 205

again wounded at Waterloo under the other ear, the ball, as before, making the circuit of the neck." Kincaid relates that the wound Worsley received at Badajoz had the effect of turning his head to the right, and that the wound he received at Waterloo restored his head to its original position. Placed on h. p. 11th Feb., 1816. M. Rose, dau. of the Rev. James Stovin, D.D., Rector of Rossington, co. York, and d. s. p. 25th Oct., 1851.

[6] H. p. 25th Dec., 1818.

[7] H. p. 1826. D. in Scotland, 1828.

[8] D. at Skibereen in March, 1822

[9] H. p. 1818.

ROYAL STAFF CORPS.

(Attached to the Quartermaster-General's Department.)

	Rank in the	
LIEUT.-COLONEL.	Regiment.	Army.

¹ Wm. Nicolay   4 Apr. 1805   Col., 4 June, 1813

CAPTAINS.

Thomas Wright, w.	23 Dec. 1813	
² Wm. Staveley	12 Jan. 1815	Maj., 15 Dec. 1814
Francis Read	16 Mar. 1815	

LIEUTENANTS.

³ George D. Hall, w.	28 Nov. 1811
Basil Jackson	6 May, 1813
A. C. G. Brauns	17 Feb. 1814

ENSIGNS.

⁴ John Sumner Sedley	6 May, 1813
⁵ John James Milliken	10 June, 1813

Facings blue.   Lace silver.

¹ C.B. for Waterloo. Maj.-Gen. 1819. Gov. of Mauritius 1832. K.C.H. and Col.-in-Chf. 1st W. I. Regt. D. 1844.

² C.B. and bt. lt.-col. for Waterloo. Aftds. Com.-in-Chf. at Madras. Lt.-Gen. and Col.-in-Chf. 24th Foot. D. whilst on a journey in his carriage, after leaving Tippicadoo, in March, 1854.

³ Afterwards Col. George Dry Hall. Retd. on h. p. in 1839. D. at Hythe, 25th Feb., 1852.

⁴ Afterwards Maj. J. S. Sedley, first-class barrack-master at the Mauritius. Retd. in Aug., 1860, on a pension of £145 13s. 9d. per annum. D. 21st Aug., 1867.

⁵ Placed on h. p. 11th March, 1819.

ROYAL WAGGON TRAIN.*

(Attached to the Quartermaster General's Department.)

		Rank in the	
	LIEUT.-COLONEL.	Regiment.	Army.
1	Thomas Aird	4 May, 1815	2 June, 1814
	CAPTAINS.		
2	Thomas Pardoe	1 Oct. 1812	
3	Basil Jackson	3 Dec. 1812	
	LIEUTENANTS.		
4	Wm. Aitkin	9 Feb. 1809	
5	Edward Smith	23 Feb. 1815	
6	Joseph McDowall	16 Mar. 1815	4 July, 1811
7	Henry O'Neil	27 Apr. 1815	
8	Robert Parkinson	4 May, 1815	
9	Charles Bott	25 May, 1815	22 Apr. 1813
10	Robert Kerr	25 May, 1815	
	CORNETS.		
11	Thos. Glendinning		9 Dec. 1813
12	John Fenn	4 May, 1815	
	SURGEON.		
	Thomas Wynne	6 Oct. 1808	20 June, 1799
	VETERINARY-SURGEON.		
13	Frederick Cherry	16 July, 1807	

Blue. Facings red. Lace silver.

---

* In 1816 the Rl. Waggon Train took up a new position in the *Army List*, viz., after the cavalry and newly-raised corps, the "Staff Corps of Cavalry," so called to distinguish it from the "Royal Staff Corps," which followed in the wake of the Rifle Brigade. The Waggon Train was reduced about twenty years after Waterloo, and after the Crimean War a corps called "The Military Train" sprung into existence, which, like its predecessor, was chiefly officered by old soldiers who had won their commissions while serving in the ranks. The Military Train was reduced in its turn, and "The Army Service Corps" may be said to be its present equivalent.

1 Placed on h. p. 25th Dec., 1818. D. 1839. (*See* note to Lieut. Elwes, 71st Regt.)

[2] In 1830 this unfortunate officer was still a capt. in the corps.

[3] Quitted the service after 1830, with rank of maj. D. 10th Sept., 1849, aged 92. His son, Basil Jackson (*see* Staff notes), wrote the military life of the Duke of Wellington, and several scientific works.

[4] Serving in 1817. H. p. 1818.

[5] H. p. 28th Aug., 1823.

[6] Serving in same corps in 1830.

[7] Adjt. 20th July, 1815. Serving in 1830.

[8] H. p. 1817.

[9] H. p. 1816.

[10] Lieut. 60th Rifles 28th Nov., 1816. H. p. 1817.

[11] Lieut. 20th July, 1815. Exchanged to 60th Rifles 18th Apr., 1816. H. p. 27th Sept., 1817. Living 1855.

[12] H. p. 25th Dec., 1818.

[13] Principal vet.-surgeon at Maidstone depôt 17th Sept., 1839. Serving in 1846.

ROYAL REGIMENT OF ARTILLERY.

STAFF.

[1] Col. Sir George Adam Wood, Kt., commanding.

[2] Lt.-Col. Sir Augustus Frazer, K.C.B., commanding Royal Horse Artillery.

[3] Lt.-Col. A. Macdonald, commanding six troops of Horse Artillery attached to the Cavalry.

[4] Adjt. Capt. Wm. Pakenham, R.H.A.

[5] Lt.-Col. Sir John May, A.A.General.

[6] Capt. H. Baynes, w., Brigade Major.

[7] Lieuts. John Bloomfield and [8] George Coles, Staff-Adjts. to Sir George Wood.

[9] Lieut. Wm. Bell, Staff-Adjt. to Sir A. Frazer.

[10] Lt.-Cols. S. G. Adye, [11] C. Gold, [12] J. S. Williamson, and [13] J. Hawker, field officers commanding two batteries of Foot Artillery attached to each division of the army.

[14] Major P. Drummond, field officer commanding Reserve Artillery.

[15] Lt.-Col. Sir Alexander Dickson, K.C.B., commanding Battering Train.

---

[1] Son of Adam Wood, Lt. of Capt. Coote's Independent Company of Foot at Landguard Fort, who d. 1773. Commanded the R.A. in Holland during the campaign of 1814, and led one of the attacking columns at Bergen-op-Zoom. Was knighted when proxy to Sir J. C. Sherbrooke at the installation of the Bath, 22nd May, 1812. C.B., K.M.T., K.St.V., and K.W. for Waterloo. A.D.C. to George IV., and K.C.H. D. a maj.-gen., 22nd April, 1831.

[2] Son of Col. Andrew Frazer, R.E., by Charlotte, dau. of Stillingfleet Durnford, of the Ordnance Office. Bn at Dunkirk, 5th Sept., 1776, and educated at the High School, Edinburgh, where he was a contemporary of Lord Brougham. Joined the Military Academy at Woolwich in August, 1790, and became 2nd lt. R.A., 18th Sept., 1793. Served in Holland in 1794. In 1795 was appointed to the Royal Horse Artillery, and in 1799 again embarked for active service in Holland. Commanded the artillery of the expedition against Buenos Ayres, and was present at the assault of that city in July, 1807. In June 1811, was made bt. maj., and in Nov., 1812, joined the British army in the Pa. Five months later was appointed to command the Horse Artillery of Wellington's army, and served in this capacity until the conclusion of the war, winning for himself, and his branch of the service, a high reputation. K.C.B. and the gold cross, with one clasp. In the Waterloo campaign, Frazer again commanded the R.H.A., and "his high reputation as an artillery officer, combined with his firmness of character, prevailed on the Duke of Wellington, who was at first not favourable to the exchange, to permit him to substitute 9-pounders for 6-pounders in the troops of Horse Artillery serving with the army. To this exchange, which preceded the battle of Waterloo, may justly be ascribed much of the success of that memor-

able day." Another instance of Frazer's firmness of character is exhibited in the speedy way in which he made the Prussians, two days after Waterloo, surrender all the French guns which had been captured by the British, and which the rapacious Prussians had annexed, and "regularly parked with Prussian sentries." Frazer's interesting letters from the Pa. and the Netherlands were published in 1859. These letters stamp the writer as a thorough soldier, a perfect gentleman, a delightful companion, and a modest and unassuming man, possessing a heart that could feel for others' woes. He m., in 1809, Emma, youngest dau. of James Lynn, of Woodbridge, in Suffolk, and had issue two sons. He d. as col., 11th June, 1835, at Woolwich, whilst holding the appointment of Director of the Royal Laboratory.

[3] One of the "Macdonalds of Glencoe." Commanded a troop of R.H.A. in the Pa. C.B. for Waterloo. Was entertained at a public banquet at Edinburgh on 18th June, 1816. Maj.-gen. 1837. D. at Leamington 21st May, 1840.

[4] Retired on h. p. as 2nd capt., 1st July, 1822. 3rd son of Edward Pakenham, M.P. for co. Donegal, by Catherine, dau. of Chambre Ponsonby-Barker. Bn. 3rd Feb., 1789. D. about 1863.

[5] Son of John May, Esq., storekeeper of the Ordnance, Fort George, Guernsey; lineally descended from Thos. May, the poet (of the family of Mays, of Mayfield, county Sussex). Bn. 1778. Md. 1819 the only child of Robt. Broff, Esq., formerly governor of Bencoolen, Sumatra. Major-Genl. in the army 1838. Was a colonel in the R.A., in which he served from 1795. Recd. the gold cross and three clasps for his services at Badajoz, Salamanca, Vittoria, San Sebastian, Nivelle, Nive, and Toulouse. Was given the order of St. Anne of Russia, 2nd class, for his services at Quatre Bras and Waterloo, also nominated a knight of the Tower and Sword of Portugal, in 1815, for his services in the Peninsula. K.C.B. 1815. K.C.H. 1822. Sir John was employed afloat in bomb service from 1st Dec., 1797, to the 16th April, 1801. Present at Copenhagen in 1807. He recd. two musket balls through the left thigh when charging the French rearguard on the morning after the battle of Salamanca, and a violent contusion at Vittoria. D., 8th May, 1847, in London. Above information communicated by Mrs. Gibbons, great-niece of Sir John May, K.C.B.

[6] Afterwards bt. maj. and K.H. Maj., unattached list, 12th Dec., 1826. D. in Guernsey, 15th July, 1844.

[7] A scion of the Tipperary family, and cousin of the late Baron Bloomfield, the diplomatist. Was attaché at Stockholm for some years. G.C.B. Gen. and col.-commandant R.H A. D. 1st Aug., 1880, in London, unm.

[8] Retired by sale of his commission, as 2nd capt., 9th April, 1825, after being some years on temporary h. p.

[9] Afterwards Gen. Sir Wm. Bell, K.C.B. Col.-comdt. R.H.A. His father was Wm. Bell, a native of Tanfield, Yorkshire, a cornet in the Yeomanry, but a surgeon by profession, who had a good practice in Ripon, and was twice mayor of that town. His mother was Ann Atkinson, one of the daughters of Henry Atkinson, town clerk of Ripon. The way W. Bell became an artilleryman was as follows :—" Old Col. Quist of the R.A., head of the riding establishment (who belonged to a Dutch family), came to Ripon to buy horses when Bell was a boy in his teens, and happening to meet the youth in Ripon society, he took a fancy to him." Col. Quist used his interest in obtaining for Bell a nomination to a cadetship at Woolwich Academy. In due course Bell obtained a commission in the R.A., and soon evinced that he

had a talent for "the music of war." He served in the West Indies from 1807-1810, and was present at the capture of several of the West Indian islands. Served in the Pa. from July, 1813, to 1814, and was present at five general actions. Slightly wounded at Toulouse. His duties were very onerous both at Quatre Bras and Waterloo, where he was employed in conveying instructions and orders to officers commanding batteries in all parts of the field. He had the narrowest escape of being crushed to death, in after life, that ever befell anyone. "He fell from his horse in front of a battery of R.H.A. at Norwich (or Ipswich), and the battery going over him at a gallop, the drag-shoe of one of the guns knocked his ear off!" Sir W. Bell resided during the latter part of his life at Ripon, and d. there, unm., 28th March, 1873. Buried at Tanfield. M.I. (The above is from information supplied by the late Gen. W. H. Askwith, R.A.)

[10] Afterwards Maj.-Gen. Stephen Galway Adye, C.B. Superintendent of the Rl. Laboratory. 2nd son of Maj. Stephen P. Adye, R.A. Served under Abercromby in Egypt, and took part in the Walcheren Expedition. Served also in the Pa. D. 13th Sept., 1838.

[11] Afterwards Col. Charles Gold, C.B. Sold his commission 31st Dec., 1827. D. at Leamington, 17th April, 1842.

[12] C.B. for Waterloo. M., 30th April, 1817, Miss Maclean, of Giese, co. Caithness. Was an officer of considerable ability, and his scientific knowledge of gunnery was most beneficial to his corps. D. at Woolwich, 26th April, 1836.

[13] Afterwards Col. James Hawker, C.B., Lt.-Gov. of Tilbury Fort. Brother to Capt. Edward Hawker, of the *Britannia*, and to John Hawker, of Plymouth. D. at Woolwich, 12th Oct., 1827, leaving a widow and three daughters.

[14] Afterwards Maj.-Gen. Percy Drummond, C.B. Son of Duncan Drummond, R.A., Director-Gen. of the Field Train. Lt.-Gov. of the R. M. Academy, 1829. Director-Gen. of Artillery, 1840. D. at Woolwich, 1st Jan., 1843.

[15] Afterwards Maj.-Gen. Sir A. Dickson, G.C.B. and K.C.H., &c. 3rd son of Adm. Wm. Dickson, by his 1st wife, Jane, dau. of Alexander Collingwood, of Unthank, in Northumberland The eminent war services of this distinguished soldier are too well known to need recapitulation. From 1798 to 1815 Sir A. Dickson was "on the war-path," in Europe, North and South America. He commanded the allied artillery at Vittoria, San Sebastian, the passage of Bidassoa, Nivelle, Nive, and Toulouse. Recd. the gold cross and six clasps. K.T.S. The Portuguese medal, and Spanish gold cross for Albuera. Good service pens. of £365 per ann. M. Miss Briones, and had issue. D. 22nd April, 1840, and was bd. at Plumstead.

ROYAL HORSE ARTILLERY.

MAJOR BULL'S TROOP.

	Rank in the	
CAPTAIN.	Regiment.	Army.
1 Robert Bull, w.	28 June, 1805	Maj., 31 Dec. 1811
SECOND CAPTAIN.		
2 Robert M. Cairnes, κ.	1 Feb. 1808	12 Apr. 1814
FIRST LIEUTENANTS.		
3 Matthew Louis	28 Dec. 1805	
4 Wm. Smith, w,	1 Feb. 1808	
5 John Townsend	1 Dec. 1811	

[1] Afterwards Lt.-Col. R. Bull, C.B. and K.H. Bn. at Stafford, 3rd March, 1778. Entered the R.A. in 1794, and saw service in the West Indies in 1796–1798. Commanded I troop of Horse Artillery in the Pa. At Waterloo " his troop effected the greatest possible service throughout the early part of the battle ; but owing to the loss sustained both in men and horses, together with the disabled condition of the guns (through incessant firing) it was obliged to retire before the close." Bt. lt.-col. for Waterloo. Retd. on f. p. in 1834. D. at Bath, 17th Aug., 1835.

[2] 2nd son of Maj. W. Cairnes, of 39th Foot, who served all through the defence of Gibraltar, and d. in India. On the female side he was of the elder branch of the same family to whom a baronetcy was granted by Queen Anne (extinct). Killed by a cannon ball. Had seen much service in the Pa. M.I. in Canterbury Cathedral.

[3] 3rd son of Rear.-Adm. Sir Thomas Louis, Bart., by Jacquetta, dau. of Samuel Belfield. M., in 1825, Mary, eldest dau. of the Rev. A. Mallock, of Cockington Court. Retd. on f. p. as lt.-col., 1st April, 1852. D. in Jersey, 19th March, 1853.

[4] Afterwards Sir W. Smith, Knt. 2nd capt. 1825. Killed by a carriage accident in Dublin, 3rd April, 1835. His son, a cadet at the R.M.A. Woolwich, met with a violent death in May, 1826.

[5] Retired on h. p. 6th Feb., 1826.

LIEUT.-COLONEL WEBBER SMITH'S TROOP.

Rank in the

CAPTAIN.	Regiment.	Army.
1 James Webber Smith	1 June, 1806	Lt.-Col., 21 Sept. [1813

SECOND CAPTAIN.

2 Edmund Y. Walcot   23 Mar. 1809

FIRST LIEUTENANTS.

3 Donald Craufurd, w.	2 Nov. 1805
4 David J. Edwards	1 June, 1806
5 Henry Forster, w.	16 Oct. 1807

1 Afterwards lt.-gen. and C.B. Commanded a troop of Horse Artillery in the Pa., and recd. the gold medal and one clasp for Vittoria and San Sebastian. C.B. for Waterloo. M. Eleanora, eldest dau. of Sir John Simeon, Bart. Director-Gen. of Artillery 1844-1848. Col.-Comdt. 1848. D. at Brighton, 21st March, 1853.

2 Retired on f. p. 10th April, 1845, as lt.-col. D. at Winkton, Hants 28th Feb., 1847.

3 4th son of Patrick Craufurd, by Jean, dau. of Lt.-Col. Donald Macdonald of the 84th Regt. D. in Perthshire, 21st Oct., 1819.

4 Retired on h. p. 29th July, 1825, as 2nd capt., and d. at Kerryside, near Carmarthen, 14th April, 1866.

5 Severely wounded in the foot by a grape shot. Served at Copenhagen in 1807, and in the Corunna campaign. Retd. on h. p. as 2nd capt., 7th Feb., 1832, and d. at Aix-la-Chapelle, 24th Oct., 1855.

LIEUT.-COLONEL SIR R. GARDINER'S TROOP *

Rank in the

CAPTAIN.	Regiment.	Army.
[1] Sir Robert Gardiner, K.C.B.	18 Nov. 1811	Lt.-Col., 3 Mar. [1814
SECOND CAPTAIN.		
[2] Thos. Dyneley	22 May, 1808	
FIRST LIEUTENANTS.		
[3] Robert Harding	6 Apr. 1807	
[4] Wm. Swabey	13 Aug. 1807	
[5] Wm. Ingilby	9 Apr. 1812	

* This troop had the old 6-pounders.

[1] Youngest son of Capt. John Gardiner (3rd Buffs), and brother of Lt.-Gen. Sir John Gardiner, Col.-in-Chf. 61st Regt. Bn. 2nd May, 1781. Joined the R.A. 7th April, 1797. In Oct. of same year was sent to Gibraltar, then partially blockaded by the French fleet. In Nov., 1798, was present at the capture of Minorca. Served under Lord Cathcart, in North Germany, in 1805, and in the Pa., and was made bt. maj. for his services in the trenches before Badajoz. Commanded a field battery at Salamanca, and at the capture of Madrid. At the siege of Burgos he volunteered with several of his men for the trenches. Was soon after appointed to the command of a troop of Horse Artillery, with which he served until the conclusion of the war. K.C.B. "His troop was most severely pressed in covering the left of the army on the retreat from Quatre Bras on the 17th, and took part in the great battle of the 18th June." Appointed principal equerry to Prince Leopold of Saxe-Coburg, on the latter's marriage with Princess Charlotte. A.D.C. to George IV., William IV., and her late Majesty Queen Victoria. In 1848 was appointed Gov. and Col.-in-Chf. of Gibraltar. G.C.B. K.St.A. and Grand Cross of Charles III. of Spain. D. as gen. and col.-comdt. R.A. at Claremont, 26th June, 1864. He m., in 1816, Caroline, eldest dau. of Lt.-Gen. Sir John MacLeod, and had issue.

[2] Afterwards Lt.-Gen. Dyneley, C.B. Served at the battle of Maida, and in the Pa. Was taken prisoner at Majalahonda, when engaged with the rearguard of the French army, 11th Aug., 1812, but escaped from the enemy. Bt.-maj. for Waterloo. D. 21st June, 1860.

[3] 4th son of John Harding. of Old Springs, co. Stafford, by Sarah Booth, Bn. 1791. Retd. on h. p. 8th April, 1825, as 2nd capt., and d. 12th Nov., 1849.

[4] Retired on h. p. as 2nd capt., 1825. D. 6th Feb., 1872. There is a short memoir of this officer's services in the *Gentleman's Magazine* for 1872.

[5] Afterwards Gen. Sir Wm. Bates Ingilby, K.C.B., col.-comdt. R.A. 2nd son of the Rev. Henry Ingilby, of Ripley, and aftds. of Kirkleatham, co. York, by Isabella, eldest dau. of Ralph Bates, of Milbourne, co. Northumberland. Bn. 30th April, 1791. Served in the Pa., and was present at the sieges of Ciudad Rodrigo, forts of Salamanca (wounded) and Burgos. Also at the battles of Busaco, Fuentes d'Onor, and Salamanca. This Sir Wm. Ingilby, who d. in 1879, unm., must not be confounded with his cousin and namesake, Sir Wm. Ingilby, of Ripley Castle, a baronet of the second creation. of whom many amusing anecdotes are still remembered in Yorkshire, and whose appearance cannot have been martial.

CAPTAIN EDWARD C. WHINYATES'S TROOP.

(*Rocket Troop—reduced in* 1816.)

Rank in the

CAPTAIN.	Regiment.	Army.
[1] Edward C. Whinyates, w.	24 Jan. 1813	8 July, 1805
SECOND CAPTAIN.		
[2] Charles C. Dansey, w.	10 Oct. 1809	
FIRST LIEUTENANTS.		
[3] Robert H. Ord	7 Apr. 1806	
[4] Amherst Wright, w.	1 Feb. 1808	
[5] Thos. Fox Strangways, w.	1 Feb. 1808	
[6] Adam Ward	9 Sept. 1810	

[1] Afterwards Gen. Sir E. C. Whinyates, K.C.B. and K.H. Col.-Comdt. R.H.A. This distinguished officer was 3rd son of Maj. Thomas Whinyates, of Abbotsleigh, co. Devon. His mother was Catherine, dau. of Adm. Sir Thomas Frankland, 5th Bart., representative of the historic family of "Frankland of Thirkleby," co. York, which has a direct descent from Oliver Cromwell. Bn. 6th May, 1782. Joined the R.A. 1st March, 1798. Accompanied the expedition, under Abercromby, to the Helder in 1799. Aftds. joined the army under the Duke of York, and took part in the campaign in North Holland. Served at the capture of Madeira in 1801. In 1807 was appointed adj. to the artillery of the army which, under Lord Cathcart, was employed in the attack on Copenhagen, and where he commanded, throughout the siege, one of the principal batteries, which went by the expressve name of the "Churchyard" battery. On his return home was appointed 2nd capt. of Capt. Lefebure's troop of horse artillery (D troop), and in Feb., 1810, embarked for the Pa. The *Camilla*, of 200 tons, having on board Capt. Whinyates, two officers, and 36 horses, nearly foundered in the Bay of Biscay, and was at last driven back to Cork, almost a wreck. This troop, arriving in the Pa. by detachments, was prevented from taking the field for some time. During the interval Whinyates served on the artillery staff, and was present at the battle of Busaco. His troop took the field before the battle of Albuera, where Whinyates commanded the half-troop which was attached to the cavalry on the right. It was here that some of the severest fighting took place. He was mentioned in public despatches for his conduct in the brilliant attack and defeat of Lallemand's cavalry at Ribera, 24th July, 1812. Promoted 1st capt. in Jan., 1813, which occasioned his return to England. At Waterloo he had three horses shot under him, was struck by a round shot on the leg, and sev. wnded. in the left arm towards the close of the day. Bt. maj., and a permanent pens. for wounds. The eminent services of Maj. Whinyates were recognised by his being promoted bt. maj. for Waterloo, and re-appointed to a troop of horse artillery by the Duke of Wellington in 1823, and nominated K.H. same year. C.B., 1831. K.C.B. 1860. Gen. and col.-comdt. of Brigade R.H.A., 1864. D. at Cheltenham

25th Dec., 1865. He had m., 22nd May, 1827, Eliz., only dau. of Samuel Crompton, of Wood End, co. York. An interesting memoir of Gen. Whinyates's military life was published by the R. A. Institution in 1867, from which the above notice is extracted. The Editor is indebted to Maj.-Gen. Whinyates, nephew of Sir Edward, for the loan of the said memoir.

² Afterwards Col. Dansey, C.B. Served in the Pa. Sev. wnded. at Waterloo. D. 21st July, 1853.

³ Afterwards Maj. Ord. K.H. Placed on temporary h. p. 1st April, 1817, and again from 1st Feb., 1819, to 1823. D. 4th Dec., 1828.

⁴ Was attached to the Swedish army in 1813–1814, and saw much service. Recd. a gold medal from the Prince Royal of Sweden for the siege of Gluckstadt, and made a Knt. of the Rl. Order of the Sword in 1814. Retd. on f. p. as maj. 15th June, 1840. D. at Malta, 27th Sept., 1840.

⁵ Afterwards Brig.-Gen. in the Crimea, where he met a soldier's death at Inkermann by the bursting of a shell. Served as a subaltern with the Rocket Troop sent to Germany, and was present at the battles of Goerde and Leipsic in 1813. K.St.A. of Russia, and the Swedish Order of the Sword. Dangerously wounded at Waterloo, and his recovery was miraculous. Eldest son of the Hon. Charles Strangways, by Jane, dau. of Rev. Dr. Haines. Bn. 28th Dec., 1790. M., 20th July, 1833, Sophia, eldest dau. of Benjamin Harenc, and had issue.

⁶ Lost a leg at Tarbes. D. in Dublin, 28th Feb., 1827.

CAPTAIN MERCER'S TROOP.

	Rank in the	
SECOND CAPTAINS.	Regiment.	Army.
¹ Alexander Cavalié Mercer	3 Dec. 1806	
² Robert Newland	20 Dec. 1814	
FIRST LIEUTENANTS.		
³ Henry M. Leathes	1 June, 1806	
⁴ John Hincks	1 Feb. 1808	
⁵ John F. Breton	15 Mar. 1811	

¹ Came of a military race. 2nd son of Gen. Mercer, R.E. Bn. 1783. Served in South America in 1807–1808. His troop came in for the hottest part of the battle on Waterloo Day, and suffered considerably in loss of men and horses. Sir George Wood, R.A., paid the battery a visit on that memorable afternoon, and was surprised to find so many cannon balls whizzing round his ears. " D——n it, Mercer," he exclaimed, " you seem to be having a hot time of it here." Hot it was for all parties concerned, but the gallant way in which the gunners worked their guns kept the French cavalry from reaching the infantry squares behind Mercer's battery. In after years Gen. Mercer published his *Journal of the Waterloo Campaign*, which is a delightful book in every respect. Attained the rank of gen. and col.-comdt., and d. at Cowley Cottage, Exeter, 9th Nov., 1868.

[2] Retired by the sale of his commission 5th April, 1831.

[3] Of Herringfleet Hall, Suffolk. 3rd son and eventual heir of Maj. George Leathes, by Mary, dau. of J. Moore. Served in the Pa. Resigned his commission in 1819. Was distinguished through life for his benevolence and philanthropy, and was equally beloved by rich and poor, young and old, soldiers and civilians. He d. at Lowestoft, 16th Dec., 1864. An interesting obituary notice appeared in the *Gentleman's Magazine* soon after his lamented death. He left issue by his marriage with Charlotte, dau. of Thos. Fowler, of Gunton Hall, Suffolk.

[4] 2nd son of Capt. Thos. Hincks, of Marfield, co. Leicester, by Joanne, eldest dau. of Lt.-Col. Roger Morris, of York. Retd. as capt. on h. p. 1826. M., 31st May, 1826, Henrietta, dau. of Henry Pulleine, of Crake Hall, co. York and d. s. p. 14th Oct., 1842.

[5] The following anecdote is taken from Gen. Mercer's *Waterloo Journal :* " Lt. Breton, who had already lost two horses and had mounted a troop horse, was conversing with me during a leisure moment. As his horse stood at right angles to mine, the poor jaded animal dozingly rested his muzzle on my thigh ; whilst I, the better to hear amidst the infernal din, leant forward, resting my arm between his ears. In this attitude a cannon ball smashed the horse's head to atoms, and the headless trunk sank to the ground ! " Retd. on h. p. 1st Oct., 1820, and d. at Lyndhurst, 17th March, 1852.

MAJOR RAMSAY'S TROOP.

	Regiment.	Rank in the Army.
CAPTAIN.		
[1] Wm. Norman Ramsay, K.	17 Dec. 1813	Maj., 22 Nov. 1813
SECOND CAPTAIN.		
[2] Alexander Macdonald, w.	1 Oct. 1812	
FIRST LIEUTENANTS.		
[3] Wm. Brereton, w.	1 June, 1806	
[4] Philip Sandilands	1 Feb. 1808	
[5] Wm. L. Robe, K.	28 June, 1808	

[1] This officer's name has been immortalised by Napier in his *Peninsular War*. He came of a Scottish family, and was the eldest of three sons of a retired naval officer who resided in Edinburgh. He was the pride and glory of the branch of the army to which he belonged, and the beau-ideal of what a Horse Artilleryman should be. He served with great credit in Maj. Bull's troop of R.H.A., in the Pa., from 1811 to 1813. It was in the campaign of 1811 that he performed the brilliant action which Napier's facile pen has so strikingly illustrated. This happened on 5th May, 1811, when, the British cavalry out-guards being far outnumbered near Fuentes d'Onor, were driven in upon their supports, and Capt. Ramsay found himself cut off. It is a matter of history how Ramsay, at the head of his battery, charged like a

whirlwind through the French squadrons who intervened between his handful of men and the British troops, and rejoined the latter in safety when given up for lost.   And at the battle of Vittoria, Ramsay again distinguished himself, but, by an unfortunate act of disobedience to Wellington's orders, he incurred the Iron Duke's iron displeasure.   The story has been told as follows by a well-known author, and differs somewhat from the account given by Col. Duncan in his *History of the Royal Artillery*:—"I remember hearing a striking instance of what, perhaps, might be called severe justice, which he exercised on a young and distinguished officer of artillery in Spain ; and though one cannot help pitying the case of the gallant young fellow who was the sacrifice, yet the question of strict duty, to the very word, was set at rest for ever under the Duke's command, and it saved much after trouble, by making every officer satisfied, however fiery his courage or tender his sense of being suspected of the white feather, that implicit obedience was the course he must pursue.   The case was this : The army was going into action.   The Duke posted an officer, with his six guns, at a certain point, telling him to remain there until he had orders from him.   Away went the rest of the army, and the officer was left doing nothing at all, which he didn't like ; for he was one of those high-blooded gentlemen who are never so happy as when they are making other people miserable, and he was longing for the head of a French column to be hammering away at.   In half an hour or so he heard the distant sound of action, and it approached nearer and nearer, until he heard it close beside him ; and he wondered rather that he was not invited to take a share in it, when, pat to his thought, up came an aide-de-camp at full speed, telling him that Gen. Somebody ordered him to bring up his guns. The officer asked, ' Did not the order come from Lord Wellington ?' The aide-de-camp said ' No,' but from the gen., whoever he was.   The officer explained that he was placed there by Lord Wellington, under command not to move unless by an order from himself.   The aide-de-camp stated that the general's entire brigade was being driven in, and must be annihilated without the aid of the guns, and asked, ' Would he let a whole brigade be slaughtered ?' in a tone which wounded the young soldier's pride, savouring, as he thought it did, of an imputation on his courage. He immediately ordered his guns to move, and joined battle with the general ; but while he was away an aide-de-camp from Lord Wellington rode up to where the guns had been posted, and, of course, no gun was to be had for the service which Lord Wellington required.   Well, the French were repulsed, as it happened ; but the want of those six guns seriously marred a pre-concerted movement of the Duke's, and the officer in command of them was immediately put in arrest.   Almost every general officer in the army endeavoured to get this sentence revoked, lamenting the fate of a gallant fellow being sent away for a slight error in judgment while the army was in full action ; but Lord Wellington was inexorable, saying he must make an example to secure himself in the perfect obedience of officers to their orders, and it had the effect."—Mr. Lover's *Handy Andy.*
To a man of Norman Ramsay's highly honourable and sensitive nature the circumstances of his arrest, coupled with the omission of his name from the Vittoria despatches, and the loss of a brevet he had well earned, may be said to have inflicted a wound which neither time nor subsequent honours could heal.   Three weeks after his arrest he was restored to the command of his battery, to the great joy of the whole army in Spain, and after the battle of the Bidassoa he was promoted bt. maj.   At Waterloo he commanded the H Troop R.H.A., and his forward gallantry in that battle attracted the fatal bullet which put an end to his noble life.   He was buried on the field by his great friend Sir Augustus Frazer, during a momentary lull in the battle, but three weeks later was disinterred and his body sent to Edinburgh, as the only

consolation to his aged father, half-demented with grief, who was fated to lose his three gallant sons in the short space of eight months. Norman Ramsay m., 14th June, 1808, Mary Emilia, eldest dau. of Lt.-Gen. MacLeod, of Macleod. Sir Augustus Frazer erected a monument to Ramsay's memory on the field of Waterloo. The hero's remains were subsequently interred in Inveresk Churchyard.

[2] Brother to Gen. Sir John Macdonald, Adjt. Gen., and to Col. Robert Macdonald, 1st Foot. Aftds. Lt.-Gen., C.B., and K.St.A. Served at the capture of the Cape of Good Hope in 1806, and was taken prisoner at Buenos Ayres in 1807. Served in the Pa. and distinguished himself at Busaco and San Sebastian. Was sev. wnded. at Waterloo. Bt. Maj. D. at Aix-la-Chapelle, 31st May, 1856.

[3] Aftds. Lt.-Gen. and K.C.B. Also K.H. and col.-comdt. R.A. Served in the Pa., and was sev. wounded at Waterloo (bt.-maj. in Jan., 1819.) Served as maj.-gen., and was second in command of the expedition under M.-Gen. D'Aguilar, who assaulted and took the forts of the Bocca Tigris in the Canton River. Served with the fleets off Sebastopol in Oct., 1854, and directed the rockets fired from the *Britannia* against the city and forts. D. 27th July, 1864.

[4] Retired on f. p. 23rd June, 1846. D. as lt.-gen. at Hythe, Oct., 1869.

[5] Son of Col. Sir Wm. Robe, R.A., a distinguished officer. He obtained his first commission 3rd Oct., 1807, and in the same year accompanied the expedition to Gothenburg. Served throughout the Par. War with much distinction. " He had the singular honour, as a subaltern, to be mentioned for his distinguished conduct by Wellington, and in consequence the gold medal and clasp for the battles of Nivelle and Nive were forwarded to his family after his death." An account of his death at Waterloo is given in a letter from Capt. Alex. Macdonald, of Ramsay's battery, to Sir Wm. Robe (*See* Appendix.)

LIEUT.-COLONEL SIR HEW D. ROSS'S TROOP.

(The historical " Chestnut Troop.")

Rank in the

CAPTAIN.	Regiment.	Army.
¹ Sir Hew Dalrymple Ross, K.C.B.	24 July, 1806	Lt.-Col., 21 June, [1813
SECOND CAPTAIN.		
² John B. Parker, w.	5 June, 1808	Maj., 21 June, 1813
FIRST LIEUTENANTS.		
³ *Richard Hardinge*	19 Dec. 1806	
⁴ James Day, w.	1 Feb. 1808	
⁵ Phipps Onslow	16 Dec. 1808	
⁶ Francis Warde	8 Mar. 1812	

¹ Afterwards F.-M. and G.C.B. He was grandson of Alexander Ross, of Balkail, co. Wigtown, and cousin to Capt. Sir James Ross. R.N., the distinguished Polar navigator. Commanded the A Troop, A Brigade, R.H.A., during the Par. War, and was dangerously wounded at the siege of Badajoz. K.C.B. and K.T.S., also the gold cross and two clasps. K.St.A. of Russia for Waterloo. He was the first artilleryman who was made a F.-M. D. lt.-gov. of Chelsea Hospital in Dec., 1868, aged 90.

² Afterwards maj.-gen. and C.B. Served in the Pa. and at Walcheren. Lost his left leg at Waterloo. Bt. lt.-col. 18th June, 1815. Was lt.-gov. of the R.M.A. at Woolwich, from 1st April, 1848, up to the time of his death in March, 1851. He was 2nd son of Adm. Sir Hyde Parker, by Anne, dau. of John Boteler, of Henley. M., in 1814, Anne, dau. of Adm. Home Popham, and had issue.

³ Brother to Henry, Viscount Hardinge. Was not at Waterloo, being otherwise employed that day, but was present both at Ligny and Quatre Bras on the eventful 16th June, 1815. Had served in the Pa. Aftds. maj.-gen. and K.H. Bn. 14th April, 1790. D. 20th July, 1864. He was twice md., and left issue by both wives.

⁴ Served in the Pa. Retd. on h. p. as 2nd capt., 3rd Feb., 1828, and d. in Jersey, 1st Aug., 1843.

⁵ 3rd son of the Rev. Arthur Onslow, Archdeacon of Berks and Dean of Worcester, by Frances, dau. of Constantine Phipps. He was distantly related to the noble family of Onslow, one of whom was satirised in the lines :—

> "What can Tommy Onslow do?
> He can drive a curricle and two.
> Can Tommy Onslow do no more?
> Yes, he can drive a curricle and four."

Retd. on h. p. as lt. 9th Dec., 1824. D. 10th May, 1867. He was twice md., and left issue.

⁶ Afterwards Gen. Sir Francis Warde, K.C.B., col. comdt. R.A. D. at Winchfield, 4th May, 1879. He was 4th son of Charles Warde, of Squerryes Court, Kent. M. Annabella, eldest dau. of Robert Adeane, of Babraham, Cambs. D. at Reading in May, 1879.

MAJOR BEANE'S TROOP.

(*Reduced in* 1816.)

		Rank in the	
CAPTAIN.	Regiment.	Army.	
[1] George Beane, ᴋ.	1 Feb. 1808	Maj.,12 Apr. 1814	
SECOND CAPTAIN.			
[2] Wm. Webber, w.	17 Apr. 1812		
FIRST LIEUTENANTS.			
[3] John E. Maunsell	1 June, 1806		
[4] James R. Bruce	1 June, 1806		
[5] Michael T. Cromie, w.	25 Jan. 1809		

[1] This officer was appointed to the command of D Troop R.H.A. in 1813. Capt. Mercer succeeded to the command after Waterloo. Served in the Pa., and was present at Corunna, Vittoria, San Sebastian, Orthes, and Toulouse.

[2] Was present at the capture of the colony of Surinam in 1804. Served through the Par. War, and saw active service in Canada in 1814. Bt.-maj. 21st Jan., 1819 ; Maj., h. p., unattached, 1826 ; Lt.-col., 1837. D. at Hexworth House, Cornwall, 1st March, 1847.

[3] Retired on h. p. as 2nd capt., 1826. D. 20th Nov., 1869.

[4] Afterwards Sir James Robertson Bruce, Bart. 2nd son of the Rev. Sir Henry Bruce, Bart., by Letitia, dau. of the Rev. Dr. Henry Barnard. Retd. on h. p. as 1st lt., 16th June, 1820. M., 20th Sept., 1819, Ellen, youngest dau. of Robert Bamford Hesketh, of Gwyrch Castle, co. Denbigh, and had issue. D. 1836.

[5] Had both his legs taken off by one shot, and d. two days after, while undergoing amputation.

ROYAL ARTILLERY.

CAPTAIN SANDHAM'S BRIGADE.*

Rank in the

CAPTAIN.	Regiment.	Army.
[1] Charles F. Sandham	14 Feb. 1814	1 June, 1806
SECOND CAPTAIN.		
[2] Wm. H. Stopford	1 Apr. 1815	
FIRST LIEUTENANTS.		
[3] George Foot	1 Feb. 1808	
[4] George M. Baynes	1 Feb. 1808	
SECOND LIEUTENANT.		
[5] Darell Jago	5 July, 1813	

* This and all the other Field Brigades were each armed with five 9-pounders and one 5½-inch howitzer.

[1] The name of Sandham has been a household word in the Artillery for nearly 140 years. The above Capt. Sandham came of the Sussex family of this name, who have for long been landholders in that county. "The first shot fired by the allied artillery at Waterloo was fired by Sandham's brigade." Retd. on h. p. as bt. maj., 7th June, 1822. D. at Rowdell, Sussex, Feb., 1869.

[2] Third son of Lt.-Gen. the Hon. Edward Stopford. Assumed the additional surname of Blair on succeeding to the Penninghame estate, co. Wigtown. Retd. on h. p. as bt. col., 20th Dec., 1841. Col. Stopford-Blair m., in 1823, a dau. of Col. R. Bull, C.B. He d. 23rd Sept., 1868, and was succeeded by his eldest son.

[3] Retired on h. p. as 2nd capt., 13th Nov., 1826, and d. 26th Oct., 1874. In 1814 he served at the attack on Merxem, and the bombardment of the French shipping at Antwerp.

[4] Served in the Pa. Retd. on h. p. as 2nd capt., 25th Sept., 1834. D. in Guernsey, 28th Oct., 1874. He was nephew of Sir John Macleod, R.A., and brother to Capt. H. Baynes, Bde.-Maj., R.A., at Waterloo.

[5] Retd. on h. p. as 2nd capt., 6th Jan., 1836. D. 22nd Dec., 1850.

CAPTAIN S. BOLTON'S BRIGADE.

	Rank in the	
CAPTAIN.	Regiment.	Army.
¹ Samuel Bolton, K.	20 Dec. 1814	

SECOND CAPTAIN.

| ² Charles Napier, w. | 16 Mar. 1812 | |

FIRST LIEUTENANTS.

³ George Pringle	1 June, 1806	
⁴ Wm. C. Anderson	1 Aug. 1808	
⁵ Charles Spearman, w.	30 Aug. 1812	
⁶ Wm. Sharpin	20 Dec. 1814	

SECOND LIEUTENANT.

| ⁷ Burke Cuppage | 17 Dec. 1812 | |

¹ This officer was killed towards the close of the battle, when directing the fire of his battery against the Imperial Guards in their historical advance.

² Succeeded Capt. Bolton in the command of the battery, and by Wellington's orders gave the advancing French column "a salvo of grape and canister" which did terrible execution among their devoted ranks. A few minutes afterwards Capt. Napier recd. eight wounds from the bursting of a shrapnel shell. On 21st Jan., 1819, recd. a tardy bt. of maj. for his services at Waterloo. Retd. by the sale of his commission, 20th March, 1827. D. at Lisburn, 20th June, 1849.

³ Retd. on f. p. as bt. maj., 16th May, 1839. D. in Edinburgh, 23rd March, 1842.

⁴ Afterwards maj.-gen. D. in Edinburgh, 30th Aug., 1865.

⁵ D. at Brussels, 27th June, 1815, of wounds recd. at Waterloo. Eldest son of Charles Spearman, of Thornley Hall, co. Durham, by Sarah, dau. and heir of Samuel Brooke, of Birchington, Kent.

⁶ Retd. on h. p. 1st July, 1823. D. 23rd July, 1857.

⁷ Afterwards Gen. Sir Burke Cuppage, K.C.B., and col.-comdt. R.A. Son of Lt.-Gen. Wm. Cuppage, R.A., by the widow of Maj. Cairnes, 39th Foot, whose son's death has already been recorded. D. 19th April, 1877.

MAJOR W. LLOYD'S BRIGADE.

(*Reduced in* 1817.)

Rank in the

CAPTAIN.	Regiment.	Army.
[1] Wm. Lloyd, w.	13 June, 1807	Maj., 4 June, 1814
SECOND CAPTAIN.		
[2] Samuel Rudyerd	24 Mar. 1809	
FIRST LIEUTENANTS.		
[3] Fortescue Wells	1 Feb. 1808	
[4] Samuel Phelps	18 Sept. 1809	
SECOND LIEUTENANT.		
[5] Wm. H. Harvey, w.	13 Dec. 1813	

[1] This gallant soldier was son of Maj. John Lloyd, 46th Foot, A.D.C. to Sir H. Clinton during the American War, by Corbetta, dau. of the Ven. George Holcombe, Archdeacon of Carmarthen. Bn. 2nd Dec., 1778. D. at Brussels 29th July, 1815, of a wound recd. at Waterloo.

[2] Son of Lt.-Gen. Henry Rudyerd, R.E. Attained rank of col. in 1846, and d. at Whitby, 29th July, 1847.

[3] Probably son of Adm. Wells, one of whose sons, in 1815, was a subaltern in the R.E. Retd. on h. p. 27th Oct., 1826. D. at Slade, 29th Dec., 1861.

[4] Appears to have been the 7th son of Joseph Phelps, of Moyallon, co. Down. Retd. on h. p. 4th Aug., 1822. D. unm., 13th Dec., 1827.

[5] Second son of John Harvey, of Mount Pleasant, co. Wexford, by Mary, dau. of Wm. Harrison, of Castle Harrison, co. Cork. " Left his bride (Eliz., dau. of Col. Paulet Colebrooke, R.A.) at the church door to join his battery in the Netherlands." Lost his right arm at Waterloo. Recd. a pens. of £70 per ann., and was appointed to the Invalid Batt. in 1817. Retd. on f. p. in 1819, and d. at Eltham, 18th Aug., 1826, leaving issue.

CAPTAIN J. SINCLAIR'S BRIGADE.

	Rank in the Regiment.	Army.
SECOND CAPTAINS.		
[1] James Sinclair	14 Feb. 1814	
[2] Forbes Macbean	20 Dec. 1814	
FIRST LIEUTENANTS.		
[3] John A. Wilson	20 Dec. 1814	
[4] Wm. H. Poole, w.	10 May, 1815	
SECOND LIEUTENANT.		
[5] Richard B. Burnaby	17 Dec. 1812	

[1] Retd. on f. p. as lt.-col., 23rd Dec., 1841. D. in Jersey, 15th May, 1851.

[2] Served at the siege of Copenhagen in 1807, expedition to Sweden 1808, Corunna campaign same year, Walcheren expedition and siege of Flushing 1809. Served in Canada during the rebellion in 1837-1838, and for his services at Prescott, in Upper Canada, in Nov., 1838, received the thanks of the lt.-gov. and a bt. lt.-colonelcy. The Editor is indebted to this officer's son, the late Col. Forbes Macbean, formerly comg. 92nd Highlanders, Sergt.-at-Arms to Her late Majesty, for the following interesting particulars regarding his family : " My great-great-grandfather was minister of the High Church (Presbyterian) at Inverness for upwards of forty years. One of his sons (Forbes) was a maj.-gen. of R.A. ; two of his sons were—one (Frederick) col.-comg. 6th Foot, the other maj. of the 14th and 71st Regts. The eldest had six sons, all in the army, viz.: Sir William, K.C.B. and K.T.S., gen. and col.-in-chf. 92nd Highlanders ; Frederick, K.H., col. 84th Regt. ; Forbes, col. R.A. ; Archibald, lt.-gen. R.A. ; Alfred, capt. 93rd Highlanders ; Alexander, lt. 83rd Regt. The last two died young. When their father took the youngest to the Duke of York, C.-in-C., to ask for a commission for him, the duke replied, ' Yes, and if you had six more sons they should all have commissions.' In the retreat on Corunna, my uncle Archibald, then in the Horse Artillery, picked up his brother Frederick off the roadside, very seriously wounded, and carried him on a gun-carriage into Corunna, and so saved his life." Forbes Macbean attained the rank of bt. col., and d. (on f. p. retd. list) in Cleveland, co. York, 19th June, 1853.

[3] D. as col. R.A. at Dinan, France, 20th July, 1857.

[4] Retd. on h. p. as 2nd capt., 22nd Jan., 1834. D. at Terrick Hall, White-church, 20th Jan., 1859.

[5] Afterwards lt.-gen. on the retd. f. p. list. D. in 1871.

MAJOR T. ROGERS'S BRIGADE.*

	Regiment.	Rank in the Army.
CAPTAIN.		
[1] Thos. Rogers	1 June, 1806	Maj.,4 June, 1814
SECOND CAPTAIN.		
[2] Thos. Scott	20 June, 1812	
FIRST LIEUTENANT.		
[3] Robert Manners, w.	13 Mar. 1811	
SECOND LIEUTENANT.		
[4] Richard Goodwin Wilson	17 Dec. 1812	

* This list is imperfect, but is an improvement on the list given in Col. Duncan's *History of the R.A.* in so far that the Editor has been able to add two officers to his list.

[1] Major Rogers's battery was hotly engaged at Quatre Bras, and rendered valuable service. C.B. for Waterloo. D. as col., 9th Aug., 1839, at Woolwich.

[2] Had his horse killed under him at Quatre Bras. D. as bt.-maj. at Ford-wich, Canterbury, 28th Dec., 1834.

[3] Was attached to Capt. Cleeves's German battery at the battle of Ligny, and recd. a wound, which proved mortal, on 18th June, 1815.

[4] Was near Picton when the latter was killed at Waterloo, and was the last survivor of Rogers's Waterloo Battery. Was superintendent at Shoe-buryness during the Crimean War. D. as maj.-gen., retd. f. p., 24th Oct., 1876.

ROYAL ARTILLERY OFFICERS AT WATERLOO WHO WERE UNATTACHED.

FIRST LIEUTENANTS.

[1] Wm. Lemoine.
[2] Edward Trevor.

[1] Afterwards maj. retd. p., 1840. D. 21st Oct., 1874.

[2] " Belonged to Capt. Tyler's Company (6 Co. 5th Batt.) in 1815. The co. was at Antwerp in June, 1815, but Lieut. Trevor was unattached at Waterloo." (Communicated by Lieut. Hubert Trevor, grandson of above officer.) Aftds. major-gen. retd. f. p. Md., 11th June, 1827, Anne, 2nd dau. of G. Goulding. D. at Plymouth, 22nd Nov., 1878.

The following R.A. officers received the Waterloo medal, but "chaotic confusion" has left a doubt as to whether they served at Waterloo, or were with the reserve forces on 18th June, 1815 :—

FIRST LIEUTENANTS.

[1] Edward Wm. Wood.
[2] George Silvester Maule.

SECOND LIEUTENANTS.

[3] Henry Dunnicliffe.
[4] Thos. Watkis.
[5] Wm. How Hennis.
[6] Chas. Geo. Kett.
[7] Gustavus T. Hume.

[1] In Capt. Ilbert's company at Brussels in June, 1815.   D. at Gibraltar, 25th Nov., 1826.

[2] In Capt. Ilbert's company at Brussels in June, 1815.   Served on board a gunboat in the Adriatic 1812.   Served in Spain 1813.   2nd capt. 31st July, 1832.   D. at Greenwich, 18th Oct., 1839.

[3] Retd. h. p. 1st Apr., 1819.   D. at Richmond, 8th Apr., 1866.

[4] 1st Lieut. 1st Aug., 1815.   D. at the Cape of Good Hope 29th Apr., 1825

[5] Retd. on f. p. as lt.-col. 1851.   Attained rank of lt.-gen. retd. list 1868, and d. at Boulogne 14th Dec., 1872.

[6] 1st Lieut. 30th Sept., 1816.   Retd. f. p. 4th March, 1835.   D. 14th Sept., 1841.

[7] In Capt. Ilbert's company at Brussels in June, 1815.   1st Lieut. 21st Nov., 1816.   Purchased a cornetcy in 15th Lt. Dragoons, 16th Dec., 1819.   Lieut. 7th Aug., 1823.   Capt. 10th June, 1824.   H. p. 1829.   Probably belonged to a collateral branch of " Hume, of Castle Hume," co. Fermanagh.

CORPS OF ROYAL ARTILLERY DRIVERS.*

Rank in the

	Regiment.	Army.
CAPTAIN-COMMISSARY.		
[1] Wm. H. Humphreys	21 May, 1806	
FIRST LIEUT.-COMMISSARIES.		
[2] George Fiske	5 June, 1804	
[3] Matthew Evans	1 Jan. 1807	
[4] Wm. Carthew	14 Jan. 1807	
[5] George Wilkinson	1 Sept. 1808	
[6] Edward Philpot	1 Sept. 1808	
[7] Thomas Reid	1 May, 1809	
[8] John Roberts	1 Dec. 1809	
SECOND LIEUT. COMMISSARY.		
[9] Joseph Jagger	16 July, 1813	
ADJUTANT.		[June, 1804
[10] Moore Jordan	1 Jan. 1813	First Lieut., 7

* "The corps of R. A. Drivers was gradually reduced after the peace of 1814—four troops on 1st Jan., 1815, two on 1st July, 1816, and two on 1st Aug., 1816—the officers being placed on half-pay. In 1822 the corps ceased to exist."—Kane's *R.A. List*, from which the following notes are taken :—

[1] Retd. 1st Aug., 1816. D. at Paris, 17th Feb., 1837.

[2] Retd. 1st Dec., 1816. D. 6th Sept., 1824.

[3] Retd. 1st Aug., 1816. D. 7th April, 1854.

[4] Retd. 1st Aug., 1816.

[5] Served at Copenhagen and in the Pa. A'so in the Walcheren expedition. H. p. 1st Aug., 1816. Appointed barrack-master at Rutland barracks. D. 1831.

[6] Retd. 1st Aug., 1816. D. 12th May, 1855.

[7] Retd. 1st July, 1816. D. 1855.

[8] Retd. 1st July, 1816. D. 20th Aug., 1858.

[9] Retd. 1st Aug., 1816. D. 28th Sept., 1862.

[10] Retd. on f. p., 11th March, 1817.

CORPS OF ROYAL ENGINEERS.

		Rank in the	
LIEUT.-COLONEL.	Regiment.	Army.
[1] Jas. Carmichael Smyth	20 Oct. 1813	
CAPTAINS.		
[2] Sir George Hoste, Kt.	21 May, 1812	Maj.,17 Mar. 1814
[3] John Oldfield	26 Jan. 1815	
SECOND CAPTAINS.		
[4] Frank Stanway	21 July, 1813	
[5] Alexander Thomson	21 July, 1813	
LIEUTENANTS.		
[6] John Wm. Pringle, w.	1 May, 1811	
[7] Marcus Anton Waters	1 May, 1811	
[8] Francis Bond Head	13 May, 1811	
[9] Francis Yarde Gilbert	10 June, 1811	
[10] John Sperling, Adjt.	1 July, 1812	
[11] Andrew Douglas White	21 July, 1813	

[1] C. B. for Waterloo. The admirable position which Wellington chose for his army on 18th June, 1815, had been surveyed by the Duke's directions in 1814, and it was Col. Smyth's plan of the ground which enabled Wellington to place his troops so rapidly and advantageously that day. Created a bart. 25th Aug., 1821. Eldest son of James Carmichael Smyth, M.D., F.R.S., the intimate friend and contemporary of Sir Robert Strange, the great engraver. Bn. 22nd Feb., 1780. M., 28th May, 1816, Harriet, only surviving child of Gen. Robert Morse, and had issue. Gov. of British Guiana. D. there 4th March, 1838.

[2] 2nd son of Dixon Hoste, by Margaret, dau. of Henry Stanforth, of Salthouse, co. Norfolk. M., in 1812, Mary, only dau. of James Borroughes, of Burlingham Hall, Norfolk, and had issue. Lt.-Col. 29th July, 1825. C.B. D. 1845.

[3] Brigade-Maj. at Waterloo. An interesting extract from his journal of the Waterloo campaign is given in Maj.-Gen. Porter's *History of the Corps of Royal Engineers*. D. as gen. and K.H. 2nd Aug., 1863.

[4] Served in Sweden and in the Pa. Capt. 23rd March, 1825. D. at Limerick, 9th Dec., 1832.

[5] Wounded at the taking of Cambray in June, 1815. D. as maj. 20th June, 1830, in Edinburgh.

[6] Served in the Pa. D. as maj., 12th Oct., 1861, at Bath.

[7] Retd. on f. p. as col., and d. in London, 14th Jan., 1868.

8 Afterwards lt.-gov. of Upper Canada, and K.C.H. Retd. in 1828 as maj. Created a bart. in 1837. Son of James Head, by Frances, dau. of George Burges. M., 20th May, 1816, Julia Valenza, sister of Mark, Lord Somerville, and had issue. D. 20th July, 1875.

9 Mentioned in Sir C. Colville's despatch for his services at the taking of Cambray, in June, 1815. 6th son of the Rev. Edmund Gilbert, Vicar of Constantine, co. Cornwall. Retd. as capt. 1825. M. Eliz., widow of Wm. Burroughs. D. at Killaloe, 30 Nov., 1871.

10 Led the Forlorn Hope at Bergen-op-Zoom in 1814. Some extracts from his Waterloo diary are given in Maj.-Gen. Porter's *History of the R.E.* One of the sons of Henry Piper Sperling, of Norbury Park, Surrey, by Sarah, dau. and co-heir of Henry Grace, of Tottenham, Middlesex. Retd. on h. p. as lt. 1824. M. Harriet, dau. of John Hanson. D. 14th Feb., 1877.

11 2nd capt. 6th Dec., 1826. H. p. 6th Oct., 1831. D. at Paramatta, N.S.W. 24th Nov., 1837.

MEDICAL STAFF.

INSPECTOR.

Date of Commission.

[1] Sir James Robert Grant, M.D.   14 July, 1814

DEPUTY-INSPECTORS.

Wm. Taylor	25 July, 1811
John Gunning	17 Sept. 1812
Stephen Woolriche	26 May, 1814
[2] John R. Hume	26 May, 1814

PHYSICIAN.

[3] George Denecke, M.D., w.   17 June, 1813

SURGEONS.

[4] David Brownrigg	18 June, 1807
Henry Gresley Emery, M.D.	11 Aug. 1808
[5] Thos. Draper	1 Sept. 1808
M. A. Burmeister	4 Jan. 1810
Robert Grant	22 Aug. 1811
John Maling	3 Sept. 1812
[6] John Callander	25 Mar. 1813
[7] Andrew Halliday	29 Apr. 1813
[8] Jas. Matthews, M.D.	9 Sept. 1813
[9] J. Gideon Van Millingen, M.D.	26 May, 1814
[10] Samuel Barwick Bruce	25 May, 1815

ASSISTANT-SURGEONS.

[11] J. W. McAuley	8 Feb. 1810
James Dease	11 Mar. 1813
Wm. Twining	10 Mar. 1814
[12] George Evers	3 June, 1815

APOTHECARY.

Wm. Lyons   9 Sept. 1813

[1] This distinguished physician was son of Duncan Grant, of Lingeston, N.B., and brother to that equally distinguished soldier, Col. Colquhoun Grant (*see* Staff). Bn. at Forres, Morayshire, in 1771. Served as assistant-surgeon and surgeon in the 11th Regt. of Foot, and was one of the very few officers who served through the whole of the war with France, viz., from 1793 to 1815. C.B. and K.H. In 1814 he recd. the order of St. Anne of Russia from the Emperor for his services when with the Russian army in France. Aftds. Inspector-Gen. of Hospitals. Retd. on f. p. about 1847. Resided in Cumberland, and d. 10th Jan., 1864. (Communicated by the late Major Walter McGregor, nephew of the above).

[2] Wellington's friend and physician for many years. "AFTER WATERLOO. —After the battle Wellington rode to Brussels, and the first person who entered his room on the morning of the 19th was Dr. Hume. 'He had, as usual,' says the doctor, 'taken off his clothes, but his face was covered with the dust and sweat of the previous day. He extended his hand to me, which I held in mine while I told him of Alexander Gordon's death. He was much affected. I felt his tears dropping fast upon my hand, and, looking towards him, saw them chasing one another in a stream over his dusty cheeks. He brushed them suddenly away with his left hand, and said to me, in a voice tremulous with emotion—" Well, thank God, I don't know what it is to lose a battle, but certainly nothing can be more painful than to gain one with the loss of so many of one's friends." ' "—*Fifty Years' Biographical Reminiscences,* by Lord William Lennox

[3] Slightly wounded at Quatre Bras, and his horse sev. wnded.

[4] Served in the Pa. "Was the first surgeon to amputate with success at the hip joint." D. in Dublin in Nov., 1836.

[5] Served in Egypt, at Maida, and in the Pa. Was surgeon to Sir John Moore. Recd. the thanks of the Govt. for his services at Waterloo. Inspector-Gen. of Hospitals. D. 28th June, 1850, at Instow, Barnstaple.

[6] Surgeon to the 7th Hussars, 7th May, 1816. H. p. 25th June, 1829, from Rl. Waggon Train. Living 1846.

[7] Afterwards Sir Andrew Halliday, Knt., M.D., F.R.S., and K.H. Was educated for the Church, but finding he had a medical turn, adopted the latter profession. Served on the medical staff both in Spain and Portugal, and aftds. at Waterloo. Was of humble parentage, but of good blood, being descended from "Thom Halliday, my sister's son, so dear," mentioned by the great Sir William Wallace. D. at Dumfries, 7th Sept., 1839.

[8] Hospital assistant 8th July, 1799. Assist.-surgn. Dec., 1799. H. p. before 1824.

[9] D. Sept., 1852.

[10] Entered the medical dept. 1804, but saw some of his earliest service afloat under Lord Nelson in 1805. Present at the capture of St. Thomas, St. Croix, and St. John in 1807. Subsequently served at Fort Dessaix, Martinique, and Guadaloupe. Proceeded to the Pa. in 1813 and America 1814-15. Present at the attack on New Orleans and Fort Bowyer. Joined the army in the Netherlands in May, 1815. Present at Waterloo and capture of Paris. H. p. 1816. Retd. in Jan., 1833. D. in London 24th Dec., 1852. Left issue a son, Lt.-Col. Robt. C. D. Bruce, h. p. 8th Foot, to whom there is a tablet in Ripon Minster.

[11] H. p. 5th Foot 22nd Aug., 1816. Living 1852.

[12] Assist.-Surgn. 14th Foot 23rd Dec., 1824. H. p. 15th Dec., 1825. Living 1846.

ORDNANCE MEDICAL DEPARTMENT.*

SURGEONS.

		Date of Commission.
1	Edward Simpson	5 Aug. 1813
2	John Morgan	16 Feb. 1814
3	James Powell	28 May, 1814
4	T. Macmillan Fogo, M.D.	26 Sept. 1814

ASSISTANT-SURGEONS.

5	Richard Hichins	11 Nov. 1811
6	James Ambrose	11 Nov. 1811
7	Alex. Macdonald, M.D.	5 Aug. 1813

SECOND ASSISTANT-SURGEONS.

8	Matthias Kenny	1 Dec. 1810
9	Edward Rudge	3 Dec. 1812
10	Thos. Beard	5 Aug. 1813
11	Henry Gatty	20 Nov. 1813
12	Edward Donovan Verner	29 Nov. 1813
13	Henry Peter Loedel	1 Feb. 1814
14	Wm. Barker Daniel	16 Apr. 1814
15	John Bingham	26 Sept. 1814
16	Walter Raleigh, M.D.	12 Oct. 1814
17	Stewart Chisholm	20 Oct. 1814

* The notes given below are taken from Kane's *R. A. List* :—

[1] Sen. surgeon 16th Jan., 1841. Retd. f. p. 24th Jan., 1844. D. at Jessfield, 23rd Sept., 1854.

[2] H. p. 1st Sept., 1817. D. at Dover, 4th Sept., 1849.

[3] H. p. 1st Oct., 1817.

[4] H. p. as sen. surgeon 25th July, 1849. D. at Tiverton, 28th Sept., 1850.

[5] H. p. 1st Apr., 1816. D. at St. Ives, 17th Jan., 1866.

[6] H. p. 1st Oct., 1816. D. at Westport, Ireland, 17th Apr., 1824.

[7] H. p. 11th Sept., 1838. D. at Aberdeen, 8th March, 1860.

[8] H. p. 1st Feb., 1819. D. in Dublin, 24th Sept., 1874.

[9] H. p. 1st June, 1816. D. at Fakenham, 29th Nov., 1854.

[10] H. p. 1st Nov., 1822. D. at Spa, 29th Aug., 1848.

[11] H. p. 31st Dec., 1824. D. 6th Apr., 1858.

[12] H. p. 30th March, 1825. D. in London, 9th July, 1861.

[13] D. at Montreal, 24th March, 1825.

[14] D. 28th Jan., 1824.

[15] H. p. 1st May, 1816. D. in Ireland, 20th Jan., 1825.

[16] Retd. 8th Nov., 1832.

[17] Sen. surgeon 18th June, 1846. H. p. 8th Nov., 1852. Staff surgeon, 1st class, 20th July, 1855. D. at Inverness, 30th Sept., 1862.

FIELD TRAIN DEPARTMENT OF THE ORDNANCE.*

* The Editor has no means of tracing the war services of the officers of this department, and can only give two Waterloo representatives of the above.

ASSISTANT-COMMISSARIES.

	Date of Commission.
[1] Samuel J. Tibbs	1 June, 1814
[2] Richard Baut	1 June, 1815

[1] Served through the whole of the Par. war, and in 1848 recd. the medal with fourteen clasps. He also recd. the Waterloo medal. H. p. 6th Aug., 1816. An interesting memoir of this veteran, with his portrait, appeared in *The Regiment*, 29th Aug., 1896.

[2] H. p. 27th March, 1816. D. in 1818. His Waterloo medal was for long in the Seaforth collection.

COMMISSARIAT DEPARTMENT.*

* The Commissariat officers who served at Waterloo were not granted the Waterloo medal, and none of them ever appeared in any *Army List* with the glorious " W " before their names, although, in after years, those who had served in the Pa. had the " P " before their names in the *Army Lists*, and they recd. the Par. medal in 1848. It is, therefore, impossible, to give any correct list of officers belonging to the above department, but the Editor gives the names of six officers who were undoubtedly at Waterloo.

DEPUTY-COMMISSARIES-GENERAL.

	Date of Commission.
[1] Randal Isham Routh	9 Mar. 1812
[2] Gregory Haines	25 Dec. 1814

ASSISTANT-COMMISSARIES-GENERAL.

[3] Tupper Carey	10 Aug. 1811
[4] Chas. Purcell	10 Aug. 1811
[5] Alex. R. C. Dallas	1 July, 1814

DEPUTY-ASSISTANT-COMMISSARY-GENERAL.

[6] Gilbert Dinwiddie	5 Sept. 1814

[1] Afterwards Sir Randal Routh, K.C.B., commissary-gen. Son of Richard Routh, Chief Justice of Newfoundland. Bn. at Poole, co. Dorset, 1787. Served in the Pa. M. in Paris, in 1815, the niece of the French Bishop of Canada. D. in Jersey, 29th Nov., 1858.

[2] Recd. the Par. medal with eleven clasps in 1848. Retd. h. p. as commissary-gen. 30th Aug., 1833. Living 1846.

[3] H. p. commissary-gen. 24th Dec., 1844. Recd. the Par. medal with seven clasps in 1848. See mention of this officer in the paper on " Waterloo " in the *Cornhill Mag.*, 1897.

[4] Dep. commissary-gen. 22nd Oct., 1816. Served with the Walcheren expedition and in the Pa. He wrote a MS. journal of his services which came into the Editor's possession a few years ago, and is now in the R.A. Institution Library.

[5] Afterwards the Rev. A. R. C. Dallas, Rector of Wonston, Hants. " He left a distinguished name behind him as a clergyman, particularly in Ireland, where his work was well recognised." Eldest son of Robert Dallas, of Dallas Castle.

[6] Afterwards commissary-gen. D. in London, 10th March, 1862.

RESERVE FORCES.

The 35th, 54th, 59th, and 91st British Foot Regts., with two brigades of Rl. Artillery, were not engaged at Waterloo, but being in the vicinity (at Hal), and forming part of Wellington's army, on 18th June, 1815, they were granted the Waterloo medal, and were also allowed the grant of two years' service, but the word " Waterloo " is not to be found on the colours of the above four regts.

35TH (OR THE SUSSEX) REGIMENT OF FOOT.*

(2nd Battalion.)

	Rank in the	
LIEUT.-COLONEL.	Regiment.	Army.
Sir George H. F. Berkeley, K.C.B., w.	13 June, 1811	
MAJORS.		
1 Charles Macalister	13 June, 1811	
2 John Slessor	7 Oct. 1813	Lt.-Col., 4 June, [1814
CAPTAINS.		
Charles Wm. Wall	19 May, 1805	
3 Wm. Rawson	4 May, 1809	
Henry Rutherford	3 Aug. 1809	
4 Thos. McNeil	11 Mar. 1813	8 Sept. 1808
5 Nich. F. Dromgoole	29 July, 1813	
Henry G. Macleod, w.	10 Dec. 1813	29 Sept. 1813
LIEUTENANTS.		
6 Samuel Scarfe	28 Nov. 1805	
J. W. Amos	13 Apr. 1809	
Francis Stenton	18 May, 1809	
John Osbourne	3 Aug. 1809	
7 Thos. McDonough	30 Oct. 1809	
8 Christ. Spencer Breary, Adjt.	2 Nov. 1809	
9 Robert Thoburn	18 Oct. 1810	12 Jan. 1809
10 Wm. Farrant	29 Jan. 1812	
Aylmer Barnewell	10 Dec. 1812	
John Hildebrand	23 Sept. 1813	
Peter Murdoch	8 Dec. 1813	
James Wilder	9 Dec. 1813	
Newland R. Tompkins	10 Dec. 1813	
Edward Shewell	22 Dec. 1813	
Wm. Rainsforth	23 Dec. 1813	
George Wilkins	1 Sept. 1814	
H. Middleton	1 Dec. 1814	7 Oct. 1813
ENSIGNS.		
11 Wm. Levitt Hedding	7 Jan. 1813	
12 John Hewetson	13 May, 1813	
13 Wm. Macalister	10 June, 1813	

35TH (OR THE SUSSEX) REGIMENT OF FOOT—*continued.*

	Rank in the	
ENSIGNS—*continued.*	Regiment.	Army.
[14] John Barwis Wyatt	22 Dec. 1813	
[15] Anthony Macdonell	7 Apr. 1814	
Herbert Potenger	7 July, 1814	
Alex. Duke Hamilton	27 Oct. 1814	
John Thomas	22 Dec. 1814	

PAYMASTER.

Wm. Bury	7 Jan. 1808

QUARTERMASTER.

Robert Foote	2 Dec. 1813

SURGEON.

Chas. Simon Doyle	31 Mar. 1808

ASSISTANT-SURGEONS.

Wm. Keoghoe	22 Feb. 1810
John Purcell	28 July, 1814

Facings orange.   Lace silver.

* The col.-in-chf. of this regt. was Charles, 4th Duke of Richmond, K.G., a gen. and gov. of Plymouth. He was present at Waterloo as a spectator, and although Wellington, his personal friend, implored him early in the day to retire to Brussels, the Duke did not beat a retreat until the battle was half over. He was accompanied by his son, Lord William Lennox (a boy of 15), a cornet in the Horse Guards, and extra A.D.C. to Gen. Maitland. By an unfortunate accident, a few days before the battle, Lord William fractured his right arm, and had the sight of one of his eyes destroyed, and although he left his sick bed at Brussels to proffer his services to Gen. Maitland, the latter felt himself obliged to decline them, so the disappointed youth followed his father and another brother to the field, *en amateur*. Gen. Mercer records in his *Waterloo Journal* how surprised he was to see "a fine, tall, upright old gentleman, in plain clothes, followed by two young ones, come across our front at a gallop, from the Brussels road, and press forward to so hot a fight." This fine old veteran died from hydrophobia, while holding the appointment of Gov.-Gen. of Canada, 28th Aug., 1819.

[1] Probably a son of Gen. Archibald Macalister, who for many years commanded this regt. D. at Axminster in Aug., 1869.

[2] Served for many years in the Rl. Irish Artillery, and was transferred to above regt. Retd. on f. p., Rl. Irish Artillery, in 1817, and d. at Sidmouth, 11th Oct., 1850. For an account of his family see the Editor's *English Army Lists and Commission Registers*, 1661-1714, Vol. V., p. 227, note 2.

[3] H. p. 27th Feb., 1818.   Adjt. 3rd West York Militia, 1827.   D. 18th July, 1850.

[4] Appointed ens. in the 35th Foot, 20th Feb., 1800.   Served at the blockade of Malta.   Lieut. 82nd Foot 1803.   Served at the siege of Copenhagen, and was wounded at Windmill Battery; recd. the thanks of Col. Sir Geo. Smith for his heroism while employed at that post.   Capt. in the army 8th Sept., 1808.   Capt. 74th Foot 2nd Nov., 1809.   Was with Sir John Moore's army during the whole of its operations until its returning from Madrid and Burgos to the north of Portugal.   Employed on recruiting service 1810–Sept., 1812.   Exchanged back to 35th Foot in 1813.   Served with Lord Lynedoch's army in the Netherlands.   Recd. the medal for Waterloo.   Transferred to 7th Veteran Battalion, 3rd Aug., 1815.   Retd. f. p. 24th May, 1816.   D. 23rd Sept., 1839.   The above information was communicated by Capt. McNeil's nephew, the late Major-Gen. McNeil, of the Indian Army.

[5] H. p. 1817.   D. in 1863.

[6] Capt. 24th Aug.., 1815.   H. p. 25th June, 1817.

[7] H. p. 34th Foot 1837.

[8] H. p. 27th Foot 1825.

[9] H. p. 25th Feb., 1816.

[10] H. p. 25th June, 1817.

[11] Lieut. 25th Sept., 1815.   H. p. 1817.

[12] Lieut. 28th Sept., 1815.   H. p. 25th Apr., 1817.

[13] Lieut. 30th Nov., 1815.   Exchanged to 20th Foot, 24th July, 1823. Exchanged to 98th Foot, 5th July, 1827.

[14] Lieut. 26th July, 1821.   H. p. in Oct. same year.   Restored to full pay as ensign 47th Foot, 8th June, 1826.   Serving in 1830.

[15] H. p. 2nd Apr., 1818.

54TH (OR THE WEST NORFOLK) REGIMENT OF FOOT.

	Rank in the	
LIEUT-COLONEL.	Regiment.	Army.
John, Earl Waldegrave	26 Nov. 1812	
MAJORS.		
[1] Sir Neil Campbell, Kt.	20 Feb. 1806	Col., 4 June, 1814
[2] Allan Kelly	31 Oct. 1811	
CAPTAINS.		
[3] Thos. Cox Kirby	25 Sept. 1806	
Richard Blakeman	15 Mar. 1809	
Walter Crofton, K.	16 Mar. 1809	
[4] James Leslie	3 Jan. 1811	
Gilhow J. Tappenham	12 Dec. 1811	
George Black	9 July, 1812	
Thos. Chartres	28 Apr. 1814	
LIEUTENANTS.		
George Fraser	11 Dec. 1806	
[5] Gonville Bromhead	23 Mar. 1809	
[6] Edward Alleyne Evanson	20 Apr. 1809	
[7] John Pillon	11 May, 1809	20 Mar. 1807
Robert Woodgate	28 Sept. 1809	
Wm. Claus	22 Feb. 1810	
Richard Kelly	14 June, 1810	
John Grey	19 Sept. 1811	
[8] Philip Mandilhon	7 Nov. 1811	
Joseph Henry Potts	12 Dec. 1811	
Robert Leacroft	21 Aug. 1812	
Francis Taylor	10 Sept. 1812	
[9] Edward Marcon	20 May, 1813	
John Reid	22 Oct. 1813	
Richard Stacpoole	15 Dec. 1813	
Francis Burgess	16 Dec. 1813	
Wm. Pilkington	12 May, 1814	
Wm. Nich. Persse	2 June, 1814	
[10] Dixon Denham	1 Dec. 1814	7 Sept. 1813
Francis Hutchinson	8 Dec. 1814	
[11] M. Stoughton H. Lloyd	2 Mar. 1815	

54TH (OR THE WEST NORFOLK) REGIMENT OF FOOT
—continued.

	Rank in the	
ENSIGNS.	Regiment.	Army.
Edward Nugent	23 Dec. 1813	
Thos. Fraser	5 May, 1814	
12 Charles Hill	12 May, 1814	
13 John Clark	2 June, 1814	
14 C. W. Thomas	17 Nov. 1814	15 July, 1814
Alexander Mathewson	8 Dec. 1814	
15 Pryce Clarke	2 Mar. 1815	
PAYMASTER.		
Henry Irwin	11 Feb. 1813	18 June, 1801
QUARTERMASTER.		
16 Wm. Coates	1 Aug. 1811	
SURGEON.		
George Redmond	11 Sept. 1806	
ASSISTANT-SURGEONS.		
Moore F. Fynan	28 Feb. 1811	
George Leech	25 Nov. 1813	

Facings green.   Lace silver.

1 " The man who let Boney go." This distinguished officer was second son of Capt. Neil Campbell, of Duntroon. Bn. 1st May, 1776. Joined 6th West India Regt. as ensign in 1797. After three years' service in West Indies returned to England and joined 95th Rifles as a lieut., and in following year purchased a company in same regt. In 1805 was promoted major in 43rd Foot, and in 1806 was removed to 54th Foot. Served with this regt. in Jamaica, and in 1808 returned home. Again sent to West Indies as a bt. lt.-col. on the staff, and in that capacity was present at the capture of Guadaloupe. Commanded a Portuguese regt. during the Par. War. In Feb., 1813, was sent to Russia by the British Government, and was employed by Gen. Lord Cathcart British Ambassador at St. Petersburg, to accompany a corps of the Russian army and report on its force and military operations. In the autumn of 1813 was detached to the siege of Dantzig, where a corps of 30,000 men was employed under Prince Alexander of Wurtemberg. On the 24th March, 1814, was severely wounded at Fere Champenoise, in France, in a cavalry charge, by a Cossack, who mistook him for a French officer and struck him to the ground. In April, 1814, was chosen by the British Government to accompany Napoleon from Fontainebleau to Elba. Author of *Napoleon at Fontainebleau.* In the following spring, whilst Col. Campbell was at Florence, having left

Elba for a few days on pressing business, Napoleon formed and carried out his plan of escape. Commanded the 54th in 1815, and was at the storming of Cambray. C.B. Gold cross for the capture of Martinique and Guadaloupe, siege of Ciudad Rodrigo, and battle of Salamanca. A knight bachelor, maj.-gen., Governor of Sierra Leone, where he died of fever, 14th Aug., 1827.

2 Bt. lt.-col. 12th Aug., 1819. D. in 1829.

3 Retd. as bt. lt.-col. 1845. D. 1850.

4 Lt.-col. unatt. 23rd Nov., 1841. D. in Edinburgh in Feb., 1853.

5 Son of Lt.-Gen. Sir Gonville Bromhead, 1st Bart., by Jane, youngest dau. of Sir Charles Ffrench, Bart. In 1830 was a maj. on the h. p. list. Bn. 22nd Jan., 1791. M., 1823, Judith Coriston, youngest dau. of James Wood, of Woodville, co. Sligo.

6 Son of Alderman Evanson, of Cork. D. as capt. in this regt. in Jan. 1827.

7 Paymaster Nov., 1818. Retd. 1825. D. in Feb., 1854.

8 Capt. 30th Jan., 1823. D. at Trichinopoly, 30th June, 1836.

9 Capt. 3rd Jan., 1822. H. p., capt. 78th Foot, 6th Feb., 1823.

10 Lieut. 64th Foot 9th Dec., 1819. Capt. h. p., 3rd Foot, 24th Oct., 1821. Given the local rank of major while serving in Africa, 22nd Nov., 1821.

11 Afterwards Maj.-Gen. M. S. H. Lloyd, h. p. unattached. Entered the army in 1813. He was present at the taking of Cambray and Paris, also served in India against the Rajah of Kolapore (1826), and in the campaign in the southern Mahratta country (1844). His commissions are dated : Ensign, Dec. 16th, 1813 ; Lieut. March 2nd, 1815 ; Capt. Sept. 13th, 1835 ; Maj. Nov. 9th, 1846 ; Lt.-col. June 20th, 1854 ; Col. May 14th, 1859 ; Maj.-Gen. March 6th, 1868. Son of Richard Bateman Lloyd, by Eliz., widow of Capt. Trant. Living 1876.

12 Capt. 5th Jan., 1826. Bt.-major 23rd Nov., 1841. Retd. Nov., 1846, on full pay. D. 1852.

13 Lieut. 27th Nov., 1821. Capt. 29th Aug., 1826. Major 25th Dec., 1829. Lt.-col. 23rd Nov., 1841. Col. 20th June, 1854. Major-Gen. 26th Oct., 1858. Served the campaign of 1824-5 in Ava, including the taking of Rangoon. Led the attack upon the fortified heights of Aracan, and was sev. wounded. K.H. and medal. At the time of his death, 22nd March, 1865, was hon. colonel of 59th Foot.

14 Lieut. 18th Apr., 1822. H. p. 30th Aug., 1826.

15 Lieut. 27th June, 1822. Adjt. 25th Oct., 1827. Capt. 16th July, 1833. Paymaster 92nd Highrs. 23rd July, 1844. D. or retd. 9th June, 1846.

16 Retd. f. p. 1827.

59th (or the 2nd NOTTINGHAMSHIRE) REGIMENT OF FOOT.

(2nd Battalion.)

	Rank in the	
LIEUT.-COLONEL.	Regiment.	Army.
1 Henry Austen	23 Sept. 1813	25 Jan. 1812
MAJORS.		
2 Fred. W. Hoysted	17 June, 1813	Lt.-Col., 26 Dec.
3 Charles Douglas	20 Apr. 1815	[1813
CAPTAINS.		
4 Francis Fuller	5 Oct. 1809	
James Cockburn	4 Sept. 1812	
5 Abraham Pilkington	17 June, 1813	
Jas. Arch. Crawford	22 July, 1813	
6 Jas. MacGregor	25 Sept. 1813	
John Fawson	11 Nov. 1813	
LIEUTENANTS.		
Robert Preedy	15 June, 1808	
Wm. F. Mayne	4 Sept. 1808	
7 Abraham Dent	4 June, 1809	
8 John Cowper	7 June, 1809	
Henry Brown	26 Oct. 1809	
9 Alexander Macpherson	21 Dec. 1809	
10 Edward Duncan	28 Feb. 1811	
Archibald Campbell, Adjt.	28 Mar. 1811	
11 Nicholas Chadwick	5 Dec. 1811	
Nicholas Hovenden	12 Dec. 1811	
12 Lewis Carmichael	7 Mar. 1812	
13 Henry Hartford	12 Mar. 1812	
14 Paterson O'Hara	2 Sept. 1812	
15 Wm. Veall	23 Sept. 1813	
16 Wm. Pittman	27 Sept. 1813	
Wm. Henry Hill	25 May, 1814	
Gilmour Robinson	1 Sept. 1814	

59TH (OR THE 2ND NOTTINGHAMSHIRE) REGIMENT OF FOOT—*continued.*

	Rank in the	
ENSIGNS.	Regiment.	Army.
[17] Andrew Clark Ross	23 Sept. 1813	
[18] Henry Keane Bloomfield	30 Sept. 1813	
[19] Rowley F. Hill	25 May, 1814	
[20] Charles Makepeace	13 Apr. 1815	
PAYMASTER.		
[21] Charles Marr	7 Mar. 1805	
QUARTERMASTER.		
[22] Wm. Baird	31 May, 1810	
SURGEON.		
[23] James Hagan	25 Nov. 1813	9 Sept. 1813.
ASSISTANT-SURGEONS.		
[24] Peter K. Lambe	8 Feb. 1810	
Andrew Colvin	9 Sept. 1813	

Facings white.   Lace gold.

[1] Placed on h. p. in March, 1816.

[2] Saw service in the Pa. Transferred to 1st Batt. in 1816. Serving in 1817.

[3] Drowned in Tramore Bay, near Waterford, when the *Seahorse* transport was wrecked in a storm, 30th Jan., 1816. Son of Capt. Wm. Douglas 11th Foot.

[4] Major 17th July, 1817. Bt. lt.-col. 19th Jan. 1826. Lt.-Col. 59th Foot 25th Nov., 1828. Recd. the gold medal for San Sebastian. Distinguished himself at the siege of Bhurtpore. C.B. D. in Jersey 19th Apr., 1868.

[5] Placed on h. p. in May, 1816. 9th son of Thos. Pilkington (of the Westmeath family), by Bridget, dau. of the Rev. Ephraim Harpur. D. 24th May, 1843.

[6] Lost in the wreck of the *Seahorse*. Brother to Col. George MacGregor of 1st batt. same regt. Had served at Corunna and Vittoria, where he was severely wounded.

7 Afterwards adjt.   Lost in the *Seahorse.*

8 Saved when the *Seahorse* was wrecked.

9 Saved when the *Seahorse* was wrecked.   This officer's Waterloo medal was for some years in the Editor's collection of war medals.

10 Capt. 48th Foot 19th May, 1837.   Retd. as maj. in 1840.

11 Capt. 13th Foot 3rd Aug., 1826.   Serving 1830.

12 Capt. 5th Dec., 1826.   Major of a corps raised for "particular service" 1st Jan., 1838, and bt. lt.-col. serving in aforesaid regt. in 1842.

13 Saved when the *Seahorse* was wrecked.

14 H. p. 1816.   D. in Dublin 1850.

15 Lost in the *Seahorse.*   A native of Portsmouth and son of a master-builder of that town.

16 Capt. 49th Foot 12th Apr., 1831.   H. p. 10th Jan., 1834.   D. 17th Nov., 1853.

17 Lost in the *Seahorse.*

18 Capt. 11th Foot 1st Apr., 1824.   Lt.-col. 11th Foot 27th June, 1845. Living 1860.

19 Lost in the *Seahorse.*

20 Capt. 4th D. G. 24th July, 1823.   Retd. as major 1841.

21 H. p. 1816.

22 Lost in the *Seahorse* with his wife and two children.

23 Lost in the *Seahorse.*

24 Lost in the *Seahorse.*

91st REGIMENT OF FOOT.

		Rank in the	
LIEUT.-COLONEL.	Regiment.		Army.
1 Sir Wm. Douglas, K.C.B.	25 Nov. 1808		Col., 4 June, 1814

CAPTAINS.

2 James Walsh	28 Aug. 1804	Maj., 12 Apr. 1814
Thos. Hunter-Blair, w.	28 Mar. 1805	Maj., 30 May, 1811
3 Wm. Steuart	17 Apr. 1806	
4 Archibald Campbell (1st Batt.)	1 Oct. 1807	
5 Dugald Campbell	23 Nov. 1809	
6 James C. Murdoch	29 Nov. 1810	
7 Alexander Jas. Callander	10 Oct. 1811	Maj., 4 June, 1814
8 Archibald Campbell (2nd Batt.)	15 Jan. 1812	
9 Robert Anderson	30 Apr. 1812	

LIEUTENANTS.

10 John Campbell	24 Aug. 1807	
11 John Russell	11 May, 1808	
12 Alexander Campbell (1st Batt.)	12 May, 1808	
13 Robert Stewart	13 May, 1808	
14 Andrew McLachlan	14 May, 1808	
15 Carberry Egan	19 May, 1808	
16 Andrew Cathcart	11 May, 1809	
17 John McDougall	15 June, 1809	
18 James Hood	3 Aug. 1809	
19 Alexander Smith	30 Aug. 1810	22 Feb. 1810
20 Thos. Lisle Fenwick	13 Sept. 1810	3 Nov. 1808
21 Thomas Murray	11 July, 1811	
22 Robert Spencer Knox	2 Jan. 1812	
23 Charles Stuart	16 Jan. 1812	
24 John McDonald	30 Apr. 1812	
25 Eugene Browne	9 July, 1812	
26 Alex. Campbell (2nd Batt.)	20 July, 1813	
27 George Scott, Adjt.	21 July, 1813	
28 Wm. Smith	21 July, 1813	
29 James Black	22 July, 1813	
30 Alexander Sword	2 Mar. 1815	

91st REGIMENT OF FOOT—*continued.*

ENSIGNS.	Rank in the Regiment.	Army.
[31] Norman Lamont	26 Aug. 1813	
[32] Wm. Trimmer	18 Nov. 1813	
[33] James Paton	30 Dec. 1813	
[34] Dugald Ducat	24 Feb. 1814	
[35] Patrick Cahill	31 Mar. 1814	
[36] Andrew Smith	14 Apr. 1814	
[37] Lawrence Lind	9 June, 1814	

PAYMASTER.

Dugald Campbell	16 May, 1808	

QUARTERMASTER.

[38] James Stewart	16 Apr. 1807	

SURGEON.

Robert Douglas	6 June, 1805	

ASSISTANT-SURGEONS.

Geo. M. McLachlan	26 Mar. 1812	
Wm. H. Young.	4 Feb. 1813	

Facings yellow.   Lace silver.

[1] Served in the Pa. and recd. the gold cross and two clasps for six general actions. Commanded the second column of attack at the assault of Cambray in June, 1815. D. at Valenciennes in Aug., 1818, and was interred there.

[2] Bt. lt.-col. 21st Jan., 1819. Retd. 1825.

[3] D. 1825.

[4] H. p. 1816.

[5] D. 1825.

[6] H. p. 1819. This officer's Waterloo medal was many years in the Tancred collection.

[7] Eldest son of James Callander of Craigforth. H. p. 1821.

[8] D. 1822.

[9] Major 23rd Sept., 1824. Lt.-Col. 91st Foot 2nd Dec., 1831.

[10] Capt. 7th Sept., 1815. H. p. 1816.

[11] H. p. 1816

[12] H. p. 1821.   D. 1835.

[13] Retd. 1823.   D. in Mar., 1851.

[14] D. as capt. in 1822.

[15] Serving in 1817.   Out of the regt. before 1824.

[16] H. p. 1821.

[17] H. p. 39th Foot 1820.

[18] Retd. f. p. 9th Rl. Veteran Batt. 1821.   D. in Jersey 1853.

[19] H. p. Lieut. 42nd Highrs. 30th Sept., 1819.

[20] Capt. 55th Foot 26th Nov., 1830.

[21] Capt. 1824.   D. 1826

[22] H. p. 1817.

[23] H. p. 1817.

[24] H. p. 1817.

[25] H. p. 1817.

[26] Lieut. 38th Foot 28th Nov., 1821.   Serving 1830.

[27] H. p. 1821.

[28] D. 1823.

[29] H. p. 1817.   Appointed Lieut. 100th Foot (Rl. Canadian Rifles) in 1841.

[30] H. p. 1816.

[31] A scion of the ancient family of Lamont, of Lamont, co. Argyll.   Capt. 7th Apr., 1825.   Major 2nd Dec., 1831.   K.H.   D. in 1845 at the Cape of Good Hope.

[32] Lieut. 2nd Mar., 1820.   H. p. 17th Foot 6th Aug., 1823.

[33] Lieut. 27th Apr., 1820.   Out of the regt. before 1830.

[34] Capt. 4th Aug. 1828.   Major 2nd. July, 1841.   Lt.-Col. in Oct., 1842. D. 1844 at Colesberg, South Africa.

[35] Lieut. 11th Aug., 1822.   Adjt. 23rd Aug., 1823.   D. in Jamaica, 1827.

[36] D. 1825.

[37] H. p. 1816.   Living 1830.

[38] H. p. 36th Foot 1821.

ROYAL ARTILLERY.*

MAJOR JOSEPH BROME'S BRIGADE.

	Rank in the	
CAPTAIN.	Regiment.	Army.
[1] Joseph Brome	13 Aug. 1804	Maj.,4 June, 1813

SECOND CAPTAIN.

[2] John E. G. Parker	20 Dec. 1814	

FIRST LIEUTENANTS.

[3] Robert J. Saunders	11 Aug. 1811	
[4] Thos. O. Cater	16 Apr. 1812	

SECOND LIEUTENANT.

[5] Anthony O. Molesworth	17 Dec. 1812	

MAJOR GEORGE W. UNETT'S BRIGADE.

CAPTAIN.

[6] George W. Unett	1 Feb. 1808	Maj., 4 June, 1814

SECOND CAPTAIN.

[7] Thos. Gore Browne	1 Feb. 1808	

FIRST LIEUTENANTS.

[8] Douglas Lawson	28 Oct. 1808	
[9] Willoughby Montagu	11 Aug. 1811	

CAPTAIN THOMAS HUTCHESSON'S FOOT BATTERY.

CAPTAIN.

[10] Thomas Hutchesson	24 Oct. 1812	10 Apr. 1805

* Major Brome's Brigade was at Hal with Sir Charles Colville's Division. Major Unett's was attached to the 6th Division, and Capt. Hutchesson's is said to have been at Ostend.

[1] Lt.-col. 24th June, 1823. Served at Copenhagen in 1807 and at Walcheren in 1809. D. in Jamaica, 4th Jan., 1825.

[2] Capt. 30th Dec., 1828. Succeeded as 4th Bart. of Basingbourn, Essex. D. 1835 without issue.

[3] H. p. 1st Apr., 1821.

[4] Served with distinction in the Pa. Retd. f. p. major-gen. 26th May, 1857. D. 1862.

[5] 2nd Capt. 10th July, 1834. H. p. 1835. D. 10th July, 1848.

[6] Sold his commission 1825. D. same year.

[7] Served at the siege of Flushing, 1809. Attained rank of col. 9th Nov., 1846. D. 23rd Jan., 1854.

[8] D. 10th Aug., 1823.

[9] 2nd Capt. 6th Nov., 1827. H. p. same year. D. 2nd Dec., 1872.

[10] Served in the Pa. and France. Attained the rank of lt.-gen. 14th June, 1856. D. at Dover, 28th Aug., 1857.

PART II.

2ND OR R.N. BRITISH REGIMENT OF DRAGOONS.

WATERLOO MUSTER ROLL.*

A TRUE COPY OF THE LIST TRANSMITTED FROM THE
HORSE GUARDS.

Those wounded have the letter " w " placed after their names.

FIELD AND STAFF OFFICERS.

Major Isaac B. Clarke, w.
    „   T. P. Hankin, w.
Adjutant Henry Macmillan.
Surgeon Robert Dunn.
Asst.-SurgeonJamesAlexander.
Vet.-Surgeon John Trigg.
Reg.Quartermast.JohnLennox.
Paymaster William Dawson.

CAPTAIN (late) BARNARD'S
TROOP.

Lieut. G. H. Falconer.
Troop Sergt.-Major Will. Perrie.
Reg. Sergt.-Major Will. Craw-
ford.
Paymaster-Sergt. Will. Bayne.
Armourer-Sergt. James Bray.
Saddler-Sergt. Alex. Wallace.
Sergt. John Gillies.
    „   Will Porteous.
    „   John White.
Corp. Alex. Hall.
    „   Alex. Litch.
    „   John Scott.
    „   Hugh Wylie.
Trumpeter Humphrey Steven-
son.

Privates—
John Aitkin.
John Andrew.
James Ballantyne.
Edward Bell.
Isaac Bell.
John Blair.
Will. Bromley.
James Bullock.
John Callander.
John Chambling.
James Clachan.
James Drummond.
George Fiddes.
James Frame.
James Gibson.
Henry Head.
John Jarvie.
Joseph Jarvie.
David Kally.
William Kidd.
James Knox.
John Livingston.
William Leeke.
Adam McCree.
James M'Millan.
John Marshall.
David Mathie.
Robert Mathews.

Privates—*continued.*
James Nairn.
Thomas Nicol, w.
William Patrick.
David Pentland.
Will. Provan.
Will Robertson.
Job Rood.
James Rowan.
Will Taylor, w.
John Watson.
Robert Watt, w.
William Wells, w.
Will Williamson.
David Wilson.
John White.
Thomas Young.

CAPTAIN PAYNE'S TROOP.

Capt. Edward Payne.
Lieut. Arch. Hamilton, w.
  „ Charles Wyndham, w.
Troop Sergt.-Maj. Will. Robertson.
Sergt. James Bullock.
  „ David Dunn, w.
  „ John M'Neil.
  „ Will Somerville.
Corp. Geo. Edwards.
  „ Geo. Milward.
  „ Michael Nelson.[1]
Privates—
David Anderson.
Alex. Armour, w.
John Bishop.
Alex. Borland.
Joseph Brazier.
John Brown.
Thomas Bullock, w.
Alex. Campbell.
Colin Campbell.
Robert Carmaly.
William Clark.

Privates—*continued.*
William Cunningham.
Daniel Dick.
Henry Eaves.
Peter Evans.
Thomas Fergus.
William Fleming.
Peter Gibson.
Alex. Gourley.
John Hamilton.
James Hart.
William Hickling.
William Hill, w.
Alex. Hunter.
Alex. Ingram.
James Lapsley.
Richard Lee.
William Levitt, w.
Geo. Longworth, w.
John M'Keching.
David M'Lelland.
Hugh M'Lelland.
Alexander McLeod.
James M'Lintock.
William Mackie.
John Martin.
James Masterton.
Geo. Manchlin.
Will. Merrie.
Robert Miller.
James Paterson.
Robert Paterson.
Hugh Pattison.
Andrew Peden.
Samuel Sifton.
James Smith.
William Smith.
James Smithers.
Joseph Tucky.
James Waite.
James Walker.
Francis Wells.
George Willet, w.
Will. Wilkerson.

Privates—*continued.*
William Wilson.
Robert Wilson.
Arch. Wright, w.

CAPTAIN CHENEY'S TROOP.

Capt. Edward Cheney.
Lieut. Francis Stupart, w.
   ,,   James Gape.
Troop Sergt.-Major Alex. Dingwell.
Sergt. Donald Campbell.
  ,,   William Dickie.
  ,,   Will Harvey, w.
  ,,   Alex. Rennie.
Corp. Robert Hare.
  ,,   William Laird.
  ,,   John Long.
  ,,   James Ross.
Trumpeter John H. Sibold.
Privates—
  Geo. Alison.
  Matthew Anderson.
  Arch. Bell.
  Hugh Bicket.
  John Brash, w.
  Charles Burges, w.
  James Bulton.
  John Calder, w.
  Samuel Clarke, w.
  Arch. Craig.
  David Crighton.
  Thomas Crowe.
  John Crombie.
  Major Dickinson.
  Peter Drysdale.
  John Fraser.
  George Gray.
  William Gunn.
  James Hamilton, Sen.
  James Hamilton, Jun.
  Robert Hamilton.

Privates—*continued.*
David Henderson.
Adam Hepburn.
Will. Hubbard.
Thomas Johnston, w.
John Judd, w.
Will. Lockead, w.
Andrew M'Clure.
Arch. M'Farlan.
John M'Intire.
Andrew M'Kendrick.
Will. M'Kinley.
Alex. M'Pherson.
Robert Makin.
James Mann.
Will. Mathie.
Thomas Oman.
David Rampton, w.
James Ronald, w.
Andrew Scott.
James Scott.
John Spraike.
John Stirling, w.
Robert Stirling.
William Stirling.
Thomas Stobo.
Thomas Timperly, w.
Robert Temple.
James Thompson.
John Toman.
John Wallace.
William Watt.

CAPTAIN POOLE'S TROOP.

Capt. James Poole, w.
Lieut. James Wemyss.
Troop Sergt.-Major James Russell.
Sergt. John Bishop.
  ,,   Arch. Johnston.
  ,,   Thomas Stoddart, w.
Corp. Alex. Gardner, w.[2]

Corp. James Nelson.

„ John Wallace, w.

Trumpeter Peter Buncle.

Privates—

John Alexander.

James Bruce.

James Crawford.

David Craig.

Joseph Crowe.

Alexander Donaldson.

William Erskine.

Gavin Gibson.

Robert Gilchrist.

Thomas Goods.

James Kennedy.

Alexander Lander.

Andrew Lees.

William Lock, w.

Robert Lawrie, w.

David M'Gown, w.

Fred. M'Vicar.

John Miller.

Andrew Muir.

John Nelson.

Edward Noaks.

Henry Palmer, w.

Thomas Philips.

James Ratcliff.

James Richardson.

Thomas Robertson.

William Robertson.

John Rowat.

John Salmon.

Matthew Scott.

Robert Smellie.

Robert Stevenson.

Adam Tait.

John Thompson.

James Tovie.

John Wark, w.

Andrew White.

Robert Wilson.

William Willis.

William Wright.

Privates—*continued.*

Alexander Young.

Nathaniel Young.

CAPTAIN VERNOR'S TROOP.

Capt. Robert Vernor.

Lieut. John Mills, w.

Troop Sergt.-Major W. McMillan, w.

Sergt. William Clarke.

„ Charles Ewart.

„ John Tannock.

Corp. John Dickson.[3]

„ Samuel Tar, w.

„ Alex. Wilson.

Trumpeter Joseph Reeves.

Privates—

John Atherley.

Francis Brown, w.

James Brown.

John Brobin.

George Butler, w.

Adam Colquhoun.

John Collier.

Robert Craig, w.

John Dalziel.

William Dunlop, w.

John Dunn.

John Gillies.

William Gordon.

Robert Gourley.

Robert Greig.

John Harkness, w.

John Henderson.

Henry Hodkinson, w.

William Jones.

Samuel Kinnier.

James King.

John Lane.

David McAll.

John McGee, w.

William Mackie.

William M'Nair.

Privates—*continued.*
John Matthews, w.
James Montgomery.
John Moore.
William Patton, Sen.
William Patton, Jun.
William Park.
Robert Reid.
William Ross.
James Smith.
William Smith.
William Sykes.
Ebenezer Thompson.
John Veazy.
Robert Wallace.[4]
Thomas Watson.
Richard Wharan.
John Wise.

CAPTAIN FENTON'S TROOP.

Capt. Thomas C. Fenton.
Lieut. J. R. T. Graham.
Sergt. James Andrew.
   „   Richard Hayward.
   „   Thomas Soars, w.
   „   William Swan.[5]
Corp. John Craig, w.
   „   Thomas Davis.
   „   Robert Thompson.
   „   John Mair.[6]
Trumpeter Henry Bowig.
Privates—
Thos. Anderson.
John Arklie.
James Armour.
William Ballantyne.
George Biddolph.

Privates—*continued.*
Alex. Blackadder.
Samuel Boulter.
Cunningham Bowes, w.
Stephen Brooks.
Adam Brown, w.
John Campbell.
John Clarke, w.
Robert Currie.
William Dick, w.
John Dobbie, w.
John Ferguson.
John Gould.
James Green.
William Howie.
Alex. Hunter.
Hugh Hunter.
Robert Hunter.
Arch. Hutton.
James Jones, w.
Arch. Kean.
James Kean.
Samuel Kinder.
John Liddle, w.
Robert Littlejohn, w. (dead).
Joseph Macro.
Peter Miller, w.
John Mitchell, w.
William Pearson, w.
William Reid, w.
John Ross.
William Smith.
Peter Swan, w.
Jonathan Taylor.
Andrew Thompson.
John Watson.
Thomas Wilmot.

* Taken presumably on 19th June, 1815.

NOTES BY CAPTAIN G. TANCRED.

Privates William Storrie and J. Liddle, of Capt. Vernor's Troop, are not mentioned in the above Muster Roll, having been returned as killed 18th June. They rejoined 19th Sept., 1815, from a French prison, the former having been wounded and his horse killed.

[1] M. Nelson became regt. sergt.-maj. 25th March, 1825.

[2] Alex. Gardner was promoted as troop sergt.-maj. 1st Jan., 1826.

[3] John Dickson became a troop sergt.-maj. He d. at Nunhead Lane, Surrey, 16th July, 1880, aged 90.

[4] Robert Wallace, a troop sergt.-maj. 2nd March, 1826, and in 1872 was a messenger in the Queen's Body Guard.

[5] William Swan became a regt. sergt.-maj., and d. as such, March, 1825.

[6] Corp. John Mair rejoined from a French prison 1st Sept., 1815, supposed to have been killed 18th June.

PART III.

NON-COMMISSIONED OFFICERS AND PRIVATES AT WATERLOO WHO SUBSEQUENTLY RECEIVED COMMISSIONS.

1st Life Guards.

Corporal-Major Robert Falconer.

Appointed quartermaster same regt. 2nd Sept., 1836. H. p. 1847. D. Apr., 1849.

2nd Life Guards.

John Ellington.

Appointed quartermaster 19th June, 1815.

Royal Horse Guards.

Corporal-Major Andrew Heartley.

Served in the Pa. Appointed quartermaster 12th Dec., 1822. H. p. 1831. D. Feb. 1861 as a Military Knight of Windsor.

Carter Fairbrother.

Appointed quartermaster 7th Nov., 1829. D. Feb., 1852.

John Frost.

Appointed quartermaster 31st May, 1828. D. Apr., 1852.

Wm. Emmett.

Appointed quartermaster 25th Sept., 1828. H. p. 1831.

1st Dragoon Guards.

Sergt.-Major Richard Hollis.

Appointed adjt. to above regt. 8th July, 1836. Lieut. 12th Jan., 1838. Lieut. Rl. Canadian Rifles 24th Oct., 1845. D. in Canada as a retd. capt. in 1856.

1st Dragoons.

Corporal Francis Stiles.

This brave soldier was promoted sergt. in the 1st Dns., and aftds. Ensign in the 6th West India Regt. (commission dated 11th April, 1816), for the gallantry he displayed at Waterloo, in helping Capt. Clark of the same regt. to capture the Eagle of the 105th French Regt. The following letter, copied from the original in the United Service Museum, throws additional light on the above exploit :—

IPSWICH BARRACKS, 31*st Jan.*, 1816.

SIR,—This day Col. Clifton sent for me about the taking the Eagle and colours. He asked me if I had any person that see me take the Eagle ; I told him that you see me, I believe, as the officer of the French was making away with it. I belonged to your troop at that time, and you gave me orders to charge him, which I did, and took it from him. When I stated it to him this day he wants to know the particulars about it, and me to rite to you for you to state to him how it was. I would thank you to rite to the Colonel, as you was the nearest officer to me that day. Sir, by so doing you will much oblige,—Your most obedient humble servant,

FRANCIS STILES,
Sergt. 1st Royal Drag.

To Lt. Gunning, 1st Dragoons,
Cheltenham, Glostershire.

Ensign Stiles was placed on h. p., 28th Dec., 1817, and d. in London, 9th Jan., 1828.

John Smith.

Appointed cornet and adjt. 26th Oct., 1815. Left the regt. in 1829.

John Partridge.

Appointed quartermaster in above regt. 18th July, 1834. H. p. 1849. Hon. capt. 1st July, 1859. D. in Aug., 1863.

2ND DRAGOONS.

[1] Sergt.-Maj. Wm. Crawford.
[2] Sergt. Charles Ewart.

[1] Promoted cornet and adjt. same regt., 17th Aug., 1815. Lt. 25th June, 1819. Paymaster, 24th March, 1829. Held this appointment for 20 years. H. p. 1849. Living in 1855.

[2] Captured the Eagle of the 45th French Regt. at Waterloo. This daring act won the admiration of the whole British Army. Ewart was rewarded with an ensigncy in the 5th Royal Veteran Battalion, 22nd Feb., 1816, and on the reduction of this regt. in 1821 he recd. a retiring pens. of 5s. 10d. per day. He was a native of Kilmarnock. D. at Davyhulme, near Manchester, 17th March, 1846. The *Edinburgh Advertiser* for 21st June, 1816, has the following :—

"Extract of a letter from Sergt. Ewart, of the Scots Greys, dated Rouen, 16th Aug., 1815 :—

"The enemy began forming their line of battle about nine in the morning of the 18th. They came down to the left, where they were received by our brave Highlanders. No men could ever behave better ; our brigade of cavalry covered them. Owing to a column of foreign troops giving way, our brigade was forced to advance to the support of our brave fellows, and which we certainly did in style ; we charged through two of their columns, each about 500. It was in the first charge I took the Eagle from the enemy ; he and I had a hard contest for it ; he thrust my horse at my groin—I parried it off, and I cut him through the head ; after which I was attacked by one of their Lancers, who threw his lance at me, but missed the mark by my throwing it off with my sword by my right side ; then I cut him from the chin upwards, which cut went through his teeth. Next I was attacked by a foot soldier, who, after firing at me, charged me with his bayonet ; but he very soon lost the combat, for I parried it, and cut him down through the head ; so that finished the contest for the Eagle. After which I presumed to follow my comrades, Eagle and all, but was stopped by the General saying to me, ' You brave fellow, take that to the rear ; you have done enough until you get quit of it,' which I was obliged to do, but with great reluctance. I retired to a height, and stood there for upwards of an hour, which gave me a general view of the field, but I cannot express the sight I beheld ; the bodies of my brave comrades were lying so thick upon the field that it was scarcely possible to pass, and horses innumerable. I took the Eagle into Brussels, amidst the acclamation of thousands of the spectators that saw it."

On 18th June, 1816, Ensign Ewart, and other Waterloo officers, were entertained at a public banquet in Edinburgh. "Nearly 400 noblemen and gentlemen sat down to an elegant dinner in the Assembly Rooms, the Rt. Hon. Wm. Arbuthnot, Lord Provost of the city, in the chair. After several toasts had been given and duly honoured, Sir Walter (then Mr.) Scott proposed a bumper to the health of Ensign Ewart, late of the Scots Greys, whose bravery was conspicuous where he took a French Eagle, and killed with his own hand three of Napoleon's guard. The toast was drank with great acclamation, and a general expectation prevailed that Ensign Ewart, who was present, would address the company. After a short pause, the Lord Provost rose, and, at the request of Mr. Ewart, stated how much he felt honoured by this mark of the company's approbation, but that he would much rather fight the battle over again and take another Eagle, than make a speech."

6TH DRAGOONS.

F. McDowell.

Appointed quartermaster 10th Dec., 1829. H. p. 1843. D. in June, 1846.

Thos. Boyd.

Appointed adjt. 19th Oct., 1815. Lieut. 18th June, 1819. Out of the regt. in 1840.

7TH HUSSARS.

Troop Sergt. Maj. Thos. Jeffs.

Promoted cornet and adjt. same regt., 7th March, 1816, for gallantry at Waterloo. Lt. 4th March, 1819. H. p. unattached, 14th June, 1827. Living 1830.

Sergt.-Major Samuel Brodribb.

Appointed quartermaster 15th Jan., 1829. Quartermaster 14th Lt. Dns. 24th Apr., 1838. D. 1846.

Thos. Blackier.

Appointed quartermaster 16th Sept., 1819. H. p. 1839. D. 1841.

10TH HUSSARS.

Fred Kinkie.

Appointed quartermaster 19th Lt. Dns. 1st July, 1824. H. p. 18th Aug., 1825. D. in Nov., 1863.

11TH LIGHT DRAGOONS.

Sergt.-Maj. G. Butcher.

Appointed adjt. 12th Oct., 1815. Lieut. 8th Nov., 1818. Capt. 13th Nov., 1834. Retd. 1837.

Sergt. Robt. Bimbrick.

Lieut. 12th Oct., 1825. Capt. 7th D. G. 25th Feb., 1843. K. in action at the Cape in Apr., 1846.

12TH LIGHT DRAGOONS.

Sergt.-Maj. John Carruthers.

Promoted cornet in same regt., 26th Oct., 1815.   H. p. 25th Dec., 1816.

13TH LIGHT DRAGOONS.

Troop Sergt. Maj. Edward Wells.

Commanded Capt. Gubbins's troop at Waterloo after all the officers had fallen.   His gallantry that day was particularly remarked.   Promoted Ensign in th· 2nd West India Regt. in 1816.   Lt., 25th Dec., 1823.   Exchanged to 54th Regt., and quitted the service as capt. same regt. in 1841.

Troop Sergt.-Maj. Thos. Rosser.

Appointed adjt. 24th June, 1819.   Out of the regt. in 1831.

15TH HUSSARS.

George Chettle.

Appointed quartermaster 9th Sept., 1824.   Out of the above regt. in 1835.

16TH LIGHT DRAGOONS.

Wm. Webster.

Appointed lieut. and riding master 25th Sept., 1832.   Serving on f p. in 1846.

18TH HUSSARS.

John Collins.

Appointed quartermaster 12th June, 1817.   H. p. 1821.

Sergt. James Robert Cruess.

Served in Capt. Ellis's troop at Waterloo.   Promoted Ensign 92nd Regt. 11th Jan., 1816.   H. p. 37th Regt., 22nd Jan., 1816.   Living 1824.

1st Foot Guards.

Sergt. John Payne.

Afterwards Capt. J. Payne, late quartermaster of the Grenadier Guards. Served in Sicily in 1806-7 and in Spain in 1808-9, and was present in several actions, including Corunna. He was also at Walcheren. He served in the campaigns of 1812 to 1815, and was present at the actions in the Pyrenees, capture of San Sebistian, passage of the Bidassoa, Nive, Nivelle, investment of Bayonne, Quatre Bras, and Waterloo. He was commissioned as a quarter-master the 31st Aug., 1815, and retd. with the rank of capt. in Dec., 1855. Living 1876. The following description of the square of the Grenadier Guards during the afternoon of Waterloo day is by Capt. Gronow of that regt., and is certainly worthy of remembrance, exhibiting as it does the desperate heroism of the British resistance :—

"During the battle our squares presented a shocking sight. Inside we were nearly suffocated by the smoke and smell from burnt cartridges. It was impossible to move a yard without treading upon a wounded comrade, or upon the bodies of the dead ; and the loud groans of the wounded and dying were most appalling.

"At four o'clock our square was a perfect hospital being full of dead, dying, and mutilated soldiers. The charges of cavalry were in appearance very formidable, but in reality a great relief, as the artillery could no longer fire on us ; the very earth shook under the enormous mass of men and horses. I shall never forget the strange noise our bullets made against the breast-plates of Kellerman's and Millhaud's cuirassiers, six or seven thousand in number, who attacked us with great fury. I can only compare it, with a somewhat homely simile, to the noise of a violent hailstorm beating against panes of glass.

"The artillery did great execution ; but our musketry did not at first seem to kill many men, though it brought down a large number of horses, and created indescribable confusion. The horses of the first rank of cuirassiers, in spite of all the efforts of their riders, came to a standstill, shaking and covered with foam, at about twenty yards' distance from our squares, and generally resisted all attempts to force them to charge the line of serried steel. On one occasion two gallant French officers forced their way into a gap momentarily created by the discharge of artillery ; one was killed by Stables, the other by Adair. Nothing could be more gallant than the behaviour of those veterans, many of whom had distinguished themselves on half the battle-fields of Europe.

"In the midst of our terrible fire, their officers were seen as if on parade, keeping order in their ranks, and encouraging them. Unable to renew the charge, but unwilling to retreat, they brandished their swords with loud cries of 'Vive l'Empereur !' and allowed themselves to be mowed down by hundreds rather than yield. Our men, who shot them down, could not help admiring the gallant bearing and heroic resignation of their enemies."

Sergt. Robt. Steele.

Appointed adjt. 66th Foot 23rd March, 1826. Lieut. 10th Foot 26th Sept., 1833. H. p. 8th Nov., 1842.

Sergt.-Maj. Christopher Main.

Appointed ens. 43rd L. I. 4th Aug., 1825. H. p. 18th May, 1826.

Wm. Hanna.

Quartermaster 4th Foot 8th Jan., 1829. H. p. 27th May, 1836. D. at Ardres en Calais 7th March, 1856.

3RD FOOT GUARDS.

Quartermaster-Sergt. Wm. Thompson.

Appointed quartermaster 6th May, 1819. H. p. 1837. D. Sept., 1851.

Jas. Davidson.

Quartermaster 41st Foot 14th Feb., 1828. H. p. 1836.

Joseph Aston.

Quartermaster 9th Aug., 1833 D. in the Tower 23rd June, 1853. Bd. within the Tower precincts with military honours.

4TH REGIMENT OF FOOT.

H. N. Shipton.

Appointed ens. in above regt. 19th Nov., 1818. D., of fever, in Barbadoes, 1823.

14TH REGIMENT OF FOOT.

Sergt. Samuel Goddard (3rd Batt.).

In the *Standard* of 5th Jan., 1868, appeared the following obituary notice regarding this gallant soldier :—

"DEATH OF A MILITARY KNIGHT, AT WINDSOR CASTLE.—On Sunday last Capt. Samuel Goddard, Military Knight of Windsor, died at his residence in the Lower Ward, Windsor Castle. This veteran and gallant officer was formerly of the 14th or Buckinghamshire Regt. of Foot, and had seen very lengthened service in the army, having served in the campaign of 1815, including the battle of Waterloo and the storming of Cambray ; in 1817, in the East Indies, he was present at the siege of Hattrass, and in the campaign of 1817-18, in the Deccan ; also at the siege and storming of Bhurtpore, in 1825–26. With the medal so well earned, he was one of the officers receiving rewards for distinguished service ; moreover, as having originated the measure by which was accorded to meritorious quartermasters of long service the nominal rank of captain, several of whom, many years since, presented him with a handsome testimonial, expressive of their obligation, and of his efficient aid.'

On Waterloo day, Sergt. Goddard was with an advanced party of skirmishers of the 14th, and about four o'clock the reflux wave of some French cuirassiers passed through them. They were, of course, fired at by the 14th skirmishers, and several bit the dust. One poor wounded Frenchman was thrown from his horse, and a comrade nobly returned and offered the soldier the help of his stirrup. An active light infantry man of the 14th, Whitney by name, who had shot one cuirassier, having reloaded, was about to fire at the mounted Frenchman, who was then rescuing his comrade, when Goddard interfered and said, "No, Whitney, don't fire ; let him off, he is a noble fellow." (Communicated by a friend of Capt. Goddard.)

23RD REGIMENT OF FOOT.

Charles Grant.

Severely wounded at Quatre Bras whilst serving in the ranks. Was acting-quartermaster to the Grenadier Guards in Canada in 1838–39. Appointed quartermaster to the 23rd Welsh Fusiliers 5th July, 1844. Retd. on h. p. with rank of capt. in 1854. D., in London, 12th Dec., 1865.

Samuel Brelsford.

Appointed 2nd lieut. and adjt. 60th Rifles 25th Aug., 1827.

Garret Moore.

Appointed quartermaster in above regt. 8th Nov., 1827. H. p. 5th July, 1844. D., Dec., 1852, at Picton, Canada.

Wm. Howe.

Appointed quartermaster 35th Foot 29th March, 1827.

27TH REGIMENT OF FOOT.

John Kennedy.

Appointed quartermaster 22nd June, 1820. Appears with the "W." before his name in Army List for 1825 only.

28TH REGIMENT OF FOOT.

Private John O'Brien, w.

In one of the charges made by the 28th, at Waterloo, "a flag belonging to the 25th French regt. was taken by Private John O'Brien, of the 8th company, who the moment after received a severe wound, which ultimately

occasioned the loss of his leg. The trophy, however, was preserved, and sent
to Maj.-Gen. Sir James Kempt, who commanded the division, when the regt.
arrived at Paris." Received a lieut.'s commission in the Sicilian Regt., and
subsequently in 61st Foot. Retd. f. p. Rl. Veteran Batt. in 1817.

Wm. Kerr.

Appointed ens. 7th July, 1837, and quartermaster 1st June, 1838. H. p.
1844.

32ND REGIMENT OF FOOT.

Sergt.-Major George Oke.

Appointed adjt. 8th Dec., 1825. Lieut. 26th June, 1828.

Sergt.-Major Wm. Pepperal.

Appointed quartermaster 15th Oct., 1818. H. p. 1827. D. 1837.

Thos. Healey.

Appointed quartermaster 29th Nov., 1827. H. p. 28th June, 1844. D., at
Quebec, in Jan., 1849.

42ND REGIMENT OF FOOT.

Sergt.-Major Finlay King.

Appointed quartermaster 31st Dec., 1818. Retd. 1840. D., in Guernsey,
1842.

Armourer-Sergt. Edwd. Paton.

Appointed quartermaster 19th June, 1840. D., at Southsea, in May, 1863.

71ST REGIMENT OF FOOT.

Thos. Creighton.

Appointed quartermaster 19th Sept., 1827. H. p. 24th Jan., 1840. D. July,
1853.

Bernard Grant.

Ens., 82nd Foot, 28th Dec., 1832. Quartermaster 28th Aug., 1836.
D. May, 1856.

73RD REGIMENT OF FOOT.

Maurice Shea.

Bn., in County Clare, in 1794 ; joined the Kerry Militia 1812, and in 1813 enlisted in 73rd Regt. and went to Holland. Served under Gen. Graham, and was at the siege of Antwerp. Was in Capt. Kennedy's company at Waterloo. In 1835 joined the British Legion at Cork as quartermaster, and was subsequently promoted lieut. Was in twenty-six engagements during the war. Received the Order of Isabella II. for his Spanish services. D., at Sherbrooke, Canada, in March, 1892. He was the last Waterloo survivor known.—*Army and Navy Gazette*, 2nd April, 1892.

Sergt. George Austin.

Appointed adjt. 30th Nov., 1815. H. p. 1817.

79TH REGIMENT OF FOOT.

Sergt. Colin Macdonald.

Served throughout the Pal. War with the 79th, and was twice sev. wnded. Was again badly wounded at Waterloo. Served in Canada during the rebellion of 1838–39. Received an ensign's commission 30th Jan., 1835, and appointed Town Major at Montreal. Living 1855.

✗ M of (4) classes for Salamanca, Pyrenees, Nivelle, Nive,

Alex. Cruikshank. and Toulouse.

Appointed quartermaster 12th Oct., 1838. H. p. 1849. Fort Major, Edinburgh Castle, 1851. Served (in ranks) at Copenhagen 1807 in Sweden, 1808; Walcheren, '09; Cadiz, 1810; and at Busaco, Fuentes d'Onor, Nivelle, Nive and Toulouse.

92ND REGIMENT OF FOOT.

Sergt.-Major Wm. Grant.

Appointed adjt. 5th Nov., 1819.

95TH RIFLES.

(1st Battalion.)

Fras. Feneran.

Appointed quartermaster to above regt. 1st Dec., 1823, and paymaster 95th Regt. of Foot 15th Dec., 1837. Serving as paymaster to the depôt battalion at Parkhurst in 1860.

Sergt.-Major Robt. Fairfoot.

A Peninsular hero who had been wounded in the breach at Badajoz; had his right fore-arm fractured by a shot on 17th June, 1815. Appointed quartermaster to above regt. 28th Apr., 1825. D. in Sept., 1838.

Wm. Hill.

Appointed quartermaster to above batt. 25th Dec., 1826. H. p. 29th March, 1839.

95TH RIFLES.
(2nd Battalion.)
Robt. Trafford.

Appointed quartermaster to above batt. 2nd June, 1837.

95TH RIFLES.
(3rd Battalion.)
Dugald Macfarlane.

Appointed 1st lieut. 18th July, 1815. H. p. Feb., 1816.

RESERVE FORCES.

54TH REGIMENT OF FOOT.
James Willox.

Appointed quartermaster to above regt. 27th Sept., 1827. H. p. 1846. D. June, 1864.

91ST REGIMENT OF FOOT.
Sergeant-Major Andrew Maclean.

Appointed quartermaster to above regt. 8th Aug., 1823. D., at Boulogne in 1869,

PART IV.

A FEW WATERLOO HEROES.

1st Life Guards.

Field-Trumpeter J. Edwards.

Sounded the bugle for the decisive charge of the 1st Life Guards at Waterloo. Was 32 years in the regt., and received a pension in June, 1841 His medal and bugle are still preserved in the regiment.

2nd Life Guards.

[1] Corp. John Shaw, k.
[2] Private Samuel Godley.
[3]   „   Johnson.
   „   Dakin.
   „   Hodgson.

[1] The well-known pugilist and "fancy man" of this regt. His prowess when charging with the Life Guards at Waterloo was exemplified by the number of cuirassiers he slew. The little that is known of his early life, and the account of his death at Waterloo, are given in his biography by Lt.-Col. Knollys, who, out of very scanty material, has compiled a very interesting little book. Shaw was born at Woolaston, co. Notts, in 1789, and enlisted 15th Oct., 1807.

[2] Known in the regt. as "Marquis of Granby," from the fact of his having a bald head. Had his horse shot under him in one of the charges at Waterloo, and was thrown. As he got up, minus his helmet, which had fallen off, a cuirassier rode at him and attempted to cut him down. Godley managed to kill his assailant, and mounting the Frenchman's horse, rode back to his regt. who welcomed him with shouts of "Well done, Marquis of Granby!" Discharged in 1824. D. in 1831. M. I. St. John's Wood Cemetery.

[3] Immediately after the first charge of his regt. at Waterloo, when the French cavalry were being pursued by ours, Johnson pursued three cuirassiers who, with a view of escaping, turned down a narrow lane. "There proved to be no thoroughfare at the end of the road, when Johnson, though alone, attacked the three, and, after a slight resistance, they surrendered themselves prisoners."

1st Dragoon Guards.

[1] Troop Sergt.-Maj. Thos. Nicholson, w.
[2] Sergt. John Hodgkins.

[1] Received a sabre wound through his body when charging at Waterloo. After being discharged he resided at York, and kept the "Light Horseman" Inn, Fulford Road.   D. there, 28th Sept., 1850, aged 66.

[2] Served at Salamanca in a dragoon regt.   Aftds. exchanged to 1st D. G. as sergt., and was present at Waterloo.   Bought his discharge after 17 years' service, and recd. a pens. of 6d. a day for two years!   He was a native of Tipperary, but spent the latter part of his life at Penrith, where he was a well-known figure, being "29 stone in weight, 6 feet 2 inches in height, and 2 feet 4 inches across the shoulders."   D., at Penrith, in 1867, aged 80.

2nd Dragoons.

[1] Troop Sergt.-Maj. Wm. Robertson.
[2] Sergt. John Weir, k.
[3] Private Thos. Stobo.

[1] A native of Renfrewshire.   Aftds. sergt.-major of the Rl. Fifeshire Yeomanry.   Was in every charge made by his regt. at Waterloo.   D., at Kirkcaldy, in Dec., 1825.

[2] "Sergeant Weir of the Scots Greys was pay-sergt. of his troop, and as such might have been excused serving in action, and perhaps he should not have been forward; but, on such a day as Waterloo, he requested to be allowed to charge with the regt.   In one of the charges he fell mortally wounded, and was left on the field.   Corporal Scott of the same regt. (who lost a leg) asserts that when the field was searched for the wounded and slain, the body of Sergt. Weir was found with his name written on his forehead by his own hand, dipped in his own blood.   This, his comrade said, he was supposed to have done that his body might be found and known, and that it might not be imagined he had disappeared with the money of the troop.   John Weir joined the Greys about 1798, and was a native of Mauchline, Ayrshire."—Copied from a MS. in possession of the regt., and communicated by Capt. G. Tancred.

[3] The oldest soldier in the Greys at Waterloo.   Served at Dunkirk under the Duke of York.   D. 1852.   His brother was aftds. a capt. in the same regt.

6TH DRAGOONS.

Troop Sergt.-Maj. Wm. Seney.
       „   „   John Laws.
1   „   „   Matthew Marshall, w.
Sergt. Hugh M'Mahon.
   „   Johnston Marlow.
Private Wm. Penfold.
     „   Robert Potters.
2   „   Jeremiah Brown.

1 " The Enniskilleners charged in line when Marshall's squadron dashed into the thickest of the enemy's phalanx, and were cut off from the other troops of the regt. Marshall, while sabreing a cuirassier on his right, had his bridle-arm broken by a stroke from his enemy on his left, and had not proceeded much further when he was beset by another crowd of French cavalry and hurled from his horse by a lance which penetrated his side. While he was falling he received a heavy blow across the body, and another which broke his right thigh. He lay unconscious except when goaded into sensibility by the hoofs of the enemy's horses passing over his mangled body. The ground afterwards becoming somewhat clear he espied a horse without any rider, towards which he crawled, and was about to mount, when a French trooper galloping up cut him down in the midst of his hopes, inflicting several severe wounds on his body. This part of the field being again occupied by the French, a French artilleryman made Marshall's body a resting-place for his foot while he rammed his gun. For two days and three nights Marshall remained on the field with 19 lance and sabre wounds. On the regt. returning home he was discharged with 2s. per day. Resided at Belfast, where he was much respected. D. there, 28th Sept., 1825."—*Scots' Magazine.*

2 Born at Enniskillen 14th March, 1792. Fought at Waterloo and in the Kaffir, Sepoy, and Maori wars. Living at Melbourne, Australia, in 1891.

7TH HUSSARS.

Sergt.-Maj. Edward Cotton.

Had his horse killed under him at Waterloo. After being discharged from the regt. he took up his abode at Waterloo, and became a guide to the battle-field. Being a clever and well-educated man, he was able to compile a very interesting little book called *A Voice from Waterloo*, which held its own among the many accounts of the great battle. Besides this he formed a Waterloo Museum, which has always been a great attraction to visitors. In 1875, when the Editor was at Waterloo, the Museum was kept by a niece of the late sergt.-maj., who d. 1st July, 1849, and was bd. in the orchard of Hougomont, by the side of Capt. Blackwood, who fell in the battle.

16TH LIGHT DRAGOONS.

Sergt.-Maj. Baxter, K.

A Pa. hero, mentioned in the records of this regt.

18TH HUSSARS.

Sergt. John Taylor.

Belonged to Capt. Ellis's troop. In the charge at Waterloo he made a cut at the head of one of the French cuirassiers, which had no other effect on the Frenchman than to induce him to cry out, in derision, "Ha ! ha !" and to return a severe blow at the sergt., which was admirably parried, and then Taylor thrust his sabre into the mouth of the cuirassier, who immediately fell, and the conqueror cried, "Ha ! ha !"

COLDSTREAM GUARDS.

Sergt. John Graham, Light Company, 2nd Batt.

Distinguished himself in the defence of Hougomont, and by his great personal strength was of great assistance in helping to close the courtyard gate against the French. "At a later period of the day, when in the ranks along the garden wall facing the wood, and when the struggle was most severe in that quarter, he asked Lt.-Col. Macdonell's permission to fall out. The colonel, knowing the character of the man, expressed his surprise at the request made at such a moment. Graham explained that his brother lay wounded in one of the buildings then on fire ; that he wished to remove him to a place of safety, and that he would then lose no time in rejoining the ranks. The request was granted ; Graham succeeded in snatching his brother from the terrible fate which menaced him, laid him in a ditch in rear of the enclosure, and true to his word, was again at his post."—Col. Mackinnon's *History of the Coldstreams*. Was selected in August, 1815, for the pension granted by the Rev. — Norcross, Rector of Framlingham, "to the most deserving soldier at Waterloo." D., at Kilmainham, 23rd April, 1843. He was a native of Cloona, co. Monaghan.

3RD FOOT GUARDS.

[1] Sergt.-Maj. Ralph Fraser.
[2]   ,,   Brice M'Gregor.

[1] Aided in closing the gate at Hougomont. Served in Egypt in 1801. "In the landing at Aboukir Bay, on 8th March, the boat in which Corporal Fraser

was, containing sixty persons, were all destroyed by the enemy's fire excepting fifteen." Served in Hanover, at Copenhagen, and in the Pa., and was
twice badly wounded. Discharged in Dec., 1818. Aftds. a bedesman in
Westminster Abbey. Living in 1861.

[2] A native of Argyllshire. Enlisted at Glasgow in 1799. Aided in barring
the door at Hougomont, and being very strong, was of much service in the
gallant defence of that farmhouse. Shot a cuirassier dead who attacked
him, and rode into the courtyard on the Frenchman's horse. Discharged in
1821 with a handsome pension. Appointed one of the Yeomen of the Guard.
D. 27th Nov., 1846.

23RD REGIMENT OF FOOT.

Col.-Sergt. Jonathan Thomas.

D., at the Union Workhouse, Swansea, in Dec., 1867, aged 85.

27TH REGIMENT OF FOOT.

Private Thos. Kerrigan.

One of the few of this regt. who escaped being blown to pieces when
standing in square on the Charleroi road, 18th June, 1815. D., at Calky,
near Enniskillen, 3rd Dec., 1862. Is said to have attained the great age
of 108.

33RD REGIMENT OF FOOT.

Private John Riches.

Was at the storming of Seringapatam, and is said to have been present at
both Quatre Bras and Ligny on 16th June, 1815. Aftds. a Chelsea Hospital
pensioner. D., at Attleburgh, in June, 1860.

40TH REGIMENT OF FOOT.

Sergt. Wm. Lawrence.

Born at Bryant's Piddle, co. Dorset, 1791. Enlisted in the 40th Foot at
age of fifteen. Served with the 1st Batt. in the expedition to Monte Video,
and throughout the Par. War. Wounded at Badajoz, where he was one of
the forlorn hope, and kept six weeks in hospital at Estremos. Soon after

made corporal. Earned Lord Wellington's praise for the gallant manner in
which he captured three French cannon, and drove off a score of French
artillerymen with only six men of his own regt. Promoted sergt. Narrowly
escaped being killed at Waterloo by a French shell, which exploded near
Lawrence, "hurling him two yards into the air." About 4 o'clock P.M. on
Waterloo day was ordered to the colours, in defending which an officer and
fourteen sergts. had already lost their lives that terrible day. M., when at
St. Germains, a Frenchwoman named Marie Louise Claire, who, under
Napoleon's *régime*, had, in common with all other "Marie Louises," been
obliged to change their Christian names, so that the Empress might be the
only one of that name in France! Pensioned on 9*d.* a day in 1819. D., at
Studland, co. Dorset, 1867.

42ND REGIMENT OF FOOT.

Private Donald Davidson, w.

The following notice appeared in the *Standard*, in April or May, 1867 :—
"There died at the village of Ardisier, Inverness-shire, a few days ago, an
old veteran named Donald Davidson, one of the fast diminishing band of
Waterloo heroes. Donald, who, it may be mentioned, had six toes on each
foot, was born in the parish of Nairn, Nairnshire, in the year 1792, and
enlisted in the 42nd Highlanders in June, 1813. He served with his regt. in
the Pa., France, and the Netherlands. from February, 1814, to December,
1816. He was wounded at the battle of Toulouse, and slightly on the head
at Quatre Bras. Notwithstanding, he stuck to his regt., and was one of the
gallant few who repulsed the grand charge of cavalry in the cornfield at
Waterloo. He was discharged with 1*s.* per day of pension, and served for a
long time as barrack labourer in Fort George. He d. at the advanced age
of 75 years."

52ND REGIMENT OF FOOT.

Private Patrick Lowe.

Served through the whole of the Par. War, and formed one of the forlorn
hope at Badajoz, where he personally captured the governor of the fortress,
by which he obtained a large reward. In 1848 he recd. the silver war medal
with 13 clasps; but it is said he would never wear this medal, because he
had claimed his right to 14 clasps and considered himself injured by receiving
one clasp less. He d., at Enniskillen, in 1852, aged 84.

69th Regiment of Foot.

Private John Slater.

Born at Ilkeston, co. Derby. Enlisted in the 52nd in 1803. Served through the whole of the Par. War with that regt. Aftds. exchanged into 69th. In 1848 Slater claimed his right to the silver war medal with 14 clasps—one clasp more than Wellington obtained—but only got a medal with 12 clasps. He d. at Nottingham in 1860.

92nd Regiment of Foot.

Sergt. Alexander Cameron, Piper Major.

Served in the Pa. during the whole of the late war, and for his zeal attracted the attention of several officers of high rank. Lt.-Gen. Sir Wm. Erskine, in a letter to a friend, after the affair at Rio del Molinos, says :— " The first intimation the enemy had of our approach was the piper of the 92nd playing 'Hey, Johnnie Coup, are ye waukin' yet?'" To this favourite air from Cameron's pipe the streets of Brussels re-echoed on the night of the 15th June, 1815, when the regt. assembled to march out to the field of Waterloo. It is recorded of this gallant Scot, on the 18th June, 1815, that " not content with piping at the head of his regt. he marched forward with a party of skirmishers, and placing himself on a height, in full view of the enemy, continued to animate by playing favourite national airs." D. at Belfast 18th Oct., 1817.—*Scots' Magazine.*

Royal Horse Artillery.

Sergt. Daniel Dunnett.

Belonged to Capt. Whinyates's Rocket Battery. The Waterloo historian (Siborne) gives the following :—" A party of horse artillery proceeded under Capt. Dansey along the Charleroi road, to the front of the centre of the Anglo-allied line, and came into action with rockets near the farm of La Haye Sainte, leaving its two guns in the rear under Lt. Wright. Capt. Dansey very soon received a severe wound which obliged him to retire ; and the party, after firing a few rockets, fell back a little to where its horses were standing. It was then commanded by a sergeant (Daniel Dunnett), who, on perceiving the advance of the nearest French column towards the farm, dismounted his men as coolly and deliberately as if exercising on Woolwich Common, though without any support whatever, laid rockets on the ground, and discharged them in succession into the mass, every one of them appearing to take effect. The advance of the column was checked, and was not resumed until Dunnett, having expended all his rockets, retired with his party to rejoin the guns in rear."

APPENDIX.

STAFF.

Col. C. H. Churchill was son of Maj.-Gen. Horace Churchill, and a descendant of the Earl of Orford. In a letter to his father from "Le Cateau, 24th June, 1815," Churchill thus graphically describes Napoleon's final effort at Waterloo :—

"It was about four o'clock. The enemy had made great efforts, but our troops foiled them everywhere. We could not follow him ; he had retired rather than be beaten back. His position was very strong. About six o'clock we perceived formation columns, cavalry and infantry, formed in a great mass—the enemy's artillery was brought to a more forward position—and again he began to cannonade us. He opened a fire, the most tremendous ever known, I believe, in the annals of war—250 pieces, very close, throwing shells and round shot, grape, and every instrument of destruction. It is really not exaggeration to say we could not ride quick over the ground for the bodies of men and horses. Under cover of this cannonade advanced Bonaparte at the head of his Imperial Guards ; cavalry in a column on the left flank, and the Grenadiers of the Guard on their right flank. They advanced most steadily up to our line in one great mass. They halted and commenced firing. Our troops were literally mowed down. The fire was so great nothing could stand." The writer then goes on to describe how he had two horses killed under him, and a third disabled by a shot in the knee before the advancing French columns were "licked back." "The Prussians," continues Churchill, "now came upon the enemy's flank, and this obliged them to hurry their retreat."

Sir De Lacy Evans.

In Kensal Green Cemetery is a handsome altar monument to the memory of Sir De Lacy Evans, his wife, and his brother, Maj.-Gen. Richard Evans, C.B., Col. of the Madras Grenadier Regt. The epitaph to Sir De Lacy and Lady Evans is as follows :—

"Beneath this monument lie the remains of
JOSETTE, Lady EVANS, the beloved and deeply mourned wife of
Gen. Sir DE LACY EVANS.
Born 1787. Died 1861.

Here, too, lie the remains of Gen. Sir DE LACY EVANS, G.C.B.,
Col. of the 21st Rl. N. Brit Fusiliers.
Born 1787. Died 1870.
He commenced his career in India.
Fought under Wellington in the Peninsula and South of France.
Served with distinction in America.
Was engaged at Quatre Bras and Waterloo.
Commanded with marked ability the British Legion in the service of Spain.
And in old age nobly led the 2nd British Division in the Crimea.
During 30 years he was M.P. for the City of Westminster.
An enterprising and skilful commander. An accomplished politician.
His comrades mourn the chivalrous soldier,
And many friends affectionately cherish his memory."

Letter from Capt. (aftds. Lt.-Gen.) Alexander Macdonald, R.H.A., to Col. Sir W. Robe, K.C.B., R.A., regarding the death of Lt. W. Robe, R.H.A., at Waterloo. From a copy in the possession of Col. F. A. Whinyates, late R.H.A. :—

"Amiens, *7th August*, 1815.

"MY DEAR SIR WILLIAM,—I should have written to you long ere this had not a wound, which deprived me of the use of my arm, prevented me. As to the fall of your son, and my esteemed friend, I can only say that few young men have left this life more sincerely regretted, and his exertions on the 18th will ever endear his memory to all who witnessed his noble conduct on that day. Major Ramsay's last words to me were as follows : ' Did you ever witness such noble conduct as that of Brereton and Robe ? ' In short, it is a most painful task to relate the history of a man whose fall I sincerely lament, and I cannot without tears of sorrow think of your son, and my esteemed friend Major Ramsay. About five o'clock on the 18th your son received a mortal wound, and about the same time the following day he died at the village of Waterloo, after twice having taken leave of me in the most friendly and affectionate manner. I was too ill to ask him any questions ; indeed, I was so distressed when I saw him at his last moments, that I could only shake him by the hand, and in the course of a few minutes he expired. His remains were interred in a beautiful spot of ground in the village of Waterloo, where I intend to raise a monument to his memory.—Yours most truly,

"A. McDONALD."

REMINISCENCES OF WATERLOO [? 1895].

" Our Paris correspondent states that a correspondent of the *Gaulois* gives an interesting account of a conversation with one of the very few surviving spectators of the battle of Waterloo, a widow named Givron, the hundredth anniversary of whose birth is about to be celebrated in the little village of Viesville, Hainault. She relates that on the morning of the day of the great battle she ran away from her parents and made her way through the woods, being curious to see what was going on. She was close to Hougomont when the place was attacked by the French troops, and remained in hiding for hours, not daring to move. The cannonade having diminished she ventured towards the farm, but fled horror-stricken at the sight—the ground, as she expresses it, being like red mud, so drenched was it with blood. She ran across the fields and reached the Bois de Planchenoit, where she fell asleep, worn out by fatigue and excitement. At dusk she was awakened by the noise of horses' hoofs, and saw a troop of cavalry, headed by a man of short stature mounted on a curveting grey horse. He was riding slowly on as if in a dream, looking straight ahead and paying no heed to what went on about him. The girl learnt on the same evening from her relatives, when she finally reached home, that the rider was Napoleon. Madame Givron is remarkably active, and is particularly proud of her eyesight, which, she declares, is as good as it was seventy-five years ago. When her daughter Marceline, who, as she says, is only seventy-two, sits down to sew, her mother threads the needles for her. The old lady has had seven children, and her descendants number ninety-two."—*Morning Post.*

A Centenarian.

Commissary-Gen. Downs writes to the *Army and Navy Gazette* in July, 1891, as follows :—

"Samuel Gibson—an inmate of the Metropolitan Asylum, Caterham—is now in his 101st year. He enlisted about the year 1803 at Sanderage, county Armagh, as a boy in the 27th Regt., his father being at that time a private in the Monaghan militia. Young Gibson accompanied the Inniskillings to the Peninsula and also served with the regt. at Waterloo. He was discharged from the army soon after on a pension of one shilling per diem, which he afterwards commuted, receiving besides, he states, £74. He has been an inmate of Caterham Asylum for some years, and although unable to leave his bed he still enjoys a pipe of tobacco, which he indulges in frequently."

Interesting Survivor.

"In the village of Rolvenden, in the Weald of Kent, there is living an old woman named Moon, who was present at the battles of Quatre Bras and Waterloo. Her father, a col.-sergt. of the 3rd batt. Rifle Brigade, served throughout the Peninsular war, and took part in the battles of Badajoz, Salamanca, and other conflicts. He died of wounds received at Waterloo some months after the battle and before he had received his pension. Mrs. Moon was born in the Peninsula, her mother doing work for the forces when operating there. Though Mrs. Moon is now infirm, her intellect is clear and her memory good."—*Morning Post*, 27th March, 1899.

Note by the Editor.—Mrs. Barbara Moon d. at Rolvenden in Oct., 1903. It was stated in an obituary notice that she was four years old at the time of the battle of Waterloo and rode in a waggon over the field on the evening of 18th June, 1815.

The Last British Eye-Witness of Waterloo.

Elizabeth Watkins, of Norwich, born 31st Jan., 1810, at Beaminster, near Bridport. Her father, one Daniel Gale, was pressed into the King's service just before Waterloo. Gale's wife and child followed him to Brussels and were in the women's camp near the field of Waterloo. The child remembers cutting up lint—saw many dead, and some stirring incidents of the battle. (*Notes and Queries*, 5th Dec., 1903). A portrait of Elizabeth Watkins recently appeared in *The Sphere*.

An Eye-Witness of Waterloo.

From a Correspondent.

In a small cottage at the little village of Chapelle, within eye-shot of the meeting-place of Wellington and Blücher after the most tremendous and fateful struggle in the world's history, there was living on June 18, 1815, a little girl, Thérèse Roland, thirteen years of age, who witnessed all that took place on that historic day. Eighty-nine years later she is still living there, a widow now, with her two sons of eighty and seventy-eight, herself a bowed and wrinkled old dame of 103 years. This aged peasant, with faculties still clear and memory unimpaired, is probably the only living witness of the death-blow dealt to all Napoleon's hopes on that midsummer day, which moulded the future history of an entire continent, and altered the balance of power of the entire world.

A representative of the *Patrie* has recently visited the battlefield, and obtained from this interesting old character, now Mme. Dupuis, some reminiscences of much that happened that day. She says :—

" As a little girl, stirred and fascinated by the long lines of horsemen, guns, and tired foot regiments passing our cottage, I stood at our door and served out water to the ' beaux soldats.' Afterwards I followed them to Waterloo. In the evening we heard the booming of great cannon, and from the windows I could see the clouds of smoke rising into the air like trees. I was in the mill, and the windows rattled. All night long we heard the tramp of silent men and the creaking, stumbling guns passing our doors. When I looked out next morning I saw wounded men lying by the roadside. In the distance I could hear a sound like a rough sea breaking against the rocks. There were clouds of smoke, and I saw men galloping, and masses of my brave soldiers moving hurriedly across the fields. Then the doctors came, and took out the bullets from the wounds of the soldiers. . . . The Prussians came by, and then the English, shouting their cries of victory.

" Not far away soldiers were digging trenches in our fields to bury the dead. There were so many of them, so many of them "—and the old peasant covered her face with her hands as though to shut out the terrible picture. " I saw one woman of Gotarville cut off the fingers of a Prussian officer, sorely hurt but still living, to secure the jewelled rings that he wore.

" At Planchenoit, a little further away, they tell me that the brave French were so beaten down by bayonet charges that the river ran with blood. Near the hill above a general was killed.

" No : I did not see Napoleon, and I still regret it. Poor Napoleon !. . . We did not like the English or the Prussians. . . . The next day we knew that Napoleon's power was broken, by the lines we heard the people singing,"—and raising herself in her chair, the tottering old dame sang in a feeble voice :—

> Les canonniers bombardaient à feu et à flamme,
> Les cuirassiers, les gardes d'honneur, sont renversés,
> Bonaparte, enfin voilà ta fin. Il faut te rendre—
> Te voilà battu, convaincu, tu n'en peux plus !

Pall Mall Gazette.

18th June, 1904.

INDEX TO COMMISSIONED OFFICERS.

Brooke, Francis, 1st Dgn. Gds., 52
——, ——, 4th Foot, 120
Brookes, Hen. Wm., 145
Broughton, Saml., 48
Brown, Alexander, 157
——, Andrew, 189
——, Evan M., 128
——, Geo., 146
——, Hen., 242
——, John, 52
——, Thos., 1st Foot, 98
——, ——, 79th Foot, 189
Browne, Barton Parker, 71
——, Donald, 185
——, Eugene, 245
——, Fielding, 153
——, John, 120
——, Hon. Michael, 153
——, Thos. Gore, 248
——, Hon. Wm., 169
——, Wm. Fredk., 62
Brownrigg, David, 231
Bruce, Jas. R., 221
——, Robt., 99
——, Saml. Barwick, 231
——, Wm., 189
Brugh, Adam, 161
Brunton, Ric., 8, 37
Buchanan, John Phillips, 86
——, Wm., 146
Buck, Hen. Rishton, 149
Buckle, Wm., 123
Buckley, Edw. P., 98
——, Geo. Ric., 107
——, Hen., 82
——, Wm., 116
Budgen, John Robt., 201
Bull, Robt., 212
Bullen, Jas., 141
Bullock, Hen. R., 71
Burgess, Francis, 239
——, Sam. W., 98
Burke, Jas., 161
——, Joseph, 198
Burmeister, M. A., 231
Burnaby, Rich. B., 225
Burnet, John, 170
Burney, Wm., 161
Burrell, Wm. G., 190
Burrows, Montagu, 124
Burton, Francis, 120
Bury, Viscount, 1, 12, 98
——, Wm., 237
Bushell, John, 120
Busteed, Christopher, 175

Butler, Jas., 98
——, Theobald, 145
——, Whitwell, 113
Byam, Edw., 82
——, Wm., 82
Byng, Sir John, 4, 20

CADDELL, Chas., 135
Cahill, Patrick, 246
Cairnes, Robt. M., 212
Callander, Alex. Jas., 245
——, John, 231
Calvert, Felix, 145
Cameron, Alexander, 79th Foot, 189
——, ——, 95th Foot, 197
——, ——, 79th Foot, 190
——, Allen, 116
——, Angus, 190
——, Archibald, 190
——, Donald, 79th Foot, 189
——, ——, 1st Foot, 99
——, Dugald, 201
——, Duncan, 189
——, Ewen, 189
——, Jas., 189
——, John, 33rd Foot, 149
——, ——, 79th Foot, 189
——, ——, 92nd Foot, 193
——, Wm. G., 1st Ft. Gds., 8, 38, 98
Campbell, Alex., 91st Foot, 1st Batt., 245
Campbell, Alex., 91st Foot, 2nd Batt., 245
Campbell, Arch., 59th Foot, 242
——, ——, 91st Foot, 1st Batt., 245
——, ——, 91st Foot, 2nd Batt., 245
——, Sir Colin, K.C.B., 8, 39, 107
——, Colin, 1st Foot, 116
——, Donald, 179
——, Dugald, 91st Foot, 245
——, ——, 91st Foot, 246
——, ——, 92nd Foot, 193
——, Ewen, 193
——, Geo., 169
——, Sir Guy, 7, 30
——, Jas., 51st Foot, 164
—— , ——, 79th Foot, 190
——, ——, 79th Foot, 189
——, John, 42nd Foot, 157
——, ——, 44th Foot, 161
——, ——, 91st Foot, 245
——, Sir Neil, Kt., 239
——, Neil, 189
——, Norman, 180
—— Patrick, 169

U

Smith, Wm., 11th Lt. Dns., 71
——, ——, 71st, 180
——, ——, R.H.A., 212
——, ——, 91st, 245
——, ——, Slayter, 68
Smyth, Chas., 4, 21, 197
——, Jas. Carmichael, 229
Snodgrass, John J., 170
Somerset, Lord Edw., 4, 21
——, —— Fitzroy, 1, 9, 97
——, H., Lieut., 4, 22, 90
——, Lord John, 1, 11
Soutar, David, 180
Sowerby, Thos., 107
Spalding, John, 180
Spearman, Chas., 223
Sperling, John, 229
Squire, Will., 120
Stables, Edw., 97
Stacpoole, Ric., 239
——, —— John, 124
Stainforth, Geo., 129
Standen, Geo. Douglas, 112
Stanhope, Hon. Jas., 97
Stanway, Frank, 229
Stapylton, H. C., 68
Staveley, Wm., 206
Stawell, Samson, 75
Steed, Geo., 55
Steele, Hen., 72
——, Samuel L., 94
Stenton, Francis, 236
Stephens, Edw., 145
Steuart, Chas., 245
——, Robt., 185
——, Wm., 245
Stevens, Matthew, 176
——, Thos., 117
——, Wm., 146
Stevenson, Chas. Butler, 55
Stewart, Alex., 146
——, Allen, 198
——, Archd., 197
——, Arthur, 180
——, Chas., 179
——, Duncan, 157
——, Geo., 116
——, Jas., 246
——, John, 42nd Foot, 158
——, ——, 92nd Foot, 194
——, ——, 69th Foot, 175
——, Robt., 73rd Foot. See Steuart.
——, Roger, 157
——, Ronald, 170
——, Wm., 82

Stewart, Wm. H., 71
Stilwell, John, 197
Stirling, Wm., 52
Stoddart, Edw., 150
Stopford, Hon. Edw. 112
——, Wm. H., 222
Storer, Ric., 164
Story, Geo., 46
Stothert, W., 4, 20, 112
Stoyte, John, 116
Strachan, Jos. Wm. H., 185
Strange, Alexr., 78
Strangeways, Thos., 128
Strangways, Thos. Fox, 215
Straton. See Muter, Joseph
Streatfield, Thos., 97
Stretton, Sempronius, 153
Strong, W. B., 161
Stuart, Charles. See Steuart
——, Hon. Wm., 97
——, Rob. Thomson, 136
Stupart, Francis, 58, 252
Sturges, Wm., 55
Sumner, Edw., 107
Swabey, Wm., 214
Swann, Fredk. Dashwood, 98
Sweeney, John Paget, 52
Sweeten, Benj., 170
Swetenham, Clement, 86
Swinburne, Thos. Robt., 98
Swinfen, Francis, 86
Sword, Alex., 245
Sykes, John C., 55
Symes, Joseph, 116

Talbot, Jas., 99
——, Wm., 132
Tallon, Jas., 69
Tappenham, Gilhow J., 239
Tathwell, Tathwell Baker, 50
Taylor, Francis, 239
——, Thos., 132
——, —— Wm., 68
——, Wm., 4th Foot, 120
——, ——, Med. Staff, 231
Terry, Hen., 124
Teulon, Chas., 135
Thackwell, Joseph, 82
Thain, Wm., 150
Thoburn, Robt., 236
Thomas, Chas, 97
——, C.W., 240
——, John, 237
——, Wm., 117
Thompson, Henry Walker, 180

Thompson, John, 190
Thomson, Alex., 229
——, Jas. Crooke, 117
Thorean, John, 153
Thornhill, Ric., 154
——, Wm., 2, 12, 65
Thoyts, John, 50
Thwaites, Wm., 164
Tibbs, Samuel J., 234
Tidy, Francis Skelly, 123
Tighe, Daniel, 99
Tincombe, Francis, 140
Tinling, Wm. Fredk., 99
Todd, John, 180
Tomkins, Wm., 161
Tomkinson, Wm., 86
Tompkins, Newland R., 236
Toole, Wm. H., 145
Torrens, Henry, 7, 34
Torriano, Wm., 180
Towers, ——, 46
——, Fredk., 65
Townsend, John, 212
Townshend, Hon. H. T. P., 97
Trafford, Sigismund, 55
Trevor, Arthur Hill, 149
——, Edw., 226
Trigg, John, 59, 250
Trimmer Wm., 246
Tripp, Baron, 1, 11
Trotter, T., 58
Troward, Thos., 164
Troy, Thos., 50
Tucker, John, 132
Tudor, Chas., 93
Turner, Michael, 52
——, Wm., 78
Turnor, Wm., 123
Twinberrow, Ralph J., 161
Twining, Wm., 231
Tyler, J., 2, 15
Tyndale, Chas. Wm., 164

Unett, Geo. W., 248
Uniacke, Robt., 65
Urquhart, Chas. Gordon, 201
Uxbridge, Earl of, 2, 12, 65

Vandeleur, John, 75
——, Sir John, 3, 17
Vane, Hen., 107
Varley, Jonas, 50
——, Thos., 50
Veall, Wm., 242

Verner, Edw. Donovan, 233
——, Wm., 65
Vernon, Hon. H. S. V., 98
Vernor, Robt., 58, 253
Vickers, Gentle, 204
Vigoreux, Chas. A., 140
Vincent, Richard, 62
Vivian, Sir Hussey, 6, 28
Vyner, Chas. Jas., 98
Vyvian, Philip. See Robinson, Philip
    Vyvian

Waddell, Wm., 55
Wakefield, Joseph, 78
Walcot, Edmund T., 213
Waldegrave, John, Earl, 239
Waldie, Jas. Hen., 90
Walker, Leslie, 179
Wall, Chas. Wm, 236
——, J. L., 154
——, Thos. B., 93
Wallace, Houston, 75
——, Jas. Maxwell, 93
——, John, 78
——, Robt., 52
Wallett, Chas., 145
Walley, Wm., 128
Wallington, J. C., 68
Walsh, Jas., 245
——, John Prendergast, 201
Walton, Wm. Lovelace, 107
Ward, Adam, 215
Warde, Francis, 220
——, J. R., 113
Warren, Wm. Ouseley, 141
Waters, J., Lt.-Col., 7, 30
——, Marcus Ant., 229
Watkis, Thos., 227
Watmough, Peter, 50
Watson, Andrew, 150
——, Hon. Geo. John, 50
——, J. Lewis, 175
——, Sam. Wm., 99
Waymouth, Sam., 48
Webb, Vere, 201
Webber, Wm., 221
Webster, H., 1, 12,
——, Jas. Carnegie, 161
——, Ric., 165
Wedgwood, Thos., 113
Wellington, Duke of, 1, 9, 50
Wells, Fortescue, 224
Wemyss, Jas., 58, 252
West, Chas., 112
Westby, Edw., 58